Rethinking and Unthinking Development

Rethinking and Unthinking Development

Perspectives on Inequality and Poverty in South Africa and Zimbabwe

Edited by Busani Mpofu and
Sabelo J. Ndlovu-Gatsheni

berghahn
NEW YORK · OXFORD
www.berghahnbooks.com

First published in 2019 by
Berghahn Books
www.berghahnbooks.com

© 2019, 2023 Busani Mpofu and Sabelo J. Ndlovu-Gatsheni
First paperback edition published in 2023

All rights reserved. Except for the quotation of short passages for the purposes of criticism and review, no part of this book may be reproduced in any form or by any means, electronic or mechanical, including photocopying, recording, or any information storage and retrieval system now known or to be invented, without written permission of the publisher.

Library of Congress Cataloging-in-Publication Data
Names: Mpofu, Busani, editor, author. | Ndlovu-Gatsheni, Sabelo J., editor, author.
Title: Rethinking and unthinking development : perspectives on inequality and poverty in South Africa and Zimbabwe / edited by Busani Mpofu and Sabelo J. Ndlovu-Gatsheni.
Description: New York : Berghahn Books, 2019. | Includes bibliographical references and index.
Identifiers: LCCN 2018056508 (print) | LCCN 2018057337 (ebook) | ISBN 9781789201772 (ebook) | ISBN 9781789201765 (hardback : alk. paper)
Subjects: LCSH: Economic development--Social aspects--South Africa. | Economic development--Social aspects--Zimbabwe. | Equality--South Africa. | Equality--Zimbabwe. | Poverty--South Africa. | Poverty--Zimbabwe.
Classification: LCC HC905 (ebook) | LCC HC905 .R48 2019 (print) | DDC 338.968--dc23
LC record available at https://lccn.loc.gov/2018056508

British Library Cataloguing in Publication Data
A catalogue record for this book is available from the British Library

ISBN 978-1-78920-176-5 hardback
ISBN 978-1-80073-645-0 paperback
ISBN 978-1-78920-177-2 ebook

https://doi.org/10.3167/9781789201765

Contents

List of Tables and Figures	vii
List of Abbreviations	viii

Introduction
Rethinking and Unthinking Development in Africa   1
Busani Mpofu and Sabelo J. Ndlovu-Gatsheni

Part I. Theory, Concepts and Discourse

Chapter 1
Rethinking Development in the Age of Global Coloniality   27
Sabelo J. Ndlovu-Gatsheni

Chapter 2
Rethinking and Reclaiming Development in Africa   50
Vusi Gumede

Chapter 3
Elusive Solutions to Poverty and Inequality: From 'Trickle
Down' to 'Solidarity Economy'   71
Tidings P. Ndhlovu

Part II. Development, Urbanism and Poverty

Chapter 4
Urban Poverty in Zimbabwe: Historical and Contemporary Issues   87
Rudo Barbra Gaidzanwa

Chapter 5
Theory of Poverty or Poverty of Theory? A Decolonial Intervention
on Urban Poverty in South Africa 105
Raymond Nyapokoto and Sabelo J. Ndlovu-Gatsheni

Part III. Empowerment, Regionalism, Identity and Development

Chapter 6
The 'Native Returns': Assessing and Reimagining Indigenisation
and Black Economic Empowerment as Development Projects
in the 'Postcolony' 129
Tamuka Charles Chirimambowa and Tinashe Lukas Chimedza

Chapter 7
Ethnopolitics and Regionalism, Discipline and Punishment:
The Matabeleland Development Question in Postcrisis Zimbabwe 152
Vusilizwe Thebe

Chapter 8
The Politics of Land Ownership in South Africa:
Self-Perceptions and Identities of Backyard Dwellers within the
Coloured Community 173
Wendy Isaacs-Martin

Part IV. Development, Social Policy and African Families

Chapter 9
Understanding the Conceptualisation of African Families:
A Social Policy Development Poser in South Africa 197
Busani Mpofu

Chapter 10
Socioeconomic and Cultural Barriers to Marital Unions and
HIV Incidence Correlates: A Public Policy Poser for South Africa 212
Busani Ngcaweni

Chapter 11
Old-Age Cash Grant Pay-out Days: How Beneficiaries Become
Victims of Abuse in South Africa 231
Gloria Sauti

Conclusion
The End of Development and the Rise of Decoloniality as
the Future 251
Sabelo J. Ndlovu-Gatsheni and Busani Mpofu

Index 267

Tables and Figures

Tables

Table 0.1	A historical overview of development studies.	5
Table 2.1	Meanings of the word 'development' in selected indigenous African languages.	52
Table 2.2	Selected conceptualisations of development.	53
Table 2.3	Human development, levels and regions.	58
Table 10.1	Civil marriages in South Africa between 2002 and 2011.	217
Table 10.2	Registered customary marriages between 2003 and 2011.	217

Figures

Figure 5.1	Diagram of the zone of being and nonbeing.	110
Figure 7.1	Excerpts from the CCJP and LRF report.	160
Figure 8.1	Content analysis format.	183

Abbreviations

AAG	Affirmative Action Group
AfCFTA	African Continental Free Trade Area
AfDB	African Development Bank
ANC	African National Congress
ANC YL	African National Congress Youth League
Aps	Assembly Points
ARP	Alex Renewal Project
ASGISA	Shared Growth Initiative for South Africa
AU	African Union
BBBEE	Broad Based Black Economic Empowerment (South Africa)
BEE	Black Economic Empowerment
BIG	Basic Income Grant
BNG	Breaking New Ground (policy housing strategy)
BRICS	Brazil, Russia, India, China and South Africa
CBD	Central Business District
CIO	Central Intelligence Organisation
COSATU	Congress of South African Trade Unions
CRU	Community Residential Units Programme
Dimaf	Distressed and Marginalised Area Fund
DMS	'Development Merchant System'
DPC	Development Planning Committee
DRC	Democratic Republic of Congo
EFF	Economic Freedom Fighters
EPWP	Expanded Public Works Programme
ESAP	Economic Structural Adjustment Program

FAO	Food and Agricultural Organisation
FMF	Fees Must Fall
FROLIZI	Front for the Liberation of Zimbabwe
GDS	Growth and Development Summit
GDP	Gross Domestic Product
GEAR	Growth Employment and Redistribution
GNU	Government of National Unity
HDI	Human Development Index
HDRs	Human Development Reports
HSRC	Human Sciences Research Council
IBDC	Indigenous Business Development Committee
IBRD	International Bank for Reconstruction and Development
IBWO	Indigenous Business Women's Organization
IDP	Industrial Decentralisation Policy
IFIs	International Finance Institutions
ILO	International Labour Organization
IMF	International Monetary Fund
LDCs	Less Developed Countries
MDC	Movement Democratic Change
MDGs	Millennium Development Goals
MPI	The Multidimensional Poverty Index
NAME	North Africa and Middle East
NATO	North Atlantic Treaty Organization
NDP	National Development Plan
NDR	National Democratic Revolution
NEET	Not in Employment, not in Education and not in Training
NGO	Nongovernmental Organisations
NICs	Newly Indutsrialized Countries
NP	National Party
NUMSA	National Union of Miners in South Africa
PSU	Police Support Unit
RBZ	Reserve Bank of Zimbabwe
RDP	Reconstruction and Development Programme
RMF	Rhodes Must Fall
SABC	South African Broadcasting Corporation
SADC	Southern Africa Development Community
SANRAL	South African National Roads Agency Limited
SAPs	Structural Adjustment Programmes
SARS	South African Revenue Service
SASSA	South African Social Security Agency
SSA	Sub-Saharan Africa
TCC	Transnational Capitalist Class

TINA	'There is No Alternative'
TNCs	Transnational Corporations
UNDP	United Nations Development Programme
UNICEF	United Nations Children's Fund
WCED	World Commission on Environment and Development
WHO	World Health Organization
WTO	World Trade Organization
ZANLA	Zimbabwe African National Liberation Army
ZANU	Zimbabwe African National Union
ZANU (PF)	Zimbabwe African National Union (Patriotic Front)
ZAPU	Zimbabwe African People's Union
ZECO	Zimbabwe Engineering Company
ZIMASSET	Zimbabwe Agenda for Sustainable Social Economic Transformation
ZIPRA	Zimbabwe People's Revolutionary Army
ZNA	Zimbabwe National Army
ZUM	Zimbabwe Unity Movement

Introduction
Rethinking and Unthinking Development in Africa

Busani Mpofu and Sabelo J. Ndlovu-Gatsheni

The intellectual and academic task of rethinking and unthinking development in Africa arises from the reality of how development has continued to be elusive in Africa. The development imperative has remained caught up in ten discernible paradoxes and contradictions that were recently delineated by Odomaro Mubangizi (2018: 1): (1) rich and complex cultural diversity; (2) ever-simmering ethno politics that underlie contemporary conflicts; (3) underdevelopment amidst enormous resources; (4) a brain drain amidst limited capacity and financial illicit flows; (5) nascent democratic and governance institutions to anchor sustainable development; (6) longstanding tensions between tradition and modernity; (7) centrifugal and centripetal political and economic forces; (8) longstanding contradictions between the sacred and the secular; (9) an ever-widening gap between rich and poor people; and (10) the quest for homegrown solutions to African problems while relying heavily on foreign aid, foreign direct investment and imported goods and services.

These above stated challenges coexist with two discourses on the state of development in Africa. On one level is the positive discourse of 'Africa rising', which is entangled with such initiatives as the African Union (AU)'s Agenda 2063, Sustainable Development Goals, Africa's demographic dividend, drives towards an African Continental Free Trade Area (AfCFTA) and 'the increasing attractiveness of Africa as a choice destination for foreign direct investment' (Mubangizi 2018: 2). On another level, there is the negative discourse of the Third Scramble for Africa, taking the form of intensified competition for Africa's abundant natural resources, which directly counters the positive discourse of a developmentally 'rising' African continent (Southall and Melber 2009).

While the process of rethinking development research set in long ago, it has been accelerating since the end of 2008, when neoliberalism lost most of its triumphalism because of the global financial and economic crises (Schuurman 2009: 831–48). In 2008, the contours of a partial meltdown of global financial capitalism and the subsequent global recession[1] in the real economy necessitated more than ever the need for critical development research to contribute to new, much-needed insights into processes of development and underdevelopment, and possible alternative roots towards a more sustainable future (Schuurman 2009: 835). The financial crisis left neoliberalism, which had created a more unequal society, wounded, but surely not yet defeated and as Hart, Laville and Cattani asked, what can we, the people, do about it (2010: 1)? For Slavoj Zizek, the global capitalist system was approaching 'an apocalyptic zero-point', in the process producing ecological crises, inequalities and poverty, struggles over raw materials, food and water, as well as 'the explosive growth of social divisions and exclusions' (Zizek 2011: x).

In Southern Africa's former settler states, South Africa and Zimbabwe, and in Africa in general, conventional development theories or practices have failed to adequately lead to social transformation that reduces unemployment, inequality and poverty, and the majority of citizens are homeless, unemployed, landless, stateless and undocumented, as well as being afflicted by various diseases. Decolonisation has remained a challenge in Southern Africa, especially in the former white settler states, Zimbabwe and South Africa, where the negative effects of colonialism and imperialism continue to linger on. In both countries, the current governing parties – the Zimbabwe African National Union-Patriotic Front (ZANU PF) and the African National Congress (ANC) – both former liberation movements, secured black majority rule through negotiated settlements that involved compromises, which left the capitalist economic structure largely intact.

In order to economically empower the majority of the black population constitutionally marginalised by the colonial and apartheid governments, the governing parties introduced various black economic empowerment, indigenisation and land reform initiatives. The extent to which these initiatives have transformed the lives of the majority of the historically disadvantaged communities is debatable, but what is clear is that the majority of the populations continue to wallow in poverty. For example, Hart and Padayachee (2010: 424) argue that the legacy of racial division excluded and still excludes the majority of South African citizens from economic emancipation. Worse still, South Africa is still racially divided economically, with an extremely advanced sector focused on mining, finance, security and retail, but a more racially mixed elite now is surrounded by black poverty. Economic growth since 2000 has failed to reduce this divide. As a result, South Africa remains a world leader in inequality, and ruling elites in most of Africa often collude with foreign extractive, commercial and military experts (Hart and Padayachee 2010: 423, 426).

National political leaders today continue the process of accumulation without development in most of Africa. As a result, Africa's underdevelopment currently should be substantially attributed to the self-serving actions of the fragmented political class serving the interests of foreign powers (Hart and Padayachee 2010: 410–11). Mbeki (2009) blamed African ruling elites for enriching themselves at the expense of their own people by serving the interests of foreign powers determined to exploit their countries' human and natural resources. Žižek (2013) questioned whether African leaders would dare to touch the capitalist mechanisms or whether they would decide to 'play the game'? The challenge, according to Žižek, is that if one disturbed the capitalist mechanisms, one was very swiftly 'punished' by market perturbations, economic chaos and the rest. What is clear is that global coloniality produced a particular form of leadership in Africa – a petty bourgeoisie that could not invent or even transform political, economic and social institutions inherited from colonialism 'into its own image' so as to 'become socially hegemonic' (Nabudere 2011: 58; Taylor 2014: 5).

Since 2015, South African universities have become a site of struggles for student protests against the deep-seated exclusionist tendencies of apartheid colonialism. According to Ndlovu-Gatsheni (2016), what began as the Rhodes Must Fall movement (RMF), targeting Cecil John Rhodes's statue at the University of Cape Town, quickly expanded into broader demands for cognitive justice. Students demanded change of curriculum; decommissioning of offensive colonial/apartheid symbols; the right to free, quality and relevant education; cultural freedom; and an overall change in the very idea of the university from its Western pedigree ('university in Africa') into an 'African university'. There has been a demand for transformation in universities that embraces the need for a diverse and cosmopolitan student cohort, and enhanced access for talented students from poor and marginalised communities (Habib 2015: 8–10). The issue of alienating institutional cultures features prominent as another grievance. University institutional cultures are deemed European, anti-black, racist, and patriarchal (Tabensky and Matthews 2015). In other words, these universities are what Francis Nyamnjoh depicted as 'European greenhouses under African skies', making them 'a space of whiteness' even if they are inhabited by black people (Nyamnjoh 2012: 129–54).

As a result, an increase in African and Coloured (people of mixed race) representation in the university and the evolution of the institutional culture where black staff and students feel comfortable within the university is deemed the solution. There are calls to reorganise the curriculum in order to incorporate African theorists and contextual challenges. The movement also called for an end to the exploitation of workers through the in-sourcing of all outsourced services. Finally, naming has to reflect the diversity of society and students (Habib 2015: 8–10). Broadly, the RMF movements are loudly calling for what Brenda Cooper and Robert Morrell term 'Africa-centred knowledges' as a form of cognitive justice (Cooper and Morrell 2014). The 'Fees Must Fall' (FMF) strand of the RMF movements specifically demands the implementation of 'the right to education' for every student as stated in the Freedom Charter in 1955 (Ndlovu-Gatsheni 2016).

Generally, millions of poor people inhabit Africa. Even if the middle class has grown substantially and, to the extent that measurements in small formal economies are useful, the measurable level of inequality is also disturbingly high and few African states seem to have comprehensive policies to better the situation. Therefore, now more than ever, we need to imagine different economic development policy alternatives. In other words, in spite of development's dismal track record, Easterly fundamentally argued that a development ideology is needed. It appeals to people in Africa and the Third World in general because they want a definitive, complete answer to the tragedy of global poverty and inequality, and ideologies usually arise in response to tragic situations in which people are hungry for clear and comprehensive solutions (Easterly 2007). In 1988, Escobar (1988: 498) succinctly argued that the concept of development was embedded in the neocolonial construction of the world and was a key ideological tool in global power relations. As a result, he argued that instead of searching for development alternatives, we must search for alternatives to development, which respect local autonomy, culture and knowledge (Escobar 1997). The problem, according to Banda (2004: 98), is that in the language of 'development', Western modernity has been projected as the ideal that others from other parts of the world have to follow, while disregarding their historical, cultural and economic differences. In other words, the 2008 financial crisis has opened up a new terrain for thinking about the economy (Hart, Laville and Cattani 2010: 4), but also about development discourses that are meant to shape the economy.

Economic growth needs to translate urgently into less poverty. However, this has been very slow and hindered by high levels of inequality. In 2013, for example, the World Bank forecast strong economic growth in Africa of about 4.9 per cent. In spite of this growth, poverty and inequality remain 'unacceptably high and the pace of reduction unacceptably slow', with almost half of all Africans still living in extreme poverty (World Bank 2013: 2). Those 'peddling' the idea of development keep on adding adjectives to the word 'development', but are actually not able to reduce poverty in general (Boaventura de Sousa Santos 2014). For example, according to Banda (2004: 101–2), in the 1950s and 1960s, the development discourse assumed that the growth of the economy would 'trickle down' to the masses in the form of jobs and other economic opportunities. Most Third World countries achieved the United Nations (UN) targeted growth expectations in the 1960s, but their economic status remained the same or even worsened. The economists shifted their emphasis from the economic growth model to the basic needs approach in the 1970s. When this failed to yield the desired results, a 'sustainable development' with 'bottom-up' planning was adopted in the 1980s. Soon after, the International Monetary Fund (IMF) introduced 'structural adjustment' policies in the 1980s, forcing governments in the Third World to cut down their expenditure on social welfare programmes. Cowen and Shenton's *Doctrines of Development* (1996) provides a comprehensive history of the origins, invention and design of the doctrines of development. Shanmugaratnam (2011) provided an excellent up-to-date historical overview of Development Studies research centred on the ideology of development (see Table 0.1 below).

Table 0.1 A historical overview of development studies (adapted from Shanmugaratnam 2011).

'Prehistory' – Nineteenth-century Europe: invention of development – Colonial studies: the lesser known connection to development studies	Related events/interventions/examples
Postwar: 1945	– 1945: World Bank International Bank for Reconstruction and Development (IBRD); IMF Keynesianism – Decolonisation – Cold War begins
1960s: development studies/Western universities	

1960s–1970s:	State-led development policies in newly independent countries
– Modernization paradigm and growth theories – Critical theories: Marxist, neo-Marxist/dependency; structuralism	– African socialism (Tanzania) – India: economic planning – East Asian Newly Industrialized Countries (NICs) emulating the Japanese success story
1980s:	Late 1970s–1980s: International Finance Institutions (IFI) criticise 'state failure' and prescribe neoliberal package Washington Consensus,
– Impasse in development theory – Critiques of Marxist and neo-Marxist structuralism – Poststructuralism; post-Marxism – Gender/feminist theories – Middle-range concepts: agency/actor – Empirical/local studies – Environment/development – Microeconomics – Methodological individualism – Washington Consensus and IFIs impact on development studies	– Market-led development (post-Keynesian) – Transnational Corporations (TNCs) – 1987: World Commission on Environment and Development (WCED) Report 'Our Common Future' – Development studies in universities in the Global South – 1989: end of the Cold War; neoliberal triumphalism
1990s:	Post-Cold War
– Rise of postmodernism – Capability approach gains currency – Critical views/studies on neoliberalism, SAPs, etc. – Discourse analysis – Post-development/antidevelopment – More focus on civil society; social movements, Nongovernmental Organisations (NGOs) – Focus on globalization and development – Post-Washington Consensus: state/market – 'New wars', conflict/peace/development, liberal peace – Listian theories (late development)/the other canon developed	– 1990: United Nations Development Programme (UNDP), Human Development Report (HDR) – UNDP popularizes the capability approach – 1995: World Health Organization (WHO) 1990s: – -Neoliberalism modified – Post-Washington Consensus – Bringing the state back in – Second-generation reforms: effective states

2000s: – Neoliberalism, 'Postims' – Listian theories (late development) – Critical modernism – Climate change/development – Emerging powers and development	'Global War on Terror' Securitisation: security–development nexus

Source: Shanmugaratnam (2011: 38)

In spite of all these 'development' efforts, the social, economic and political inequality of the poor, marginalised and exploited people in the Global South is worsening. Where development takes place, some people get excluded because of their gender, ethnicity, regionalism, age, sexual orientation, disability or poverty or other factors.

As a result, the idea of development, peddled under the hegemony of neoliberal economics since the end of the Cold War, has been one of the most globally contested ideas across different historical timeframes. While it originated from and is hugely uncontested in the West, the process towards 'achieving' development has been contested greatly in the non-Western world. According to Easterly (2007), the main challenge is that like Marxism to some extent, development aspires to be scientific, and finding one correct solution to poverty is seen as a scientific problem to be solved by experts, the international aid bureaucrats, 'the self-appointed priesthood of Development'. It favours collective goals such as national poverty reduction, national economic growth and the global Millennium Development Goals (Easterly 2007). In other words, according to Easterly, the ideology of development promises a comprehensive final answer to all of society's problems. It shares the common ideological characteristic suggesting that there is only one correct answer and it tolerates little dissent. It deduces this unique answer for everyone from a general theory that purports to apply to everyone universally. The 'one correct answer' referred to 'free markets' and, for the poor world, was defined as doing whatever the IMF and the World Bank prescribed. For Easterly (2007), the ideology of development is not only about having experts design the free market for states; it is about having the experts design a comprehensive, technical plan to solve all the problems of the poor. These experts see poverty as a purely technological problem, to be solved by engineering and the natural sciences. However, countries having the potential to develop are wise to avoid too strong and one-sided Western-centric ideas that emanate from the World Bank, the IMF and the World Trade Organization (WTO), among others (Easterly 2007).

Human economists advocate that development policies in the public and private sectors should enhance people's concrete activities and aspirations in societies, a development approach that is rooted in the local people's lived experiences (Hart 2008a). This involves the use of approaches that emphasise endogenous efforts that have sustained local communities in the light of the failure of states to provide for them. Economic anthropologists have argued that the project of economics needed to be rescued from economists, who have tended to portray the economy as an impersonal machine, remote from the everyday experience of most people, but with devastating consequences (Hart et al. 2010: 4–5). Hart (2008a) argued that economics, which ought to be a science for human emancipation, has become a dehumanised expert ideology remote from people's practical concerns and from their ability to understand what to do. The twentieth-century market economy, sustained by a concern for individual freedom, generated huge inequalities, but submission of the economy to the political will on the pretext of equality led to the suppression of freedom (Hart 2008b: 2).

Easterly (2014) reiterated that the experts' idea that they can have a purely technical approach to resolving problems of poverty without any moral implications was an illusion. He noted that development tactics (in the fight against global poverty) trampled over the individual freedom of the world's poor, and in doing so suppressed a vital debate about an alternative approach to solving poverty: freedom. An understanding of 'how can people be more free to find their own solutions' can contribute to the development of a more appropriate development ideology. Easterly thus argues that only a new model of development, one predicated on respect for the individual rights of people in developing countries and one that understands that unchecked state power is the problem and not the solution, will be capable of ending global poverty once and for all. He regards the attitude that views the poor as helpless individuals without any dignity to be respected as condescending and paternalistic. He therefore criticised experts as being too arrogant in their own knowledge and too oblivious to the moral consequences of their overconfidence and about how this can lead to damaging other people. In other words, there is a technocratic blindness to the moral dimension of development. Worse still, according to Easterly, in development, people at times tend to ignore the following question: who has the power (interview between William Easterly and Kent Annan, 2 April 2014)? James Ferguson (1990) correctly postulated that development is not neutral of power and cannot be understood outside of current power dynamics.

Those seeking to promote development that reduces inequality and poverty, but from within the confines of neoliberal economics, talk of inclusive approaches to development in Africa. Inclusive development is one of the human development approaches and it integrates the standards and principles of human rights, including participation, nondiscrimination and accountability. It originated from the realisation that many people in societies tend to be excluded from development because of their gender, ethnicity, age, sexual orientation, disability or poverty. Inclusive development refers to the improvement of the distribution of wellbeing along many dimensions (falling poverty, narrowing inequality, education and health) alongside the improvement in average achievement (Kanbur and Rauniyar 2009).

Decoloniality thinkers push for the interrogation of the contradictions between the epistemic location of development theory in the academy and the social location of the intended beneficiaries of development in the non-Western world. They contend that the hand of 'invisible power structures' still haunts the majority of the citizens now long after the end of formal colonialism (Ndhlovu 2016). The strength of the decolonial epistemic perspective is that it does not attempt to claim universality, neutrality and singular truthfulness. It is decidedly and deliberately situated in those epistemic sites, such as Latin America and the Caribbean, Asia and Africa, that experienced the negative consequences of modernity and that are facing development challenges. At the same time, it openly accepts its partiality, the awareness that all knowledges are partial (Ndlovu Gatsheni, Chapter 1 in this volume). Decolonial epistemic perspectives are predicated on the concepts of power, knowledge and being. Coloniality of power locates the discourse of development within the context of the politics of constitution of a racially hierarchized Euro-America-centric, Christian-centric, patriarchal, capitalist, heteronormative, hegemonic, asymmetrical and modern global power structure (Grosfoguel and Cervantes-Rodriguez 2002; Grosfoguel 2007). Deploying decolonial epistemic perspectives can reveal the coloniality embedded in development discourses.

Easterly (2007) also argued that development's simple theory of historical inevitability is highly hypocritical. In other words, experts argue that poor societies are not just poor, but that they are 'developing' until they reach the final stage of history, or 'development', when they 'catch up' with the West, at which stage poverty will soon end. However, and unfortunately, development ideology has had a dismal record of helping any country actually develop and the regions in which the ideology has been most influential – that is, Latin America and Africa – have done the worst. From the above, it is therefore clear that there is now a need to embrace an interdisciplinary approach in attempts to solve development conundrums and avoiding pretensions of 'the [purported] superiority of [the narrow focussed orthodox] economics' (Ndhlovu 2016: 188–9; Fourcade et al. 2015: 89). In 1991, Immanuel Wallerstein argued that the presumptions of nineteenth-century social science, which were previously considered to possess a 'liberating of the spirit, serve today as the central intellectual barrier to useful analysis of the social world' (Wallerstein 1991: 1–2). Chabal reiterated this in 2012 when he argued that:

> Those instruments – that is, the social sciences we employ to explain what is happening domestically and overseas – are both historically and conceptually out of date … I show that these theories are now obstacles to the understanding of what is going on in our societies and what we can do about it (Chabal 2012: viii) … The end of conceit is upon us. Western rationality must be rethought. (Chabal 2012: 335)

Therefore, trying to reform the development ideologies, but from within the confines of mainstream neoliberal ideologies, is very problematic. Ideologies cloned from mainstream neoliberal ideologies fail to confront present structural and agential sources of social injustices, asymmetrical power structures, patriarchal ideologies, logics of capitalist exploitation, resilient imperial/colonial reason, and racist articulations and practices (McNally 2005; Santos 2008). In this volume, we argue that racism, the slave trade, imperialism, colonialism, apartheid, and neocolonialism do not only constitute global coloniality as a modern power structure but are also manifestations of the 'dark side/underside' of modernity (Mignolo 1995, 2011, 2012). As Ngugi wa Thiong'o (1986: 2) argued, African predicaments are 'often not a matter of personal choice', but are a product of a 'historical situation'. Africans do not yet have a choice to choose the type of economy they prefer. Ngugi wa Thiong'o identified imperialism and colonialism as well as neocolonialism not as mere slogans, but 'real'. This meant that if the problems of development arose from a historical situation and were structural, then 'their solutions are not so much a matter of personal decision as that of fundamental social transformation of the structures of our societies starting with a real break with imperialism and its internal ruling allies. Imperialism and its comprador alliances in Africa can never develop the continent' (Ngugi wa Thiong'o 1986: xii). This structuralist decolonial argument provokes the question of possibilities and potentialities of African people being able to create African futures within a modern world system structured by global coloniality.

Even after the entry of China, Russia, Brazil and India into the African market, which has boosted the sale of primary commodities, Africa is still forced to celebrate an economic growth that is premised on a problematic 'intensification of resource extraction through diversification of partners, while inequality and unemployment increase and deindustrialization continues apace' (Taylor 2014: 160). China's presence in Southern Africa (Angola, Mozambique, Zimbabwe, Namibia and South Africa) gained prominence through its support to liberation movements in the region from the 1960s and the construction of the Tazara railway in the 1970s (Moyo 2016: 59). Its presence has increased in Africa since 2001, when the Chinese economy grew sharply and its demand for raw materials increased (Moyo 2016: 61). Today its presence is more visible in those countries with extensive energy resources, which it is increasingly extracting (Moyo 2016: 59). New Chinese small and medium-scale commercial enterprises have also become active players in the construction of new infrastructures, including the rehabilitation of new roads, railways, dams, stadiums, office complexes and so on (Moyo 2016: 62).

Chinese leader Xi Jinping committed to a new round of loans and aid totalling $60 billion in 2015, with a large portion of the funds directed at South African infrastructure, Zimbabwean projects and other initiatives (Wengraf 2017). In Zimbabwe, while Chinese companies have invested in mining chrome, diamonds and platinum, South African, American and British companies remain the dominant investors in these minerals in Southern Africa. South African supermarkets are also becoming a dominant commercial force in Africa in general (Moyo 2016: 62). However, in spite the involvement of China, industrialisation has failed to gain any momentum in much of Africa (Wengraf 2017).

According to Moyo (2016: 59), China's presence is viewed from three perspectives. The first is that China is recolonising Africa. The second view sees China's presence in Africa favourably in the global arena, with the diversification of markets and its presence as an emerging power providing room for manoeuvre for African states, which have been marginalised by Eurocentric domination for longer periods. Third, China's presence in Africa is viewed as a 'sub-imperial/ force leading the new scramble for African resources hand in hand with the Eurocentric-American capitalism' (Moyo 2016: 59). For Moyo, while China has become influential in Africa through trade, investments and geopolitical relations, it is far from being a hegemonic recoloniser (2016: 58). Stephen Marks (2006) argued that for China, Africa represented a key source of raw materials and a market for cheap Chinese-made products. As a result, Moeletsi Mbeki labelled the trade relations between South Africa and China 'a replay of the old story of South Africa's trade with Europe'. According to Marks (2006), Mbeki noted that the selling of raw materials to China and importing their manufactured goods resulted in an unfavourable balance of trade against South Africa. In March 2018, Chinese companies topped the list of businesses entities that were identified by President Emmerson Mnangagwa as 'looters' who illegally externalised foreign currency from Zimbabwe (Share 2018). Therefore, any development in Africa based on the intensification of resource extraction by diverse powers, whether European, North American, Brazilian, Indian, Chinese or Russian, rather than industrialisation is simply a manifestation of the coloniality of markets, which is at the centre of capitalism and is driving the new scramble for African resources today (Ndlovu-Gatsheni 2015: 35). The tragedy is that those who have been advocating empowerment of the poor or the distribution of the world's riches also indirectly support the reproduction of neocolonial power relations (Banda 2004: 99).

It is clear that African intellectuals need to come up with policies and trajectories that can be implemented easily. Perhaps development prospects for African countries may lie in initiatives anchored by some form of an African modernity. The challenge is how Africa can adapt some Western development models to suit its political, economic, social and cultural circumstances. If successful, while they would make Africa very much more Western in most respects, perhaps like Japan or China, they will not be lacking in distinctiveness and will certainly not be following self-interested advice from Western sources of mainstream technocratic approaches (Easterly 2007). For example, the AU's Agenda 2063 envisions an African future that emphasises pan-African unity, integration, prosperity and peace. Africans have to drive the processes of self-improvement unencumbered by external forces that want to maintain the status quo. While global coloniality works through the division and atomisation of Africans, the AU has identified pan-Africanism as the overarching ideological framework for unity, self-reliance, integration and solidarity (African Union 2013). Before gaining political independence from colonial rule, Africa's political leaders often embraced the pan-African ideal, unifying all people of African descent to drive out colonial rulers (Hart and Padayachee 2010: 423).

In 2006, the AU conference issued the 'Livingstone Call for Action', which emphasised that every African country should have social programmes, 'including the social pension and social transfers to vulnerable children, older pensions and people with disabilities' (Hanlon et al. 2010: 2). This was perhaps after the increasing realisation of the failure of the belief that low-income countries should focus on market-based economic growth in order to grow before they could 'start redistributing wealth and combating poverty'. Equity and social protection are now accepted as crucial prerequisites to growth and development (Hanlon et al. 2010: 143).

However, South Africa has a complicated history of relations within the Southern African region. Since 1994, Africans in South Africa's 'rainbow' nation have been hostile to their African neighbours that supported them in the struggle against apartheid (Hart and Padayachee 2010: 412, 413). According to Hart and Padayachee (2010: 420), under the African National Congress (ANC), South Africa has increased, rather than reduced, the sense of division between its own citizens and the many Africans who emigrate there to live and work. Social movements in the country do not possess a broader vision of Africa's emancipation comparable to pan-African resistance to colonial empire, which was the most inclusive political movement in the first half of the twentieth century (Hart and Padayachee 2010: 412). As a result, there have been tight restrictions on the movement of people, goods and money within the Southern African Development Community (SADC), with South Africa restricting the entry into its relatively more developed economy (Hart and Padayachee 2010: 412–13). Currently, visas are still required for travel between many SADC countries, and a plethora of bilateral deals and tariff barriers prevent the establishment of any meaningful economic cooperation or community. This is in spite of the attempted revival of the pan-African impulse that former President Thabo Mbeki supported through his African renaissance ideas. However, on the ground, African communities have since colonial times perfected clandestine patterns of transborder movement and exchange, which persist despite their rulers' attempts to force the economy and society into national boundaries (Hart and Padayachee 2010: 423–25).

Ferguson (2015: xi) now believes that simply 'giving' money directly to the poor could yield better results in terms of reducing poverty than spending development project funds on Land Cruisers and foreign consultants. In his book *Give a Man a Fish: Reflections on the New Politics of Distribution*, he focuses on the rise of social welfare programmes across Southern Africa through which governments have adopted noncontributory social protection schemes transferring small amounts of cash to the elderly, disabled and women caring for children. Citing South Africa, which has led the way in this, Ferguson noted that by 2013, more than 30 per cent of the entire population received the monthly cash payments from the national government (2015: 5). He believes that this is a 'quiet revolution' in development practice in the Global South, where capitalism has rendered a growing percentage of the population chronically unemployed (Ferguson 2015: 5). Traditional (industrial capitalist-based) development initiatives that sought to prepare people to work have not yielded the desired results in the economies of the Global South, where many people are not in formal employment. Ferguson thus believes that the social welfare grant in South Africa could be the firm basis upon which the radical proposal circulating in South Africa and Namibia that every member of society should receive a basic income grant (BIG) without reference to their age, gender, employment and family configuration could be implemented. He believes that this could be the basis of the 'new politics of distribution' that he is proposing (2015: xii). The cash transfer programmes are not unique to Southern Africa, as they have been implemented in Latin American countries.

Hanlon et al. (2010: 1) characterised the cash payment transfers as a 'development revolution from the global South' that pointed to 'a wave of new thinking' rooted in the conviction that 'it is better to give money to poor people directly so that they can find effective ways to escape from poverty' (Ferguson 2015: 13). The key message of Hanlon et al.'s book *Just Give Money to the Poor: The Development Revolution from the Global South* (2010) is that direct transfers to households are a key component of effective poverty reduction and development strategies in the Global South. They argue that four conclusions can be drawn from the cash payments: (1) the programmes are affordable; (2) recipients use the money well and do not waste it; (3) cash grants are an efficient way of reducing current poverty directly; and (4) they have the potential to prevent future poverty by facilitating economic growth and promoting human development (Hanlon et al. 2010: 2). For Hanlon et al., cash transfers represent a paradigmatic shift in poverty reduction. While acting as palliatives for current poverty, they also build productive capacity among those in poverty and promote development programmes. This is a direct affront to the traditional aid and development industry, which is built on the belief that development and the eradication of poverty depended on what international agencies and consultants could do for the poor, while ignoring what the citizens of the developing countries, including the poor, could do for themselves (Hanlon et al. 2010: 4).

This volume is therefore a continuous search for more sustainable and appropriate strategies for communicating development in developing countries (Sachs 1992). It adopts a broader and inclusive view of development than the narrow desire to achieve economic growth in terms of national or regional statistics. It seeks to historicise the present state of development (or lack of it) by placing it within a long-term process of social transformation, while simultaneously analysing South Africa and Zimbabwe's development challenges that exacerbate the prevalence of inequality and poverty. This is not a comparison between the two countries. We also do not restrict ourselves to specific times, as the elusiveness of development has always been ever present. Ferguson (2015: 4) decried the fact that many critical accounts of neoliberalism have settled into the politics of denunciation without offering convincing and realistic alternatives and strategies. However, our intention in this volume is not to simply reject ideas of development based on exploitative capitalist tendencies, but to free it from coloniality if it has to be attainable in the Global South in general and Africa in particular.

We need to rethink and unthink the current development discourses that are linked to economic growth, but have failed to reduce unemployment and poverty in most of Africa. In other words, we need to rethink our thinking (Odora-Hoppers and Richards 2012: 7) about development. This, according to Odora-Hoppers and Richards (2012: 7), needs to go beyond 'the clutches of mere dissent or post-colonial critiques, to transformative post-colonial action'. This can enable the light that was initially cast on colonialism and the legacy of domination and abuse to be changed to 'vigilant analyses of its failures, silences, and a systematic spotting of transformative nodes that were not recognizable before, but which are now released into public spaces' (Odora-Hoppers and Richards 2012: 7). In our task of rethinking thinking, Odora-Hoppers and Richards note that we need 'to recognize the cultural asphyxiation of those numerous "others" that has been the norm, and work to bring other categories of self-definition, of dreaming, of acting, of loving, of living into the commons as a matter of universal concern' (2012: 8).

As development, inequality and poverty studies are conducted across disciplines by practitioners such as anthropologists, economists, human economists, development workers, geographers, sociologists, and urban planners and historians, a multidisciplinary approach has been adopted here. The contributors to this volume come from different academic persuasions, including anthropologists, historians, economists and decolonial thinkers. Theoretical and empirical contributions in the volume analyse development quagmires militating against efforts to reduce poverty, inequality, social disintegration, lack of social justice, weak citizenship, the collapse of institutions of community and family, and other societal ills. We therefore have chapters on the histories of development studies research, inequality, urban poverty, ethnopolitics, empowerment and indigenisation, land and identity struggles, challenges in conceptualising family social policy, how socioeconomic and cultural barriers may promote the spread of HIV, and the abuse of state pension grants given to the elderly in South Africa. Some contributions adopt a historical approach because a thorough understanding of past historical stages of development policies enables informed debates on processes that can contribute to social transformation for the majority of historically disadvantaged citizens.

The book opens with Sabelo J. Ndlovu-Gatsheni's chapter, 'Rethinking Development in the Age of Global Coloniality'. Ndlovu-Gatsheni argues that when history meets development studies, the encounter between the two disciplines invokes an inquiry into the past, a critical reflection on the murky present, and imaginations of a mysterious future. This entry point is vital in order to understand the challenges that have been faced by the African people in their struggles for development in their troubled continent. The chapter seeks to harnesses historical knowledge to reflect on development studies as an academic field, as well as ideology, discourse, and practice from decolonial epistemic perspectives and the world-systems approach. The chapter is organised into four sections. The first of these introduces the concept of decolonial epistemic perspectives, which illuminates how development studies has been colonised and held hostage by global imperial designs, and highlights the need for its decolonisation. The second section discusses development challenges as an integral part of the African national project, highlighting how African political economies have remained hostage to invisible colonial matrices of power. The third section analyses the reality of neoliberal imperialism and its impact on current thinking about development issues. The final section grapples with how to transcend the global development impasse and outlines the complex contours of decolonial options that can lead us into the post-Euro-American neoliberal hegemony.

If development is such a desirable end for both African leaders and their so-called partners, why has it become so elusive and difficult to achieve? This is the question posed by Vusi Gumede in Chapter 2, 'Rethinking and Reclaiming Development in Africa'. Gumede argues that it is important to further problematise the notion of development, including what development is, in whose interest is it being pursued and by whom as well as how. He looks into whether there are alternatives to the dominant paradigm of what is generally accepted as development and whether there are alternative routes to the desired end of inclusive development. His chapter therefore attempts to pull together the various perspectives on the notion of development and to propose a better approach to inclusive development in Africa. He begins by looking at how selected earlier writers on development characterise development. He then moves on to discuss post-development and modernisation, as well as functionalism, and the character and nature of development in post-independence Africa. He then follows this with a discussion of how to make development happen in Africa and then proposes an approach to development in Africa.

Analysts hold divergent views regarding poverty and its solutions. Apart from the disagreements concerning the definitions of poverty and inequality, there is no consensus on the appropriate indices for evaluating the suggested programmes, let alone how to address aggregation problems and construct a comprehensive composite index. This is the subject of Chapter 3, 'Elusive Solutions to Poverty and Inequality', by Tidings P. Ndhlovu. Ndhlovu highlights how the neoclassical 'trickle-down', top-down analysis defines poverty and inequality as a natural phenomenon whose only solution is to 'get prices right', while the International Labour Organization (ILO)-inspired basic needs approach regards deprivation of consumption as the primary cause, with the solution being the provision of consumption bundles and productive employment. Ndhlovu also discusses Sen's entitlements and capability approach that focuses on deprivation of basic individual capability, and suggests 'functionings' and freedom as the key to the alleviation of poverty and inequality, and of how Yunus goes further in showing the potential of participatory approaches in Bangladesh and other countries. For the Marxian and/or 'solidarity economy' approaches, poverty and inequality are explicable from the conflictual process of accumulation, while deprivation of power is the central cause.

The next two chapters deal with the perceptions and dynamics of poverty in Zimbabwe and South Africa respectively. While Africa's poverty is well described and discussed in the development literature, at times there is a tendency to focus on rural poverty and underdevelopment, while urban poverty tends to receive less attention. This is the subject of discussion in Chapter 4, 'Urban Poverty in Zimbabwe', by *Rudo Barbra Gaidzanwa*. This chapter focuses on urban poverty, its structure and manifestations in Zimbabwe. Using data from research carried out in Zimbabwe after the infamous Operation *Murambatsvina* (clean-up) exercise of 2005, it describes urban poverty, its profile and the determinants. It argues that urban poverty is distributed amongst specific strata, such as the youth, the elderly and people with disabilities and income-earning challenges. In comparison to poverty in the previous century, urban poverty in Zimbabwe has evolved, taking on a younger profile and endangering social and economic development in urban and rural areas.

In Chapter 5, 'Theory of Poverty or Poverty of Theory?', Raymond Nyapokoto and Sabelo J. Ndlovu-Gatsheni propose a decolonial intervention on urban poverty in South Africa. They argue that what sets South Africa apart is the uneasy coexistence of poverty and opulence, which led former President Thabo Mbeki to articulate the situation in terms of a 'two nations' thesis. They thus propose deploying a Fanonian decolonial theory to critically explore the genesis of poverty and inequality in the country in order to unmask foundational structural causes of poverty, tracing them back to the unfolding of colonialism, the rise of industrial capitalism, and urbanisation patterns and processes. The chapter uses case studies of Alexandra Township and Sandton as epitomes of poverty and opulence respectively. Sandton symbolises the 'zone of being', whereas Alexandra represents the 'zone of nonbeing'. They posit that the road (M1) separating Alexandra and Sandton represents the abyssal line dividing the two. The zone of being is a site for good living and opulence, whereas the zone of nonbeing is the locale of hellish conditions, depravity and poverty. They argue that these two zones are not natural, but a product of particular histories and deliberate policies, which their chapter seeks to reveal.

The next three chapters in the book address issues relating to empowerment, regionalism, ethnicity, identity and development challenges in Zimbabwe and South Africa. Blaming colonialism can never be sufficient answer for the existence of poverty and inequality in postcolonial Africa. There is thus a need to ponder over whether ruling African elites have a vision and decisiveness to come up with new forms of regulating their own economies. Does affirmative action, indigenisation or black economic empowerment benefit the poor strata of society or those already-privileged elites? This is the subject of discussion in Chapter 6, 'The "Native Returns"', by Tamuka Charles Chirimambowa and Tinashe Lukas Chimedza. Chirimambowa and Chimedza assess whether indigenisation and black economic empowerment are development projects in the 'postcolony' or are just a decoy used by ruling elites for their primitive accumulation. They argue that Southern Africa's former liberation movements and their governments in power have argued for and implemented some sort of 'indigenisation' (in Zimbabwe) or Broad-Based Black Economic Empowerment (BBBEE) in South Africa. Such polices have been presented and implemented as a strategy to 'empower' citizens, but mostly as a political and policy response to 'develop' the nation, reduce poverty and inequality. Politically, 'empowerment' is framed as a nationalist liberation project to achieve 'decolonisation' and or 'desettlerisation'. The chapter focuses on Zimbabwe and South Africa, and attempts to critically analyse historical and contemporary contestations around 'indigenisation/empowerment' and the possibility of the emergence of a 'patriotic' black capitalist class capable of leading and driving social and economic transformation.

While development has been an attractive catchphrase in most African countries, power, patronage, ethnicity, nepotism, regionalism and other issues are the ones that count the most, not just for politicians but also for the entire elite and the general population. Vusilizwe Thebe's chapter, 'Ethnopolitics and Regionalism, Discipline and Punishment', argues that ethnopolitics and regionalism have characterised Zimbabwe's development trajectory since independence in 1980. After a failed process of moderation, reconciliation and nation building, the postcolonial state increasingly leaned towards patronage and ethnic and regional politics, using its physical, politically and financial might not only to co-opt but also to punish perceived dissident social groups. According to Thebe, this unfortunate process alongside natural and economic events after 1990 left certain regions politically and economically disenfranchised and underdeveloped as development stalled.

Issues of development and identity remain sensitive in the former white settler states of Southern Africa. Chapter 8, 'The Politics of Land Ownership in South Africa', by Wendy Isaacs-Martin explores whether backyard dwellers perceive that racial identifiers are linked to spatial planning and (re)distribution, as issues of spatial (re)distribution are contentious and emotive in South Africa, particularly for backyard tenants. Backyard dwellers are individuals or families who rent and reside in the yard of main houses, usually council-owned properties, in temporary homes made of wood, plastic and corrugated iron. These are impoverished areas composed predominantly of a single ethnic racial group, the Coloured (people of mixed race). This chapter adopts a desktop research method, conducting structural content analysis of national newspapers following the democratic elections of 1994. Newspaper articles associated with the topic were retrieved from the NewsBank Access South Africa database using a stratified random sample and analysed. An electronic IOL database was used to supplement NewsBank. The period under consideration is from 1997 to 2014. According to Isaacs-Martin, perceptions of entitlement and relative privilege are linked to issues of identity in these impoverished areas. Coloured backyard dwellers perceive this as the reason why they do not have access to land and housing, and that this exclusion and marginalisation is responsible for their economically depressed predicament.

The last three chapters in this book deal specifically with challenges afflicting African families in relation to social policy issues, socioeconomic and cultural barriers to marital unions, threatening diseases and abuse of seniors receiving old-age pension grants. Chapter 9, 'Understanding the Conceptualisation African Families', by Busani Mpofu is an introduction to the ongoing study on the conceptualisation of a family policy in South Africa, focusing on the Eastern Cape, KwaZulu-Natal and Limpopo Provinces, which were identified as containing the majority of poor and more child-headed families. Mpofu argues that developing an African family policy from an African perspective is even more crucial now because black African families in South Africa are in a state of crisis, which manifests itself in the form of escalating family breakdowns and very negative effects on children and the youth (see Holborn and Eddy 2011). The major source of concern here is that while the *White Paper* acknowledged that various kinds of families exist in the country, it concluded that the nuclear family is the most common type in South Africa (Department of Social Development, Republic of South Africa 2012: 15). The problem with this assumption is that, at the end, the Western nuclear family, which is regarded as the norm due to the hegemony of Western imperialism, continues to be the basis of many social policies, despite the fact that this family form is not the most dominant among black African families (Sunde and Bozalek 1995: 65). This chapter argues that living in nuclear households in urban or semi-urban areas should not be conflated with having a nuclear family. A historical understanding of the conceptualisation of a black African family, which was incorrect at certain levels, is necessary before one can think of conceptualising about a family policy.

Can Africa's current problems be divorced from the limitations of its historical development (precolonial as much or more than colonial)? In order for real progress to occur, does social and cultural life in Africa have to change? This is Busani Ngcaweni's subject of discussion in Chapter 10, 'Socioeconomic and Cultural Barriers to Marital Unions and HIV Incidence Correlates'. Ngcaweni explores socioeconomic and cultural barriers to marital unions and HIV incidence correlates in South Africa. He argues that the cultural practice of *lobola* (payment of a dowry) forms part of the causes of low marriage rates among Africans because *lobola* is overpriced and out of reach of most unemployed and underemployed Africans. This leaves more black Africans unable to marry and more exposed to the risk of HIV, as recent studies have shown that single and cohabiting individuals tend to have higher exposure to HIV compared to married people. The chapter therefore ask whether or not, if marriage presents some 'form of protection' against HIV, the national government should actively promote marriage as a public policy response to the HIV pandemic. In addition, should government and other concerned stakeholders actively engage with traditional leaders and other role players to address concerns about the abuse of *lobola* and therefore depressing marriage rates among Africans who happen to be the most afflicted by the AIDS epidemic?

While Ferguson (2015) highlighted the increasing importance of cash pay-outs in the Southern African region, some intended beneficiaries may not benefit much from them. This is the subject of discussion in the last chapter of this book, 'Old-Age Cash Grant Pay-out Days', in which Gloria Sauti argues that seniors (the elderly) attract unprecedented attention just before or during the Old-Age Pension or the 'Old Age Grant' pay-out days in South Africa. Vendors, local stores and taxi drivers claim to significantly reduce prices in their stalls, shops and transport fares respectively around grant pay-out points in order to attract seniors. Some seniors are forced to become 'money lenders' by family members who borrow from them. In order to survive for the whole month, seniors have to eventually borrow and thus fall victim to loan sharks or the so-called 'machonisas' who charge exorbitant interest rates. Seniors are abused in the process, a situation to which the government and other humanitarian actors seem oblivious. Sauti demonstrates how this abuse of the old-age grant jeopardises the government's goal to combat poverty and improve the wellbeing of seniors.

Busani Mpofu is a senior researcher at AMRI, College of Graduate Studies, University of South Africa. His main research interests include Third World urbanisation and the history of African cities, urban poverty, inclusive development, development discourse and theory. His publications include 'The Urban Land Question, Land Reform and the Spectre of Extrajudicial Land Occupations in South Africa', *Africa Insight* (2017) and 'The Land Question, Agriculture, Industrialisation and the Economy in Zimbabwe: A Critical Reflection', in O. Akanle and J.O.T. Adesisa (eds), *Development of Africa: Issues, Diagnoses and Prognoses* (2018).

Sabelo J. Ndlovu-Gatsheni is the Acting Executive Director of Change Management Unit (CMU), Vice Chancellor's Office at the University of South Africa (Unisa). He has published extensively in African history, African politics, and development. His major publications include *The Ndebele Nation: Reflections on Hegemony, Memory and Historiography* (2009); *Do 'Zimbabweans' Exist? Trajectories of Nationalism, National Identity Formation and Crisis in a Postcolonial State* (2009); *Redemptive or Grotesque Nationalism? Rethinking Contemporary Politics in Zimbabwe* (2011); *Empire, Global Coloniality and African Subjectivity* (2013); *Coloniality of Power in Postcolonial Africa: Myths of Decolonization* (2013); *Nationalism and National Projects in Southern Africa: New Critical Reflections* (2013); and *Bondage of Boundaries and Identity Politics in Postcolonial Africa: The 'Northern Problem' and Ethno-Futures* (2013).

Note

1. For more information on the main causes, responses and effects of the 2008 global financial crisis, see Robinson (2014).

References

African Union. 2013. *Agenda 2063 Vision and Priorities: Unity, Prosperity and Peace*. Addis Ababa: African Union.

Banda, R.M.R. 2004. 'Development Discourse and the Third World'. Proceedings of the Second Academic Sessions. Retrieved 6 September 2018 from http://www.ruh.ac.lk/research/academic_sessions/2004_mergepdf/98-103.PDF.

Chabal, P. 2012. *The End of Conceit: Western Rationality after Postcolonialism*. London: Zed Books.

Cooper, B., and R. Morrell (eds). 2014. *Africa-Centred Knowledges: Crossing Fields and Worlds*. Oxford: James Currey.

Cowen, M.P., and R. W. Shenton. 1996. *Doctrines of Development*. London: Routledge.

de Santos, B.S. 2014. *Epistemologies of the South: Justice against Epistemicide*. Boulder, CO: Paradigm Publishers.

Department of Social Development, Republic of South Africa, 2012. *White Paper on Families in South Africa*, September.

Easterly, W. 2007. 'The Ideology of Development'. June 11. Retrieved 17 July 2014 from http://www.foreignpolicy.com/articles/2007/06/11/the_ideology_of_development.

―――. 2009. 'The Ideology of Development'. Retrieved 6 September 2018 from http://foreignpolicy.com/2009/10/13/the-ideology-of-development.

―――. 2014. *The Tyranny of Experts: Economists, Dictators and the Forgotten Rights of the Poor*. New York: Basics Books.

Escobar, A. 1988. 'Power and Visibility: Development and the Intervention and Management of the Third World', *Cultural Anthropology* 3(4): 428–43.

―――. 1997. 'Anthropology and Development', *International Social Science Journal* 49(4): 497–516.

Ferguson, J. 1990. *The Anti-politics Machine: 'Development', Depoliticization, and Bureaucratic Power in Lesotho*. Cambridge: Cambridge University Press.

―――. 2015. *Give a Man a Fish: Reflections on the New Politics of Distribution*. Durham, NC: Duke University Press.

Fourcade, M., E. Ollion and Y. Algan. 2015. 'The Superiority of Economists', *Journal of Economic Perspectives* 29(1): 89–114.

Grosfoguel, R. 2007. 'The Epistemic Decolonial Turn: Beyond Political-Economy Paradigms', Cultural *Studies* 21(2–3): 211–23.

Grosfoguel, R., and Cervantes-Rodriguez, A.M.C. 2002. 'Introduction: Unthinking Twentieth Century Eurocentric Mythologies: Universalist Knowledges, Decolonization, and Developmentalism', in R. Grosfoguel and A. M. Cervantes-Rodriguez (eds), *The Modern/Colonial/Capitalist World-System in the Twentieth Century: Global Processes, Antisystemic Movements, and the Geopolitics of Knowledge*. Westport: Praeger, pp. xi–xxx.

Habib, A. 2015. 'Accelerating Transformation for an Inclusive and Competitive Wits', *Focus: The Journal of Helen Suzman Foundation* 76: 8–14.

Hanlon, J., A. Barrientos and D. Hulme. 2010. *Just Give Money to the Poor: The Development Revolution from the Global South*. Sterling, VA: Kumarian Press.

Hart, K. 2008a. 'The Human Economy', *asa online* 1(1): 1–12.

_____. 2008b. 'After the Disaster', *Anthropology Today* 24(2): 1–3.
Hart, K., J.-L. Laville and A. D. Cattani. 2010. 'Building the Human Economy Together', in K. Hart, J.-L. Laville and A. Cattani (eds), *The Human Economy*. Cambridge: Polity Press, pp. 1–17.
Hart, K., and V. Padayachee, 2010. 'South Africa in Africa: From National Capitalism to Regional Integration', in V. Padayachee (ed.), *The Political Economy of Africa*. London: Routledge, pp. 410–27.
Holborn, L., and G. Eddy, 2011. 'First Steps to Healing the South African Family', research paper by the South African Institute of Race Relations, sponsored by the Donaldson Trust, Johannesburg.
Kanbur, R. and G. Rauniyar. 2009. 'Conceptualising Inclusive Development: With Applications to Rural Development and Development Assistance'. Retrieved 6 September 2018 from http://www.kanbur.dyson.cornell.edu/papers/ADBCompendiumInclusiveDevelopment.pdf.
Marks, S. 2006. 'China in Africa: The New Imperialism'. Retrieved 6 September 2018 from https://www.pambazuka.org/global-south/china-africa-new-imperialism.
Mbeki, M. 2009. *Architects of Poverty: Why African Capitalism Needs Changing*. Johannesburg: Picador Africa.
McNally, D. 2005. *Another World is Possible: Globalization and Anti-capitalism*. Winnipeg: Arbeiter Ring Publishing.
Mignolo, W.D. 1995. *The Dark Side of Renaissance: Literacy, Territory, and Colonization*. Ann Arbor, MI: University of Michigan Press.
_____. 2011. *The Dark Side of Western Modernity: Global Futures, Decolonial Options*. Durham, NC: Duke University Press.
_____. 2012. *Local Histories/Global Designs; Coloniality, Subaltern Knowledges, and Border Thinking*. Princeton: Princeton University Press.
Moyo, S. 2016. 'Perspectives on South-South Relations: China's Presence in Africa', *Inter-Asia Cultural Studies* 17(1): 58–67.
Mubangizi, O. 2018. 'Dr Abiy Ahmed's Ethiopia: Anatomy of an African Enigmatic Polity', *Pambazuka News*, 15 May. Retrieved 6 September 2018 from https://www.pambazuka.org/democracy-governance/dr-abiy-ahmed%E2%80%99s-ethiopia-anatomy-african-enigmatic-polity.
Nabudere, D.W. 2011. *Archie Mafeje: Scholar, Activist and Thinker*. Pretoria: Africa Institute of South Africa.
_____. 2011. *Afrikology, Philosophy and Wholeness: An Epistemology*. Pretoria: Africa Institute of South Africa.
Ndlovu-Gatsheni, S. 2015. 'Genealogies of Coloniality and Implications for Africa's Development', *Africa Development* XL(3): 13–40.
_____. 2016. '"Rhodes Must Fall": South African Universities as Site of Struggle', unpublished Draft (the first draft of this article was delivered as a public lecture at the London School of Economics' Africa Public Talk Lectures, Hong Kong Theatre, London, 9 March).
Ndhlovu, T.P. 2016. 'Colonialism and the Economics of Unequal Exchange', in B. Avari and G.G. Joseph (eds), *The Interwoven World: Ideas and Encounters in History*. Champaign, IL: Common Ground Publishing, pp. 188–205.
Ngugi wa Thiong'o. 1986. *Decolonizing the Mind: The Politics of Language in African Literature*. London: James Currey.

Nyamnjoh, F. 2012. 'Potted Plants in Greenhouses: A Critical Reflection on the Resilience of Colonial Education in Africa', *Journal of Asian and African Studies* 47(2): 129–54.

Odora-Hoppers, C., and H. Richards. 2012. *Rethinking Thinking: Modernity's 'Other' and the Transformation of the University*. Pretoria: University of South Africa.

Robinson, W.I. 2014. *Global Capitalism and the Crisis of Humanity*. New York: Cambridge University Press.

Sachs, W. (ed.). 1992. *The Development Dictionary*. London: Zed Books.

Share, F. 2018. 'UPDATED: President Names, Shames Looters • Nearly $1bn Remains Outstanding • Funds Stashed in China, Botswana, SA', *The Herald*, 20 March. Retrieved 6 September 2018 from https://www.herald.co.zw/president-mnangagwa-exposes-externalizers.

Schuurman, F. 2009. 'Critical Development Theory: Moving out of the Twilight Zone', *Third World Quarterly* 30(5): 831–48.

Shanmugaratnam, N. 2011. 'Development in Historical Perspective and an Overview of Development Studies'. Retrieved 6 September 2018 from http://www.umb.no/statisk/noragric/staff_cv/shanmugaratnam_development_theory_2011.pdf.

Sunde, J., and V. Bozalek, 1995. '(Re)Presenting "The Family": Familist Discources, Welfare and the State', *Transformation* 26: 63–77.

Southall, R., and H. Melber (eds). 2009. *A New Scramble for Africa?: Imperialism, Investment and Development*. Pietermaritzburg: University of KwaZulu-Natal Press.

Tabensky, P., and S. Matthews (eds). 2015. *Being at Home: Race, Institutional Culture and Transformation at South African Higher Education Institutions*. Pietermaritzburg: University of KwaZulu-Natal Press, 2015.

Taylor, I. 2014. *Africa Rising: BRICS – Diversifying Dependency*. Oxford: James Currey.

The Livingstone Call for Action. 2006. Adopted at the African Union Intergovernmental Regional Conference 'A Transformative Agenda for the 21st Century: Examining the Case for Basic Social Protection in Africa', Livingstone, Zambia, 20–23 March 2.

Wallerstein, I. 1991. 'Introduction: Why Unthink?', in I. Wallerstein (ed.), *Unthinking Social Science: The Limits of Nineteenth Century Paradigms*. Cambridge: Polity Press, pp. 1–30.

Wengraf, L. 2017. 'Imperialism in Africa: China's Widening Role'. Retrieved 6 September 2018 from http://roape.net/2017/04/13/imperialism-africa-chinas-widening-role.

World Bank. 2013. *Africa's Pulse, October 2013: An Analysis of Issues Shaping Africa's Economic Future*. Washington, DC: World Bank. https://openknowledge.worldbank.org/handle/10986/20237. License: CC BY 3.0 IGO.

Žižek, S. 2011. *Living in the End Times*. London: Verso.

———. 2013. 'If Nelson Mandela Really Had Won, He Wouldn't Be Seen as a Universal Hero', *The Guardian*, 9 December. Retrieved 6 September from http://www.theguardian.com/commentisfree/2013/dec/09/if-nelson-mandela-really-had-won.

Part I

Theory, Concepts and Discourse

Chapter 1

Rethinking Development in the Age of Global Coloniality

Sabelo J. Ndlovu-Gatsheni

Introduction

Development is simultaneously an ideology, a discourse and a practice. Genealogically speaking, development is part of Cartesian thought, Enlightenment reason and Euro-North American-centric modernity. It ranks alongside linear notions of social evolution, progress and emancipation. Its links with modernity can in particular be seen in the notions of 'rapture' and 'difference' (Bhambra 2007), which form part of the relegation of Africa and other areas outside Europe and North America to the categories of premodern and primitive. It is such thinking that provoked the need for rethinking development and indeed even unthinking it from a decolonial epistemic perspective. A decolonial epistemic perspective is by nature a historical analysis as it delves into genealogy of knowledge, power and being as it consistently unmasks and drills into how embedded these are matrices in coloniality.

Thus, the first section of this chapter introduces the concept of decolonial epistemic perspectives, which illuminates how development studies as a field of knowledge has been colonised and held hostage by global imperial designs, and highlights the need for its decolonisation. The second section discusses development challenges as an integral part of the African national project, highlighting how African political economies have remained hostage to invisible colonial matrices of power. The third section analyses the reality of neoliberal imperialism and its impact on current thinking about development issues. The final section grapples with how to transcend the global development impasse and outlines the complex contours of decolonial options that take us into the post-Euro-American hegemony.

The decolonial epistemic perspective, which embraces a world-systems approach, makes it possible to grapple with pertinent global imperial designs, and facilitates the laying of the foundations for a decolonisation of development studies as a field of study, which has remained deeply interpellated by its Euro-American modernist and 'civilising mission' genealogy. A combination of a world-systems approach and decolonial epistemic perspectives form an ideal entry point to interrogate claims of objectivist-universalist knowledges, challenges of decolonisation of Euro-American power structure, and problems of developmentalism (Grosfoguel and Cervantes-Rodriguez 2002: xi–xxx).

Decolonisation as a political, epistemological and economic liberatory project has remained an unfinished business, giving way to coloniality. Coloniality is an invisible power structure that sustains colonial relations of exploitation and domination long after the end of direct colonialism (Maldonado-Torres 2007: 240–70). Coloniality of power works as a crucial structuring process within global imperial designs, sustaining the superiority of the Global North and ensuring the perpetual subalternity of the Global South using colonial matrices of power (Mignolo 2007: 155–67).

Colonial matrices of power are a set of technologies of subjectivation that consist of four types. The first is control *of economy*, which manifests itself through dispossessions, land appropriations, the exploitation of labour, and control over African natural resources. The second is *control of authority*, which includes the maintenance of military superiority and monopolisation of the means of violence. The third is control of gender and sexuality, which involves the reimagination of 'family' in Western bourgeois terms and the introduction of Western-centric education, which displaces indigenous forms of knowledge. The last is *control of subjectivity and knowledge*, which includes epistemological colonisation and the rearticulation of African subjectivity as inferior and constituted by a series of 'deficits' and a catalogue of 'lacks' (Grosfoguel 2007: 214; Quijano 2007: 168–87).

In terms of the definition of development, the Bandung Conference of 1955 articulated development from the perspective of decolonisation, in which it is understood as a liberatory human aspiration to attain freedom from political, economic, ideological, epistemological and social domination that was installed by colonialism and coloniality (Mkandawire 2011: 7). In the Bandung version, development entailed overcoming those major obstacles to human happiness and the attainment of material welfare, civil and political liberties, social peace and human security, which can be named as colonialism and coloniality (Ndlovu-Gatsheni 2012, 2013).

This definition of development is opposed to what Thandika Mkandawire terms the 'Truman version of developmentalism', where development is interpreted as Euro-American missionary task of developing the Global South in general and Africa in particular (Mkandawire 2011: 7-8). In the Bandung Conference version of development, it is conceived as a rational human response to historical experiences and human needs, whereas in the Truman version, development falls neatly within global imperial designs articulated in terms of 'civilising mission' and 'Westernisation' of the non-Western world (Mehmet 1995). As will become clear in the course of this chapter, decolonising development studies entails rescuing it from the Truman version of developmentalism.

The enormity of the task of decolonising development studies cannot be fully realised in the absence of deployment of a well-thought-out theoretical framework capable of unmasking the beast of coloniality, which has been assuming different colours and wearing different masks in its endeavour to disguise itself. Therefore, I specifically deploy the concept of 'coloniality of power' as a major component of the world-systems approach and critical concept underpinning decolonial epistemic perspectives, which highlights the darker side of modernity that has resulted in the underdevelopment of Africa.

Development studies and development discourses are not free of the colonial matrices of power that underpin coloniality. Development studies continues to suffer from a crisis of ideas, which culminated in the development impasse of the 1980s. The recent economic crisis affecting global capitalism that has manifested itself as a financial crisis is a further indicator of troubled economic epistemologies that have implications on discourses and practices of development. As noted by James Ferguson, development is not neutral of power and cannot be understood outside of the current power dynamics. It is part of what he terms the anti-politics machine (Ferguson 1990). It cannot be reduced to simple real-life problems of hunger, water scarcity, disease, malnutrition and poverty, as if these were untouched and unshaped by broader questions of power, epistemology, representation and identity construction (Tripathy and Mohapatra 2011: 93–118).

The Case for Decolonising Development Studies

The exercise of decolonising development studies entails four tasks. The first is that of probing development's relative amnesia about coloniality

(Kapoor 2008: xv). The second is that of revealing its embeddedness in Enlightenment and modernity's notions of scientific progress, civilising mission and universal economic prescriptions. The third is that of interrogation of development's deep imbrications in Euro-American knowledge and global imperial designs. The last is that of critiquing the current neoliberal tendencies that masquerade as salvation for Africa (Kapoor 2008: xv).

The best approach to use in order to achieve the decolonisation of development studies is to deploy decolonial epistemic perspectives that reveal coloniality embedded in development discourse. Decolonial epistemic perspectives are predicated on the concepts of power, knowledge and being. Coloniality of power locates the discourse of development within the context of the politics of the constitution of a racially hierarchised, Euro-America-centric, Christian-centric, patriarchal, capitalist, heteronormative, hegemonic, asymmetrical and modern global power structure (Grosfoguel and Cervantes-Rodriguez 2002; Grosfoguel 2007). Within this structure, development exists as one of the technologies of subjectivation in the same league as ideas of modernity, progress, civilisation and modernisation.

Coloniality of knowledge enables an investigation into the epistemological foundations of development as a modernist form of apparatus that has been utilised to construct what became known as the 'Third World'/'developing world' inhabited by people whose being was constituted by a series of 'lacks' and a catalogue of 'deficits' that justified various forms of external intervention in Africa, including the notorious structural adjustment programmes (SAPs) (Escobar 2012: viii). Coloniality of being extends the debates to the realm of the making of modern subjectivities and conceptions of humanism, where racial hierarchisation and classification of people according to race pushed Africans to the lowest rank of human ontology, where even their being human was doubted and where they existed as objects of development (Maldonado-Torres 2007).

The concepts of power, knowledge and being help to unmask coloniality as an underside of modernity, without necessarily rejecting the positive aspects of modernity. Through decolonial epistemic perspectives, we seek to discover the benefits of analysing development discourse from the perspective of 'colonial difference'. Colonial difference is a reference to the spaces, borders and peripheries of empire that have suffered the negative consequences of modernity, such as the slave trade, imperialism, colonialism, apartheid and neocolonialism (Mignolo 2000: 49–88).

What distinguishes the decolonial epistemic perspective from dominant Euro-American-centric hegemonic neoliberal discourses is its locus of enunciation. Locus of enunciation here refers to the geographical spaces from which academics and intellectuals speak, their ideological orientations, subject positions (racial, gender and class identifications), and the historical processes and events that inform their knowledge claims (Grosfoguel 2007: 213). The decolonial epistemic perspective does not attempt to claim universality, neutrality and singular truthfulness. It is decidedly and deliberately situated in those epistemic sites such as Latin America, Asia, the Caribbean and Africa that experienced the negative consequences of modernity and that are facing development challenges. At the same time, it openly accepts its partiality, in the awareness that all forms of knowledge are partial.

The overarching objective of the decolonial epistemic perspective is to unveil epistemic silences hidden within Euro-American epistemology as well as the deceit and hypocrisy that conceal epistemicides. It challenges what Aime Cesaire termed 'the fundamental European lie', which articulated colonisation as a vehicle for civilisation (1955: 84). In short, a decolonial perspective is meant not only to change the content of intellectual and academic conversations on development, but also the terms of this conversation so as to engage with the crucial issues of epistemology, being and power that maintain the present asymmetrical global relations.

Coloniality of power is at the core of the present global power structure, where ideas of development fall neatly within a genealogy of discourses that presented Africans as people whose being was constituted by negations and lacks: lacking writing, lacking history, lacking civilisation, lacking development, lacking democracy and lacking human rights (Grosfoguel 2007: 213). At the same time, the human population has been undergoing social classification according to invented racial categories of inferior/superior, primitive/civilised, rational/irrational, traditional/modern and developed/underdeveloped (Quijano 2000).

The agenda of decolonising development studies entails revealing what development meant within the context of colonialism (and now coloniality). How was (and is) it defined? In the first place, understood from the perspective of empire as the locus of enunciation, imperialism and colonialism were grand 'civilising missions'. Europeans were agents of development and Africans were the objects of development (Mehmet 1995).

Within colonial discourses, development meant opening up the African continent for economic exploitation and the permanent relocation of white settlers. Development also meant defeating African resistance (read as the pacification of barbarous tribes resisting modernity) to pave the way for the construction of colonial states. Development meant the designation of land as the private property of white settlers in those areas that fell victim to settler colonialism, like South Africa, Algeria, Zimbabwe and Kenya (Magubane 1996). Development meant the rearrangement of African agrarian systems to make sure they produced the cash crops needed in Europe and America.

Development meant the dispossession of Africans, forcing them off the land and transforming them into peasants, workers and domestic servants. At the same time, acquired land was quickly transformed into plantations and farms owned by victorious white settlers. In other words, development in the colonial context meant pushing Africans out of their modes of life and production, and into the evolving capitalist system, where they participated mainly as sources of cheap labour. Mbembe argued that 'in implementing its projects, the colonial state did not hesitate to resort to brute force in dealing with natives, to destroy the forms of social organisation that previously existed, or even to co-opt these forms in the service of ends other than those to which they had been directed' (2000: 8).

Within the colonial context, development meant the transformation of African society according to the needs, demands and imperatives of colonial regimes. Frederick Cooper noted that colonialism never provided a strong national economy to benefit African people because the colonial economies were 'externally oriented and the state's economic power remained concentrated at the gate between inside and outside' (Cooper 2002: 5). It was Cooper who described the colonial state as a 'gatekeeper state' that was not embedded in the society over which it presided, that stood astride the intersection of colonial territory and the outside world, and that drew revenue from imposing duties on goods and taxing Africans (Cooper 2002).

Socially, colonial development entailed the reorganisation and classification of the colonial population according to race. Mahmood Mamdani (1996) described the colonial states as bifurcated social formations inhabited by 'subjects' and 'citizens'. In order to prevent the coalescence of colonised peoples into nations, colonialists used cartography, censuses and the law to classify and categorise the population. Political and legal identities were enforced via the issuing of identity cards. Through its technologies of governance, colonialism transformed fluid and accommodative precolonial cultural identities into rigid, impermeable, singular, nonconsensual and exclusionary political identities.

Within this, 'races' were acknowledged as having a common future as citizens, whereas tribes, as subjects, were to be excluded from this common future. Further, colonial governments denied the African people the space to coalesce into a majority identity by splitting them into different and competing tribes and minorities (Mamdani 2007). One good example of this is the establishment of Bantustans by the apartheid regime in South Africa that enabled the exclusion of black people from belonging to South Africa.

Politically, colonial governance assumed the character of a hybrid military/civilian model where violence was a norm of governance. Paramilitary authoritarianism was a core component of colonial governance, with disciplining of the 'natives' being the order of the day. Mbembe has argued that 'the colonial state model was, in theory as in practice, the exact opposite of the liberal model of discussion or deliberation' (2000: 6). Three forms of violence underpinned colonial governance: 'foundational violence', which authorised the right of conquest and had an 'instituting function' of creating Africans as its targets; 'legitimating violence', which was used after conquest to construct the colonial order and routinise colonial reality; and 'maintenance violence', which was infused into colonial institutions and cultures, and was used to ensure their perpetuation (Mbembe 2000: 6–7).

Under colonialism, citizenship rights for Africans were a scarce resource. Participation of Africans in elections was impossible. Largely, the colonial state became an institution for the exploitation of black labour and a vehicle of repression. Coercion rather than consent formed the DNA of colonial governance. Through its social, economic and political engineering processes, colonialism created a complex 'native-settler' question – permeated by white supremacist ideas – that prevented the formation of multiracial nation-states out of colonial encounters (Mamdani 1996: 12–18).

In countries like South Africa and Zimbabwe, with large white European populations, the resolution of the colonially created native-settler question has proven to be difficult and continues to impinge on nation building and development. Thinking about how this question could be resolved, Mamdani located it within the politics of identity reconstruction and asked how could 'a settler become a native' (see Mamdani 1998a, 1998b; Ahluwalia 2001: 67). He elaborated on the intractability of the 'native-settler' question thus:

> In the context of a former settler colony, a single citizenship for settlers and natives can only be the result of an overall metamorphosis whereby erstwhile colonisers and colonised are politically reborn as equal members of a single political community. The word reconciliation cannot capture this metamorphosis ... This is about establishing for the first time, a political order based on consent and not conquest. It is about establishing a political community of equal and consenting citizens. (Ahluwalia 2001: 67)

The reality is that colonialism did not bequeath modernity to Africa. Olufemi Taiwo (2010) argues that by the time of colonisation, Africa was already becoming modern on its own terms. Colonialism disrupted these indigenous initiatives by imposing such structures as indirect rule, which masqueraded as the preservation of precolonial institutions of governance while at the same time crippling African agency and impulses towards progress. Taiwo concluded that 'colonialism was the bulwark against the implantation of modernity in Africa' (Taiwo 2010: 237).

Decolonising development studies is urgent today because modernity has created numerous modern problems – ranging from climate change to the global financial crisis – for which it has no modern solutions. Neoliberalism as a solution has proven to be problematic because it has not enabled a radical transformation of Euro-American hegemonic epistemology, North–South asymmetrical power relations and racialised perceptions of being in which black races suffer subalternity.

As a result of the dominance of neoliberal thinking, what is driving development studies today is a positivist re-evaluation and consolidation of previous concepts and techniques, as opposed to the formulation of new ideas per se. Eric Thorbecke noted that the 'important contribution to development doctrine in this decade is technique rather than theory' (2007: 3). This means that the ability to formulate grand theories like modernisation and dependency has been substituted with a concentration on methodological innovations that do not challenge knowledges of equilibrium. What is lost is a clear understanding of the underlying structural factors sustaining a global system of relationships generating negative development outcomes in Africa.

According to Slavoj Žižek, 'weak thought', which is 'opposed to all foundationalism', takes the form of heavy empiricism that misses the bigger picture of coloniality of power and celebrates African agency without considering the structural constraints in place, has been celebrated as progressive since the fall of the Soviet Union (Žižek 2008: 3–5). The development community has run out of 'big ideas' and 'strong thought'. This reality led David L. Lindauer and Lant Pritchett to argue that 'what is of even deeper concern than the lack of an obvious dominant set of big ideas that command (near) universal acclaim is the scarcity of theory and evidence-based research on which to draw' (Lindauer and Pritchett 2002: 2).

'Weak thought' promotes a shallow understanding of global and local power dynamics, to the extent that at times 'experts' from the developed North are still given space to deliver their 'pedagogy of development' on Africa, in spite of the dismal failure of the SAPs of the late 1970s and 1980s. What is often missed is John Henrik Clarke's warning that 'powerful people will never educate powerless people on what it means to take power away from them' (n. d.). The reality remains that 'the aim of the powerful people is to stay powerful by any means necessary' (Clarke n. d.). This is as true for African dictators as it is for the 'experts' from the Global North, as well as for those who primitively accumulated wealth in Africa during the colonial and apartheid eras. There is no doubt that developmental disparities in Africa are informed by deliberately constructed power asymmetries that in turn underpin and maintain socially constructed hierarchies of a 'superior' West and an 'inferior' Africa.

Žižek has railed against 'weak thought', which, according to him, has resulted in the 'culturalisation of politics' that ignores the broader historical, discursive and structural processes responsible for human developmental tragedies. He posed the following question:

> Why are so many problems today perceived as problems of intolerance, rather than as problems of inequality, exploitation, or injustice? Why is the proposed remedy tolerance, rather than emancipation, political struggle, even armed struggle? (Žižek 2009: 119)

The field of development studies is terribly affected by 'weak thought' as opposed to 'strong thought' (Žižek 2008: 1). To Žižek, strong thought produces 'large-scale explanations' and 'true ideas' that are 'indestructible' (2008: 5). Large-scale explanations have the capacity to 'always return every time they are proclaimed dead' (Žižek 2008: 8). Decolonial epistemic perspective is a good example of the cocktail of all those strong liberatory ideas that have proven resistant to neoliberal mystifications.

Weak thought has even blinded some academics to such an extent that they continue to uncritically believe in the innocence of development discourses and to defend wrong causes – which have appropriated acceptable terms such as democracy, reform, development, good governance and humanitarian intervention – without sifting out the dangerous colonial matrices embedded therein. The same weak thought has seen Africans annually celebrating decolonisation, which Grosfoguel has correctly depicted as 'the most powerful myth of the twentieth century' that 'led to the myth of a postcolonial world', while in reality 'we continue to live under the same colonial power matrix' (2007: 219).

In 2010, Achille Mbembe posed a crucial soul-searching question: 'Here we are ... 50 years after decolonisation: Is there anything at all to commemorate, or should one on the contrary start all over again?' (Mbembe 2010). The answer came from Ali Mazrui, who argued that 'the 50th anniversary provides a suitable occasion not only to evaluate what has happened to Africa as a whole, but also to estimate the impact of the colonial experience on the African peoples' (Mazrui 2011: 1). What is telling is that Mazrui decided to use the fiftieth anniversary of decolonisation as an occasion to judge '100 years of colonial rule' (Mazrui 2011: 1). Does this mean that the fifty years of decolonisation was not worth judging? The response is borrowed from Grosfoguel, who clearly stated that 'the heterogeneous and multiple global structures put in place over a period of 450 years did not evaporate with the juridical-political decolonization of the periphery over the past 50 years' (Grosfoguel 2007: 219).

There are also crucial epistemological issues such as those identified by Mahmood Mamdani, particularly the proliferation of 'corrosive culture of consultancy' that has substituted diagnostic research in developmental issues for shallow technicist prescriptions informed by a symptomatic reading of the African development malaise (Mamdani 2011). The pervasiveness of this 'consultancy culture' manifests itself in many forms, including an emphasis on training in descriptive and quantitative data collection methods. These empiricist tools enable efficient 'hunting and gathering' of raw data and the production of consultancy reports that are eventually processed into theories and developmental policy documents in Euro-American academies. This 'consultancy culture' ends up turning Africans into pure 'native informants' rather than authentic, rigorous and robust producers of knowledge who can drive African development (Mamdani 2011).

The pervasiveness of 'consultancy cultures' was also identified by Mamdani as manifesting itself in the tendency of academics to rely on what he termed 'corporate-style power point presentations', dominated by the parroting of buzzwords at the expense of lively, engaged and rigorous intellectual debate (Mamdani 2011). The outcome has been the reduction of academic research from a long-range diagnostic enterprise to a quick prescriptive exercise. It is within this context that 'weak thought' has occupied centre stage in many debates on development and has led to the glossing over of pertinent questions concerning the role of empire and Western epistemology in hampering development in Africa.

A further downside to this has been attempts to characterise the humanities and social sciences as irrelevant to development, because development is conceived in simplistic and shallow terms of 'technicism' and 'innovation', or in 'bricks and mortar' terms where there is little space for debate and the critique of knowledge claims (Stewart 2007: 141). This thinking has resulted in what Peter Stewart has termed 'the current dominance of instrumental reason', resulting in knowledge being reduced to the 'polytechnic/technikon and industry mode of know-how' (Stewart 2007: 141). The outcome of this weak thought has been a combination of the commodification, marketisation and pervasive managerialism invading universities as sites of knowledge generation.

Development studies is terribly affected not only by the heavy empiricism but also by a failure to distinguish between alternatives to the systems and structures that generate underdevelopment, and the alternatives within the same systems that lead to development dead-ends. Indeed, there is development literature that blames the problems of Africa on Africans themselves and totally exonerates imperial global designs of responsibility for this. It is this different reading of the African development predicament that decolonial epistemic analysis seeks to partly challenge. The point is that the scale of African development challenges cannot be understood clearly outside of a distinct understanding of the historical, discursive and structural contexts of modernity, imperialism, colonialism, decolonisation, neocolonialism, neoliberalism and globalisation (Ndlovu-Gatsheni 2012).

African conceptions of development are locked into the Truman version of developmentalism, and the Bandung version of development has been struggling to transcend coloniality. The African national projects that embraced development as a core component assumed modernist-elitist formats and unfolded as impositions by undecolonised postcolonial states on society.

The African National Project and Development Challenges

Tukumbi Lumumba-Kasongo defined the national project as an important aspect of state building involving the creation of new institutions, defining new culture, forging new citizenship, formulating new policies, putting in place new political and economic programmes aimed at addressing people's demands, and institutionalising the idea of sovereignty of the state (Lumumba-Kasongo 2011: 70). At the centre of the African national project has been the preoccupation with development, which was simplistically embraced as involving 'catching-up' with the Euro-American world on the one hand, and a rectification of colonially created economic and social problems on the other hand (Mkandawire 2011: 10–12). The intimate connection between the national project and development is well articulated by Arnold Rivkin, who said:

> Nation-building and economic development ... are twin goals and intimately related tasks, sharing many of the same problems, confronting many of the same challenges; and interrelating at many levels of public policy and practice. (Rivkin 1969: 156)

Due to the drive to 'catch up', the postcolonial states tried to achieve multiple national tasks as quickly as possible and simultaneously. These tasks began with the drive toward nation building and state consolidation involving uniting different races and ethnicities into one national identity, as well as the entrenchment of African political power in terms of building institutions, monopolising violence and forging hegemony (Olukoshi and Laakso 1996: 7–39). The postcolonial state promised to eradicate colonial autocracy and repression so as to build accountability, legitimacy and transparency, and ensure popular participation in governance. This was to be accompanied by the eradication of poverty, ignorance and disease, and the promotion of economic growth so as to improve the standard of living. The more radical postcolonial states, like Ghana, Tanzania, Mozambique and Zimbabwe, also promised to reverse colonial dispossession through the redistribution of national resources. All postcolonial states became preoccupied with the challenge of securing the hard-won political independence against external threats (Mkandawire 2005: 10–55).

What indicated that development occupied the heart of the African national project was that every African state was busy implementing some form of five-year development plan or another soon after the achievement of political independence (Nugent 2004: 214). The crucial question is why did the African national project not succeed in realising its core objectives? Why has development eluded Africa? Julius Ihonvbere squarely blames African leaders and the African elite for the failures of the African national project and development (1994: 17).

Ihonvbere's explanation is familiar and shared by many Africanist and African scholars, such as George Ayittey, who argued that it is naïve to blame Africa's misery on external factors when African leaders themselves betrayed both the aspirations of their people and their indigenous political systems (Ayittey 1994: 15–20). Moeletsi Mbeki (2009) reinforced Ihonvbere's and Ayittey's views, and identified African leaders and elites as 'the architects of poverty' in Africa, keeping their fellow citizens poor while they enriched themselves. It is clear that African leaders and elites are not innocent when it comes to squandering opportunities for development, betraying the objectives of the African national project and looting the resources meant to help poor people.

Yet this explanation leaves a number of questions unanswered. For instance, how do we explain why the African postcolonial state is best known for aberrant behaviour such as repression, brutality, corruption, inefficiency and failure to promote the collective wellbeing of its citizens? Some scholars have responded to this question by articulating an 'African exceptionalism' thesis premised on a static, cultural relativist reading of the African condition and development (Chabal and Daloz 1999). One good example is the work of Patrick Chabal and Jean-Pascal Daloz, which deployed Weberian notions of modernity and progress to arrive at the conclusion that development in Africa is informed by a different logic from that which shaped the Western world. In the first place, they assert that development in Africa is concerned with short-term consumption – the politics of the belly (Chabal and Daloz 1999: 55–58). Second, they argue that in Africa there is a preference for reliance if not dependence on outside resources rather than productive activities or proper savings (Chabal and Daloz 1999: 58–60). Third, they argue that what appears as disorder to outsiders appears as order to the African beholder (Chabal and Daloz 1999: 65–67).

What this orientalist thinking ignores is the role of coloniality of power in making it difficult for development to take root in Africa. Coloniality of power has positioned Africa at the interface between different value systems and different forms of logic: Western and African, urban and rural, patriarchal and matriarchal, religious and secular, nationalist and tribal/ethnic, modern and traditional, progressive and conservative, cultural and technical – the list is long. Until today, Western values and concepts have coexisted uneasily with African concepts, partly because colonialism manipulated and deployed both Western and African concepts as tools of control, domination and subjection, destroying some of the concepts and values originating in precolonial Africa and reinventing others.

The net effect of all this was the creation of an African elite that dreamt in both Western and African languages. From these African elites came African leaders. However, colonialism created elites who aspired to a capitalist lifestyle, but had no capital. The black elite had seen how white colonialists used the state to engage in primitive accumulation and authoritarianism in order to silence African voices. Although never exposed to democracy under colonialism, they were expected to run postcolonial governments along democratic lines.

Emerging from this context, the African national project unfolded as a top-down enterprise informed by a strain of pedagogical nationalism that was intolerant of questioning and dissenting voices. Development was to be delivered in an authoritarian fashion. Single-party and military regimes emerged from the same context of intolerance informing the African national project. The postcolonial state became a leviathan suffocating and disciplining any form of opposition. Questions of state illegitimacy emerged as development projects failed and authoritarianism deepened towards the end of the first decade of decolonisation (Olukoshi and Laakso 1996).

SAPs emerged within the context of economic stagnation in Africa and the global shift from Keynesianism to neoliberalism, which privileged market forces over the role of the state, in the late 1970s and early 1980s. At the same time, economic globalisation was accelerating, with enormous implications for the management of national economies. The World Bank and the International Monetary Fund (IMF) began to play a leading role globally. SAPs came with antistatist philosophies, where the postcolonial state was seen as nothing but a 'giant theft machine' (Mkandawire 2003: 10). This thinking inaugurated what Mkandawire described as the 'wanton destruction of institutions and untrammeled experimentation with half-baked institutional ideas' (2003: 10).

There is little doubt that SAPs were a wrong diagnosis of the causes of the failure of development in Africa. Pushing the state out of the development project was based on the wrong assumption that the state per se was the culprit. What *was* wrong was that the state had been tasked with promoting development beneficial to the African people without having been fully decolonised and thus able to serve African interests. As noted by Fantu Cheru, the implementation of SAPs reinforced the hold of imperial global designs over African economies, and African leaders lost the little remaining policy space they had left (Cheru 2009: 275–78).

Cheru concluded that: 'What is normally accepted as "development" in Africa has been essentially an imperial project, derived and financed by the dominant Western powers to serve Western needs' (2009: 277–78). He went further to state that, under SAPs, 'policy making, an important aspect of sovereignty, has been wrenched out of the hands of the African state. This is colonisation, not development' (Cheru 2009: 277). Africa has not yet recovered from this blow and the emerging consensus is that the state has to be reconstituted into a democratic institution and allowed to regain lost policy space so as to play a positive role in development. The neoliberal dispensation in place since the end of the 1970s is in trouble today – it is riddled by crises of legitimacy and methodology.

Neoliberal Imperialism and the Present Global Crises

The present moment can best be described as a troubled time in which the fate of humanity seems uncertain. At the global level, a devastating economic crisis has rocked the Global North, calling into question triumphalist views of the capitalist mode of production as the only viable global economic system. The ripple effects of this crisis have been felt in Africa and other parts of the world simply because the capitalist system has assumed global proportions. At the same time, there is an intense drive by the United States and its North Atlantic Treaty Organization (NATO) partners to intervene militarily in other states like Iraq, Afghanistan and

Libya under the cover of humanitarian intervention and the 'right to protect' people suffering from the excesses of dictatorships.

This has revived debates on what has come to be termed 'neoliberal imperialism' hidden within the wave of globalisation. Development studies is yet to be well equipped to deal effectively with this rising phenomenon accompanied by a new scramble for African natural resources (Quijano 2000). Michael Hardt and Antonio Negri (2000) argued that empire was alive and resurgent, carving a new economic, cultural and political globalised order. Negri (2008) emphasised that, today, empire no longer has an 'outside' and that it no longer tolerates any realities external to itself.

Since the fall of the Soviet Union, no alternative discourse of development has emerged. A closer look into the current dynamics of imperial global designs vis-à-vis Africa indicates a looming danger of 'recolonisation', beginning with those African countries endowed with strategic natural resources like oil, gas and diamonds. It would be simplistic to just accept recent events in Iraq and Libya as military interventions in support of democracy and human rights.

The reality is that neoliberalism has gradually managed to naturalise a notion of politics that is dismissive of any radical thinking questioning the current status quo privileging the West. Such thinking is often dismissed as sentimental, nostalgic, antisystemic and, at worst, terrorism (Ndlovu-Gatsheni 2012). At the same time, all Euro-American interventions – including military ones – are cast as humanitarian and developmental. Radicalism has been beaten into support for the neoliberal status quo. The veteran journalist John Pilger unpacks some of the dangers embedded in popular conceptions of development informed by mystifying neoliberal thought in this way:

> 'Democracy' is now the free market – a concept bereft of freedom. 'Reform' is now the denial of reform. 'Economics' is the relegation of most human endeavour to material value, a bottom line. Alternative models that relate to the needs of the majority of humanity end up in the memory hole. And 'governance' – so fashionable these days – means an economic approval in Washington, Brussels and Davos. 'Foreign policy' is service to dominant power. Conquest is 'humanitarian intervention'. Invasion is 'nation-building'. Every day, we breathe the hot air of these pseudo ideas with their pseudo truths and pseudo experts. (Pilger 2008: 4)

To Pilger, neoliberal discourses of development, which ideally sound like noble concepts, have been manipulated into 'the most powerful illusions of our time' having been 'corporatised and given deceptive, perverse, even opposite meanings' (Pilger 2008: 5). The net impact of this thinking has been the increasing articulation of development issues in terms provided by Euro-American hegemonic discourse.

At the centre of neoliberal practices are the World Bank and the IMF as key drivers of the neoliberal agenda predicated on Washington Consensus. As noted by Arturo Escobar, Washington Consensus is constituted by 'the set of ideas and institutional practices that have seemingly ruled the world economy since the 1970s, most commonly known as neoliberalism' (Escobar 2012: Preface). Robert Calderisi, a long-time World Bank official, being a neoliberal, argued that most of the misfortunes bedevilling Africa were self-imposed. He linked the failures of development in Africa to kleptocratic governments, mismanagement, antibusiness behaviour, family values, cultural fatalism, corruption and tribalism. He called for what he termed 'new tough-love' in dealing with Africa, which involved cutting foreign assistance by half and channelling the remainder to those countries that strictly and obediently pursued the neoliberal democratic trajectory dictated by the West (Calderisi 2004: 15).

Of course, Africans are not only victims of underdevelopment; invariably, they have contributed to some of the miseries. Yet problems like corruption are linked to the colonial logic of primitive accumulation. For instance, mercantilism, colonialism and apartheid are typical grand corrupt systems. The fact that the postcolonial state was bequeathed by the grand corrupt system of colonialism to some extent explains its predatory tendencies. Colonialism structured the state in such a way that it did not serve the interests of ordinary African people.

It must be remembered that it was the World Bank and the IMF, under such leaders as Calderisi, who worked for the World Bank for over thirty years in various senior positions, including as the bank's international spokesperson for Africa, who constructed the SAPs that wreaked havoc on Africa, including the cutting of subsidies on basic commodities and opening up Africa to trade liberalisation. Even in the face of the failures of SAPs, Calderisi still urged Africans not to point fingers at the West, but rather to blame themselves (Calderisi 2004). This denialism of the contribution of some Western-concocted policies to the development problems in Africa increases scepticism and doubts about the genuineness of the West to help with the development of Africa.

Even in 2011, when the African masses in North Africa engaged in what became known as the 'Arab Spring', which unfolded as an open indictment on both the limits of neoliberalism and juridical freedom bequeathed to Africa by decolonisation, Euro-American powers did not hesitate to intervene, pretending to be on the side of the struggling masses of Africa while in reality setting old scores with such leaders as

Muammar Gaddafi. While the Arab Spring was unleashed against both dictators and the neoliberal economic policies responsible for widespread poverty and unemployment, the NATO intervention in Libya during the course of the Arab Spring indicated how Euro-American powers were always ready to hijack popular movements, pretending to be on their side while pursuing their permanent strategic interests. A combination of claims to advance humanitarianism, development and the antiterrorist struggle is today used to justify what Mignolo terms 're-westernization' that began with the invasion of Iraq and involves the task of trying to save capitalism (Mignolo 2011).

Beyond Development Impasse: Towards a Decolonial Turn

A development impasse has taken the form of crisis of ideas, alternatives and options within an era that has witnessed not only the collapse of socialism but also the occupation of the Wall Street. According to Žižek (2011: xi), there are five responses to this development impasse, which he described as 'forthcoming apocalypse'. He mapped the reactions as follows:

> The first reaction is one of ideological denial: there is no fundamental disorder; the second is exemplified by explosions of anger at the injustices of the new world order; the third involves attempts at bargaining ('if we change things here and there, life could perhaps go on as before'); when the bargaining fails, depression and withdrawal set in; finally, after passing through this zero-point, the subject no longer perceives the situation as a threat, but as the chance of a new beginning – or, as Mao Zedong put it: 'There is great disorder under heaven, the situation is excellent. (Žižek 2011: xi–xii)

Attempts to move beyond the development impasse have involved calling into question a narrative of modernity, progress, civilisation and modernisation cascading from Euro-American epistemic sites. From inside Europe and America, a Euro-centric critique of 'modernity within modernity' commenced with Marxism and psychoanalysis (Mignolo 2011). It involved Christian, liberal and socialist options. It has grown into poststructuralism, postmodernism and postcolonialism as critical forms of critique of 'modernity within modernity.'

From outside of Europe and America, the longstanding critique has sought to reveal how the achievement of development in the Euro-American zone was entwined with the overseas conquest of the non-Western zones. It also sought to reject the tendency of consignment of 'non-Western world' to 'static backwardness regardless of how those regions' fates were shaped by interaction with Europe, including the sidetracking of other modes of change and interaction' (Cooper 2005: 6).

The Euro-centric critique of modernity resulted in a series of 'turns', such as the 'historical turn', the 'cultural turn' and the 'linguistic turn', that failed to radically transform Euro-American hegemony (Cooper 2005: 6–8). The critique of modernity from non-Western epistemic sites inaugurated the 'decolonial turn' that not only questions modernity but also calls for the end of Euro-American hegemony that generates underdevelopment. As noted by Nelson Maldonado-Torres:

> The decolonial turn does not refer to a single theoretical school, but rather points to a family of diverse positions that share a view of coloniality as the fundamental problem in the modern (as well as postmodern and information age), and decolonization or decoloniality as a necessary task that remains unfinished. (Maldonado-Torres 2011: 2)

Broadly speaking, the decolonial turn involves many initiatives, including decoloniality and de-Westernisation, which have locked horns with re-Westernisation. Decoloniality originated as a response to the capitalist and communist imperial designs. The Bandung Conference of 1955 was one of the major decoloniality projects that sought to chart development beyond capitalism and communism building on decolonisation and solidarity in the Global South. Present-day decolonial options also include Islamic, feminist, nationalist and Afrocentric options. Decoloniality became an epistemic and political project involving epistemic disobedience, decolonisation of power, decolonisation of being and decolonisation of knowledge as those people who experienced the negative aspects of modernity continue the struggle for a new humanism (Fanon 1968).

Today, the discourse of development is caught up in four global trajectories. The first is re-Westernisation, which seeks to save and to reimagine the 'future of capitalism' (Mignolo 2011). The second is 'reorientations of the Left' with a view to building what is known as 'socialism of the 21st century' associated with some Latin American leaders such as Lula and others (Mignolo 2011). The third is 'de-Westernisation', which originated in East and Southeast Asia and has seen such countries as Malaysia, Indonesia, India and China appropriating and adapting modernity and shifting the centre of development from Europe into Asia. As put by Mignolo:

> Dewesternization means the end of long history of Western hegemony and of racial global discrimination projecting the image and the idea that Asians are yellow and that yellow people cannot think. Like many others, East and Southeast Asians have come out of the closet, and in this regard

dewesternization means economic autonomy of decision and negotiations in the international arena and affirmation in the sphere of knowledge, subjectivity. It means above all deracialization ... . (Mignolo 2011: 48)

The fourth trajectory is the decolonial option, which is a longstanding and long-term liberatory process ranged against coloniality, which denied African humanity. It embraces de-Westernization and envisages a pluriversal world in which Africa has a dignified space. Within decoloniality, development is understood as a graduation from coloniality into liberation and from 'objecthood' into 'subjecthood' (Ndlovu-Gatsheni 2013b). At the power level, development is defined as a triumph over an unsustainable Euro-American centric global status quo that has been in place since the fifteenth century.

At the level of being, development entails graduation of the African people from a 'zone of non-being' to a 'zone of being' (from objecthood to subjecthood) (Santos 2007: 45–87). Development becomes a consistent and persistent struggle for new humanism that was defined clearly by Frantz Fanon to mean liberation and self-determination (Fanon 1968). It is the same struggle that Marcus Garvey described as 'universal negro improvement' that was predicated on self-help principles (Hill 1983).

At the level of epistemology, development means the successful 'provincialization' of Euro-American epistemological hegemony and opening up for ecologies of knowledges that reflect the plurality of human experience, including the restoration of those forms of knowledge that had been displaced and silenced (Santos 2007: 80–87). It involves turning the previously colonised peoples who have been reduced to objects of Euro-American knowledge into participants and generators of knowledge from the vantage points of their geopolitical and biographical locus of enunciation.

Conclusion

There is no doubt that Africans have been worked over by colonialism and coloniality since the first colonial encounters, and this reality has made it very hard for them to find a way out of the snares of colonial matrices of power. The decolonial turn predicated on unmasking invisible global imperial designs that work to keep Africa in a subordinate position forms the ideal beginning of thinking of another world of equality. The decolonial turn promotes a shift away from the delusions of a world naturalised by global imperial designs. It calls for the definitive entry of Global South subjectivities into the realm of thinking and imagining another world.

The fact that there is emerging critical thinking that accepts that the Euro-American hegemony in place since the beginning of colonialism is no longer sustainable and that modernity has created modern problems to which there are no modern solutions makes it imperative that we rethink the dominant thinking that has underpinned development discourse and informed development practice in Africa. Already Jean Comaroff and John L. Comaroff in their book *Theory from the South* have posed penetrating questions such as:

> But what if, and here is the idea in interrogative form, we invert that order of things? What if we subvert the epistemic scaffolding on which it is erected? What if we posit that, in the present moment, it is the global south that affords privileged insight into the workings of the world at large? (Comaroff and Comaroff 2012: 1)

In order for a meaningful and systematic decolonisation of development studies to take place, there is a need to shift the geography and biography of knowledge and to begin to articulate the experience of development from Africa as a privileged epistemic site capable of formulating its own development trajectory. This is now possible because, as noted by Patrick Chabal, the Euro-American 'conceit' is coming to an end and the 'Western societies are no longer sure of how to see themselves' (Chabal 2012: 3). This moment of doubt engulfing the Western world must be seized with both hands by Africa in particular and the Global South in order to push forward the decoloniality project involving 'unthinking' some ideas cascading from Euro-American renditions of development as a simple exercise of 'catching up' with the Euro-American world. Indeed, the world is ripe for a shift in the geography and biography of thinking about development, and Africa must take advantage and relaunch its development projects while continuing to push for the final collapse of the Euro-American hegemony with the aim of creating another world order that is truly pluriversal.

Sabelo J. Ndlovu-Gatsheni is the Acting Executive Director of Change Management Unit (CMU), Vice Chancellor's Office at the University of South Africa (Unisa). He has published extensively on African history, African politics and development. His major publications include *The Ndebele Nation: Reflections on Hegemony, Memory and Historiography* (2009); *Do 'Zimbabweans' Exist? Trajectories of Nationalism, National Identity Formation and Crisis in a Postcolonial State* (2009); *Redemptive or Grotesque Nationalism? Rethinking Contemporary Politics in Zimbabwe* (2011); *Empire, Global Coloniality and African Subjectivity* (2013); *Coloniality of Power in*

Postcolonial Africa: Myths of Decolonization (2013); *Nationalism and National Projects in Southern Africa: New Critical Reflections* (2013) and *Bondage of Boundaries and Identity Politics in Postcolonial Africa: The 'Northern Problem' and Ethno-Futures* (2013).

References

Ahluwalia, P. 2001. 'When Does a Settler Become a Native? Citizenship and Identity in a Settler Society', *Pretext: Literacy and Cultural Studies* 10(1): 63–73.
Ayittey, G. 1994. *Africa Betrayed*. London: Macmillan.
Bhambra, G.K. 2007. *Rethinking Modernity: Postcolonialism and the Sociological Imagination*. New York: Palgrave Macmillan.
Calderisi, R. 2004. *The Trouble with Africa: Why Foreign Aid isn't Working*. New York: Palgrave Macmillan.
Cesaire, A. 1955. *Discourse on Colonialism*. New York: Monthly Review Press.
Chabal, P. 2012. *The End of Conceit: Western Rationality after Postcolonialism*. London: Zed Books.
Chabal, P., and J. P. Daloz. 1999. *Africa Works*. Oxford: James Currey.
Cheru, F. 2009. 'Development in Africa: The Imperial Project versus the National Project and the Need for Policy Space', *Review of African Political Economy* 36(120): 275–78.
Clarke. J. H. n. d. 'A Great and Mighty Walk'. Video. Retrieved 23 August 2014 from https://archive.org/details/JohnHenrikClarke-AGreatAndMightyWalk.
Comaroff, J., and Comaroff, J. L. 2012. *Theory from the South: Or, How Euro-America is Evolving toward Africa*. Boulder: Paradigm Publishers.
Cooper, F. 2002. *Africa since 1940: The Past of the Present*. Cambridge: Cambridge University Press.
———. 2005. *Colonialism in Question: Theory, Knowledge, History*. Berkeley: University of California Press.
Escobar, A. 2012. *Encountering Development: Second Edition*. Princeton: Princeton University Press.
Ferguson, J. 1990. *The Anti-politics Machine: 'Development', Depoliticization, and Bureaucratic Power in Lesotho*. Cambridge: Cambridge University Press.
Fanon, F. 1968. *The Wretched of the Earth*. New York: Grove Press.
Grosfoguel, R. 2007. 'The Epistemic Decolonial Turn: Beyond Political-Economy Paradigms', *Cultural Studies* 21(2–3): 211–23.
Grosfoguel, R., and A.M.C. Cervantes-Rodriguez. 2002. 'Introduction: Unthinking Twentieth Century Eurocentric Mythologies: Universalist Knowledges, Decolonization, and Developmentalism', in R. Grosfoguel and A.M. Cervantes-Rodriguez (eds), *The Modern/Colonial/Capitalist World-System in the Twentieth Century: Global Processes, Antisystemic Movements, and the Geopolitics of Knowledge*. Westport: Praeger, pp. xi–xxx.
Hardt, M., and A. Negri. 2000. *Empire*. Cambridge, MA: Harvard University Press.

Hill, R.A. 1983. *The Marcus Garvey and Universal Negro Improvement Association Papers, Vol. 1 1828–August 1919*. Berkeley: University of California Press.
Ihonvbere, J. 1994. 'Pan-Africanism: Agenda for African Unity in the 1990s'. Unpublished keynote address delivered at the All-Africa Students' Conference, University of Guelph, Canada, 27 May.
Kapoor, I. 2008. *The Postcolonial Politics of Development*. New York, Routledge.
Lindauer, L., and L. Pritchett. 2002. 'What's the Big Idea? The Third Generation of Policies for Economic Growth', *Economia* 3(1): 1–39.
Lumumba-Kasongo, T. 2011. 'The National Project as a Public Administration Concept: The Problematic of State Building in the Search for New Development Paradigms in Africa', *Africa Development* XXVI(2): 63–96.
Magubane, B. 1996. *The Making of a Racist State: British Imperialism and the Union of South Africa 1870–1910*. Trenton, NJ: Africa World Press.
Maldonado-Torres, N. 2007. 'On the Coloniality of Being: Contribution to the Development of a Concept', *Cultural Studies* 21(2–3): 240–70.
_____. 2011. 'Thinking Through the Decolonial Turn: Post-Continental Interventions in Theory, Philosophy, and Critique – An Introduction', *TRANSMODERNITY: Journal of Peripheral Cultural Production of the Luso-Hispanic World* 1(2): 1–25.
Mamdani, M. 1996. *Citizen and Subject: Contemporary Africa and the Legacy of Late Colonialism*. Princeton: Princeton University Press.
_____. 1998a. 'When Does a Settler Become a Native? Reflections on the Roots of Citizenship in Equatorial and South Africa', Inaugural Lecture, A.C. Jordan Professor of African Studies, University of Cape Town, 13 May.
_____. 1998b. 'When Does a Settler Become a Native? The Colonial Roots of Citizenship', *Pretexts* 7(2): 249–258.
_____. 2007. 'Political Violence and State Formation in Post-colonial Africa', *International Development Centre Working Paper Series No. 1*. International Development Centre, Open University.
_____. 2011. 'The Importance of Research in a University', *Pambazuka News*, 21 April. Retrieved 7 September 2018 from http://www.pambazuka.org/en/category/features/72782.
Mazrui, A. 2011. 'Using 50 Years of Independence to Judge 100 Years of Colonial Rule'. Unpublished paper presented at the Centre for African Studies, University of Free State, June 2011.
Mbeki, M. 2009. *Architects of Poverty*. Johannesburg: Picador Africa.
Mbembe, A. 2000. *On Private Indirect Government: States of the Literature Series No. 1-2000*. Dakar: CODESRIA. ——. 2010. 'Fifty Years of African Decolonization', *Chimurenga*, 25 December. Retrieved 22 August 2012 from http://www.chimurenga.co.za/page-147.html. *Version translated by Karen Press now available on* https://chimurengachronic.co.za/fifty-years-of-african-decolonisation/.
Mehmet, O. 1995. *Westernizing the Third World: The Eurocentricity of Economic Development Theories*. New York: Routledge.
Mignolo, W.D. 2000. *Local Histories/Global Designs: Coloniality, Subaltern Knowledges, and Border Thinking*. Princeton: Princeton University Press.
_____. 2007. 'Introduction: Coloniality of Power and De-colonial Thinking', *Cultural Studies* 21(2–3): 155–67.

_____. 2011. *The Dark Side of Western Modernity: Global Futures, Decolonial Options*. Durham, NC: Duke University Press.

Mkandawire, T. 2003. 'Institutions and Development in Africa'. Unpublished paper presented at the Cambridge Journal of Economics Conference, 17–19 September, 10. Retrieved 7 September 2018 from http://13.111.165.101/cjeconf/delegates/mkandawire.pdf.

_____. 2005. 'African Intellectuals and Nationalism', in T. Mkandawire (ed.), *African Intellectuals: Rethinking Politics, Language, Gender and Development*. London: Zed Books, pp. 10–55.

_____. 2011. 'Running While Others Walked: Knowledge and the Challenge of Africa's Development', *Africa Development* XXXVI(2): 1–36.

Ndlovu-Gatsheni, S. J. 2012. 'Coloniality of Power in Development Studies and the Impact of Global Imperial Designs on Africa', *ARAS* 33(2): 48–73.

_____. 2013a. *Coloniality of Power in Postcolonial Africa: Myths of Decolonization*. Dakar: CODESRIA Books.

_____. 2013b. *Empire, Global Coloniality and African Subjectivity*. New York: Berghahn Books.

Negri, A. 2008. *Reflections on Empire*. London: Polity Press.

Nugent, P. 2004. *Africa since Independence*. New York: Palgrave Macmillan.

Olukoshi, A., and L. Laakso (eds). 1996. *Challenges to the Nation-State in Africa*. Uppsala: Nordic Africa Institute.

Pilger, J. 2008. 'Honouring the Unbreakable Promise'. Unpublished address delivered at Rhodes University, 6 April 2008.

Quijano, A. 2000. 'The Coloniality of Power and Social Classification', *Journal of World Systems* 6(2): 342–86.

_____. 2007. 'Coloniality and Modernity/Rationality', *Cultural Studies* 21(2–3): 168–78.

Rivkin, A. 1969. *Nation-Building in Africa*. New Brunswick, NJ: Rutgers University Press.

Santos, B. de S. 2007. 'Beyond Abyssal Thinking: From Global Lines to Ecologies of Knowledge', *Review*, XXX(1): 45–89.

Stewart, P. 2007. 'Re-envisioning the Academic Profession in the Shadow of Corporate Managerialism', *Journal of Higher Education* 5(1): 131–47.

Taiwo, O. 2010. *How Colonialism Preempted Modernity in Africa*. Bloomington: Indiana University Press, 2010.

Thorbecke, E. 2007. 'The Evolution of Development Doctrine, 1950–2005', in G. Mavrotas and A. Shorrocks (eds), *Advancing Development: Core Themes in Global Economics*. New York: Palgrave Macmillan, pp. 3–36.

Torfing, J. 1999. *New Theories of Discourse: Laclau, Mouffe and Žižek*. Malden, MA: Blackwell.

Tripathy, J and D. Mohapatra. 2011. 'Does Development Exist outside Representation?', *Journal of Developing Societies* 27(2): 93–118.

Žižek, S. 2008. *In Defence of Lost Causes*. New York: Verso.

_____. 2009. *Violence: Six Sideways Reflections*. London: Profile Books.

_____. 2011. *Living in the End of Times*. New York: Verso.

Chapter 2

Rethinking and Reclaiming Development in Africa

Vusi Gumede

Introduction

Many important questions have been posed but not satisfactorily answered regarding the notion of development. For instance, I have asked the following question: if development is such a desirable end for both African leaders and their so-called partners, why has it been so elusive and tedious to achieve? As argued elsewhere, it is important to further problematise the notion of development, including what development is, in whose interest is it being pursued and by whom as well as how. In addition, I have probed whether there are alternatives to the dominant paradigm of what is generally accepted as development and whether there are alternative routes to the desired end of inclusive development.

This chapter is an attempt to pull together the various perspectives on the notion of development and to propose a better approach to inclusive development in Africa. The central argument of the work I have been undertaking on this subject is that the development that Africa needs is not the development of the market or development that is dictated from outside. As Plaatjie (2013: 119) puts it, 'development is an imposition on the Africans, of a Euro-American "truth" about the idea of development'. The next section broadly looks at how selected earlier writers on development characterise development. I also discuss post-development and modernisation as well as functionalism, and also touch on modernity. I then discuss the character and nature of development in post-independence Africa. That is followed by a discussion of how to make development happen in Africa. Before concluding, I propose an approach to development in

Africa, taking forward the work I have been undertaking regarding the possible/new socioeconomic development approach for Africa.

What Is Development?

The debate about what development refers to is an old debate. All countries or regions in the world are concerned with development. Europe, as Prah (2006: 175) discusses, was concerned with the notion of development as 'part of the philosophical assumptions of the European Enlightenment', as an example. This Enlightenment – the age of reason – can be viewed as 'a pedagogical movement led by the philosophers to build a new scientifically ordered discourse of nature, authority, social existence and of virtually everything in the universe' (Lushaba 2006: 6). This is linked to the idea of modernity, which has been critiqued by many on different grounds. Lushaba (2006: 3), for instance, makes the point that: 'Africa cannot possibly develop by modernizing or becoming like the modern west.' It is in this context that many argue that development cannot be equated to modernity – or, rather, that modernity is not an appropriate form of development that Africa needs.

From the 1960s, Japan and the so-called Asian Tigers (Singapore, Taiwan, Hong Kong and South Korea) grew rapidly in economic terms and in social development, resulting in the idea of a developmental state. A developmental state is a state that is preoccupied with development and vigorously pursues development, working in tandem with other sectors of society. Post-independence Africa was understandably very preoccupied with development, and some argue that certain countries in Africa became developmental states in the 1980s before the structural adjustment programmes (SAPs) decimated development in Africa.

However, as many have argued, it is not clear what many refer to when talking of development. Linked to that is what has influenced the conceptualisation of and approaches to development. As Mokoena (2018: 96) puts it, 'the linear stages of development and the continuous suggestions of emulation of Western development by the developing countries is grounded on this logic of progress [Western idea of progress] … This logic of progress informed the constant and unending expansion through ceaseless accumulation, colonization, dispossession and imperialism'. Indeed, as many have argued, development (or lack thereof) and/or underdevelopment are normally viewed through Eurocentric lenses. It tends to be forgotten that the so-called development of the West was based on the exploitation of the Third World, and Africa in particular, as Walter Rodney (1973) explained. It is in this context that some of us argue that what was termed the Industrial Revolution was mainly the plunder and exploitation of Africa (which was informed by the Enlightenment ideals). To deal with the 'Western idea of progress', the hierarchies that characterise relations should be dismantled, as decolonial scholars have been arguing. In addition, for Africa, African agency should be accentuated, as Afrocentric scholars argue.

There is also a more fundamental issue: is development similar to progress? Arguably, as Prah (2006) demonstrates, the preoccupation of many countries and/or regions has historically been about *progress*. For the purposes of this chapter, progress and development are conceived of as similar. This is not the same conceptualisation of development or progress as 'progress measured in linear temporal terms' (Mokoena 2018: 97). Table 2.1 shows that development and progress can indeed be viewed as implying the same process. Although (indigenous) African languages may have different names for the same concept such as development, the actual meaning of these different but related languages converge to imply a similar process. In the 'actual meaning of the translated word(s)' column, development is viewed as 'progress'. See Table 2.1 below.

Prah (2006: 178) explains that 'in many African languages, the idea of progress is metaphorically interpreted as a notion of movement forward, or backwards to denote stagnation or retrogression'. Prah confirms that in the various indigenous African languages, using the examples of what the Ga, the Akan, the Xhosa, the Luo and the Senufo say when referring to progress, 'the idea of progress translates easily as development'.

Examining what leading scholars say about development, as Table 2.2 shows, there is an overlapping conceptualisation of what development is about. Development is about improvements in wellbeing, involving socioeconomic progress. Essentially, development is an indispensable aspect of socioeconomic progress and civilisation — development should

Table 2.1 Meanings of the word 'development' in selected indigenous African languages.

Language	Country/region	Literal translation	Actual meaning of the translated word(s)
KiSwahili	Tanzania	Maendeleo	*Progress/continuation*
Sesotho	Lesotho	Tswelopele	*Progress/continuation*
IsiZulu	South Africa	Ukuthuthukisa/Inqubekela Phambili	*Continuation/progress*
Shona	Zimbabwe	Budiriro/Kubudirira	*To prosper*
Bissa	Burkina Faso	Yiure'	*To prosper*

be thought of as far more than just economic growth, as I have argued elsewhere.

Table 2.2 Selected conceptualisations of development.

Author	Source	Conceptualisation
Prah (2001: 91)	'Culture: The Missing Link in Development Planning in Africa'	The notion of development prominently implies the improvement and raising of the quality of life of people, that they are able, to a large measure, to attain their potential, build and acquire self-confidence, and manage to live lives of reasonable accomplishment and dignity.
Clark (1991: 36)	'Democratizing Development: The Role of Voluntary Organizations'	Development is a process of change that enables people to take charge of their own destinies and realise their full potential. It requires building up in people the confidence, skills, assets and freedoms necessary to achieve this goal.
Myrdal (1974: 735)	'What is Development?'	Development must be understood as the movement upward of the entire social system, where there is circular causation between conditions and changes with cumulative effects.
Slim (1995: 143)	'What is Development?'	Development is essentially about change: not just any change, but a definite improvement – a change for the better. At the same time, development is also about continuity.
Sen (1999: 3)	'Development as Freedom'	Development can be seen as a process of expanding the real freedoms that people enjoy.
McFadden (2011: 271)	'Re-crafting Citizenship in the Postcolonial Moment: A Focus on Southern Africa'	Developmentalism involves the mobilisation of African women's agencies to define their own futures, on and off the continent.
Ake (1996: 125)	'Democracy and Development in Africa'	Development is not economic growth; it is not a technical project, but a process by which people create and re-create themselves and their life circumstances to realise higher levels of civilisation in accordance with their own choices and values. Development is something that people must do for themselves.

Although there appears to be a cross-cutting meaning or overarching view of what development is, the fundamental question about how the concept of development has been used is important to address, at least in the context of Africa. The concept of development in Africa, which often hinges and is determined by the notion of 'good governance' and respect for human rights, has for years been exogenously imposed on African governments. As many others have argued, concepts such as civilisation, development, globalisation and democratisation are some of the buzzwords that have been used and perverted by the West to make the 'other' aspire to be like them. The West uses these words as a barometer to judge other societies according to Western standards, which are supposed to be the norm and yardstick for all societies, as the works of Marimba Ani and others demonstrate.

As many thinkers acknowledge, development is relative, and it is also subjective. Swantz (2009: 34) posits that 'development cannot be transferred; it has to develop in the social conditions of each place'. Tandon (2015: 145) is of the view that 'a major challenge for the theoreticians of not only the global south but also of the marginalized peoples and sub-nationalists of the north is to provide an alternative definition of development'. Latouche (1993: 460) argues that 'development has been and still is the Westernization of the world', while Ziai (2009: 198) sees 'development [as] an empty signifier that can be filled with almost any content'.

Ziai (2013) also argues that the concept of development has depoliticised Eurocentric and authoritarian implications, even arguing that the concept of development should be abandoned. This is linked to the notion of post-development, which argues that development practice and the concept of development reflect Western hegemony, and that development projects and theories of development do not benefit the developing world. Post-development thinking has, like development (or development theory), been critiqued for not being theoretically developed and being uneven. Pieterse (2000: 183) also says that 'for all those concerned with discourse analysis, the actual use of language is sloppy and indulgent [in post-development thinking]'. Ziai (2013: 126) makes the point that 'post-development has been widely criticized ... for homogenizing development and neglecting its positive aspects, for romanticizing local communities and legitimizing oppressive traditions, and for being just as paternalistic as the chastised development experts'.

Coming to the discourses of/on development, Escobar (1995: 53) makes the point that 'development is thus a very real historical formation, albeit articulated around an artificial construct (underdevelopment) and upon a certain materiality (the conditions baptized as underdevelopment), which must be conceptualized in different ways if the power of the development discourse is to be challenged or displaced'. Further, he argues that 'the discourse of development is not merely an ideology that has little to do with the real world nor is it an apparatus produced by those in power in order to hide another, more basic truth, namely, the crude reality of the dollar sign. The development discourse has crystallized in practices that contribute to regulating the everyday goings and comings of people in the Third World' (Escobar 1995: 104), hence his argument that when development is properly conceptualised, it has been happening for a long time and is driven by the people themselves from below.

Shivji (2006), in the context of Africa, periodises development discourse into: (1) the age of developmentalism (the 1960s and 1970s); (2) Africa's lost decade (the 1980s); and (3) the 'age of globalization' (which is ongoing). In the age of developmentalism, development was a process of class struggle. During Africa's lost decade, the 'neoliberal package' (i.e. SAPs) reigned supreme. The 'age of globalization' was accompanied by pan-Africanist resistance and the discourse sees no role for the (developmental) state. Mkandawire (2011: 7), on the other hand, breaks down development discourse since the Second World War into two parts:

> Almost from its very inception, the post-World War II development discourse has had two strands: the Truman version, for which development involved both geopolitical considerations and humanitarianism, and the 'Bandung Conference' version that saw development in terms of 'catching up', emancipation and 'the right to development'.

With regard to development theory, Ziai (2013: 124–25) states that 'development theory has two roots: nineteenth-century evolutionism and nineteenth-century social technology. Evolutionism assumed that social change in societies proceeds according to a universal pattern while social technology claimed that social interventions based on expert knowledge (possessed by a privileged group that acts as a trustee for the common good) are necessary to achieve positive social change. Both roots can be found in twentieth- century development theory'. Prah (2006: 185), on the other hand, makes the point that 'Western post-Second World War development theory can be historically identified and periodized as a three-phased phenomenology ... the hegemony of Modernization theorists of the 1950s and 60s, the *Dependencia* and the Neo-marxian paradigms of the 60s and 70s, to IMF Adjustment packages of the late 70s and 80s. Today, neo-liberal paradigms hold sway'. It is worth highlighting that modernisation theories were associated with functionalism, the 'idea [that] saw societies as harmonized and integrated systems' (Prah 2006: 186).

Another important issue relates to the so-called 'Right to Development'. As Lumumba-Kasongo (2002: 85) puts it:

development should be guided and supported within the framework of rights as defined by the African Charter on Human and Peoples' Rights adopted by the Organization of the African Unity (OAU) in 1981. They include political and civil rights; economic and social rights; and the rights of peoples. Peoples' rights include freedom from discrimination, oppression, and exploitation; and the right to self-determination, national and international peace and security and a satisfactory environment for economic and social development.

A new book by Kamga (2018) goes into a lot of detail on the relevant history and debates regarding the notion of the 'Right to Development'.

Essentially, as Kamga (2018) explains, soon after the political independence in Africa, African countries acknowledged that development in Africa was affected by global inequities characterised by unfair trade rules, global postcolonial arrangements through various global institutions etc. As a response, developing countries and African countries in particular gathered in the G77 and called for the establishment of the New International Order that would enable inclusive development. In 1967 in Algiers, Dudu Tiam, the then Minister of Foreign Affairs for Senegal, made a statement that 'development is human right'. Kamga (2017) argues that the right to development concept is a legal concept in the fight against poverty. It is a composite right made of civil and political rights as well as socioeconomic rights all put together in the interest of human dignity. Arguably, M'baye (1972) introduced the concept to academia in an inaugural lecture in Strasburg in France. In 1986, the United Nations adopted the declaration on the right to development. The right to development is now a recognised human right, as Kamga (2018) indicates.

Although many (e.g. Sengutpa, Andreassen and Marks) argue that development is an entitlement (i.e. a right to development), many others (e.g. Donnelly, Bello and Whyte) reject the notion of a right to development and argue that proponents of the right to development are making up a non-existing right. Largely, the controversy around the notion of the right to development is largely because the international community is obliged under the discourse to provide development assistance as well as capacity to the developing world.

Development in Africa

So much has been written about development in Africa. Besides the neoliberal perspectives that argue for the development of the market or a developmental approach that is dictated from outside, the debate regarding development in Africa has dealt with whether (inclusive) development has taken place or not and, if not, why not. As indicated earlier,

Ake (1996) argued that development was not really on the agenda of the political elite in post-independence Africa, while many others argued that development was the main preoccupation of leaders in the early years of political independence. Ake (1996) makes the point that the main reason why development has not taken place in Africa is because the agrarian revolution (which is an important phase for development) was overlooked. Others have argued that the reason why development has been weak in Africa is because of inappropriate policies, an incorrect socioeconomic development approach, and the fact that languages and cultures have not been given space to thrive and support development. Among the factors that are said to have constrained development in Africa are: poor economic development, which results from a lack of appropriate policies/reforms, overreliance on natural resources, an absence of an original economic development model, poor implementation etc. Numerous social problems (e.g. unnecessary civil wars, poor educational outcomes and xenophobia) also make development intractable. Then there is the challenge posed by political and institutional weaknesses (which allow negative external influences and interference, weak leadership, corruption etc.).

However, Mkandawire (2015) is among those who hold the view that we have not fully understood what has constrained development, and particularly economic development in Africa. For the record, Mkandawire (2015) argues that attributing the slow economic performance of African economies to neopatrimonialism is problematic. As Mkandawire (2015: 2) puts it, 'while neopatrimonialism can be used to describe different styles of exercising authority, idiosyncratic mannerisms of certain individual leaders, and social practices within states, the concept offers little analytical content and has no predictive value with respect to economic policy and performance'. He describes 'neopatrimonialism [as] a marriage of tradition and modernity with an offspring whose hybridity generates a logic that has had devastating effects on African economies' (Mkandawire 2015: 3) and that it is factually incorrect that the African economy has not performed well, as the neopatrimonialism logic suggests.

At issue should be why economic development has not been fast enough. The related question is: why has economic development not resulted in effective human development? As argued and shown by Gumede (2016), human development in Africa remains very low. Looking at the period from 1980 to 2015 as an example, Sub-Saharan Africa's Human Development Index (HDI) has remained comparatively low, even compared to South Asia. Comparing Sub-Saharan Africa with Latin America and the Caribbean, the point made above – that Africa remains behind other regions – is glaring; see Table 2.3 below.

Table 2.3 Human development, levels and regions.

	1980	1990	2000	2010	2011	2012	2013	2014	2015
Very high human development	0.766	0.791	0.858	0.888	0.889	0.884	0.887	0.890	0.892
High human development	0.614	0.574	0.687	0.739	0.741	0.728	0.736	0.744	0.746
Medium human development	0.420	0.465	0.548	0.625	0.630	0.613	0.620	0.626	0.631
Low human development	0.316	0.356	0.383	0.453	0.456	0.486	0.490	0.494	0.497
Arab States	0.444	0.556	0.578	0.639	0.641	0.684	0.685	0.686	0.687
East Asia and the Pacific	0.428	0.516	0.581	0.666	0.671	0.700	0.709	0.717	0.720
Europe and Central Asia	0.644	0.652	0.68	0.744	0.751	0.745	0.750	0.754	0.756
Latin America & the Caribbean	0.582	0.626	0.68	0.728	0.731	0.739	0.745	0.750	0.751
South Asia	0.356	0.438	0.468	0.545	0.548	0.601	0.607	0.614	0.621
Sub-Saharan Africa	0.365	0.399	0.401	0.460	0.463	0.510	0.515	0.520	0.523

Source: Human Development Report (2016)

The pace of growth of the HDI for Sub-Saharan Africa is the lowest compared to the other regions. In the last four years (2011–15), the annual HDI level for Sub-Saharan Africa has effectively stood still. HDI levels for South Asia, East Asia and the Pacific have improved relatively faster than the HDI level for Sub-Saharan Africa. Although HDI levels for Latin America and the Caribbean, Europe and Central Asia, and for Arab States have not grown substantially during 2011–15, the HDI levels of those regions are high relative to the HDI level for Sub-Saharan Africa.

As is argued elsewhere, the crisis of development in Africa is underpinned by the ideological and epistemological confusion and imposition that define the pursuit of development, justice and freedom. The pursuit of development has generally followed a pattern defined by the West, in which a unilinear process is deemed to be sacrosanct. Following Walt Whitman Rostow's stages of economic growth, development planning efforts in Africa were geared towards the path of a sequential change, progress and transformation on the continent. Also, a Western conception of development ensures that it is seen as a process for a high rate of accumulation and industrialisation.

As a project grounded in nationalism, African countries are expected to 'catch up' or achieve 'convergence' with so-called developed countries, as Mkandawire (2011) has put it. This version of understanding development feeds into what Mkandawire (2011), cited in Sabelo Ndlovu-Gatsheni's 2012 Inaugural Professorial Lecture, calls the 'Truman Version of Developmentalism', where development is interpreted as the Euro-American missionary task of developing the Global South in general and Africa in particular. An uncritical acceptance of this definition of development has resulted in the subservience of the political elites in Africa to subordination of 'politics to economics'. The demonisation of the state as an incapable agent of transformation gave way to the hegemony of the market as the more effective agent for the allocation of resources. The ascendance of neoliberal thought in development discourse has led to emphasis on the depoliticisation of development strategies, thus giving way to technocratic governance.

It is not surprising that Samir Amin (1990), for instance, argued for 'delinking'. Amin (1990: 67) argues that in order for Third World countries to experience true development, they should 'delink' from the world capitalist system through the adoption of new market strategies and values different from the so-called developed countries. Amin's hypothesis supposes that countries in the Third World can develop economically by changing approaches to production systems. As Mokoena (2018: 87) argues, 'the capitalist world system continues to hierarchically and dichotomously configure the world culturally, epistemologically, aesthetically, ontologically at the exclusion, oppression, exploitation of *Othered* populations such as African people thus reproducing the crisis of inequalities ... This world's system is Euro-American-centric, capitalist, patriarchal, hetero-normative, and hierarchical, Christian-centric and characterized by an interstate system'. Oloruntoba (2015: 123) also argues that 'inequality remains one of the most fundamental challenges of the contemporary world' and that 'capitalism in its current form is unsustainable for the human society. Consequently, the structure of power that informs and maintains the current order must be transformed to foster inclusive development'.

There are other problems with the world capitalist system, as Mokoena (2018: 88), explains:

> Patriarchy and neoliberal ethic of contractual transactions also informs private relationships whereby certain commodities are traded and exchanged with women's commodified bodies. The marginal position of women in society and struggles relating to material exclusion reproduce women's dependency on men for survival. Transactional sex, which is common among young women who exchange sex for gifts, is another tool characterizing this neoliberal ethos of trade whereby the body becomes a resource of trade for the disadvantaged.

It is in this context that Nkenkana (2018: 67) has argued that: 'Gender equality, especially the rights of women, occupy an increasingly important place in the global and African political discourse and, by implication, has significance for the development discourse as enshrined in the ideals of the futures and visions of Africa.' As many have argued, without gender equality, we cannot talk of true development. Thomas Sankara, among others, elaborates upon this point in his many speeches (in the context of Burkina Faso) contained in a new book edited by Jean-Claude Kongo and Leo Zeilig. Taking Samir Amin's view forward, an argument is made that Africa can 'disengage' from the Global North because Africa connected with the rest of the world incorrectly – Africa can then re-engage at a later stage on its own terms. I will discuss this in detail later.

Realising Development in Africa

Many proposals have been made that are aimed at ensuring that development becomes a reality in Africa. As I have been arguing, the starting point should be revisiting those proposals, assuming that there is a consensus about what the term 'development' means for Africa and also assuming that there is agreement on why development has not been inclusive and/or effective in Africa. Arguably, African countries should work harder in the pursuit of inclusive development without relying on the notion of a 'right to development' and such.

Although it is true that the Global North makes it difficult for Africa to advance its wellbeing, more thinking and action should go into what Africa itself must do. The rest of the world can contribute too. Also, the bigger fight against imperialism and the skewed distribution of global power should not distract from what Africa, and Africans wherever they are, should be doing to improve the wellbeing in African countries. It is in this context that this section focuses on what Africa can or must do. The notion of Africa adopted in approaching this subject is that Africa means the geographical space in the south of the Sahara and Africans are those originating in Africa as a geographical entity who have had to endure many centuries of brutal Arab and European slavery and other forms of repulsive oppression, plunder and exploitation, and have suffered white racism and have been at the receiving end of white supremacy.

The following points are worth mentioning before delving into the discussion of how to make inclusive development a reality in Africa. It must be acknowledged that development has traditionally been viewed from an economic perspective. This chapter rejects this notion of development. So much has been written to make a case that economic development, or the oft-celebrated economic growth, does not equate to inclusive development. Many countries that have been, on different occasions, listed as having high economic development/growth also face many socioeconomic challenges. As argued by Gumede (2016), many high-growth economies in Africa are mineral-dependent countries, of which many come from a relatively low economic base. In other words, these mineral-rich countries have not benefited the majority of their citizens and are also growing rapidly because the baseline of economic growth has been low. It is in this context that I have joined those who reject the notion of development as 'development of the market'.

This is linked to the notion of the African middle class. Besides the fact that the measure(s) used to classify the middle class in Africa is/are questionable, there are many issues that suggest that the very notion of an African middle class is an oxymoron – how could a people who have no control over the economies of Africa, a people without consciousness and a people trapped in debt be categorised as 'middle class'? There are also those who argue that the black middle class is illusionary because it is simply a midway between extreme poverty and affluence, and does not address power or infrastructure. A similar argument can be made in relation to the bourgeoise and the corporate sector in Africa. Prah (2001) talks of 'penny capitalism'. There is a challenge in Africa that the bourgeoise and domestic capital are not patriotic and are predominantly parochial in the sense that capital in African countries is very inwardly looking (though this seems to be changing). In order for Africa to advance, it is necessary that domestic capital in the various African countries expands to other parts of Africa.

Another important issue worth highlighting before delving into the discussion of how to make inclusive development a reality in Africa is that we must address the question of what we want to see in 'development' in the context of Africa. In other words, what could be the features/characteristics of development that are important for Africa? From a pan-Africanist perspective, arguably development must speak to the people – advancement must mean human freedoms from want, oppression, poverty and other ills that engulf many people in Africa. Fundamentally, the communities should drive development because they know what their members value. In other words, development cannot be effective or inclusive if communities are not empowered to run their affairs in a manner that they prefer. This implies that the language through which development occurs is critical. As Prah (2017: 6) has explained, 'language provides the transactional and vehicular instrumentation for the representation of culture'.

By implication, and as Cheikh Anta Diop (1955) argued (and many others have taken that forward), there is no nation that can develop in a foreign language. Language is central to inclusive development, for one cannot know anything that is not in one's language. Prah (2001: 91) argues that 'the notion of development prominently implies, the improvement and upliftment of the quality of life of people that they are able, to a large measure, to attain their potential, build and acquire self-confidence and manage to live lives of reasonable accomplishment and dignity'. In order for communities to 'attain potential, build and acquire self-confidence and manage to live lives of reasonable accomplishment and dignity', language is the most fundamental factor in development, so is culture.

As Prah (2001) has argued, culture (i.e. 'tangibles and intangibles created by humanity or human groups and which provide them with a collective environment in which they transact their everyday lives') is the missing link for development to take place in Africa. Culture, in its evolving sense, should be embraced and languages must be allowed to thrive, for language is also critical, as it ensures and sustains people-to-people relations. The view that languages must be allowed to thrive, which is Kwesi Kwaa Prah's argument, is different from what Ngugi wa Thiong'o (1986) and others have proposed (i.e. that Africa needs one single language). I am now more persuaded that indigenous languages should not be suffocated. This is better than pushing for one language for the whole of Africa (something I have also supported). The works of Cheikh Anta Diop and Théophile Obenga have demonstrated, among other things, that indigenous African languages are similar. This implies that it is feasible that different cultural groups can hear each other while using their each respective languages. It might very well be that a *lingua franca* can be cultivated through adopting or creating a common language by sub-regions in Africa and ultimately culminating in a single language for all the peoples in Africa.

Another important factor for making development a reality in Africa relates to the political or ideological orientation of our societies. As many have argued, there is still an important need for African nationalism in tandem with pan-Africanism. African nationalism brings us back to why we fought for political independence, while pan-Africanism reminds us that we must fight imperialism if we are to get anywhere as Africans. To bring about the African renaissance, pan-African unity is paramount. Linked to this is the perspective that each of the countries in Africa is not able to ensure inclusive development because none of them was created to serve all its citizens. Although there are still issues to be resolved about the nature of a single 'African nation', there are no doubts in the minds of many pan-Africanists that pan-African unity is the answer to many of the challenges that Africa and Africans face. Effective development would be better pursued in a single nation of Africa (comprised of all the countries) where all languages thrive, cultures are embraced, communities are empowered and Africans are united in their diversities. If we are able to confront the crisis of a neocolonial construct that we call African countries, we would be better placed to advance development.

Approaching Development in Africa

Given all that I have said, the question remains: how should inclusive development be approached in Africa? As argued elsewhere, the starting point has to be to revisit the main proposals that have been made. For instance, as discussed earlier, Amin (1990) argued for 'delinking'. Ake (1996) proposed that an agrarian revolution is critical for the development of Africa. Some have argued for 'Afro-capitalism'. Some insist that we must dismantle the 'artificial borders'. Many argue for 'homegrown' policies, and the importance of social policy and the link between social and economic policies.

With regard to Afro-capitalism, Elumelu (2010) views it as an economic philosophy that embodies the private sector commitment to the economic transformation of Africa through investments that generate both economic prosperity and social wealth, while Amaeshi (2013) describes Afro-capitalism as a powerful emotional economic tool for sustainable African economic development, which speaks to African identity. It would seem that Afro-capitalism is essentially about the bourgeoisie and capital that is patriotic in Africa. It could also be viewed as complementing or an alternative to foreign direct investment because Afro-capitalism is about capital in Africa investing within Africa.

Amin (1990: 67) argues that in order for effective development to occur in the Third World countries, the Third World must 'delink' from the global capitalist system. He suggests that underdeveloped countries need to adopt new market strategies and values that are different from those in the developed world. The 'delinking' agenda is essentially a preparatory phase for the 'socialist transition' in the Third World. I am suggesting that Africa must 'disengage' from the rest of the world rather than just 'delinking' together with the rest of the Third World. Africa was wrongly integrated into the rest of the world, mainly through (or starting with) the slave trade. The process of 'disengaging' goes further than 'delinking'. It is not about preparing for socialism, although it could result to socialism. Disengaging would allow Africa to get its house in order, so to speak, then reintegrate with the rest of the world in its own terms rather than the terms that were imposed on it. Therefore, disengaging is not an economic process like delinking. It goes a step further in the sense that it would not only allow Africa to adopt market and production strategies that are different from the global capitalist system, but would also allow Africa to resolve many pressing issues.

Linked to the idea of disengaging is the need for a philosophical or conceptual framework that can guide social and economic relations in Africa. I have been arguing for communalism, or rather a modified version of communalism. Rodney (1973: 12) defines communalism as a system where 'property [is] collectively owned, work done in common and goods shared equally'. This is in sharp contrast to capitalism, which came with colonialism, which, according to Rodney, resulted in the 'concentration in a few hands of ownership of the means of producing wealth and by unequal distribution of the products of human labour' (Rodney 1973: 12). Although Marxism is a powerful tool of analysis, Karl Marx and the original thinkers of Marxist theory studied a society that was profoundly different from African society. Therefore, we should not be preoccupied with preparations for socialism, although this is important. For Africa, the opportunity that disengaging provides would be for Africa to think thoroughly about the possibilities regarding a socioeconomic development approach or model.

Others argue for other ways that can bring about true development in Africa from a philosophical or conceptual perspective. For instance, an argument has been advanced that African modernity would bring about development in Africa. Communalism is seen as an old (i.e. traditional) way of doing things. The case made for African modernity is problematic, given that, as Lushaba (2006: 19) argues, 'modernity is nothing more than Europe's transition from feudal to the capitalist mode of production and its attendant social relations'. That is why it is problematic that 'in a bid to develop Africa must modernize where to modernize means replicating the western historical and development trajectory' (Lushaba 2006: 23). Interestingly, Lushaba (2006: 49) concludes that '(the African) struggle to escape from the present and construct own modernity can no longer be a bourgeoisie led one just as national liberation struggles were'. So, by implication, African modernity has a place, except that it should be pursued differently. This is not convincing; thus, I have been arguing for a modified version of communalism.

Although communalism was not only in Africa during the pre-mercantilist era or early Africa, it was overwhelmingly predominant in Africa. It was not an economic system per se, but a way of life. Indeed, there is value in the pursuit of socialism and ultimately communism. However, the hypothesis of disengaging suggests that Africa can experiment with any ideological approach. The approach I am arguing for is a modified version of communalism. There is no reason why communalism cannot graduate over time into a class-less society, as Marxism envisages a graduation from capitalism to socialism and ultimately to a classless society. It might very well be that decades later, all regions will be classless societies, at a point when Africa reintegrates with the rest of the world. This proposal for Africa to disengage privileges African agency – Africans should do something about their own circumstances. More thinking still needs to go into this proposal. To be sure, I am not arguing that people in Africa should cut ties with peoples in other parts of the world. Fundamentally, the proposal is that Africa as a continent should focus on getting its house in order without interference from other parts of the world.

So, what could be the pillars of a different socioeconomic model for Africa (operating in the communalism mode)? As argued elsewhere, these could be: (1) intra-Africa trade (and regional integration); (2) state ownership; (3) social policy; (4) industrialisation; and (5) entrepreneurship. These five pillars make up what I have termed an economic renaissance model for Africa. Africa needs to trade among its countries (while there are countries) that would hopefully be gone (and one African nation would exist) when Africa ends disengagement.

To increase or ensure intra-African trade, the different subregions in Africa could focus on certain sectors. For example, Southern Africa could focus on manufacturing, while East Africa could focus on services. Africa could 'appoint' anchor economies, for example, Nigeria, South Africa, Kenya and Ethiopia. These 'leaders' could be supported and capacitated to boost economic development in the surrounding countries. Linked to this is the importance of ensuring that regional integration deals with both economic and noneconomic factors. Regional integration that focuses on markets and is top-down cannot advance true development in Africa. Regional integration should also be about people-to-people relations, hence the importance of languages and the need to embrace different cultures.

As for state ownership, having governments in the different countries in Africa temporarily owning the means of production and land would ensure that governments could ensure the proper use of such resources, and empowered communities would guide governments. Perhaps we should dispense with the term 'government' and use 'council'. In other words, representatives of the people would be 'councils' that are constituted through democratic participation. Other aspects of the new approach to development would most likely come naturally as soon as there were no further constraints imposed by the current governance arrangements and global capitalism. Entrepreneurship, for instance, would thrive when people are able to undertake commerce in their varied languages. Social policy would also come naturally as an obvious component of advancing the wellbeing of those who may not be able to fend for themselves – the key issue regarding social policy is that it should work in tandem with economic policy. Industrialisation would be a natural process that would also ensure the agrarian revolution that we have overlooked.

The fundamental precondition of all this is pan-African unity. It is not insurmountable. Starting with people-to-people relations and allowing languages to thrive, unity will happen (although it is going to take a long time, as the imperialist forces will do everything possible to stifle African unity). Among other things, mobilisation across the continent of Africa and the Diaspora will assist in ensuring that Africans unite again. Critical consciousness and thought liberation, as I have argued, are critical. Critical consciousness implies that all Africans would be alive to the realities that assign a lower rank to Africans than other races globally. Thought liberation implies that Africans would be free from ways of thinking and ways of living that do not advance the interests of Africans wherever Africans are. All of this is easier said than done. It is still early days.

Conclusion

Although it is still early days, it would seem that there is a groundswell that is pushing for African unity – and many are working hard towards giving meaning to the African nation. Indeed, African unity will happen, but, understandably, it will take a while. In the meantime, indigenous African languages must be allowed to thrive and people-to-people relations encouraged so that true development can occur. As the works of Kwesi Kwaa Prah show, without embracing indigenous languages and cultures and empowering communities, effective development will remain a pipedream.

It is critical to pursue all aspects that matter for Africa's development. This chapter has viewed development as advancement in people's lives as opposed to the development of the market. The chapter has drawn inspiration from and is influenced by the leading African scholars who have engaged with the notion of development and discourses on development in Africa. The central argument of the chapter is that inclusive development will not be satisfactory in Africa until Africa disengages from the rest of the world. The disengagement argued for is temporary, say fifty years, so that Africa can get its house in order in the meantime and reintegrate with the rest of the world on its own terms, because originally it integrated incorrectly into the rest of the world.

This chapter has problematised the notion of development and discourses in development, as an effort to rethinking and reclaiming development in Africa. It also examined the levels of development in post-independence Africa, and concluded that development – measured through conventional United Nations measures – has been weak relative to other regions. The chapter has also proposed how inclusive development could better be approached in Africa. Although others argue that Africa's past should not be romanticised and/or that being Africa or African should not be essentialised, I argue that there are important lessons that can be distilled from how early Africa was organised and functioned. It is in this context that I have argued for a modified version of communalism as a possible philosophical framework that can underpin Africa's (new/different) approach to socioeconomic development.

Vusi Gumede is Professor and Head of the Thabo Mbeki African Leadership Institute at the University of South Africa. He was previously an associate professor at the University of Johannesburg. From 2009 to 2014, he also lectured on public policy at the Graduate School of Public and Development Management (now the School of Government) of the University of Witwatersrand in South Africa. He worked for the South

African government, in various capacities, for about twelve years. He was once *Distinguished Africanist Scholar* at Cornell University and *Yale World Fellow* at Yale University, among others. He serves on various boards, committees and other structures and processes, including as Deputy President of the National Council of the South African Association of Political Studies. He holds postgraduate qualifications in economics and policy studies, including a Ph.D. in Economics (2003) at the erstwhile University of Natal (now the University of KwaZulu-Natal). He publishes on macroeconomics and political economy – his current research and teaching focus is broadly on the African political economy. He also holds an Honorary Professorship at the University of Cape Town.

References

Ake, C. 1996. *Democracy and Development in Africa*. Washington DC: Brookings Institution.
Amaeshi, K. 2013. 'Africapitalism: Unleashing the Power of Emotions for Africa's Development?', *African Argument*, 2 October 2013. Retrieved 11 September 2018 from http://africanarguments.org/2013/10/02/africapitalism-unleashing-the-power-of-emotions-for-africas-development-by-kenneth-amaeshi.
Amin, S. 1990. *Delinking: Towards a Polycentric World*. London: Zed Books, 1990.
Andreassen, B., and Marks, S. 2006. *Development as a Human Right: Legal, Political and Economic Dimensions*. Harvard School of Public Health, Francois Xavier Bagnoud Center for Health and Human Rights, Harvard University.
Bello, E. 1992. 'Article 22 of the African Charter on Human and Peoples' Rights', in E. Bello and B. Adjibola (eds), *Essay in Honour of Judge Taslim Olawale Elias*. Dordrecht: Martinus Nijhoff Publishers, pp. 447–84.
Clark, J. 1991. *Democratising Development: The Role of Voluntary Organisations*. Boulder, CO: Lynne Rienner Publishers.
Diop, C.A. 1955. *The African Origin of Civilisation: Myth or Reality*. Paris: Presence Africaine.
Donnelly, J. 1985. 'In Search of the Unicorn: The Jurisprudence and Politics of the Right to Development', *California Western International Law Journal* 15: 473–509.
Elumelu, T. 2010. 'Why Africa Needs Capitalism That is Aligned with its Development Needs'. Retrieved 11 September 2018 from http://tonyelumelufoundation.org/africapitalisminstitute/why-africa-needs-capitalism-that-is-aligned-with-its-development-needs.
Escobar, A. 1995. *Encountering Development: The Making and Unmaking of the Third World*. Princeton: Princeton University Press.
Gumede, V. 2016. 'Towards a Better Socio-economic Development Approach for Africa's Renewal', *Africa Insight* 46(1): 89–105.
_____. 2018. 'Social Policy for Inclusive Development in Africa', *Third World Quarterly* 39(1): 122–39.

_____. (ed.). 2018. *Towards Inclusive Development in Africa: Transforming Global Relations*. Pretoria: AISA & CODESRIA Press.
Kamga, S. 2017. 'The Right to Development and the Post-2015 Agenda', in S. Zondi and P. Mthembu (eds), *From MDGs to Sustainable Development Goals*. Pretoria: Institute of Global Dialogue, pp. 43–46.
_____. 2018. *The Right to Development in the African Human Rights System*. New York: Routledge.
Kongo, J.-C., and L. Zeilig. 2018. *Voices of Liberation: Thomas Sankara*. Pretoria: HSRC Press.
Latouche, S. 1993. *In the Wake of the Affluent Society: An Exploration of Post-development*. London: Zed Books.
Lumumba-Kasongo, T. 2002. 'The National Project as a Public Administration Concept: The Problematic State Building in the Search for New Development Paradigms in Africa', *Africa Development* XXXVI(2): 63–96.
Lushaba, L.S. 2006. 'Development as Modernity, Modernity as Development', African Studies Centre Working Paper 69/2006. Leiden: ASC.
M'baye, K. 1972. 'Le droit au développement comme un droit de l'homme', *Revue des droits l'homme* 5 (1972): 505–34.
McFadden, P. 2011. 'Re-crafting Citizenship in the Postcolonial Moment: A Focus on Southern Africa', *Works and Days* 29(1–2): 26–279.
Meillan, L. 2003. 'Le Droit au Dévelopment et les Nations Unies: Quelques Réflexions'. *Droit en Quart Monde* 34: 13–31.
Ouguergouz. *The African Charter on Human and Peoples' Rights: A Comprehensive Agenda for Human Dignity and Sustainable Democracy in Africa*. The Hague: Martinus Nijhoff Publishers.
Mkandawire, T. 2011. 'Running While Others Walk: Knowledge and the Challenge of Africa's Development', *Africa Development* XXXVI(2): 1–36.
_____. 2015. 'Neopatrimonialism and the Political Economy of Economic Performance in Africa: Critical Reflections', *World Politics* 67(3): 563–612.
Mokoena, D. 2018. 'Capitalist Crisis and Gender Inequality: Quest for Inclusive Development', in V. Gumede, (ed.), *Towards Inclusive Development in Africa: Transforming Global Relations*. Pretoria: AISA & CODESRIA Press, pp. 84–102.
Myrdal, G. 1974. 'What is Development?' *Journal of Economic Issues* 8(4): 729–36.
Ndlovu-Gatsheni, S. 2012. 'Coloniality of Power in Development Studies and the Impact of Global Imperial Designs on Africa'. Inaugural Professorial Lecture. University of South Africa, 16 October.
Nkenkana, A. 2018. 'No African Futures without the Liberation of Women: A Decolonial Feminist Perspective', in V. Gumede (ed.), *Towards Inclusive Development in Africa: Transforming Global Relations*. Pretoria: AISA and CODESRIA Press, pp. 67–83.
Oloruntoba, S. 2015. 'Politics of Financialisation and Inequality: Transforming Global Relations for Inclusive Development', *Africa Development* XL(3): 121–37.
Pieterse, V. 2000. 'After Post-development', *Third World Quarterly* 21(2): 175–91.
Plaatjie, S.R. 2013. 'Beyond Western-Centric and Eurocentric Development: A Case for Decolonizing Development', *Africanus* 43(2): 118–130.
Prah, K.K. 2001. 'Culture: The Missing Link in Development Planning in Africa', *Présence Africaine* 163/164: 90–102.

———. 2006. *The African Nation: The State of the Nation.* Cape Town: CASAS.
———. 2016. *Pan-African Concerns: Keeping Our Eyes on the Ball.* Cape Town: CASAS.
———. 2017. *Reflections: On Goldberg's Variations on Africanist Themes.* Cape Town: CASAS.
Rodney, W. 1973. *How Europe Underdeveloped Africa.* Dar-Es-Salaam: Tanzanian Publishing House.
Sen, A. 1999. *Development as Freedom.* New York: Oxford University Press.
Sengupta, M. 2002. 'On the Theory and Practice of the Right to Development', *Human Rights Quarterly* 24: 837–89.
Shivji, S. 2006. 'The Changing Development Discourse in Africa', Africa Notes, Newsletter (January–February). Institute for African Development, Cornell University.
Slim, H. 1995. 'What is Development?' *Development in Practice* 5(2): 143–48.
Swantz, M.-L. 2009. 'What is Development?', in P. Mikko (ed.), *Perspectives to Global Social Development.* Kalevantie: Tempere University Press, pp. 29-37.
Tandon. Y. 2015. 'Development is Resistance', *Africa Development* XL(3): 139–59.
Thiong'o, N. 1986. *Decolonizing the Mind: The Politics of Language in African Literature.* London: James Currey.
Whyte, J. 2007. 'Book Review: *Development as a Human Right*, B. Andreassen, and S. Marks, Harvard University Press', *Journal of Sustainable Development* 1(1): 1–3.
Ziai, A. 2009. 'Development: Projects, Power, and a Poststructuralist Perspective', *Alternatives: Global, Local, Political* 34(2): 183–201.
— —. 2013. 'The Discourse of "Development" and Why the Concept Should Be Abandoned', *Development in Practice* 23(1): 123–36.

Chapter 3

Elusive Solutions to Poverty and Inequality
From 'Trickle Down' to 'Solidarity Economy'

Tidings P. Ndhlovu

Introduction

The parable about the blind men and the elephant and how, after touching different parts of the elephant, each man arrived at different conclusions about what the elephant looked like best illustrates the different views that are held by analysts regarding poverty and its solutions. Depending on their ideological and political views, theorists' perspectives range from 'trickle down' theories that posit poverty and inequality as a natural phenomenon, a social 'fact of life', to arguments about poverty and inequality being an outcome of the conflictual process of accumulation, of the power relations in capitalism. While the former is a one-dimensional view of poverty and inequality, the latter is based on a multi-dimensional conception. The latter contends that there is no doubt that inequality, although seemingly self-evident or 'intuitively easy to understand' as Alkire et al. (2013: 71) put it, raises complex economic, social, political and ideological questions (Ndletyana 2013: 51–71).

Our specific concern in this chapter is to provide some historical and theoretical context within which to analyse concepts of poverty and inequality and their purported solutions. We will briefly contextualise the concepts of poverty and inequality. What follows is a discussion of neoclassical arguments, ILO ideas about basic needs, Sen's entitlements and capability approach and participatory models, and Marxian arguments that may also involve concepts of the 'solidarity economy', before we arrive at some tentative conclusions.

Context: Equity, (In)Equality and Poverty

Given the different interpretations that have been alluded to, that is, a distinction between 'formal equality' (equal treatment of everyone) and 'substantive equality' (emphasis on 'equality of results and opportunity'), we can best 'disentangle' inequality by first establishing some ground rules on what we mean by 'equality'. There are a number of facets to this issue. First, equality, when seen in legalistic terms, refers to the notion that members of society should be equal in the eyes of the law. Second, equality of opportunity conjures up an image of a meritocracy, that is, that each member of society has an equal chance of fulfilling their potential, developing their talents and applying themselves to the 'task at hand'. Finally, equality of outcome can be couched in terms of a benchmark against which we can judge unequal distribution of income, deep-seated poverty and so on. By identifying unequal distribution, we are at the same time comparing this situation with a hypothetical one where everyone receives the same income. For the political economy approach, as will be evident below, these concepts are not only contradictory, but also meaningless when seen through the prism of the capitalist system that is 'structured' along the lines of class relations of exploitation.

Similarly, the concept of poverty can be defined as either a natural occurrence or one that is caused by the deprivation of minimum requirements and capabilities, or one that is explicable from the contradictory accumulation process in capitalist societies. For Alkire and Santos, like Sen, 'the Multidimensional Poverty Index (MPI) [is] a measure of *acute poverty*, understood as a person's inability to meet simultaneously minimum international standards in indicators related to the Millennium Development Goals and core functionings' (Alkire and Santos, 2013; see also Ross, 2013: 447–48). In addition, Alkire et al. (2013) argue that such analyses and proposed solutions have broader societal implications: '"empowerment" is a broad concept that is used differently by various writers, depending on the context or circumstance. Indeed, one can argue that many policy reports ... make links between gender equality and development outcomes, not necessarily between *empowerment* and desired outcomes' (Alkire et al. 2013: 71). They define agency and empowerment as 'domain specific', hence their multidimensional, survey-based index for measuring 'domains' of empowerment, whilst also using the gender parity index (GPI) and the incidence of inequality (Alkire et al. 2013: 73–77).

In his theoretical model of 'habitas', Bourdieu (1977) advises us to take account of the environment in which people live, one that comprises of practices, habits, cultures, inherited expectations and rules. The latter are a 'product of history' and he describes 'this system of dispositions' as 'habitas' (Bourdieu 1977: 82, 164). Such a system determines limits to usages and opportunities, as well as disclosed possibilities, norms and sanctions both of the law and neighbourhood pressures. In the circumstances, the observer must not impute meaning to 'objects' of analysis and must not assign a set of rules to validate a set of predetermined narratives and behaviour (see also Siegmann and Cameron 2012). Even though Bourdieu contends that social life and social behaviour, cannot be 'codified', every now and again he does fall into the trap of referring to 'common codes' vis-à-vis power relations and his railing against male domination. Regarding the particular problem that we are trying to address, a sense of deprivation may be likened to being in an incarcerated state until the barriers begin to fall away. Thompson's (1995) polemic against Althusser's (1969) structuralist model is also instructive in this regard. He argues that we must be mindful of teleological arguments, that is, cherry-picking arguments or imposing theory to fit the evidence. For him, there must be a 'dialogue' between the conceptual 'thought' and its object ('real' history or social reality), between human agency (and process in history) and practice (the evidentiary).

From 'Trickle Down' Theory to a Basic Needs Approach

From an orthodox neoclassical approach, poverty is a natural phenomenon that reflects the poor's deficit in capabilities and thus arguably explains their low levels of productivity and even their alleged indolence (Ndhlovu 2012). This dominant neoliberal ideology seeks to convince the poor that their poverty is a natural 'fact of life' about which they can do nothing (Ndhlovu 2012). To the extent that the division of labour also reflects the poor's inherent individual weaknesses and how things are naturally ordered, all that matters in development policy terms is to 'get prices right' (Lal 1983) and facilitate this via International Monetary Fund (IMF)/World Bank structural adjustment policies. As Edwards paraphrases the point: 'The fewer the "price distortions" there are in LDCs, the faster their growth in exports and the higher their rate of economic growth' (Edwards 1985: 292). Thus, in the absence of distortions such as subsidies, it is argued that the free market system will promote greater total welfare and income distribution.

In other words, the so-called 'problems' of poverty and inequality can only be solved by ensuring freely operating markets and, in turn, open market prices of goods, services, natural resources, labour and so on that reflect relative scarcities. The contention is that free market prices are also the 'right' prices, and only when prices are 'right' can the economy effectively allocate resources to their most efficient use. In such a free market society, rational individuals with talents and tastes act in their own best interests, maximise utility (welfare/happiness) and profit, have preferences that are known only to them, and make choices (*Free to Choose*, as Milton Friedman's classic book is entitled). While the pursuit of efficient economic growth may initially worsen income distribution, it is argued that eventually income will naturally 'trickle down' to the poor. In fact, in this top-down approach, inequality can arguably ensure higher levels of savings that result in higher investment and that are followed by higher levels of economic growth and, consequently, more income trickling down.

Clearly, workers and capitalists receive income that is proportional to their contribution to production (see, for example, Jevons 1871; Samuelson 1937, 1938, 1947; Friedman and Friedman 1981). In other words, the price of labour is 'earned' income (wages, salaries and income accruing from self-employment), while the price of capital is 'unearned' income (interest, dividends and profit). Using per capita income as an indicator of inequality, orthodox economists contend that any differences in earnings can only be explicable through differences in people's contributions to production. Some people are (arguably) naturally more talented, more skilled and more intelligent than others. Therefore, when choosing between work and leisure – or indeed between different types of work that necessitate different types of skills – some people are prepared to work longer or more intensively than others. Some people will take on more difficult, dangerous or responsible jobs, whilst others will sacrifice earnings and leisure in order to acquire the necessary skills for particular jobs that will pay them handsomely in the future. Inequalities in earnings are therefore defined as 'fair' and desirable, since scarce talent is used in the most efficient ways, thus benefiting society from this standpoint.

Emphasis is placed on equality of opportunity rather than equality of outcome. In her 1975 address, the former British Prime Minister Margaret Thatcher encapsulated this 'business-as-usual, do-nothing' viewpoint: 'The pursuit of equality is a mirage. What is more desirable and practical than the pursuit of equality is the pursuit of the equality of opportunity, and opportunity means nothing unless it includes the right to be unequal.' Inequalities in income and wealth could thus be justified as merely reflecting inequalities in people themselves. To the extent that people are arguably different in terms of their intelligence, enterprise, etc., then logically, so the argument goes, each person must do the job for which they are most suited or most able. Differentials in income are thus essential in encouraging people to do the more 'valuable' jobs that are determined by society and by consumer wants. As far as it is asserted that competition shapes how we understand society, it stands to reason that 'there is no such thing as society', to use Thatcher's dramatic language to emphasise individualism.

The basic needs (BN) approach that was introduced at the 1976 World Employment Conference of the United Nations (UN) (International Labour Organization 1976) sought to address the perceived failures of the 'trickle down' theory to tackle absolute poverty. To the extent that population growth and urbanisation were said to manifest themselves in starvation, malnutrition, illiteracy, housing problems, etc., this alternative bottom-up approach defined poverty as the deprivation of certain consumption bundles. The BN strategy stressed the provision of certain basic needs to the poor – that is, basic needs for sustaining life – and productive employment (see also Jolly and Santos 2016; ODI 1978). Minimum requirements (such as 'adequate food, shelter and clothing' and 'certain household equipment and furniture') were identified as ensuring survival, whilst other public services (such as 'safe drinking water, sanitation, public transport, and health, education, and cultural facilities' and free participation in democratic processes and decision-making) were seen as essential for a healthy society. Productive employment would provide individuals with income and would also give them 'a feeling of self-respect, dignity and of being a worthy member of society'.

Clearly, the successful implementation of the BN strategy depended on adequate finance, on identifying minimum nutritional or dietary needs that would starve off hunger and absolute poverty, and the necessary service networks to ensure distribution in ways that reflected appropriate consumption patterns of the poor. China and Sri Lanka were often cited as countries that had either achieved industrial development (geared towards the needs of the agricultural and rural sector) and provided basic needs (China) or introduced reforms designed to distribute income more equitably (Sri Lanka). Indeed, the latter made great strides in improvements in the provision of housing, food, education and health services, despite the constraints of relatively low income levels per capita and limited resources.

Notwithstanding this, different interpretations of and contradictions within the BN approach eventually led to its demise. The BN strategy was reduced to 'sloganisation' of poverty alleviation and reduction of inequality. The BN approach had focused on supply and demand, on the provision of economic opportunities to the poor and expenditure on education to improve productivity, all of which were designed to contribute to sustained growth. The World Bank's 1990 Review on Third World Poverty went so far as to declare that basic needs would be difficult to achieve without economic growth. Yet there were still voices that posited income distribution as a prerequisite for growth. Moreover, the enthusiastic promotion of the BN approach by the World Bank raised suspicions within less developed countries (LDCs) about whether such campaigns were a direct attack on their national sovereignty. Apart from its patronising aspects, in some quarters this approach was seen to be fostering or reinforcing dependency.

In addition, there was no consensus on the definition of basic needs (ODI 1978) and the construction of social indicators, let alone the selection of variables and their significance in different settings. In other words, Western-determined BN requirements did not always reflect the societies in which the policies were implemented. Moreover, while the 'physical quality of life' index did provide some insights into the human condition, the methods for constructing an all-inclusive (composite) human welfare index for evaluating the effectiveness of the strategy ran afoul of aggregation problems and/or problems of selecting social indicators, as well as the arbitrary way of assigning weightings. In the final analysis, success of the BN strategy was crucially dependent on the extent to which respective governments actively sought to address problems of inadequate basic needs and/or distribution of income and wealth.

Sen's Entitlements and Capability Approach, and Participatory Approaches

For his part, Sen (1992, 1999) argues that neoclassical economics fails to address questions of wellbeing and welfare, tending to regard the market as superior to the state. He challenges the Rostow (1971) 'stages of growth' model that is often used by autocratic regimes to rationalise the denial of political freedoms and human rights on the grounds of growth today and manna (welfare improvements) tomorrow (O'Hearn 2009), especially in the light of Jevons and the 'marginalists' 'having taken the social out of economics' (Fine 2004: 100). Ironically, Sen, like the neoclassical economists he criticises, emphasises individualism and does not challenge the World Bank's post-Washington Consensus (Cameron and Gasper 2000; Devereux 2001; Fine 2001: 11–12; O'Hearn 2009). While seeking to go further than the BN approach, his analysis displays the same tensions that are immanent in the former, tensions 'between micro and macro, between the individual and the social, and also between generality/formalism as opposed to specificity/context' (Fine 2004: 97). His analysis is arguably ahistorical (O'Hearn 2009). Despite these misgivings, poverty and inequality are defined here as the deprivation of opportunities or options or, as Sen himself often puts it, the deprivation of basic (individual) capabilities (in the case of South Africa, see also Ross (2013: 451–52)).

Given that entitlements – that is, 'a set of alternative commodity bundles' that can be bought by a person in the face of constraints – 'depend on … [a person's] ability to find a job, the wage rate for that job, and prices of commodities that he or she wishes to buy' (Sen 1992: 15), increases in income will thus not necessarily guarantee entitlements to education, medical treatment, etc. Here real income is used as a proxy for entitlement to food, etc., and one's endowments (ownership of assets and resources that include labour) can be converted into exchange possibilities or exchange entitlements (see also Devereux 2001: 246). One can be '*entitled* to free food *if* there is a relief system offering that. Whether, in fact, a starving person will have such an entitlement will depend on whether such a public relief operation will actually be launched. The provision of public relief is partly a matter of political and social pressure' (Sen 1992: 17).

It is against this background that enhanced human capabilities are likely to enable people to access entitlements to education, etc. Freedom (capability) will allow people to make choices about living the lives they 'have reason to value', about which 'functionings' (actual achievements) they consider to be most important to them (that is, their ability or the space they are afforded for achieving). Functionings or states of 'being and doing' or people's achievements refer to commodities and facilities that enable people to live, as well as psychological, social and political dimensions of their lives. For Sen, freedom does not refer to the neoliberal concept of self-interest and 'getting prices right' (Lal 1983); instead, it is concerned with people's ability to access entitlements in a social atmosphere that enables capabilities to shine through.

We can only judge how far progress has taken place by the extent to which freedom has been enhanced, such success being measured by the Human Poverty Index. In Sen's analysis, freedom encompasses not only material needs, but also spiritual wants. It involves the extent to which people engage in social and political deliberations, how vocal they can express their views, and how far they can participate in the decision-making process. An example of this participatory 'economic and social development from below' approach is the case of Professor Muhammad Yunus' Grameen Bank (or Village Bank) in Bangladesh. Yunus, who was a winner of the 2006 Nobel Peace Prize, set up the bank in 1983 with the precise aim of giving 'micro-loans' to poor women to enable them to lift themselves out of poverty. The small loans were used to enable women to escape 'a life of grinding poverty and physical abuse' (Yunus 1999: 114). In Sen's terms, the question then is how far individuals are presented with the opportunities or social circumstances under which they can live the 'Good life they desire'.

According to Sen, Adam Smith led the way in showing us that 'necessaries' can enable the poor 'to appear in public without shame' and to hold their heads up in public. Unlike the one-dimensional conception of poverty in neoclassical economics, Sen argues that his multidimensional approach traces poverty to race, ethnicity, gender, etc. In the circumstances, capability deprivation tends to knock an individual's dignity, making them feel inadequate and dealing a mortal blow to their self-confidence.

Marxian Approaches and the Concept of 'Solidarity Economy'

For the political economy approach, attention must be trained on the social relations of production, on power relations as the explanation for poverty and inequality in the capitalist system. It is contended that private ownership creates a class that, by virtue of its ownership of the means of production, can lay claim to the surplus gained in production (see, for example, Marx 1859, 1887, 1894). In other words, the key to understanding unequal distribution of wealth and income from this perspective is through the process of accumulation rather than merely biological disposition. For example, those people who have higher incomes, be it via inheritance (transmission of wealth between generations), (social) networking, corruption or (forcible) expropriation, will be able to command a greater proportion of the surplus and will have greater opportunities to accumulate. In any case, without the abolition of inheritance, equality of opportunity merely implies inequality of outcome. There is also a greater chance that these people will hold large holdings of capital, enabling them to cushion themselves against risk and uncertainty, and have more control over privately owned resources and financial institutions, contributing to the ever-widening inequalities under the capitalist market system. Inequality is thus couched in a broader context that encompasses power relations. In the circumstances, and as long as there is private property, equality of opportunity will thus not be guaranteed, let alone lead to equality of outcome and condition.

Clearly, the division of labour is used to justify unequal rewards within capitalist societies. Incentives exist in order to motivate workers, as well as hire and fire them in accordance with the patterns of commodity demand. Moreover, workers could be 'persuaded' to acquire more or different skills in order to perform particular functions. It has also been argued that such division of labour ensures that (executive) managers allocate jobs accordingly, while keeping in reserve their 'right to manage', that is, discipline the workforce, coordinate production and preserve their authority. If these duties are accepted as legitimate tasks of managers, requiring specialised skills of decision-making and responsibility, then this can be used to justify their higher salaries. Further emphasis on differences rather than a community of interest ensures that workers are divided according to skills, responsibilities, manual and nonmanual tasks, etc., whilst their cohesiveness and organisation is reduced. Indeed, sexual and racial differences can then be exploited in ways that raise barriers to occupational mobility and break down the unity of experience of workers, thus dividing them into distinct groups. Thus, throughout history, there has been production and reproduction of inequality and poverty.

Since gender is a social and cultural construct within different historical contexts, women's subordination involves economic and racial oppression as well as patriarchal relations (Cameron and Ndhlovu 2000, 2001; Cole, Cameron and Edwards 1991; Ndhlovu and Spring 2009; Ndhlovu 2011, 2012). As Collins puts it, 'power as domination' is structured through 'a system of interlocking race, class and gender relations' (2000: 73, 76, 79, 203, 284, 288–90). Not only does this system of oppression manifest itself as a matrix 'politic of domination', but it is also experienced at different levels: at the interpersonal level, at the 'group or community level' and at the 'systemic level of social institutions' (Collins 2000: 288–90). The resilience of this interlocking system of oppression also stems from the state's 'political, cultural and ideological role in the process of legitimation. Ideological factors in particular involve education, the popular media and press, the family, force of habit and/or "common sense", that is, the ability to convince the working class that the dominant social organisation of production is self-evident, that it has always been so and need not be challenged' (Ndhlovu 2012: 106). Referring to 'the growing sophistication of mass media in regulating intersecting oppressions', Collins also observes that 'hegemonic ideologies concerning race, class, gender, sexuality and nation are so pervasive that it is difficult to conceptualize alternatives to them, let alone ways of resisting the social practices that they justify' (2000: 284).

Thus, theoretical analysis must be interrelated with praxis. In a word, people are 'moulded' by society, while at the same time they also strive to reshape and reconstitute that society (human agency). It is with this view in mind that we turn to the examination of the 'solidarity economy' and how far it reflects these principles in practice.

The concept of 'popular economy' is often used interchangeably with 'solidarity economy', although the former has a longer history and combines political and sociocultural sectors with 'traditional popular participatory institutions' (Bauwens and Lemaitre 2014: 66), while the latter is a newer framework (1980s and 1990s) that puts greater emphasis on 'collective initiatives' and 'collective action' (Bauwens and Lemaitre 2014: 99; see also Nobrega 2013; Razeto 1991, 1993 for Chile and Brazil). Thus, although the common theme is emphasis on social goals rather than profit gain, that is, 'collective/associative forms' (Bauwens and Lemaitre 2014: 65), these concepts mean different things to different people and in different contexts, according to time and place.

A Solidarity economy in particular is variously described as: (i) enlightened (financial) institutions that enrich the market with collective values that enable informal workers and the self-employed to eke out a living and lift themselves out of poverty, and bring about social changes, as in the United Kingdom; (ii) 'associations, cooperatives and mutuals' (Safri 2013: 2), as in French-speaking Europe; (iii) worker cooperatives that are operated and collectively managed by workers involving decisions on socially sustainable development and emancipation of women, as in Brazil (Safri 2013; Nobrega 2013); or (iv) social transformation that goes further in seeking to abolish the oppressive and dehumanising capitalist social relations of production, as described earlier in the Marxian analysis of poverty and inequality. Indeed, this 'spectrum of definitions ... [ranges] from a third sector that strengthens and stabilizes capitalism to the more radical view in which the social economy has a transformative, post-capitalist agenda' (Kawano 2013: 5).

It has been suggested that Southern African movements can learn from either the Brazilian and Chilean cases, or the Marxian analyses of fundamental social change that were discussed earlier. With regard to the Latin American cases, Kawano (2013) argues that solidarity economy embraces the radical elements of workers' self-management and collective ownership, empowerment and sustainable development, whose outcomes are enhanced social justice and social cohesion, prioritising people's welfare and community concerns, that is, socially and environmentally responsible forms of organisation, thus arresting and alleviating poverty and inequality. Indeed, Nobrega (2013) argues that, at a time of economic crisis in the 1990s and facilitated by microcredit and small loans, an alternative solidarity economy approach in Brazil 'helped [to] decrease poverty in Brazil. [The] Poverty rate fell by 57% between 2001 and 2011 ... while small businesses accounted for 39% of income of Brazilians' (Nobrega 2013: 2). While Kawano (2013: 4–5) argues that Marxian revolutionary approaches and other social change movements do not have the flexibility of the solidarity economy movement, it must be noted that the suggested pluralist approaches face the same difficulties and contradictions that confronted the entitlements, capability and participatory approaches. As indicated earlier, these problems include tensions between the micro and macro, between the individual and the social, amongst others.

In striving for a more humanistic economy, one that is not predicated on profit gain, there have also been suggestions that we must take cognisance of power relations and of social relations; indeed, of concerns that speak to ownership structures, land reform and long-term structural transformation. Indeed, social reorganisation of society will entail, amongst other things, 'correction' of health inequalities/inequities and material deprivation through redistributive measures that ensure greater access to housing and health facilities and/or services (Ngepah and Mhlaba 2013: 84–93; Pieterse and van Donk 2013: 98–108, 117–20; van Rensburg and Heunis 2013: 469–73). While seeking to arrest or, rather, rectify the skewed distribution between public and private sectors, the South African government, for example, is formulating the National Health Insurance. Like Obamacare in the United States or the more established British National Health System (NHS), this is being articulated against the backdrop of the contested positions and different ideological standpoints of stakeholders (Shisana 2013: 520–32). Those who particularly want to see an end to the dominance of private health insurance (which is out of reach of the poor) advocate a unified/universal healthcare system that will cut across the economic, racial, gender, age and (geographical) locational divide (Shisana 2013: 532; van Rensburg and Heunis 2013: 472–78). It is in this regard that self-empowered groups are crucial to the struggle for emancipation and/or alleviation of poverty and inequality.

Conclusion

From 'trickle down' theory to 'solidarity economy', it has increasingly become clear that political and ideological positions shape the way in which we conceive inequality and poverty and their measurement, as well as implications for empowerment. Indeed, the transformation of society hinges upon not only the direction taken by theorists, but more crucially upon how this plays itself out in practice.

The political economy approach arguably gives us insights into the difficulties involved in tackling issues of equity, inequality and empowerment within a capitalist society. The 'system of interlocking race, class, gender and national' oppression, together with the ideological glue that binds it together and ensures its resilience, requires that analysis be married to praxis. What is required is a multidisciplinary and multidimensional approach by historians and political economists to examine the historical roots of inequalities in Southern Africa. Apart from economic factors, what role do racial and patriarchal relations play? Has historical experience not shown us that culture, like any other facet of society, is changing and dynamic? In this dialectic relationship, Southern Africa could be a model for the rest of the world in terms of gender equity, as well as the liberation of both men and women from class, racial and cultural oppression. However, this requires redoubled activism to demonstrate/evaluate effectively.

Tidings P. Ndhlovu is Senior Lecturer in Economics at Manchester Metropolitan University Business School, UK; and Visiting Research Fellow at the Graduate School of Business Leadership, University of South Africa. He is also the Executive Secretary, International Academy of African Business and Development (IAABD).

References

Alkire, S., R. Meinzen-Dick, A. Peterman, A. Quisumbing, G. Seymour and A. Vaz. 2013. 'The Women's Empowerment in Agriculture Index', *World Development* 52: 71–91.

Alkire, S. and M.E. Santos. 2013. 'Measuring Acute Poverty in the Developing World: Robustness and Scope of the Multidimensional Poverty Index', *Oxford Poverty & Human Development Initiative (OPHI) Working Paper*, No 59, University of Oxford, March.

Althusser, L. 1969. *For Marx*. London: Allen Lane.

Bauwens, T., and A. Lemaitre. 2014. 'Popular Economy in Santiago de Chile: State of Affairs and Challenges', *World Development* 64: 65–78.

Bourdieu, P. 1977. *An Outline of a Theory of Practice*. Cambridge: Cambridge University Press.

Cameron, J., and D. Gasper (eds). 2000. 'Amartya Sen on Inequality, Human Well-Being, and Development as Freedom', *Journal of International Development* 12(7): 985–88.

Cameron, J., and T.P. Ndhlovu. 2000. 'Development Economics: An Institutional Bastion', *Journal of Interdisciplinary Economics* 11(3–4): 237–53.

_____. 2001. 'The Comparative Economics of EU "Subsidiarity": Lessons from Development/Regional Economic Debates', *Journal of Urban and Regional Research* 25(2): 327–45.

Cole, K., J. Cameron and C.B. Edwards. 1991. *Why Economists Disagree: The Political Economy of Economics*. London: Longman.

Collins, P.H. 2000. *Black Feminist Thought: Knowledge, Consciousness, and the Politics of Empowerment*. London: Routledge.

Devereux, S. 2001. 'Sen's Entitlement Approach: Critiques and Counter-critiques', *Oxford Development Studies* 29(3): 245–63.

Edwards, C. 1985. *The Fragmented World: Competing Perspectives on Trade, Money and Crisis*. London: Methuen.

Fine, B. 2001. 'Amartya Sen: A Partial and Personal Appreciation', *CDPR Discussion Paper 1601*, 1–12.

———. 2004. 'Economics and Ethics: Amartya Sen as Point of Departure', *New School Economic Review* 1(1): 95–103.

Friedman, M., and R.D. Friedman. 1981. *Free to Choose: A Personal Statement*. London: Penguin.

International Labour Organization (ILO). 1976. *Employment: Growth and Basic Needs: A One World Problem*. Geneva: ILO, UN.

Jevons, W.S. 1871. *The Theory of Political Economy*. London: Macmillan & Co.

Jolly, R. 1976. 'The World Employment Conference: The Enthronement of Basic Needs', *Development Policy Review* A9(2): 32–44.

Jolly, R. and Santos, R. 2016. 'From Development of the "Other" to Global Governance for Universal and Sustainable Development', *IDS Bulletin: Development Studies – Past, Present and Future* 47(2): 1–12.

Kawano, E. 2013. 'Social Solidarity Economy: Toward Convergence across Continental Divides', *United Nations Research Institution for Social Development (UNRISD)*, 26 February. Retrieved 7 September 2018 from http://www.unrisd.org/unrisd/website/newsview.nsf/%28httpNews%29/F1E9214CF8EA21A8C1257B1E003B4F65?OpenDocument.

Lal, D. 1983. *The Poverty of Development Economics*. London: Institute of Economic Affairs.

———. 1992. 'The Misconceptions of "Development Economics"', in C.K. Wilber and K.P. Jameson (eds), *The Political Economy of Development and Underdevelopment*. New York: McGraw-Hill, pp. 37–35.

Marx, K. 1859. *A Contribution to the Critique of Political Economy*. Moscow: Progress Publishers.

———. 1887. *Capital: A Critique of Political Economy, Volume 1*, trans. Frederick Engels. Moscow: Progress Publishers.

———. 1894. *Capital: A Critique of Political Economy, Volume 111*, trans. Frederick Engels. Moscow: Progress Publishers.

Ndhlovu, T.P. 2011. 'Corporate Social Responsibility and Corporate Social Investment: The South African Case', *Journal of African Business* 12(1): 72–92.

———. 2012. 'Globalisation: A Theoretical Reflection', *World Journal of Entrepreneurship, Management & Sustainable Development (WJEMDS)* 8(2): 95–112.

Ndhlovu, T.P., and A. Spring. 2009. 'South African Women in Business and Management: Transformation in Progress', *Journal of African Business* 10(1): 31–49.

Ndletyana, M. 2013. 'Policy Incoherence: A Function of Ideological Contestations?' in U. Pillay, G. Hagg and F. Nyamnjoh with J. Jansen (eds), *State of the Nation: South Africa 2012–2013*. Cape Town: HSRC Press, pp. 51–71.

Ngepah, N., and S. Mhlaba. 2013. 'The Role of South African Government Policies in Economic Growth, Inequality and Poverty', in U. Pillay, G. Hagg and F. Nyamnjoh with J. Jansen (eds), *State of the Nation: South Africa 2012–2013*. Cape Town: HSRC Press, pp. 72–97.

Nobrega, C. 2013. 'Solidarity Economy: Finding a New Way out of Poverty', *The Guardian*, 9 October.

Overseas Development Institute (ODI). 1978. 'Basic Needs', *ODI Briefing Paper No. 5*, December: 1–8.

O'Hearn. D. 2009. 'Amartya Sen's Development as Freedom: Ten Years Later', *Policy & Practice: A Development Education Review* 8: 9–15.

Pieterse, E., and M. van Donk. 2013. 'Local Government and Poverty Reduction', in U. Pillay, G. Hagg and F. Nyamnjoh with J. Jansen (eds), *State of the Nation: South Africa 2012–2013*. Cape Town: HSRC Press, pp. 98–123.

Razeto, L. 1991. *Empresas de Trabajadores y Economia de mercado*, Programa de Economia del Trabajo (PET): Santiago de Chile.

——. 1993. *De la Economia Popular a la Economia de Solidaridad en un Proyecto de desarrollo alternative*, Programa de Economia del Trabajo (PET): Santiago de Chile.

Ross, F.C. 2013. 'Ethnographies of Poverty', in U. Pillay, G. Hagg and F. Nyamnjoh with J. Jansen (eds), *State of the Nation: South Africa 2012–2013*. Cape Town: HSRC Press, pp. 446–465.

Rostow, W.W. 1971 [1960]. *Stages of Economic Growth*. Cambridge: Cambridge University Press.

Safri, M. 2013. 'Connecting the Right Dots: Economic Integration and Solidarity Social Economy Supply', *United Nations Research Institution for Social Development (UNRISD)*, 9 April. Retrieved 7 September 2018 from http://www.unrisd.org/unrisd/website/newsview.nsf/%28httpNews%29/8118D082CD070B7FC1257B480053C056?OpenDocument.

Samuelson, P.A. 1937. 'A Note on Measurement of Utility', *Review of Economic Studies* 4(2): 155–61.

——. 1938. 'A Note on the Pure Theory of Consumers' Behaviour', *Economica* 5(17): 61–71.

——. 1947. *Foundations of Economic Analysis*. Cambridge, MA: Harvard University Press.

Sen, A. 1992. 'Development: Which Way Now?', in C.K. Wilber and K.P. Jameson (eds), *The Political Economy of Development and Underdevelopment*. New York: McGraw-Hill, pp. 5–26.

——. 1999. *Development as Freedom*. Oxford: Oxford University Press.

Shisana, O. 2013. 'Is National Health Insurance the Solution for South Africa's Inequitable Healthcare System?', in U. Pillay, G. Hagg and F. Nyamnjoh with J. Jansen (eds), *State of the Nation: South Africa 2012–2013*. Cape Town: HSRC Press, pp. 517–535.

Siegmann, K.A., and J. Cameron. 2012. 'Why Did Mainstream Economics Miss the Crisis? The Role of Epistemological and Methodological Blinkers', *On the Horizon* 20(3): 164–71.

Thompson, E P. 1995 [1978]. *The Poverty of Theory or an Orrery of Errors*. London: Merlin Press.

Van Rensburg, D., and C. Heunis. 2013. 'Towards Greater Equality and Equity: Introducing Health and the Environment', in U. Pillay, G. Hagg and F. Nyamnjoh with J. Jansen (eds), *State of the Nation: South Africa 2012–2013*. Cape Town: HSRC Press, pp. 469–484.

Yunus, M. 1999. 'The Grameen Bank', *Scientific America* 281(5): 114–19.

Part II

Development, Urbanism and Poverty

Chapter 4

Urban Poverty in Zimbabwe
Historical and Contemporary Issues

Rudo Barbra Gaidzanwa

Introduction: Understanding Poverty

Poverty is a phenomenon that is associated with people's lack of access to services such as food, shelter, health, electricity, water and education. Education, training and other services enable people to acquire important skills, which structure and shape the opportunities available to them. Poverty also influences the relational aspects between humans, such as loss of or lack of human dignity, powerlessness, susceptibility to violence and abuse. Thus, poverty is a broad phenomenon that involves lack of income and material requirements for living decent lives, as well as non-material and relational issues between human beings. It is prudent to differentiate the types of poverty.

Poverty is built into and reinforced by societal structures of resource ownership and control, which are experienced differently by people depending on their age, class, gender and race within specific communities. These factors also affect how people respond to poverty. Money-centric measures of poverty are often used because they are regarded either as sufficient on their own or as an adequate proxy for poverty. When used alone, definitions of poverty that are restricted to income are as inadequate as those that incorporate such factors as autonomy, self-esteem or participation when used on their own. Each definition tends to underplay the impact of one type of deprivation or lack, while giving prominence to another when in fact both income and non-income-related aspects of poverty are critical to the understanding of poverty.

Urban Poverty in Historical Perspective in Zimbabwe

Poverty has been characteristic of urban life, affecting a significant proportion of black men and women's lives in Zimbabwe. After colonisation in 1893, African male labourers were required to carry passes with them all the time and each African needed a pass to secure paid work in the towns. The Africans were allowed to stay in the towns as long as they had paid work and their passes were stamped to reflect their status as wage workers. However, their wives and children were not allowed to visit them, and male workers were expected to exercise their conjugal rights during their holidays from work (Barnes and Win 1992). Only the few Africans who were church and state functionaries such as teachers, ministers of religion, court interpreters and policemen were able to access housing for married couples at police camps, government compounds and church properties. Through the Urban Areas legislation, 'townships' were set aside in urban areas for housing the black, male working class that was needed to work in the colonial economy in the railways, public works, domestic, farm and mining areas of the colony.

Dube (1996) notes that in colonial Bulawayo and Harare, in the urban native locations in which poor black workers lived, there were illegal drinking places called *shebeens*, where musicians performed for cash. Beer was served and consumed as part of the entertainment. The liquor brewers of the urban areas and the entertainers included women who followed their husbands into towns or women migrants who sought better lives in urban spaces in colonial Zimbabwe (Barnes and Win 1992). Most musicians and instrumentalists expressed themselves through live performances. Some of these musicians were itinerant, solo performers called *omasiganda* (the plural of *umasiganda*, a single performer who performed on trains and buses, and in homes and other public and private places where audiences could be garnered). Jenje-Makwenda (2005) conducted extensive research on musicians in Zimbabwe and she indicates that *omasiganda* were often shown appreciation by their audiences through coins that were thrown to them as they performed. These musicians comprised some of the informal workers in the entertainment industry in the colonial cities of Zimbabwe.

In 1960, the government passed the Vagrancy Act, which proscribed any African from maintaining a presence in white areas such as the city centre after 7 pm unless they had a permit or were employed in that area. Many African musicians lost their livelihoods because they could not perform in the clubs located in white areas. By 1946, it is estimated that Africans in Southern Rhodesian cities numbered over 99,000, although many of the labourers in the towns and cities were undocumented and therefore had no legal right to stay there according to the Land Apportionment Act (1930). Due to demands for black labour in urban areas, the Land Apportionment Act was amended to allow blacks to seek wage work in the towns. Local authorities were allowed to develop 'native' urban areas to house the black working population. In 1946, the Native (Urban Areas) Accommodation and Registration Act was passed and one of its main provisions was that urban employers had to provide free housing for their African employees within the native urban areas.

Together with pass laws, the major objective of this legislation was to control the movement of black populations between rural and urban areas. Dube (1996) noted that there was an influx of people from the rural areas into the urban areas of colonial Zimbabwe after this legislation was passed. Tax obligations forced young men into the towns to seek wage work, whereas pass control measures hampered the movement of women into the towns. Barnes and Win (1992) and Gaidzanwa (1985) argue that there was collusion between the colonial and African traditional authorities in confining women in the rural areas reserved for blacks because women safeguarded the land rights of migrant men, produced food and socially reproduced the peasant households, enabling the colonial system to utilise the wage labour of black men cheaply.

The black presence in urban areas was very circumscribed and subject to rules and regulations associated with black people's roles as providers of cheap labour to the colony of Southern Rhodesia, as Zimbabwe was called at that time. In urban areas, black men and women worked in factories as unskilled, general workers performing the arduous work requiring little or no skill. Hooker (1964) describes the attempts by the Industrial and Commercial Workers' Union (ICU) to organise black workers in Southern Rhodesia. From the beginning of colonisation, black wages were very low and black labour was exploited in the context of a racist and classist society. As a colony, Southern Rhodesia was expected to generate wealth for the colonists without necessarily ensuring social, economic and political equality between the colonised peoples and the colonists. Thus, in the urban areas, black workers were subordinated through unequal pay, legislation on separate facilities, standards and education, ensuring that the relationship of subordination of the blacks by the whites was not undermined.

In urban areas, black and white populations lived separate though connected lives since they depended on each other. Black men and women provided cheap manual labour in the factories, railways, households and other places of work, while white workers performed semi-skilled and skilled work in the industrial and commercial enterprises. Barnes and Win (1992) have described how black female workers in the town of

Harare tried to live better their lives where they were employed or made livelihoods that enabled them to survive. Yoshikuni (2007) described the Old Bricks township in colonial Harare, pointing out the lack of shops, clinics, churches and other services, save for the ubiquitous beer hall that seemed to be a fixture in all black settlements and in all colonial Zimbabwean workplaces, be they mines, farms, residential or work areas.

Different respondents who were interviewed by Barnes and Win (1992) described the squalor of urban settlements. Most of the women respondents worked in menial jobs washing dishes in the eating houses of Chinese hotels or performed domestic work in white private residences, doing laundry, cooking, minding children and helping with other miscellaneous tasks. Women who could not secure or did not desire paid employment under constricting regimens sold vegetables and fruit, while others worked as dressmakers and wood vendors near their lodgings to raise money. Some urban workers who lived on privately held land belonging to whites grew sorghum, rice and sweet potatoes for their own consumption as well as for sale. Others moulded bricks, started and operated small businesses, and yet others went into prostitution and illegal alcohol production to survive in the colonial towns. In addition to the alcohol trade, many poor women sold vegetables and hand-produced items to other workers as a means of survival. In general, male workers vastly outnumbered their female counterparts. Barnes and Win (1992) indicate that in 1936, 167 black women worked in formal jobs in Salisbury (colonial Harare), while 12,000 black men worked in the city. Observing that it was unusual for women to hold formal jobs, Barnes and Win also indicate that by 1969, 10 per cent of the female population had formal jobs. Thus, 10,000 women and 113,000 men worked in formal jobs in Harare.

Men in the towns and cities worked in domestic service as gardeners, cooks and cleaners, and were paid more than black female workers performing the same or similar jobs. The gendered wage disparity was a disincentive for women to work in domestic service. Schmidt (1992) observed that men, on the other hand, were not keen to work on farms, where pay was poor and conditions were rough. Men also worked in factories, shops and other commercial enterprises, where there was better pay. In the urban areas, men had an advantage over women because they were awarded housing based on their employment in the factories. Bachelors' housing comprised basic rooms, which were shared and had very poor sanitation. Married men with better jobs such as clerks, junior civil servants and other colonial functionaries were able to secure houses in 'married quarters' in many urban areas. However, majorities of urban workers were quite poor and were housed in squalid lodgings in the urban areas.

Workers in the towns lived under the shadow of urban township superintendents who oversaw activities in the 'townships', as the areas for blacks were called. Many townships had tower lights that were switched on at night for surveillance purposes. The war of national liberation, beginning in the late 1960s, disrupted the towns and drew in the young, disgruntled men who joined the guerrillas, whose recruitment for the war was centred in the rural areas. Urban men and women in the townships were very active in the political parties, the Zimbabwe African People's Union (ZAPU) and the Zimbabwe African National Union (ZANU), which had long been present in the urban areas. Their recruitment drive for the war of national liberation drew in significant numbers of urban, educated young men and some women who responded to the calls to join the guerrilla ranks.

Post-independence

After the war of liberation, independence resulted in a black-dominated Patriotic Front government comprising both the ZAPU and ZANU cadres who came to power. Most of the black rural poor focused on claiming rural arable land, while the white and black middle classes were focused on gaining access and some control over the economy through the use of industrial, commercial and residential urban land and arable farmland in rural Zimbabwe. The post-independence era was characterised by an initial period of economic boom resulting from the cessation of the war and reconstruction. The government embarked on ambitious programmes in health and education, providing free primary schooling and health services for the poor. However, after the initial boom in the 1980s and 1990s, the economy underperformed as the welfare policies became more difficult to fund and economic growth faltered. As a result, an Economic Structural Adjustment Programme (ESAP) was adopted.

Kanyenze (1999) and Stoneman (1992) noted that structural adjustment prescribed demand management and supply-oriented measures targeting growth and efficiency driven by exports. Structural adjustment programmes (SAPs) advocated liberalisation of market regimes and of the financial sector, as well as privatisation of service provisions and reductions in the role of the state in economic life. This led to reduced governmental expenditure on social welfare and subsidies. The retrenchments of men from waged employment placed more pressure on the resources and incomes generated by women's small economic enterprises, such as petty trading, vegetable vending and informal food stalls. In these operations, municipal police hounded women and they competed with many other poor people to sell very low-priced food and nonfood commodities (Gaidzanwa 1992). Potts (2000) and Potts and Mutambirwa (1998) have described extensively the impact of structural adjustment on the urban poor in Harare and other parts of Zimbabwe, showing the high rates of unemployment that resulted from retrenchments and loss of livelihoods in the wake of the SAP. Thus, urban incomes from the informal sector proved not to be as effective as wages in securing the livelihoods of the marginal urban populations.

Housing Deprivation as a Facet of Urban Poverty

Sithole-Fundire (1995) highlighted that men and women experienced housing deprivation in Marondera, a town neighbouring Harare. Schlyter (1989) observed that more men than women returned to rural areas permanently following long periods of wage employment. Schlyter observed that significant proportions of women-headed households in Chitungwiza and Kuwadzana in Harare were households of divorced and widowed women who had permanently abandoned the rural areas. These observations were validated by censuses since 1990, which show that young women emigrated from rural areas at rates equal to those of young men. Poverty, landlessness and the marginalisation of women were the drivers impelling them to move from rural areas because of divorce, widowhood or other marital and social breakdown. As a result, men and women under the age of thirty were equally represented in rural to urban migration in Zimbabwe by 1991.

The crisis in communal areas, characterised by the emigration of successive generations of relatively young women who considered the lifestyles of wives of migrant workers to be unacceptable, indicated resistance by women of lives as exploited household labour. At the same time, the ESAP was implemented at a time when the towns were experiencing an influx of young men and women who resisted rural lives dominated by male elders who controlled land and other resources in the communal and resettlement areas. Thus, when the SAP was rolled out, a more youthful cohort of urbanites had already swelled the informal sector in Zimbabwe's urban areas, where formal sector jobs were declining. This was noted in the GEMINI survey of 1994, where micro-enterprises employed large numbers of women in vending, retail, bars, pubs and unlicensed *shebeens*, the last three being the enterprises with the highest profits.

Mutopo (2011) noted that cross-border trade boomed as women went into this easy-entry sector requiring low investment and offering relatively high profit. As the economic crisis deepened, the migration into towns by women increased, resulting in the feminisation of cross-border trade in the new millennium. Increasingly, young, divorced, widowed and distressed women and poor men in urban areas have turned to the informal economy to improve their livelihoods in the urban areas. Potts (2006) also noted that by 2000, the urban workers in both the formal and informal sectors had experienced declines in incomes and standards of living since 1990, and these declines accelerated from 1997 through 2 000 and beyond. The Poverty Assessment Study Survey (2003) indicated that a huge increase in poverty levels in Zimbabwe from 25 per cent in 1990 to 63 per cent in 2003 had occurred.

Under the conditions described above, economic, social and political dissatisfaction peaked. This dissatisfaction was expressed publicly by students, women, trade unionists and wage workers, the landless, civil rights activists and business interests who were all trying to push for economic, social and political reform in Zimbabwe. The strikes that occurred in 1997, 1998 and 1999 and the economic decline that had taken place since 1990 catalysed the emergence of a strong civil rights movement in 1999. The rejection of the government-led draft constitution in 2000 signalled the growth in the strength of the forces of democratisation led by the Movement for Democratic Change (MDC) under the leadership of the late Morgan Tsvangirai.

Land and factory invasions by war veterans followed the rejection of the draft constitution in 2000. However, these invasions worsened the economy's performance, which depended significantly on agriculture. While the ZANU-PF government took the stance that the democratisation forces were a part of an alliance led by the MDC, funded by Western governments and donors for the purposes of regime change, the consistent gains by the opposition in elections since 2000 showed that a growing range of forces in the population supported democratisation. By 2005, economic assessments showed that GDP had declined by 40 per cent in the previous eight years and halved the income per head. Two-thirds of the population lived below the poverty datum line on less than Z$1.00 a day and unemployment was estimated to be close to 70 per cent. Inflation stood at 1,200 per cent and the fiscal deficit-to-gross domestic product (GDP) ratio doubled from 7.1 per cent in 2004 to 14.2 per cent in 2005. Domestic debt rose from Z$3 trillion in January 2005 to Z$12 trillion in June 2005. Approximately two million people, including many with high-level skills, had left the country, while Zimbabwe's share of the Southern African Development Community (SADC)'s GDP declined from 3.6 per cent in 1996 to 1.4 per cent in 2006, and the country moved from its position as the second-largest economy in the SADC to a ranking of tenth place in 2006 (Games 2006; Hawkins 2006).

Environmental Health in Zimbabwe

Access to water and sanitation by urban populations was believed to be nearly 100 per cent by 1999, but with declining capacity and budgets, municipalities increasingly struggled to maintain water and sanitation facilities. The World Health Organization (WHO) (2009) noted that in Zimbabwe, 2,048 and 5,385 cholera cases were recorded in 1992 and 1993 respectively. According to the WHO, the fatality rates were high at 5.1 per cent in 1992 and 6.1 per cent in 1993. The WHO also noted that 995 cases of cholera and 44 deaths were recorded in 1998 in the Chipinge District of Manicaland and in the Chiredzi District in Masvingo Province. It also highlighted the occurrence of a large cholera outbreak in 1999, which resulted in 5,637 cases and 385 deaths. In January 2002, a cholera outbreak was reported, with Manicaland experiencing the worst outbreak. Mashonaland East and Masvingo also reported cases and in these provinces, 3,125 cases, including 192 deaths, were registered.

Surveys carried out by the WHO and other entities in 2000 noted that 48 per cent of water points were not working and in 2002, the figure was 35 per cent. These observations were borne out by the sporadic outbreaks of cholera in 2002, culminating in the countrywide outbreak in August 2008. Urban sewage systems were and still are badly maintained and overburdened, resulting in sewer overloads, blockages and spills of untreated effluent, some of which discharge into rivers supplying water to cities such as Harare.

Operation Murambatsvina

In June 2005, in the middle of winter during a drought, through Operation Murambatsvina, (Remove the Filth), the state forcibly removed poor people from the city by demolishing illegal and informal structures and settlements in the townships, peri-urban areas and in some growth points in rural areas. The numbers removed are contested. The state alleged that only 58,000 people were affected by the operation, while the United Nations' figure stood at 700,000 (Tibaijuka 2005). This exercise was based on historically continuous conceptions of the city as a place of order, which were mobilised to justify the forced decongestion and removal of poor people from the illegal settlements in urban and peri-urban areas. The colonial city has historically been conceptualised first as a white space and a predominantly male space. At independence, the city became a predominantly middle-class space whose norms and values dominated urban governance and existence. Historically, there has never been sufficient land or housing for the urban working classes, and the shortage of accommodation for the poor in towns has always stood in sharp contrast to significant public and private development of non-poor housing schemes.

This inequitable situation has been a source of violence against the poor in Zimbabwe, forcing them to live in squalid accommodation with poor sanitation and health services as lodgers and as independent households. Even after independence, when the government allowed spouses and families to be co-resident in urban areas, there was too little land and too few loans and council, state or private housing schemes available to make spousal and family coresidence a reality. This has resulted in the exclusion of many poor women and some men from the towns, facilitating commercial sex, multiple relationships and promiscuity by men who live and work in cities separately from their wives and children. The meltdown in the economy in the new millennium intensified poverty, fuelling transactional relationships and HIV infection, and eroding the social ties that enabled black families to survive colonialism.

Operation Murambatsvina, although the state prefers to use the inaccurate English derivation 'Operation Restore Order', was disowned by many ministries and it was not possible to trace its origins. It caused divisions within the ZANU-PF ruling party and angered the urban poor. In policy terms, it was a huge problem because it brought the wrath and condemnation of the international community on Zimbabwe, undermining the government's chequered record on human rights. It was widely perceived to be a political programme to displace the supporters of the opposition parties from urban areas and to relocate them in rural areas, where the rural populace has traditionally constituted the backbone of ZANU (PF) support. During elections, the ZANU rural peasant vote was expected to swamp and outnumber the displaced urban working-class voters with clear alignment to the MDC who were displaced by Operation Murambatsvina.

The Urban Impact of Operation Murambatsvina

In urban areas, there was some support for Operation Murambatsvina as ratepayers who had experienced water problems as a result of the pressure on urban services discovered that their water supplies improved after it had been enacted. For example, in Ruwa, houseowners experienced water shortages for most of 2004 and part of 2005 because the Mabvuku Township had many lodgers living in small rooms illegally attached to houses by owners who charged desperate lodgers exorbitant rents for these makeshift rooms. Water pipes were vandalised in order to access unmetered water, resulting in water supply shortages to the middle- and low-density areas in Ruwa. In addition, lodgers congested the sewers, overburdened refuse removal and electricity services. In a house intended for a family of four, it was possible to take on six to eight lodgers if two inside rooms were let and a line of four rooms was added onto a house. Thus, the average high-density area house could provide shelter to two or three people per room, raising the occupancy of the house to fifteen people per house intended for four people. Supporters of Operation Murambatsvina pointed to Mbare's high tuberculosis infection rate, the highest in the country in 2005, and applauded the operation. In the central business districts of towns and cities, illegal structures used as kiosks, stalls in markets and pavements were demolished. Overcrowded offices used by small businesses were closed down so that thousands of tailors, seamstresses, import-export and trading enterprises were shut down.

The tenants whose shacks and rooms were demolished were forced to move in with relatives or return to the rural areas from where they were supposed to have originated. However, significant proportions of urban dwellers were born in towns and, as such, had no rural areas to return to, and the assumption that every black person has a rural home to which they can return – the same assumption made by the colonial authorities – was quite erroneous. Thousands of children of urban tenants had to leave school midterm without any provision for alternative schooling. Schools in many high-density suburbs (formerly called 'townships') suddenly had small classes as the children were sent off to the rural areas or to relatives who could provide them with shelter.

Small businesses folded because of a lack of affordable premises from which they could operate. Employers suddenly found their employees homeless and lost them if they had to migrate to rural areas. Rents in urban areas also rose dramatically as those houseowners with legal structures to rent out capitalised on the desperation of thousands of homeseekers. Overcrowding intensified as urban and rural people tried to accommodate their relatives in small homes and rooms in the legal structures. Vendors and hawkers, cobblers and small repair shops were closed down, forcing poor people to seek services from the more expensive and established businesses with higher overheads. Elderly people, retirees and other people with older housing stock in the high-density areas, which they rented out to subsidise their miniscule pensions, were immediately affected by the demolition of their 'cottages' and rooms for rent. Their incomes diminished by over 80 per cent in many cases, resulting in their destitution in old age after decades of working as professionals in teaching, nursing, supervisory and lower level semi-skilled work.

Health programmes for the poor were affected adversely because poor people on treatment for conditions such as HIV, hypertension, asthma and other ailments suddenly had to leave the cities and discontinue their drug regimes involuntarily. Monitoring those suffering from tuberculosis and other ailments became impossible after these people moved and interrupted their treatment regimens. Tracing the infected became impossible and holding camps were set up for the homeless who had nowhere to go in the middle of winter. Poor, pregnant women in need of antenatal services and children requiring immunisation were no longer able to access these services once they were pushed out of the cities, towns and growth points.

No alternative accommodation was available for the homeless, many of whom were given humanitarian aid by donor agencies. Many of these people were placed in holding camps while they waited for housing to be provided for them. To date, very few homeless people have accessed housing in the aftermath of Operation Murambatsvina. The retention and achievement of pupils in many schools declined and dropout rates escalated in urban areas amongst the poor strata in the society.

Urban schools in low-density areas became more run down as civil servants' salaries devalued and they were unable to fund the upkeep of the former group 'A' schools, which had been thrown open to poorer people following independence. Affluent people in the low-density areas deserted the schools in their neighbourhoods and moved their children into private schools. The private sector shrank and austerity programmes focusing on investment in capital stock, benefits to mid-level and upper management employees were reduced drastically, resulting in growing pressure for state schools in low-density areas to accommodate some of their children. The affluent schools also attracted the better-qualified and able teachers, resulting in the poorer schools attracting and retaining only the most inexperienced and least-trained teachers.

School-based education, especially at the primary and secondary school level, rapidly devalued as its returns declined in a speculative economy, which rewarded the politically connected, the already wealthy and the empowered, while worsening the plight of the poor. The decline of the social sectors, education and health, which in the first decade of independence absorbed the products of the public education system, worsened the plight of the poor, especially in urban areas, where there was very little land to fall back on as a residual welfare resource. Poor people were unable to continue to defer gratification and bear the costs of sending children to school for eleven years or more, only to have those children unable to find work in adulthood and continuing to act as a drain on family resources.

The Collapse of Urban Sanitation and Regulation Post-Murambatsvina

While in 2012, 95,1 per cent of Zimbabwe's urban population had access to clean drinking water, this situation had deteriorated by 2014 because of the collapse of the water and sanitation infrastructure in most areas of Zimbabwe. Most urban areas receive water occasionally and some not at all. Water quality is now questionable and most urban areas are served by boreholes and unprotected wells. In Harare, the water infrastructure is over fifty years old, loses over 60 per cent of water and is subject to frequent pump breakdowns due to poor maintenance. Given the rampant corruption in the running of council affairs, such as land allocations, the failure of service delivery has resulted in poor water availability in Harare. Harare has inadequate pumping capacity, resulting in water rationing, and Bulawayo has almost permanent water rationing because of inadequate water supplies. Thus, urban people's health is compromised by the ever-present problem of communicable diseases such as diarrhoea and typhoid and the threats of other diseases such as cholera.

In addition, most urban roads are pitted with potholes and there is little management capacity in the local authorities, resulting in the deterioration of the urban infrastructure. Despite the existence of the Environmental Management Act (Chapter 20:27), there is little enforcement of the law and many local authorities such as Harare Municipality flout the law by allowing the erection of residential and business premises on wetlands and other areas not designated for such structures. There is heavy pollution of Lake Chivero in Harare under the watch of the Harare City Council. Shanty settlements, businesses and other enterprises of the urban poor with no water or sanitation have sprung up in many urban areas. In Harare, the council is currently locked in a conflict with vendors who have moved into the central business district to sell food, clothes, electronic goods and other wares as the customer bases in the impoverished high-density residential areas have eroded. There is generally poor regulation of the environment and the population throughout the country as poverty emboldens the poor against the urban authorities.

Refuse removal in the major towns and cities is sporadic or nonexistent because of the shortage of vehicles and fuel. Pollution of cities has increased as solid waste removal decreases in frequency and as smoke, dust and other noxious substances pollute the air. This has fuelled a continuous confrontation between the urban authorities and ratepayers. Affluent and poor ratepayers have joined forces to agitate for better public sanitation in urban areas in particular. This is already happening in Harare, as ratepayers across the city organise to demand better services and resist rate and services payments. In some affluent parts of cities and towns, the privatisation of sanitation services has occurred as ratepayers organise their own refuse removal, road repairs and security. In the wake of such developments, resistance to payment of rates without service delivery is likely to intensify. In Harare, ratepayers' attempts to claim credit in areas where no services such as water have been delivered have failed because the council is cash-strapped and resistant to efforts to reimburse, defer or accept concessions to the affected ratepayers. Rate default amongst residents in many urban local authorities is high and plans to give concessions to those who do pay their rates have been developed, with mixed success given that in many areas, local authorities have little to deliver and cannot therefore use the threat of withdrawal of services to compel people to pay. Thus, illegal power and water connections, a boom in the sale of solar and alternative power appliances such as generators and the borehole drilling business provide ample evidence of the failure of service delivery in urban and other areas. Resistance to the power of local government entities linked to political parties has developed in the wake of the failure by ZANU (PF) to improve public health and sanitation services and the economy. Thus, there is a stand-off between the vendors, informal traders and the local and national authorities in the city of Harare.

The informal sector and the parallel economy reward those who are daring and unashamed of 'hustling', and those who have resources to cash in on speculative activities that are highly rewarding. The crisis-ridden Zimbabwean economy has shed jobs in the urban formal sector, resulting in working people bunching in the informal sector, where livelihoods are insecure and returns on labour and investment tend to be low. The unemployment rate rose to over 88 per cent by 2011, when 72.3 per cent of Zimbabwean wage earners were living below the Total Consumption Poverty Line for a family of five. A total of 75 per cent of households of employed people were in vulnerable types of employment in the informal sector performing casual work, which is erratically remunerated. The situation has steadily worsened since then.

Poor people with little capital have been drawn into the lower reaches of the informal and parallel economy, which does not require higher or tertiary education. As the economic crisis in Zimbabwe unfolded, a boom in trade and commerce in used clothes, textiles and other cheap manufactured goods provided urban people, particularly women, with new opportunities to earn incomes outside the formal economy. Initially, these efforts were considered innovative in an economy that was contracting and failing to generate decent, stable jobs and safe and sustainable work for the majority of jobseekers. However, regulation of the informal sector became less viable as more people entered this sector. State and local authorities became less sanguine about this sector and its continued growth and encroachment on bus termini, roads, streets, pavements, alleys, storefronts and the resultant crowding out of legitimate, ratepaying entities.

The municipal police in Harare attempted to clear out informal traders vending and conducting business in undesignated areas. However, the wife of the former President, Mrs Grace Mugabe, chided the police and directed them to be considerate to vendors and to desist from harassing them or confiscating their wares. This emboldened the traders, who poured into the city centre in larger numbers. Some of the vendors' and traders' organisations adopted names that suggested links to Grace Mugabe as a means of self-protection. The numbers of traders grew until there was a public outcry about the state of the central business district. Many rate paying businesses deserted the city centre and retreated to the less congested former white suburbs, where their clients could access them more easily without being accosted by traders selling used clothes, fruits and vegetables, cheap gadgets from China, cars and office machinery.

This situation was embarrassing for both the local authority as well as for the government since Harare, the capital, was the site of many international meetings and the state of the streets, especially in the central business district, was an embarrassment. Traders have resisted efforts to clear them off the streets, while ZANU (PF), the ruling party that was held responsible for failing to create the two million jobs promised during the election campaign in 2013, was compromised by the unemployment that put these traders onto the streets and alleys of the capital. Thus, ZANU (PF), wary of any move that could alienate the working classes and ignite resistance and civil unrest in the capital, expected the local authority, which was dominated by the MDC, to move traders off the streets. In turn, the traders dared any authority that desired to move them off the streets to provide them with jobs. A stalemate ensued as the numbers of street traders escalated. In frustration, a minister in the ZANU (PF) government suggested that the army be mobilised to move the traders off the streets, but the utterance was quickly countered by opposition figures who pointed out that the military had no business dealing with the movement of civilians off the streets.

The saga with the vendors shows the depth of the economic problems currently bedevilling Zimbabwe's government and the impoverished populace. After the disastrous experience with Operation Murambatsvina, which resulted in the strengthening of the opposition MDC party, in the general election that was held following the operation, the government is not likely to tread heavily on the poor, particularly those in urban areas who have voted for the opposition in the past four elections. With the government's poor record of economic management, stratospheric unemployment above 85 per cent and underemployment, high debt, isolation and inability to secure soft loans even from China, its purported 'all-weather friend', there is a palpable sense of helplessness in government circles, despite the bravado that is publicly expressed by the ruling, strife-torn ZANU (PF) party. It is highly unlikely that the two million jobs promised by ZANU (PF) during its election campaign in 2012–13 will materialise. However, the prospect of losing power to the MDC or any new formation arising from the splinters such as the Zimbabwe-People First (ZPF) party fronted by the expelled former Vice President, Joyce Mujuru, is very frightening to ZANU (PF). Therefore, there is a likelihood that the vendors' interactions with the local authority and the state apparatus will be less violent than those that characterised Operation Murambatsvina.

Conclusion

Urban poverty is very visible and likely to be destabilising to the political dominance of ZANU (PF) in contemporary Zimbabwe. While the war for national liberation was fought mainly in the rural areas, the mobilisation and visible political activity that preceded it was undertaken in the urban areas where ZAPU and ZANU were able to convince the urban poor and other classes to back the cause of national liberation. The MDC recruited its most committed activists from the urban working classes and the youth, the students and the section of the middle classes who have traditionally supported and voted for the MDC since 2000. These constituencies are likely to be joined by the urban poor whose fortunes have declined under ZANU (PF). Navaya and Matenga (2015) reported on a clash between the council police and vendors in the Harare central business district. The National Union of Vendors threatened to retaliate against ZANU-PF through the ballot box in the July 2018 presidential elections, citing promises of jobs by ZANU (PF) in the runup to the 2013 election. However, ZANU (PF) won the elections.

As the conflict plays itself out, it is clear that urban poverty has generated harder feelings of deprivation and destitution amongst the poor, regardless of who their backers, sponsors and promoters are purported to be. What is clear is that urban poverty has generated a potentially volatile situation in urban areas and that this might destabilise situations in urban areas as conflict between the poor, the state and its agents sharpens. Given the breakdown in urban social services, particularly in health and education, there is a high likelihood of increased social strife in urban areas as ZANU (PF) has failed to deliver jobs and has been rejected in urban areas since 2000 because of the deterioration in urban services.

Poor urban people who were affected by Operation Murambatsvina and are now threatened by the removal from the central business districts of towns and cities will likely turn to other political parties than ZANU (PF). Escalating food, education, health and housing costs are also likely to alienate poor people and render their politics more transactional and instrumental, resulting in demands for tangible benefits in exchange for votes. Ultimately, for the urban poor who did not access land from the state, hard-nosed political and material considerations will trump any historical attachments to liberation rhetoric. Thus, any political party campaigning for power will have to deliver tangible economic benefits to the urban poor and ameliorate many of the negative social and economic problems that assailed the urban poor during the era of ZANU (PF) rule in Zimbabwe.

Rudo Barbra Gaidzanwa is Professor of Sociology at the University of Zimbabwe. She specialises in Social Policy and Gender Studies and has published on gender and land, extractivism, social policy. She is also a gender and human rights activist. Her publications include *Images of Women in Zimbabwean Literature* (1985); *Voting with their Feet* (1999) and the edited volume *Speaking for Ourselves: Masculinities and Femininities amongst University of Zimbabwe Students* (2001).

References

Barnes, T., and E. Win. 1992. *To Live a Better Life*. Harare: Baobab Books.
Chimhowu, A., J. Manjengwa, and S. Feresu (eds). 2012. *Moving Zimbabwe Forward: Reducing Poverty and Promoting Growth*. Harare: Institute of Environmental Studies, University of Zimbabwe.
Dube, C. 1996. 'The Changing Context of African Music Performance in Zimbabwe' *ZAMBEZIA* 23(2): 99–120.
Gaidzanwa, R.B. 1985. *Images of Women in Zimbabwean Literature*. Harare: College Press.
———. 1992. 'Structural Adjustment and Debt'. Paper prepared for EURODAD, the European Network on Debt and Development.
———. 1999. *Voting with Their Feet: Migrant Zimbabwean Nurses and Doctors in the Era of Structural Adjustment*. Research Report No 113. Uppsala: Nordiska Afrikainstitutet.
———. 2008. 'Gender Issues in Post-primary Education'. Background paper prepared for the ADEA BIENNALE on Education in Africa, Maputo, 5–9 May.

_____. 2011. 'Women and Land in Zimbabwe'. Paper presented at the Conference on 'Why Women Matter in Agriculture', Swedish International Agricultural Network Initiative, 4–8 April.
Gaidzanwa, R.B., and F.C. Chung. 2011 'The Situation of Women and Girls in Zimbabwe'. Presentation to the International Parliamentary Conference on the Millennium Development Goals, Reaching for 2015: Governance, Accountability and the Role of the Parliamentarian. London: House of Parliament.
Games, D. 2006. 'A Nation in Turmoil: The Experience of South African Firms Doing Business in Zimbabwe'. *SAIIA Business in Africa Report* No. 8. Braamfontein: SAIIA.
Hawkins, T. 2006. 'Still Standing: The Economic, Political and Security Situation in Zimbabwe in 2006 and its Implications for the SADC Region'. Paper presented at the Institute of Strategic Studies, University of Pretoria, 4 May.
Hooker, J.R. 1964. 'The African Worker in Southern Rhodesia: Black Aspiration in a White Economy: 1927–36', *Race and Class* 6(2): 142–51.
Jenje-Makwenda, J. 2005. *Zimbabwe Township Music*. Harare: Storytime Promotions.
Kanyenze, G. 1996. *Beyond ESAP: Framework for a Long-Term Development Strategy in Zimbabwe beyond the Economic Structural Adjustment Programme (ESAP)*. Harare: ZCTU.
_____. 1999. *The Implications of Globalization on the Zimbabwean Economy*. Mimeo.
Malaba, J. 2006. 'Poverty Measurement and Gender: Zimbabwe's Experience'. Paper presented to the Inter-Agency and Expert Group Meeting on the Development of Gender Statistics, 12–14 December. New York: United Nations.
Mupedziswa, R., and P. Gumbo. 1998. 'Structural Adjustment and Women Informal Sector Traders in Harare, Zimbabwe'. *Research Report* No. 106. Uppsala: Nordic African Institute.
Mutopo, P. 2011. 'Women's Struggles to Access and Control Land and Livelihoods after the Fast Track Land Reform in Mwenezi District, Zimbabwe', *Journal of Peasant Studies* 38(5): 1021–46.
Navaya, K., and M. Matenga. 2015. 'Multimedia: We Will Meet in 2018 – Vendors', *News Day*, 9 July. Retrieved 11 September 2018 from https://www.newsday.co.zw/2015/07/we-will-meet-in-2018-vendors.
Ndlela, D. 2002. 'The Economic Dimensions of the Social Crisis in Zimbabwe'. Paper presented to the Conference on the Social Crisis in Zimbabwe, Harry Frank Guggenheim Foundation, 14–16 June.
Nussbaum, M. 2000. *Women and Human Development: The Capabilities Approach*. New York: Cambridge University Press.
Potts, D. and C. Mutambirwa. 1998. 'Basics are Now a Luxury: Perceptions of Structural Adjustment's Impact on Rural and Urban Areas in Zimbabwe', *Environment and Urbanisation* 10(1): 55–76.
_____. 2000. 'Urban Unemployment and Migrants in Africa: Evidence from Harare, 1985–1994', *Development and Change* 31(4): 879–910.

_____. 2006. '"All My Hopes and Dreams are Shattered": Urbanisation and Migration in an Imploding African Economy: The Case of Zimbabwe', *Geoforum* 37(4): 536–51.

Ravallion, M. 1998. 'Poverty Lines in Theory and Practice, Living Standards Measurement Study', *World Bank Working Paper*, No. 133.

Razavi, S. 1999. 'Gendered Poverty and Well-being: Introduction', *Development and Change* 30(3): 409–433.

Razavi, S. 2004. 'Is Poverty Gendered?' Policy Brief. New York: Gale Group and United Nations Publications.

Robertson, J. 'August 2007 Forecast Paper', Robertson Economic Information Services for Zimbabwean Statistics. Retrieved 20 May 2015 from http://www.economic.co.zw.

Robeyns, I. 2005. 'The Capability Approach: A Theoretical Survey', *Journal of Human Development* 6(1): 93–117.

Reddy, S.G., and T. Pogge. 2003. 'How Not to Count the Poor'. Retrieved 20 July 2015 from pdf.wri.org/ref/reddy_03_how_not_to.pdf.

Sachikonye, L. 1999. *Restructuring of De-industrialisation? Zimbabwe's Textile Industries under Adjustment*. Uppsala: NordiskaAfrikainstitutet.

Schlyter, A. 1989. *Women Householders and Housing Strategies: The Case of Harare, Zimbabwe*. Gavle: Swedish Institute for Building Research.

Schmidt, E. 1992. 'Race, Sex and Domestic Labour: The Question of African Female Servants in Southern Rhodesia 1900–1939', in K.T. Hansen (ed.), *African Encounters with Domesticity*. New Brunswick, NJ: Rutgers University Press, pp. 221–241.

Sithole-Fundire, S. 1995. 'Gender Issues among Dombo Tombo Lodgers: A Case Study Approach', in S. Sithole-Fundire et al. (eds), *Gender Research on Urbanisation, Planning, Housing and Everyday Life*. Harare: Zimbabwe Women's Resource Centre and Network, pp. 115–134.

Stewart, F. et al. 2003. 'Does it Matter That We Don't Agree on the Definition of Poverty? A Comparison of Four Approaches'. Oxford: Oxford University, Queen Elizabeth House Working Paper Series 107.

Stoneman, C. 1992. 'The World Bank Demands its Pound of Zimbabwe's Flesh', *Review of African Political Economy* 19(53): 94–96.

Tibaijuka, A.K. 2005. 'Report of the Fact-Finding Mission to Zimbabwe to Assess the Scope and Impact of Operation Murambatsvina by the UN Special Envoy on Human Settlements Issues in Zimbabwe, 18 July 2005'. Retrieved 11 September 2018 from http://www1.umn.edu/humanrts/research/ZIM%20UN%20Special%20Env%20Report.pdf.

World Health Organization. 2009. 'Global Task Force on Cholera Control. Cholera Country Profile: Zimbabwe'. Retrieved 11 September 2018 from http://www.who.int/cholera/countries/ZimbabweCountryProfileOct2009.pdf.

Yoshikuni, T. 2007. *African Urban Experience in Colonial Zimbabwe*. Harare: Weaver Press.

Chapter 5

Theory of Poverty or Poverty of Theory?
A Decolonial Intervention on Urban Poverty in South Africa

Raymond Nyapokoto and Sabelo J. Ndlovu-Gatsheni

Introduction

The advent of majority rule in South Africa in 1994 promised a new era in a country that for close to four hundred years had been polarised along racial lines. This polarisation had resulted in a deep socioeconomic chasm and poverty for blacks. However, inequalities have deepened in the country. Former President Thabo Mbeki, in a speech to the National Assembly in 1998, captured this scenario as follows:

> South Africa is a country of two nations, one black and the other white ... One of these nations is white, relatively prosperous, regardless of gender or geographic dispersal. It has ready access to a developed economic, physical, educational, communication and other infrastructure. The second and larger nation of South Africa is black and poor ... This nation lives under conditions of a grossly underdeveloped economic, physical, educational, communication and other infrastructure. (*Hansard* 1998, Col. 3378)

Crawford (2012) observed that South Africa is one of the most unequal countries in the world, with more than half of the population living in poverty. Woolard (2002) reported that the country was full of stark contrasts [where] one sees destitution, hunger and overcrowding side-by-side with affluence. Alexandra Township and Sandton city in Johannesburg epitomise the coexistence of poverty and opulence respectively in South Africa. This ambivalent nature compelled our focus on these two areas, as they clearly illustrate the social inequalities that were inculcated during the era of imperialist control of South Africa. Alexandra Township emerged as a place for peasants who were forced off their ancestral land to sell their labour cheaply in emerging urban settlements. Sandton city crystallised as a place for the owners of the means of production. Wilson and Ramphele (1989: 190) pointed to the inauguration of systematic exploitation of Africans as the South African capitalist political economy gathered momentum that, propelled by the mineral revolution, 'pushed [blacks] off the land or absorbed onto it as conquered labourers' (Wilson and Ramphele 1989: 190). Nzula, Potekhin and Zusmanovich (1979: 69) observed that by the 1970s the British imperialists had exploited about 93 per cent of peasant land in South Africa and set up large farms, 'tied half of the peasantry to those farms and ... herded the other half onto the reserve's pool of labour'. Cohen (1997) argued that by the 1930s the chains of proletarianisation and peasantisation were well established in colonial African cities especially on public works programs, in mines, in building of roads and railways, and in the development of harbour and port facilities.

Legassick (1977: 175) noted that mining and manufacturing industries led to the growth of cities. Witwatersrand became the economic, social and ideological focus of a subcontinent, and in a parallel process to the international dialectic of the metropole and satellite, Southern Africa proceeded from *un*development to *under*development. The growth of cities, Legassick (1977: 175) added, resulted in 'rural underdevelopment, economic decay, and pauperisation'. In the city, a new and unique catalogue of problems beset blacks, which included:

> a net of legislation and regulations ... pass laws, in which the poor became entangled because of the fact that virtually all the strategies individuals can adopt against poverty involve breaking the law in some way [and] ... forced removals in urban ... environments ... and ... the bureaucratic jungle of red tape woven by officials. (Wilson and Ramphele 1989: 161)

All of these factors resulted in fraternal twins – Alexandra Township (black and poor) and Sandton (white and affluent) – and these two are a microcosm of the generality of urban setups in South Africa.

This chapter deploys a Fanonian decolonial theory to critically explore the genesis of poverty and inequality, and to unmask structural causes of poverty in South Africa. It delves deeper into the foundational structural causes of poverty in the country, tracing them back to the unfolding of colonialism, the rise of industrial capitalism, and urbanisation patterns and processes. The focus of the chapter is on Alexandra African Township and affluent Sandton as epitomies of poverty and opulence respectively. Using the Fanonian critical decolonial theory, Sandton city symbolises the zone of being, whereas Alexandra Township represents the zone of nonbeing. The chapter posits that the road (M1) separating Alexandra and Sandton represents the abyssal line separating the zone of being from the zone of nonbeing. The zone of being is a site of good living and opulence, whereas the zone of nonbeing is the locale of hellish conditions, depravity and poverty. These two zones are not natural; they are a product of particular histories and deliberate policies. Throughout the chapter, the poverty of existing theories of poverty are revealed as we attempt to construct a Fanonian decolonial theory of poverty that is far more profound and relevant.

The Theoretical Framework

The Fanonian critical decolonial thinking is deployed here as the framework through which we can explore how poverty amongst the poor (blacks as a community) and privilege amongst the rich (whites as a community) came into being. Decoloniality is deemed superior to all other theories, which attempt to explain poverty because it traces the root causes of poverty and, most importantly, offers solutions to this anomaly. It is a plurality of schools of thought that acknowledge that Euro-American universalism does not solve global challenges. It advocates pluriversalism based on the contextual nature of challenges facing the different parts of the globe.

Decoloniality theorises from the perspective of the oppressed as opposed to the generality of Eurocentric theories, which take the perpetrators' side. Since knowledge itself has been colonised, Fanon engages in 'epistemic disobedience and delinking' from Eurocentricism. Suárez-Krobe (2009) observes that this nullifies the idea of 'the West as the logical starting point of valid and relevant theory and as a privileged site of knowledge production'. Ndlovu-Gatsheni (2012) sums up decoloniality as 'a pluriversal epistemology of the future – a redemptive and liberatory epistemology that seeks to delink from the tyranny of abstract universals ... [and] informs the ongoing struggles against inhumanity of the Cartesian subject'.

Decoloniality, according to Santos (2007: 65), is a post-abyssal thinking involving 'a radical break with modern western ways of thinking and acting, since Euro-centric theories are ahistorical and colour-blind'. Fanon's decolonial racial optic, as Kane (2007) observed, exhaustively explores and offers a genealogy of race as the organising principle for ontological polarisation and the structural organisation of global formations. Centuries of colonial dispossession stripped the Global South of wealth and simultaneously deposited the fruits of 'civilisation' in the Global North. Kane (2007) also posits that decoloniality breaks down the binaries of an oppressor-oppressed world', thus creating what Santos (2007) calls 'a radical co-presence [where] practices and agents on both sides of the line are contemporary in equal terms'. Inequality has its roots in the structure of contemporary racism.

Understanding Abyssal Lines

Originally, people were equal since God was the standard used to classify people. Mignolo (2009: 146–47) observed that 'with secularisation of the world, knowledge became attached to reason and theory (instead of God) and [became] supported by a new global design, the civilising mission'. The white man became the classifying standard buoyed by the Cartesian '"I" think therefore "I am" and later the Dusselian "I conquer, therefore "I am" abyssal thinking' (see Grosfugel 2013: 77; Mignolo 2009: 146–47).

Quijano (quoted in Mignolo 2009) observed that 'only Europe [became] rational and [could] have subjects. Other cultures [were] not rational'. Nursey-Bray (1980) points out that '[r]acism is only the emotional, affective sometimes intellectual explanation of this inferiorisation' and subsequent domination of blacks by whites. Racism is subtly embedded in all existential aspects of life, even in South Africa currently. It is slowly being erased from our memory through media, school and university. Santos (2007) observed that modern Western thinking is an abyssal thinking and it 'consists of a system of visible and invisible distinctions, the invisible ones being the foundation of the visible ones'. These '[g]lobal] designs', according to Mignolo (2009), are brewed in metropolitan countries.

Fanon (1952) observed that for blacks, their 'narrow world is strewn with prohibitions'. Mignolo (2009) observed that globalisation 'is the most recent configuration of a process that can be traced back to the 1500s, with the beginning of transatlantic exploration'. Abyssal lines change forms, but with the same result: the impoverishment of blacks. Fanon (1961: 32) observes that 'the native is declared insensible to ethics. He is... the enemy of values, and in this sense he is the absolute evil'.

Consequently, Maldonado-Torres (2011) observed that this is why even perverted acts of war are visited upon blacks. Such 'beings' can only be brutes needing brutalising forces to civilise and Christianise them. Brutalisation takes away agency and subsequently poverty is handed down to succeeding generations. This systemic inferiorisation and impoverishment of blacks by whites make the blacks dependent. For

Fanon (1952: 79), 'the white man is governed by a complex of authority'. This abyssal mentality, Dussel (quoted by Mignolo 2000: 117) believes, stems from the fact that colonialism 'in the form of a categorical imperative, as it were, was to 'develop' [civilise, uplift, educate] the more primitive, barbarous, underdeveloped civilisations'.

Santos (2007: 59), through what he terms 'social fascism', which he divided into two categories – 'fascism of social apartheid' and 'contractual fascism' – shows how blacks have been disadvantaged. Under 'social fascism', the world is delineated into 'savage' and 'civilised' zones. 'Savage' zones are neglected, whilst 'civilised' zones are kept well. 'Contractual fascism, Santos (2007: 59) posits, 'occurs in situations in which power inequalities between the parties in the civil contract are such that the weaker party [the inferiorised black man], rendered vulnerable for having no alternative, accepts the conditions imposed by the stronger party'. Santos (2007: 59, 60) cites 'privatisation of public services, such as healthcare, welfare, utilities' as a form of 'contractual fascism' and observes that the net effect of all this is that 'privatised services agencies take over the functions of social regulation earlier exercised by the state' and that 'workers and popular classes are being expelled from the social contract through the elimination of social and economic rights, thereby becoming discardable populations'. Therefore, owners of capital benefit at the expense of the poor.

Manichaeism: The Zone of Being and Nonbeing

Santos (2007) states that abyssal thinking brings out distinctions (black/white) and radicalizes them. This is the Manichaean Structure. Fanon (1952: 196) observed that the 'colonial [and postcolonial] world is a Manichaean world' divided into 'compartments' where 'black and white represent two [conflicting] poles'. This black/white binary is not natural. Kane (2007) observed that race is culturally and historically situated as opposed to a reified fact of biology. Nursey-Bray (1980) pointed at the role of racism in the structuring of colonial social relations. For Maldonado-Torres (2007), this colonial difference is the first by-product of the coloniality of power, of knowledge and being. Apartheid South Africa was Manichaean in structure: separate development for races. The whites' side is a salubrious world, whilst the world of the black person is hellish. Santos (2006), quoted in (Grosfoguel 2013) observed that:

> The way conflicts are managed in the zone of being is through ... mechanisms of regulation and emancipation. Regulation refers to civil/human/women/

labour/rights codes, relations of civility, spaces of political negotiation and action that are recognised for the oppressed 'Other' in their conflict with oppressor 'I' within the zone of being. 'Emancipation' refers to discourses of liberty, autonomy and equality that form part of the discourses and institutions used for the management of conflicts in the zone of being. As a trend, conflicts in the zone of being are regulated through non-violent means. Violence is always an exception and used only in exceptional moments [this is illustrated in Figure 5.1]. (Grosfoguel 2016: 13)

In contrast, according to Fanon (1961), the zone of nonbeing is a place of ill-fame, peopled by men of evil repute where men live there in very overcrowded environments. Here 'being' is characterised as absent.

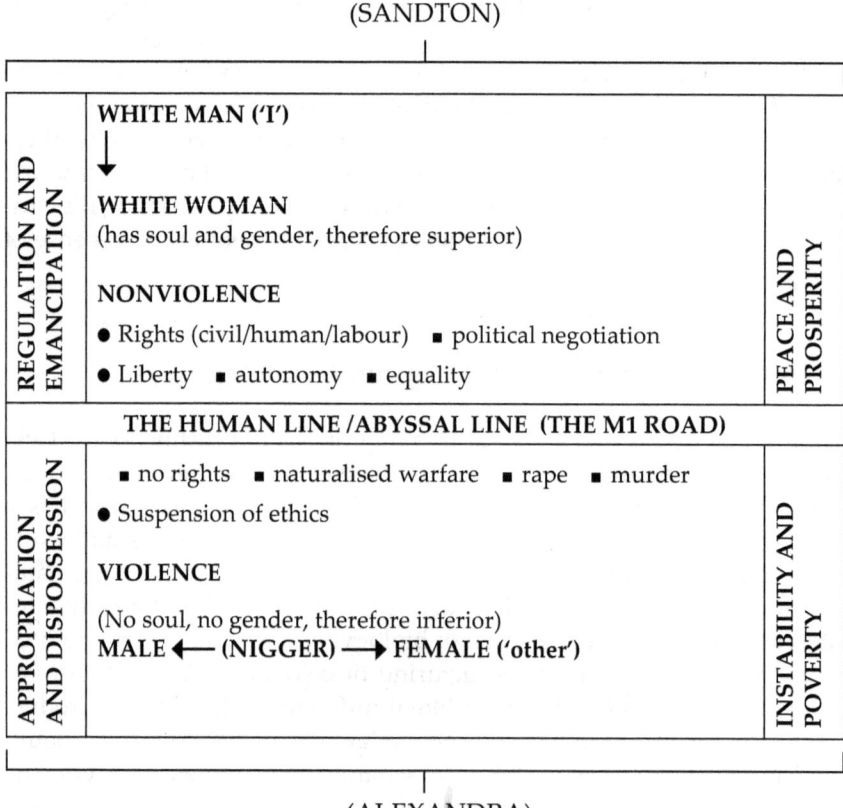

Figure 5.1 Diagram of the zone of being and nonbeing.
Source: Created by the authors, adapted from Grosfoguel (2013)

Maldonado-Torres (2010: 100) observes that 'the idea of progress in modernity is progress for a few and [that is] why the rights of Man do not apply equally to all'. Santos explains that:

> in the zone of non-being ... people are dehumanized in the sense of being considered below of the human as non-humans/sub-humans, the methods used ... [in] managing and administering conflicts, is by means of violence and overt appropriation/dispossession. As a trend ... only in exceptional moments are methods of emancipation and regulation used. (Santos 2006: 10, cited in Grosfoguel 2016: 13)

Fanon posits that Manichaenism 'dehumanizes ... or so to speak plainly it turns [blacks] into animal[s]'. Over time, blacks internalise the inferiority complex and Fanon (1952: 152) states that blacks will be convinced that: 'All those white men ... can't be wrong. I am guilty ... I'm a wretch.' Consequently, blacks seek the approval of the white man to assert their own humanness. The Manichaean structure turns blacks into zombies ready to be (ab)used and lacking entrepreneurial strength. Figure 5.1 below shows a diagram portraying the zones of being and nonbeing.

Coloniality of Being: The Black Condition

Coloniality of being has its genesis in the secularisation of the world, which brought in new identities in humanity, with the net result that non-European people, because of their darker skin colour, were delineated as constitutively inferior and fit to assume a position of slavery and serfdom (Maldonado-Torres 2011). Damnation continues even long after colonialism ends with the black skin lacking in ontological density even though blacks live among whites. This is the coloniality of being.

Daily ordeals characterise the lives of blacks. This also constitutes coloniality of being. Maldonado-Torres (2011: 245–6, 255) to this as the cruel reality of damnation and naturalisation of war. This happens through what he calls 'Manichaean misanthropic skepticism' or the dislike and questioning of the very humanity of black bodies and that coloniality of being primarily refers to the normalization of the extraordinary events that take place in war. "Killability" and "rapeability" are inscribed into the images of the colonial bodies' Maldonado-Torres (2011: 255).

Coloniality in the form of structural violence mutates from a strictly physical form during colonialism to subtle forms afterwards. Maldonado-Torres (2007) sums it up as involving long-standing patterns of power that emerged as a result of colonialism, that define culture, labour, intersubjective relations, and knowledge production well beyond the strict limits of colonial administrations. Coloniality empowers some sections of people and dispossesses another side simultaneously. Nursey-Bray (1980) observes that consequently, this leads to 'psychological dependency and distorted consciousness' in blacks. Downstream generations inherit coloniality with perpetual poverty and inequalities as its most visible byproduct.

Maldonado-Torres (2007: 257) observes that: 'The *damné* exists in the mode of not being there, which hints at the nearness of death, in the company of death.' When visible blacks become 'illegal', they are lynched, arrested and imprisoned. Visibility, sanctioned by the pass system, recognised blacks only for their utilitarian benefits as labourers. This forms part of structural violence. Structural violence is a subtle and systematic way in which social structures harm and/or disadvantage individuals. Victims never know of its existence until some 'shock' occurrence happens, 'yet these problems were not exactly invisible' (Fanon 1952: 132). It is historically given processes that conspire to constrain individual agency. The physical setup of the Manichaean 'compartmentalised' world is deliberately engineered to ensure the failure of blacks; thus, according to Fanon (1961: 28), the black man is 'beaten from the start'. Fanon (1952: 162) states that:

> the white society has crushed his old world without giving him a new one. [and] bars the road to his future after having closed the road to his past ... Apartheid aspires to banish the black man from participating in modern history as a free and independent force.

Fanon observes that structural violence is shown through blacks 'who have toiled without great success' because 'the structure of South Africa is a racist structure' (1952: 68). The education system of the blacks under apartheid was inferior and was meant solely to produce servants and labourers. Religion is also 'abused' to tame the blacks into being obsequious servants of the white masters. Neocolonialism/capitalism, which Fanon (1952) terms a 'completely new international situation', supported by new local leaders perpetuates the same hierarchical logic of disempowerment engendered during colonialism.

The Decolonial Turn and Shifting the Geography of Reason

As an 'other' thinking, this undertaking moves away from Euro-American theorising. This deployment of the Global South's perspective constitutes a 'decolonial turn and the shifting geography of reason' Fanon (1961: 78) states definitively that '[c]apitalist exploitation and cartels and monopolies are the enemies of under-developed countries'. (Mignolo 2000: 209) posits that 'everything needs to be reformed and everything thought anew'. Epistemologically, the Global South is a rich source of knowledge. Universalism, which privileges the West, has to give way to 'pluriversalism', a standpoint that recognises all parts of the globe as sources of knowledge. Grosfoguel (2013) cautions that the Global South has been basically reduced to learning theories born of the experience and problems of a particular region of the world with its own particular time/space dimension.

Wallestein (quoted in Mignolo 2000: 190) contends that there are no 'universal truths about human behaviour that hold across all space and time'. Therefore, every geopolitical entity can only be 'of and about' itself. Moya (2011) states that 'all knowledge is situated knowledge', while Mignolo (2000: 109) contends that 'there is no geographical or epistemological location that holds property rights for theoretical practices'.

Cesaire (1955) warns us that 'no-one colonizes innocently'. Mignolo (2000: 107) observes that 'it is ... consciousness on [the part of] colonialism ... that created the conditions for subaltern theorizing'. Colonisation was an epistemic genocidal project. Gordon (2011) noted that subsequently there was 'organisation of knowledges into knowledge' – the Euro-Western knowledge.

Gordon (2011: 97, 99) points out that there is 'colonization at the methodological level' and calls for 'teleological suspension of disciplinarity ... [meaning going] beyond disciplines in the production of knowledge'. Under decoloniality, the problem, not the means (method) to the problem is the main factor of theorising. It is a problem-centric quest. More importantly, critical decoloniality is not an anti-Euro-Americanism project per se, but just 'another' way of theorising. Grosfoguel (2013) posits that it is recognition of epistemic diversity' and 'against capitalism, patriarchy, imperialism and coloniality. Mignolo posits that it is 'an epistemology of and from the border of the modern/colonial world system' and it 'opens a new perspective for a geopolitical order of thinking' (2012: 61). Ultimately decoloniality brings 'perspectives that will call to account the distorted representations of peoples, ideas, and practices whose subjugation is fundamental to the maintenance of our unjust social order' (Moya 2011: 85). Ultimately, this creates a new world order inhabited by what Fanon (1961: 67) terms 'a new man'. This 'new man' is both black and white, coloniser and colonised. In the black man, Fanon (1961) envisages a 'fully conscious' human being free from coloniality and in the white man, a human being free from all prejudices. Nursery-Bray (1980) observes that Fanon advocates for the creation of a new set of human possibilities, not just for the colonised, but for all mankind. It is a liberatory project.

Alexandra Township as a Zone of Nonbeing in South Africa

Alexandra Township, situated thirteen kilometres northeast of the Johannesburg central business district, covers close to eight square kilometres and is separated by a road, the M1, from the affluent Sandton. Bonner and Nieftagodien observe that: 'The township was perceived as a quintessential "black spot", incongruously surviving in the heart of white suburbia in Africa's wealthiest city' (2008: 386).

The *Rand Daily Mail* (1980) observed that: 'Most of Alex's residents work in Sandton. Geographically and logically it should form part of the town and should not be treated as a separate leper colony.' Although planned to have a carrying capacity of 30,000 people, today, the township has around 950,000 people residing in it. Since its inception in 1905, Alexandra has been punctuated by violence. White buyers shunned Alexandra because the land was wet and diseased. Against the prevailing legislation under which blacks could not own land in towns, Papenfus, the developer, decided to sell the land to Coloureds (people of mixed race) and African (black) buyers in 1912 to recoup his investment.

Settlers in Alexandra were peasants fleeing rural poverty and those displaced from the Johannesburg inner city. With uncontrolled in-migration, Alexandra soon became overcrowded. Ferrinho, Robb, Mhlongo, Coetzee, Phakathi, Cornielje and Ngakane (1991) observed that the neglect of housing and other basic services, essential for a dignified family life, resulted in a dense urban slum, violent and poor. Callinicos (1993: 33) observed that demolished multi-racial inner city housing also compounded overcrowding.

In 1916, without resources, the Alexandra Health Committee was established to run the affairs of Alexandra. Bonner and Nieftagodien (2001: 21) records that in eight short years, the population from 1916 to 1924 rose from 900 to 2,640, and that it had shot up to 16,747 by 1936 and 80,000 in 1948. Until 1994, no jurisdiction was ever financially responsible for Alexandra. The Johannesburg City Council neglected Alexandra, arguing that it was outside its jurisdiction. Thus, 'by the late 1980s Alexandra had ... been transformed into a squatter township and was probably the most congested residential area in the country' (Bonner and Nieftagodien 2008: 311). In early 1991, about 400 people were crammed into a hectare in Alexandra, compared to a paltry 18 in Sandton. It was estimated in 1992 that there were between six and eight people living in each shack in Alexandra (Bonner and Nieftagodien 2008: 332). The *Weekend World* (2008) described Alexandra as 'a stinking cesspool of overflowing dustbins, litter-lined streets and angry residents'. Babich (1990) observed 'the stench of human excreta, filth, dust and indescribable squalor ... fear ...

intolerable living conditions'. Reminders of death pervade the residents' lives all the time. This is vividly revealed by the *Sunday Times* (1990), narrating a shack dwellers' story: 'When Martha Nana opens her shack door in the morning, she breathes the sort of stench that most people encounter only when they open their dustbins.'

Uncontrolled in-migration, idleness and want saw gangsters become a feature of the township, that is, the Spoilers and the Msomi gangsters. These spawned gang violence, rape, molestation and murders. The gangsters made blacks destitute through 'protection fees' ranging from 'five shillings to R50 a month', the gangsters swindled people of their meagre salaries.

Apartheid criminalised life of all blacks if they were not oiling the capitalist machine. Joyce explains that:

> From 1951 ... the pillars of what came to be known as 'grand apartheid' were steadily erected ... to consign the entire African population ... to its traditional 'homelands' where it would, according to theory, develop its own political and cultural institutions. Blacks would continue to reside in the Union, but only to the extent dictated by labour demands. They would have no citizenship, rights or vote. (Joyce: 1990: 16)

The Slums Act of 1934 trebled the population of Alexandra as the City Council cleared slums from central Johannesburg. The 1943 industrial boom also swelled the population of Alexandra. The Group Areas Act legitimised racial, residential and business segregation. Caldeira (2000: 213) observes that 'rules organising urban space are patterns of social differentiation and separation'. In the 1950s, the population of Alexandra had to be reduced, resulting in evictions to Zone 8 in Meadowlands. Forced removals were carried out to dispossess African landlords of their properties. African domestic workers were simultaneously being moved out of white suburbs. For Bonner and Nieftagodien (2008: 231), years of control, forced removals and attacks on urban African families severely destabilised the social cohesion of the community. Besides overpopulation, the *Sunday Times* (1990) reported that garden refuse and building rubble from Sandton was being dumped in Alexandra.

Joyce observes that the Abolition of Passes Act of 1952 replaced the pass with 'the ultimate control document ... containing the entire life and job history of its owner, his movement rights and his fingerprints' (1990: 17). Raids for permits were violent and regular. Those arrested were taken for farm labour at places like Bethal, which provided free labour. The pass laws rent into shreds the social fabric of the township.

Thus, since blacks were only tolerated for their utility value, instead of annihilating Alexandra Township completely, the idea of single-sex, prison-like hostels was mooted to house labourers. Davie (2003) records that after the Sharpeville killings of 1960, the government decided to move Alexandra altogether and rebuild the area as a 'hostel city'. Twenty-five hostels were to be built, each housing 2,500 people, for single men and women. Bonner and Nieftagodien point out that hostels were hellish and 'epitomised the crass objectives of apartheid: to control the lives of urban African workers' (2008: 124). The subhuman nature of the hostels turned them into 'potential universities of crime ... [with] dehumanising and eventually brutalising effects'.

In the hostels, residents were housed along tribal lines and this triggered tribal wars. Black-on-black violence prevented blacks from forming a force against racial oppression. Claiming to 'know' blacks and what was good for them, the Chairman of the Transvaal Board for the Development of Peri-Urban Areas opined that 'this ambitious project was tackled ... with knowledge of ... the needs, interests and comforts of those people who are to occupy the hostels' (Bonner and Nieftagodien 2008: 187–88). This abyssal thinking is what Gordon (2010: 193–214) calls 'reasoning with unreasonable reason reasonably'.

Employment and Education

Blacks arrived in Alexandra to seek work as labourers in mines and industries in Johannesburg. Hendrik Hoffman, a white South African, said 'we older folks – believe that the black man should be in his place ... We didn't have much to do with him. If he worked for you, he must just do his job and finish. Beyond that, you had nothing to do with him' (quoted in Callinicos 1993: 32). Government policies favoured whites over blacks. Callinicos (1993: 78) reports that before the Second World War, most industrial workers on the Rand were whites. The government did a great deal to assist them to upgrade their industrial qualifications and schooling, while black workers' training was either neglected or forbidden by law. This systematic exclusion ensured that blacks were unskilled and poorly paid, and had no wealth to pass on to later generations. Education is a useful tool for social mobility, but the education system for blacks was of inferior quality and was designed to produce labourers and inferior beings in society. Fanon posits that 'in capitalist societies, the educational system serves to create around the exploited person an atmosphere of submission' (Fanon 1961: 29). Tabata states that the Bantu education was:

> Calculated to serve as an instrument for creating and ensuring the continuance of a voteless, rightless and ignorant community ... [and] to rob the African of

education, cut him off from the mainstream of modern culture and shut him into a spiritual and intellectual ghetto. (Quoted in Gumede 2014: 6)

Dr Verwoerd said that: 'There is no place for him [blacks] in the European community above the level of certain forms of labour' (quoted in Dustin 1983: 23). These 'certain forms of labour' meant menial jobs. Consequently, African schools were heavily underresourced. Seekings and Nattrass (2006: 134) report that 'in 1953, the expansion of state spending on schools for African children was tied once more to ... the level of African taxation'. This was low.

In 1991, about 96,000 students resided in the area, but there was only sufficient space for 20,000. At Eastbank High, the ratio was 1:100. Consequently, some children went to schools in distant Soweto. Endless protests against the inferiority of education, powered by the 'revolution today and education later' motto by blacks, compounded illiteracy amongst blacks. The Soweto uprising of 1976 uprising was ignited by the government's decision to impose Afrikaans as a medium of communication.

The township was also occasionally ravaged by taxi wars caused by the city's planning and infrastructural neglect, and the need to control the market – one of the few informal industries in which black entrepreneurs could thrive. Black-on-black violence stood the apartheid government in good stead as it left the black community heavily divided. To date, taxi wars are still very much a feature of Alexandra and most townships.

1994–2014: The Enigma of Arrival

The year 1994 was a watershed year as the country gained its independence with the ANC at the helm of government. The new dispensation promised a new era of equality and the improvement in the lives of black people in South Africa. Bonner and Nieftagodien (2008: 386) observed that while democracy also promised an inclusive Johannesburg, a city of equality for its residents – white and black, rich and poor, inequality and exclusion persists, and these are nowhere more evident than in the contrast between Alexandra and Sandton.

Trevor Manuel observed that ANC solved problems relating to the political order, but that this is incomplete for as long as people feel they are not included in the outcome of democracy (quoted in the National Planning Commission 2013: 1). During interviews, Twala (2014) summed up the general mood of Alexandrians: 'This is not the freedom we fought for. We are free because we no longer carry the dompass (passes, dumb pass) but we are not yet free because we are still poor. Our government should start governing now.' Cox (2004) also argued that many people in Alexandra argue that they see no significant impact on their material conditions.

The liberal capitalist market claim that economic benefits 'trickle down' to everyone has remained a distant myth. As the Alex Renewal Project (ARP) began working in Alexandra, the technologies of apartheid were shown to have skipped into new South Africa. Cox (2005) reported that three houses were demolished without notification, consultation or compensation. An ARP official told residents that the homes belonged to the council because the former government in the 1950s and 1960s had appropriated them.

Red tape involving 'the Land Claims Court, the national Land Claims Commission, the Gauteng Housing Department and the City of Johannesburg Region 7' have been some of the hurdles in the way of development in Alexandra to date. Jobs have not become available to people. Mbongwa (*The Star*, 24 March 2005) quoted one resident as saying 'Alexandra looks like a Sunday every day. People don't work' and catalogues the major post-independence problems as being 'unemployment, overcrowding in schools and clinics, insufficient access to water and electricity, sewage and waste overflowing on the streets and HIV/AIDS'. These are the 'visible' problems. From a Fanonian perspective, we know that pathetic fallacy is also at play here – the inner man is never confident, firm and assertive under such barren, hellish conditions brought about by a brutal force.

Structural Violence

Abject poverty has declined, but inequalities have grown. Apartheid has been abolished, but apartheid's systematic, spatial, socioeconomic engineering remains. Visible violence has subsided, but poverty remains a stark reality. Physically, Alexandra is still a slum township and still very much symbolises evil.

A new form of discreet violence, structural violence, is at play in the township, resulting in unemployment, deaths and impoverishment. Blacks are free, yet poverty keeps them in chains. Children are going to schools, but the quality of education is very poor, with forty being a standard number in classes. STIs and AIDS are ravaging the township. The queue for people collecting ARVs on Tuesdays at Alexandra Clinic snakes around the whole clinic. McDonald's, KFC and Debonairs Pizza at the Pan Africa Mall churn out obesity. Poverty is real in the township. Functional family structures are absent from the township. Grandmothers raise children in Alexandra. Without a family structure, there is no society. Family is the microcosm of society in every aspect.

Sandton City: A Zone of Being in South Africa

Before the turn of the eighteenth century, prosperous and autonomous black middle stone age hunters occupied the plains of Sandton. Carruthers (1993: 14) observes that this group of people moved into Sandton some 30,000 years before the white settlers. Until the early 1800s, flourishing Tswana clans inhabited almost all of South Central and Western Transvaal. However, white Afrikaner farmers fleeing from the British rule in the Cape Colony began to arrive in this area.

Besides the onslaughts of the British, these Afrikaners were seeking cheap labour and arable land. Though traces of gold had been discovered since 1853, the discovery of the main reef was in 1886. Carruthers (1993: 22) explains that this 'influenced the development of Sandton and linked its fate directly with that of Johannesburg', which led to increases in land values. The Voortrekkers subdivided their farms and sold out. They augmented their fortunes through supplying the fresh produce to Johannesburg town.

The South African War (1899–1902) and Urbanisation from 1902 Onwards

During the period from 1899 to 1902 the British and the Afrikaners in South Africa fought for control of the country. Sandton was disrupted, albeit briefly. The Voortrekkers also joined the Afrikaners' side. When the war ended and the farmers of Sandton rebuilt their lives, Sandton began to grow at a phenomenal speed.

Carruthers (1993: 26) points out that from the early 1900s, there was increased prosperity on the Rand and long-term security under the British after the war. Urbanisation occurred at an unprecedented rate. Carruthers (1993) observes that wealthy Joburgers looking for recreational outlets and "gentleman's farms" joined the farmers in the Sandton area whilst Sandton was booming:

> very close by was growing an enormous working-class population ... characterised generally by poverty and deprivation. Although providing much of the labour upon which Sandton depended, Alexandra was always an entity

distinct from Sandton. Segregationist attitudes and legislation – and later apartheid – precluded any sense of community from developing among the white and African inhabitants of the area, although, in the economic sphere, they were closely linked. (Carruthers 1993: 30)

Sandton, white and middle class, was so salubrious that: 'The quiet country atmosphere of Sandton brought the Carmelite nuns to the village of Rivonia in 1931 ... [who] sought peaceful surroundings for prayer' (Carruthers 1993: 31). Other buyers of note included Adolf Wilhelmi, Ernst Eriksen, W.F. Tillet, Thomas Cullinan and Sammy Marks. Many other rich business owners and industrialists bought and built in Sandton in order to transform it into a 'suburban' paradise forming an interface between city and countryside – 'where town meets country'.

The Johannesburg Town Council proclaimed Sandton a new municipality on 1 July 1969. Residents were consulted extensively on all developmental matters as Sandtonians sought to have control of their destiny. The name 'Sandton' is a combination of the names of two suburbs: Sandown and Bryanston. In order for this name to be adopted by the town, extensive public input was sought. *The Sandton* (1978) reports that the councillors discussed the name at a meeting with provincial officials, and the name 'Sandton' was acceptable to all at this meeting.

Before the municipality came into being, predominantly English Sandton was administrated by the Peri-Urban Board and Sandtonians sought autonomy, which was won because Sandton had educated and wealthy residents who could not stomach remote control from Pretoria, which was Afrikaans. Minutes of the Sandton City Town Council on 10 August 1978 reveals many challenges tackled and the meticulous planning that the Sandton Town Council went through to turn Sandton into a real heaven on earth. The council borrowed and received money for all road infrastructure, for sewage and water reticulation, and floated a public loan for the financial good of the council. A clear traffic policy was laid down. The council enlisted the services of experts: '309 European' staff members to sort out labour challenges. A health clinic was set up and libraries for unemployed and unskilled white youths were established especially during the 1930s by the Hertzog government during the Depression. When the economy improved, these youths would have been skilled enough to secure jobs.

Sandton grew according to the expressed will of the residents and it continues to grow, and thanks to the magnetic power exerted by the glossy Sandton City mall and business district, it has flourished into becoming the financial hub of South Africa and the most expensive real estate in Africa.

As the Johannesburg central business district faced decay, many corporates took flight from Johannesburg Central to Sandton, where as many as 300 established their headquarters. Sandton City in Sandton is the largest shopping mall in Africa and, together with Nelson Mandela Square, forms the largest shopping mall in the Southern Hemisphere. Sandhurst is the most affluent suburb in Sandton. It borders Sandton City, has a total area of 2.45 km² and a population totalling 2,471 residents, thus giving a population density of 1,000 per km². *News24.com* (19 January 2014) reported that Sandhurst has 127 houses valued at more than R20 million, not including holiday homes and any property owned by foreigners. So upmarket is Sandhurst that Skurie (2013) observes that: 'It is difficult to differentiate between what is a house and what is consulate or hotel there.' Houses are all valued above R8,000,000. The country's best architects like Louis Louw and Ian Gandini designed most of these houses.

Sandhurst is a typical 'gated community' Money Web (2014) points out that '[t]he area is secure and enclosed with controlled access for privacy and exclusivity' and 'most importantly for security'. Sandhurst and many gated communities in urban South Africa are reproducing social apartheid. Caldeira (2000: 213) observes that:

> Rules organising urban space are patterns of social differentiation and separation. Different social groups are again closer to one another but are separated by walls and technologies of security ... these [spaces] are privatised, enclosed, and monitored.

Fanon explored the perception that the white man has for the black man as waiting to pounce on a white man to rob him and rape his female family members. This form of abyssal thinking brings about the idea that the outside world is dirty, undesirable and dangerous, and has to be fenced off.

The Socioeconomic Setup

Whites who bought into Sandton, especially when urbanisation was starting in earnest, were rich industrialists and highly skilled professionals. These people have always enjoyed a superior socioeconomic status over poor blacks who resided in townships and provided cheap labour to industries and mines. Even those whites who came to the Witwatersrand to seek employment had an edge over the blacks. Seekings and Nattrass reported that: 'White workers had a strong hand in negotians on the industrial councils ... White unions also succesfully prevented the training of African workers as artisans' (2006: 138). This shows that white skin holds more ontological density than black skin. Callinicos (1993: 12) explains that:

> [There] was the state's privileged treatment of white workers ... [it] introduced welfare policies for whites: free medical services, subsidised low-cost housing, and free education. It also protected whites by reserving a number of unskilled and skilled jobs for whites only.

News 24.com (11 December 2012) revealed that 'Sandhurst [and central Cape Town] are the preferred suburbs for South Africa's multi-millionaires ... [and] that 36 multi-millionaires reside in Johannesburg's leafy northern suburbs of Sandhurst [with Bryanston following in at a close second]'. It also has the highest multimillionare population density in the country, with one in every twenty residences being owned by a multimillionare (IOL 2012). Money Web (2014) stated that twelve per cent of residents in Sandhurst earn more than R2.45 million a year. This translates roughly into R204,000 per month. A maid in Alexandra Township earning a conservative figure of R3,000 per month would take five years to earn this amount. Every month, a maid in Alexandra Township is being left behind economically by five years by their neighbour in Sandhurst.

Educationally, Sandton boasts state-of-the-art educational facilities with low teacher/child ratios. Quality education leads to upward social mobility and liberates the mind. The apartheid government deployed education to empower the white population over the black population. Seekings and Nattrass posit that 'differential education was integral to the apartheid distributional regime ... Education was important because it ensured white South Africans were given huge advantages in the labour market, which in turn meant higher wages' (2006: 133).

Sandton schools, just like the suburb itself, have operated with unhindered success. Schools that are in and around Sandhurst School are top schools such as St David's Marist Inanda, Crawford College and Sandhurst Preparatory School. Redhill School, which prides itself on having achieved a '100% pass rate for [the past] 39 consecutive years ... and 100% of [its] university aspirants have been successful', states that it:

> provide[s] an enriching experience and a stimulating environment, which will provide each child with the opportunity to develop as fully as his/her abilities, talents, determination and ambition will allow ... to stimulate curiosity, mental dexterity and awareness and to encourage initiative, self-reliance and self-discipline. Pupils also thrive in the free-spirited nature ... Pupils are allowed to question, to debate robustly and to reach conclusions themselves ... pupils must be taught to make choices. (Redhill High School 2014)

The quality of this education is liberatory and prepares children to adapt creatively to the capitalist global political economy. These children have the added advantage that their community is peopled with role models – their own parents and the residents of Sandhurst – people who themselves are transforming the world. After twenty-four years of independence, Sandton is a success story:

> Sandton boasts world class suburbs, state-of-the-art shopping malls, rapid rail transport [the Gautrain], conference facilities, nearby sporting arenas, medical facilities, theatres, art galleries and restaurants. It is a magnet for those who seek vibrant innovation and the opportunities that only the African continent can offer. (Sandton Exclusive 2014)

Conclusion

Violence of all sorts is the hallmark of the zone of nonbeing. Violence came in the form of laws/acts, removals and so on that curtailed social mobility of blacks leaving them earning low incomes. This had many ripple effects and ensured that blacks could not hand down wealth to subsequent generations. The fact that the township suffered neglect resulted in the slum conditions that we witness even today. This is the thesis on why blacks as a community in South Africa are poor.

On the other hand, nonviolence is the hallmark of the 'zone of being'. Peace and tranquillity are ensured in the suburbs and today Sandton, over forty-five years later, stands strong as one of the most sought-after real estate locations in the whole of Africa, even attracting the attention of international buyers. Sandtonians became prosperous and handed down wealth to subsequent generations, which is a reason why whites as a community are rich in South Africa.

Raymond Nyapokoto is a doctoral student in Development Studies at the University of Pretoria. He is an independent contractor at the Development Studies Department of the University of South Africa (Unisa). His research interests include urban poverty, inequalities, informality and nation building.

Sabelo J. Ndlovu-Gatsheni is the Acting Executive Director of the Change Management Unit (CMU) of the Vice Chancellor's Office at Unisa. He has published extensively on African history, politics and development. His major publications include *The Ndebele Nation: Reflections on Hegemony, Memory and Historiography* (2009); *Do 'Zimbabweans' Exist?*

Trajectories of Nationalism, National Identity Formation and Crisis in a Postcolonial State (2009); *Redemptive or Grotesque Nationalism? Rethinking Contemporary Politics in Zimbabwe* (2011); *Empire, Global Coloniality and African Subjectivity* (2013); *Coloniality of Power in Postcolonial Africa: Myths of Decolonization* (2013); *Nationalism and National Projects in Southern Africa: New Critical Reflections* (2013); and *Bondage of Boundaries and Identity Politics in Postcolonial Africa: The 'Northern Problem' and Ethno-Futures* (2013).

References

Babich, J. 1990. 'Alexandra in Shambles', *Sandton Chronicle*, 20 February.
Bonner, P., and N. Nieftagodien. 2001. *Alexandra: A History*. Johannesburg: Wits Press.
Caldeira, T.P.R. 2000. *City of Walls: Crime, Segregation and Citizenship in Sao Paulo*. Berkeley: University of California Press.
Callinicos, L. 1993. *A Place in the City: The Rand on the Eve of Apartheid*. Johannesburg: Ravan Press.
Cesaire, A. 1955. *Discourse on Colonialism*. New York: Monthly Review Press.
Cohen, R. 1997. *Global Diasporas: An Introduction*. Washington, DC: University of Washington Press.
Cox, A. 2004. 'Misery and Squalor Continue to Haunt Alex', *The Star*, 13 December.
_____. 2005. 'Land Claims Could Delay Alexandra Regeneration Plans', *The Star*, 30 June.
Crawford, A. 2012. 'South Africa Poverty Survey Shows Slow Progress', *Sky News*, 18 December.
Davie, L. 2003. 'Why Alexandra Survived Apartheid'. Retrieved 23 February 2014 from http://www.theheritageportal.co.za/article/why-alexandra-survived-apartheid.
Dustin, J. 1983. *Alexandra, I Love You: A Record of Seventy Years*. Johannesburg: Future Marketing.
Fanon, F. 1952. *Black Skin, White Masks*. Paris: Edition du Soleil.
_____. 1961. *The Wretched of the Earth*. London: MacGibbon & Kee.
Ferrinho, P.D., D. Robb, A. Mhlongo, D. Coetzee, G. Phakathi, H. Cornielje and P. Ngakane. 1991. 'A Profile of Alexandra', *South African Medical Journal* 80(8): 374–78.
Fin24. 2010. 'SA Billionaires Double in 2010', 5 December 2010. Retrieved 15 September 2018 from https://m.fin24.com/Economy/SA-billionaires-double-in-2010-20101205.
Frith, A. 2012. 'Sandton: Main Place 77424 from Census 2001'. Retrieved 15 September 2018 from http://census.adrianfrith.com/place/77424.
Gordon, L.R. 2010. 'Theory in Black: Teleological Suspensions in Philosophy of Culture', *Qui Parle* 18(2): 193–214.

_____. 2011. 'Shifting the Geography of the Reason in an Age of Disciplinary Decadence', *Transmodernity: Journal of Peripheral Cultural Production of the Luso-Hispanic World* 1(2): 95–103.

Grosfoguel, R. 2013. 'The Structure of Knowledge in Westernized Universities: Epistemic Racism/Sexism and the Four Genocides/Epistemicides of the Long 16th Century', *Human Architecture: Journal of the Sociology of Self-Knowledge* 11(1): 73–90.

_____. 2016. 'What is Racism', *Journal of World-System Research* 22(1): 9–15.

Grosfoguel, R., A. Oso and A. Christou. 2015. 'Racism, Intersectionality and Migration Studies: Framing Some Theoretical Reflections', *Identities: Global Studies in Culture and Power* 22(6): 635–52.

Gumede, V. 2014. 'Thought Leadership, Thought Liberation, and Critical Consciousness for Africa's Development and a Just World'. Inaugural Professorial Lecture, Senate Hall, Pretoria, Unisa, 19 March.

Hansard, 29 May 1998, Col. 3378.

IOL. 2012. 'Study Reveals South Africa's Wealthiest Areas', 29 August. Retrieved 15 September 2018 from http://www.iol.co.za/news/south-africa/study-reveals-sa-s-wealthiest-areas 1.1371969#.VFOjLzSUcfQ.

Interview with L. Twala, 17 January 2014, Johannesburg.

Joyce, P. 1990. *The Rise and Fall of Apartheid*. Cape Town: Struik.

Kane, N. 2007. 'Frantz Fanon's Theory of Racialisation: Implications for Globalization. Human Architecture', *Journal of the Sociology of Self-Knowledge* 5(3): 353–61.

Legassick, M. 1977. 'Gold, Agriculture and Secondary Industry in South Africa, 1885–1970: From Periphery to Sub-metropole as a Forced Labour System', in R. Palmer and N. Parsons (eds), *The Roots of Rural Poverty in South and Central Africa*. Lusaka: Heinemann Educational Books, pp. 175–200.

Maldonado-Torres, N. 2007. 'On the Coloniality of Being: Contribution to the Development of a Concept', *Cultural Studies* 21(2–3): 240–70.

_____. 2010. 'On the Coloniality of Being: Contribution to the Development of a Concept', in W.D. Mignolo and A. Escobar (eds), *Globalization and the Decolonial Option*. London and New York: Routledge, pp. 94–124.

_____. 2011. 'Thinking Through the Decolonial Turn: Post-Continental Interventions in Theory, Philosophy and Critique-An Introduction', *Transmodernity: Journal of Peripheral Cultural Production of Luso-Hispanic World* 1(2): 1–23.

Mbongwa, L. 2005. 'Forced to Live in Squalor'. *The Star*, 24 March.

Mignolo, W.D. 2000. *Local Histories/Global Designs: Coloniality, Subaltern Knowledges and Border Thinking*. Princeton: Princeton University Press.

_____. 2009. 'Epistemic Disobedience, Independent Thought and De-colonial Freedom', *Theory, Culture and Society* 26(7–8): 159–81.

Money Web. 2013 'Johannesburg's Most Exclusive Address for R45m', 14 April. Retrieved 15 September 2018 from http://www.moneyweb.co.za/moneyweb-property/joburgs-most-exclusive-sandhurst-address-for-r45m.

Moya, P.M.L. 2011. 'Who We are and from Where We Speak', *Transmodernity: Journal of Peripheral Cultural Production of the Luso-Hispanic World* 1(2): 79–94.

National Planning Commssion. 2013. *National Development Plan 2030: Our Future-Make It Work*. Department: The Presidency, Republic of South Africa. Retrieved 20 July 2016 from http://www.dac.gov.za/sites/default/files/NDP%202030%20-%20Our%20future%20-%20make%20it%20work_0.pdf.

Ndlovu-Gatsheni, S.J. 2012. 'Coloniality of Power in Development Studies and the Impact of Global Imperial Designs on Africa', *ARAS* 33(2): 48–73.

Ndlovu-Gatsheni, S.J. 2013. 'Why Decoloniality in the 21st Century?', *The Thinker* 48: 10–15.

News 24.com. 2012. 'SA's Rich Nestled in Sandton, Cape Town', 11 December. Retrieved 15 September 2018 from https://www.fin24.com/Companies/Property/SAs-rich-nestled-in-Sandton-Cape-Town-20121211.

News24.com. 2014. 'Where the Rich Live'. 19 January. Retrieved from 15 September 2018 from https://www.news24.com/Archives/City-Press/Where-the-rich-live-20150430.

Nursey-Bray, P. 1980. 'Race and Nation: Ideology in the Thought of Frantz Fanon', *Journal of Modern African Studies* 18(1): 135–42.

Nzula, A.T., I. Potekhin and I. Zusmanovich. 1979. *Forced Labour in Colonial Africa*. Johannesburg: Zed Press.

Palmer, R., and N. Parsons (eds). 1977. *The Roots of Rural Poverty in South and Central Africa*. Lusaka: Heinemann Educational Books.

Rand Daily Mail. 1980. 'The Proposed Merging of Sandton and Alexandra', 18 March.

Redhill High School. 2014. Retrieved 15 September 2018 from www.redhill.co.za.

Sanai, D. 1991. 'Half in Alex are without Jobs'. *Business Day* (15 July).

Sandton Exclusive. 2014. Retrieved 15 September 2018 from http://www.sandtonexclusive.com/touristinfo/sandton.html.

Santos, B. de S. 2006. *Renova la teoria critica y reinventar la emancipacion social (encuentros en Buenos Aires)*. Buenos Aires: CLASCO.

_____. 2007. 'Beyond Abyssal Thinking: From Global Lines to Ecologies of Knowledges', *Review* XXX(1): 45–89.

Seekings, J., and N. Nattrass. 2006. *Class, Race, and Inequality in South Africa*. Scottsville: University of KwaZulu-Natal.

Skurie, J. 2013. 'Where Africa's Rich Live', *The City Press*, 26 May.

Suárez-Krobe, J. 2009. 'Coloniality of Knowledge and Epistemologies of Transformation', *Kult* 6: 1–9.

Sunday Times. 1990. 'Home Sweet Home', April 1.

Swanepoel, H., and de Beer, F. 1989. *Community Development: Breaking the Cycle of Poverty*. Lansdowne: Juta.

The Sandton. 1978. Sandton: Sandton Town Council. Sandton.

The Weekend World. 2008. 'The Shame of Alexandra'. 20 April.

Wilson, F., and M. Ramphele. 1989. *Uprooting Poverty: The South African Challenge*. Cape Town: Carnegie, Norton Publishers.

Woolard, I. 2002. 'An Overview of Poverty and Inequality in South Africa', DFID. Retrieved 15 September 2018 from http://www.sarpn.org/documents/e0000006/Poverty_Inequality_SA.pdf.

Yin, R.K. 2011. *Qualitative Research from Start to Finish*. New York: Guilford Press.

Part III

Empowerment, Regionalism, Identity and Development

Chapter 6

The 'Native Returns'
Assessing and Reimagining Indigenisation and Black Economic Empowerment as Development Projects in the 'Postcolony'

Tamuka Charles Chirimambowa and Tinashe Lukas Chimedza

Introduction: Theory, Conceptualisation and Political Economy Context

This chapter critically evaluates the political and ideological contestations characterising the Zimbabwean and South African political economy, pointing particularly to the emergence of the Movement for Democratic Change (MDC) in Zimbabwe and the Economic Freedom Fighters (EFF) in South Africa. It begins by introducing the Southern Africa political-economy context after 'colonial-settlerism' (including apartheid) and the contradictions of politics and ideology within the global political economy contours. It then assesses the empirical configurations and variations in the political economy of Zimbabwe under what the ruling Zimbabwe African National Union (Patriotic Front) (ZANU (PF)) has called the *Third Chimurenga* (the third war of economic liberation).

The chapter then moves on to trace the development and accumulation patterns attendant to the Broad-Based Black Economic Empowerment (BBBEE). The objective is to evaluate the magnitude to which these policies are reconfiguring capital accumulation patterns in post-apartheid South Africa and whether these 'decolonising' projects are designing inclusive development projects. After that, the next section makes two main observations – the nature of accumulation patterns in both countries while having some divergences point to a postcolonial state facilitated the accumulation process captured by ruling elites or their networks, as predicted by Fanon (1963), with the effect that *redistribution without growth* is becoming a defining feature of the emerging contemporary political economy. The chapter concludes by arguing for the need of a more intense debate over the possibility of a *democratic developmental state* within the two countries, as this presents perhaps an approximate postcolonial development project envisaged by the *National Democratic Revolution*.[1] We also point to critical policy issues related to *state structures* and their role in development, and how the state can be central to broaden development projects by deliberately eroding the 'enclave' nature of the existing political economy (Mhone 2002) and lack of 'capabilities' (Sen 1999) in the postcolonial setting.

Conceptually, the chapter utilises two theoretical approaches. Because our methodology is historical, we use Fanon's (1963) 'warning' on the limitations of the nationalist liberation movements. In terms of the contemporary postcolonial accumulation patterns, we utilise the concept of 'dualism' and 'enclave' economy explored by Mhone (2000). To begin with, Fanon warned about the limitations of a bourgeoisie, which is state-dependent and only interested in speculative activities and living only as a conduit of 'metropole' capitalism. This is what he had to say about the dangers of such an extractive and consumptive class:

> From the beginning, the national bourgeoisie directs its efforts toward activities of the intermediary type. The basis of its strength is found in its aptitude for trade and small business enterprises, and in securing commissions. It is not its money that works, but its business acumen. It does not go in for investments and it cannot achieve that accumulation of capital necessary to the birth and blossoming of an authentic bourgeoisie. At that rate it would take centuries to set on foot an embryonic industrial revolution, and in any case it would find the way barred by the relentless opposition of the former mother country, which will have taken all precautions when setting up neo-colonialist trade conventions. (1963: 179)

Apart from the deformities (for example, lack of accumulation and investment) entrenched by this postcolonial 'fake business class' stated above, Mhone (2000) argued that the postcolonial political economy was also structurally deformed as a result of how capital accumulation was facilitated, resulting in a 'dual' and 'enclave economy' characterised by low labour absorptive capacity. Here we quote this seminal analysis extensively:

> Capitalism emerged in Africa without the need to transform both agriculture and industry and without the need to commodify all of the active population

the majority which remains outside the sphere of influence of capitalist relations of production. This incomplete subordination of non-capitalist forms of production by capitalism is manifested in what may be seen as an *economic dualism* ... there is a coexistence of mutually interrelated major segments of the labour force, a minority, which is engaged in dynamic activities propelled by the capitalist imperative for accumulation, and another, comprising the majority, which is trapped in non-capitalist forms of production and engaged in low productivity economic pursuits that are static from the point of view of accumulation. The capitalist sector, which we shall label as the formal sector, exists as an *enclave* in a sea of under-employment, which we shall refer to as the non-formal sector. (2002: 7, emphasis added).

In the case of Zimbabwe, these concepts were further developed by Kanyenze et al. (2011), who explored how the colonial political economy characterised by 'dualism' and 'enclavity' has continued to dominate the structure of Zimbabwe's postcolonial political economy. The same disarticulations are evident in South Africa because of the legacy of apartheid, and Mbeki (cited in *Hansard*, Col. 3378) would argue that there were 'two nations' in post-apartheid South Africa: one South Africa that was rich, skilled, developed and white, and the one South Africa that was poor, unskilled, underdeveloped and black. In this chapter, we will combine these analyses by Fanon (1963) and Mhone (2000) to assess the postcolonial 'development' trajectory associated with the national liberation movements in Zimbabwe and South Africa. We also undertake these analyses cognisant of the fact that the global financial crisis (2008–9) has forced 'free market fundamentalism' into retreat, especially after Western governments extensively intervened through various measures like 'quantitative easing' and direct support of some industries (UNECA 2011). This ideological and policy shift in the international political economy presents a unique opportunity where the policies pursued by the Washington Consensus through 'neoliberalism' (structural adjustment) are being partially abandoned and perhaps 'developmental states' (Edigheji 2010) can emerge instead.

'Rhodes Must Fall' and a 'Few Cheers for Mugabe?' Turbulence in the Southern African Political Economy

When Robert Gabriel Mugabe, the former leader of ZANU (PF) and leader and President of Zimbabwe for more than thirty years appeared on different occasions in Africa, he received 'thunderous applause'. The first and most significant of these occasions was when he was 'elected' to be the Chair of the African Union (AU) in 2015; the second cheer was at the inauguration of the incoming President of Namibia; the third cheer was at Nelson Mandela's funeral; the fourth cheer was at the funeral of the late Zambian President Michael Sata; and the fifth cheer was at the inauguration of Edgar Lungu as President of Zambia. When he arrived to visit the Hector Peterson Memorial in Soweto in South Africa, some residents who were interviewed called him an 'African giant' and he gleefully played to the gallery, declaring that 'I don't like the white man'.[2] These cheers and idolisation raised very puzzling questions, especially in the context of how ZANU (PF) had consolidated power through rabid authoritarianism (Matombo and Sachikonye 2010: 117) and a much-contested 'grotesque nationalism' (Ndlovu-Gatsheni and Muzondidya 2011).

Electoral contests have often been very bloody and electoral outcomes have often been viewed as illegitimate. Widespread allegations of violence resulted in a negotiated Government of National Unity (GNU) in Zimbabwe in 2009. This crisis has led some to say that Zimbabwe's winds of change had been defied (Masunungure 2009) or that Zimbabwe was 'mired in transition' (Masunungure and Shumba 2013). Within Zimbabwe, former President Mugabe's electoral victories were widely condemned as lacking legitimacy, and a former Finance Minister from the opposition, Tendai Biti, described the ruling party as a 'phalanx of gangsters' who have cornered the state into a vehicle of a 'patronage economy'. What made these 'few cheers' for Mugabe puzzling is that they came within the context of what has been called Africa's 'development impasse' (Andreasson 2010), while Jauch and Muchena (2011) has argued that the 'inequalities' in Southern Africa are 'tearing us apart'. Some have even argued that Africa is being 'looted' (Bond 2006) and in Zimbabwe specifically some have noted the 'Zimbabwe crisis' and the 'lost decades' (Sachikonye 2011).

As a corollary to this, two very fascinating historical political processes have taken place in Southern Africa. First, in Zimbabwe, there was the launch of the Fast Track Land Reform Program, commonly known as 'jambanja' (violent land seizures), in 2000 and subsequent to that the launch of the *indigenisation* programme (ZANU (PF) Manifesto 2013). Second, in South Africa, Julius Malema, who had been expelled from the African National Congress Youth League (ANCYL), launched the Economic Freedom Fighters (EFF), and within nine months the EFF had received over a million votes and was allocated twenty-five Members of Parliament. Analysed through the controversial men who dominated these movements – Robert Mugabe in Zimbabwe and Julius Malema in South Africa – these historical processes can be dismissed as vehicles of power grabbing by two political demagogues. In Zimbabwe, the electoral process was violently contested and if the Khampepe Report (2014) is considered, then the elections which kept Mugabe and ZANU (PF) in power north of the Limpopo were anything *but* free and fair. Julius Malema's personality has been dented by statements like 'we will kill for Zuma', while his in and out of court movements and sparring with the South African Revenue Service (SARS) have not helped his credibility.

First, when one strips ZANU (PF) of the violence and what has been called 'nationalist authoritarianism' and, second, when one strips the EFF of the demagoguery and perhaps the flawed character of Julius Malema, there is a pattern emerging which highlights that the 'unfinished business' Hammar et al. (2003) of liberation is returning to haunt the postcolonial political economy and the results are indeed 'messy'. In Zimbabwe, ZANU (PF) claimed that the 'land is the economy, the economy is the land', and in 2013 the motto was 'indigenize, empower and employ' (ZANU (PF) Manifesto 2013). In South Africa, the EFF changed the historical motto 'Freedom in Our Lifetime' to 'Economic Freedom in Our Lifetime' and pointed out that as a political party, it wanted 'to expropriate land without compensation' and nationalise 'mines, banks, and other strategic sectors of the economy, without compensation' (EFF Manifesto 2014). The ANC also attempted to reconfigure the post-apartheid political economy by introducing BBBEE and eventually a National Development Plan (NDP) committed to 'eliminate poverty and reduce inequality by 2030' (National Development Commission 2013). The ANC government has also expressly committed to building a 'democratic development state' (Edigheji 2010: 2).

'Unfinished Business': Demands for Decolonisation outside of the 'Party-State'

In analysing the trajectory of the contestations around 'indigenisation', 'black economic empowerment' and 'land reform' in Zimbabwe and to some extent in South Africa, there has been an overwhelming tendency to focus on the state and political parties. This is a very easy and tempting but rather narrow analysis of the trajectory of this contestation. This section therefore points out that there have been subcurrents of 'other' social forces outside the state that have been pressing for the completion of the 'decolonisation' project in Southern Africa in general. We have pointed out elsewhere that partial analyses that limit the 'African crisis' to one of narrowly defined 'democracy and good governance' have tended to ignore what have been radical demands for asset redistribution (Chirimambowa and Chimedza 2014). In Zimbabwe, there have been groups like the Indigenous Business Development Committee (IBDC), the

Indigenous Business Women's Organisation (IBWO) and the Affirmative Action Group (AAG). Chirimambowa (2007) has also traced the historical development of these social groups and we have to point out that the study of these groups has been marginal, as they have been considered 'uncivil' and their demands have tended not to fit the archetypical civil society organisation in Africa, which tends to check state power. While the prevalent interpretation of the land reform and indigenisation has been that Mugabe and the ruling elites had to 'buy off' social groups in order to retain power, there have also been other arguments. Ndlovu-Gatsheni has pointed out the following:

> Indeed a large section of emerging black/national bourgeoisie aligned to ZANU-PF frustrated by the slow pace of embourgeoisement, some sections of the academic fraternity, war veterans, ex-detainees and unemployed youth combined to support the Third Chimurenga with its nativist claims and its hostility towards whites. (2009: 69)

Sadomba (2009) has argued strongly that land reform and indigenisation were pushed onto the national political landscape by what he calls a 'social movement' of the war veterans' 'vanguard' and was later on hijacked by the elites. Moyo and Yeros' 'radicalised state' (2007) was from that perspective a consequence and not an antecedent to either the Fast Track Land Reform Program or subsequently the indigenisation programme. It is this reconfiguring of the postcolonial political economy that Ndlovu-Gastheni (2009) has called the 'nativist revolution', and this chapter seeks to unpack and raise critical questions about the trajectory that this 'return of the native' is taking. This chapter specifically analyses the nature and substance of the political economy that is emerging as a result of state power being leveraged to intervene very radically in order to reconfigure political economic relations. Drawing on Fanon's (1969) theorisation of the economy that emerges in the postcolonial period, we would like to point out that there is a distinctive political economy under formation and the hallmark of this political economy is that the political parties in power are becoming central to accumulation. In Zimbabwe, the distinctive feature might be violence, while in South Africa the BBBEE is 'orderly', yet the process seems to be achieving a very similar result: rewarding party-linked elites. In both countries, the state bureaucracy has also been strangled of its capacity to be developmental by a policy of 'cadre deployment' that often places political interests above competency (this is opposed to the model of the developmental states in East Asia, which placed able and skilled bureaucrats to drive policy-making and practice).

'Indigenisation' and 'Land Reform': The Contested Ideology and Politics

Since about 2000, a distinctive political economy has emerged in Zimbabwe that is characterised by an increased interventionist state that others have called 'nationalist authoritarianism' (Raftopolous 2003). The ruling political party, ZANU (PF), has become very authoritarian and has become instrumental in the accumulation process. Moore and Mawowa (2010) and Mawowa (2011) noted the emergence of a party-state apparatus directing accumulation, especially in mining, including extending into illicit mining activities carried out by 'makorokoza'. Politically, ZANU (PF) projected itself as a political party completing the 'revolutionary' demands of the liberation process and has therefore ideologically placed its post-2000 manifestos as a successor to the *Second Chimurenga* (war of liberation that began in the 1960s and led to the 1979 negotiations for Independence in 1980). In the tightly contested 2000 election, for example, the ZANU (PF) Manifesto claimed that 'The Land is the Economy, the Economy is the Land' and by 2013, the same 'People's Manifesto' boldly declared 'Taking Back the Economy: Indigenise, Empower, Develop and Create Employment (ZANU (PF) Manifesto 2013). Under the Fast Track Land Reform Program that started in about 2000, the white-settler class monopoly on land ownership was wiped out. The indigenisation programme is supposed to facilitate the ownership of 51 per cent of all businesses worth over US$500,000 by 'indigenous Zimbabweans'; the government has also facilitated the formation of a Sovereign Wealth Fund, Community Share Ownership Trusts and Employee Share Ownership Trusts. Some have dismissed these policy measures as 'reverse racism' (Matyszak 2011), while others like Levitsky et al. (2009) have emphasised that the ideological reorientation by the ZANU (PF) elites must not be overlooked as it was used to re-align social forces that have been a historical support block for the liberation movement (including the military and peasants).

The policies pursued by ZANU (PF) have not been without internal contestations, unpredictable variations and in certain cases outright uncertainty. In financial services, for example, where a number of 'indigenous banks' have been liquidated, the Governor of the Reserve Bank of Zimbabwe (RBZ) was very critical. He even took the extraordinary step of writing a published opinion pointing out that a 'one-size-fits-all' approach' was inappropriate, disruptive and dangerous, and hence any deals that foreign banks in this market voluntarily or involuntarily enter into and sign-off without RBZ prior approval were to remain just deals on paper that were basically null and void (Reserve Bank of Zimbabwe

2013). The same statement went on to highlight that the financial sector was already 97 per cent indigenous and any attempt to forcibly take over 'foreign owned banks' was almost like 'shooting ourselves in the foot with a financial bazooka' (Reserve Bank of Zimbabwe 2013: 11). It is important to note here that almost all the banks that have collapsed as a result of scandals ranging from 'nonperforming loans' to 'insider loans' and 'related party transactions' and have struggled to raise capital have been indigenous-owned.[3] Others who have studied the crisis in the banking sector have called it a corporate governance failure and legalised theft (Mambondiani 2011).

'Comrades in Business': Patronage and Elite Accumulation in Zimbabwe

In the case of Zimbabwe, the so-called *Third Chimurenga* (refers to the so called for for economic liberation in post-independence Zimbabwe) has not lived up to its ideological and policy pronouncements, except to feed the accumulation patterns of the elites in the party-state. A few observations can be made here. First, as observed by Moore and Mawowa (2010), the party-state had become central in terms of facilitating accumulation, often in a very authoritarian manner. Second, the accumulation patterns were dominated by ruling-elite networks, especially state security networks. Third, the discovery of commodities (gold, diamonds, etc.) spurred the emergence of a 'resource curse', and the companies in this sector are closely related to Zimbabwe's security services like the army, intelligence, police, prison services or highly placed party and state bureaucrats with access to and protection by state power. Furthermore, land reform in Zimbabwe has been marred by allegations of multiple farm ownerships by the ruling elite and the politically connected. This was highlighted by the government-commissioned Flora Bhuka and Dr Charles Utete Reports.[4] Temba Mliswa, former Mashonaland Central ZANU (PF) chairperson and Hurungwe West legislator, in a moment of sour grapes in the aftermath ZANU (PF) Congress fallout, exposed the messy affair:

> The programs (indigenization and land reform) are then manipulated by individuals and corruption starts to raise its head. Whilst the program is noble its implementation is now corrupt and marred by cases of multiple farm ownership ... in land reform you have 'big guys' now being owners of multiple farms ... yet there is a term called 'warehousing'. Indigenization is another policy which is supposed to be broad based ... but there is a total reversal of empowerment. We are indoctrinated to fight whites but the ZANU (PF) leadership is dining and wining with the whites. *If you don't toe*

the line you lose the farm. There is no tenure. There is no certainty. (Temba Mliswa interview, emphasis added)[5]

When one takes a closer look at the networks that are actively supported, they are heavily related to political power – in fact, these lines of accumulation from the control of parastatals; diamond mining has been dominated by military and security elites, leading to the conclusion that Zimbabwe's economy is now run by the 'securocrats' (Mangongera 2014). These networks of accumulation also extend into the region, especially going back to the deals that were facilitated in the Democratic Republic of Congo (DRC) when the Zimbabwe National Army was deployed to support the presidency of Laurent Kabila. A United Nations (UN) report found that Zimbabwe's military elite and ministers in government had benefited immensely from illegal diamond and other mining activities in the Congo. What has emerged in Zimbabwe is what Alexander and McGregor et al. (2014) have called the 'patronage economy', or almost what Reno (1995) would have called the 'shadowy economy', which is related to but in some ways has flows that are hidden from the formal state and cannot be taxed or disciplined in any way by the regulatory apparatus.

'Stirring the Nest': BBBEE and the Native Club in South Africa

South Africa as a late decoloniser with an advanced industrial economy presents an interesting case in terms of assessing the trajectory of the National Democratic Revolution (NDR). Increasingly, the fissures of race, class and dispossession have occasionally boiled to the surface, but thus far the South African liberal democratic architecture negotiated by Nelson Mandela has held forth, although the fissures have already started to show. As early as 2000, Bond (2000) was arguing that South Africa had gone from apartheid to neoliberalism via an 'elite transition' and a few years later, he would argue that South Africa's political was 'unsustainable'. To begin with, the rate and intensity of what has been called 'service delivery' protests has increased and the black middle-class 'impatience' with the remnants of the apartheid economy has started to show in various ways. In 2006, a group of black intellectuals launched a Native Club and while its force seems to have petered out, here is why it was important:

> the formation of the Native Club is not seen as an isolated event, but as a consequence of some embers which have been burning since the beginning of

the struggle against apartheid and is situated historically within the broader terrain of power contestations and continuous reflections by different sections of South African society on the gains of the anti-apartheid struggle, post-apartheid development failures and disappointments as well as the future direction of democratic social and political transformation at this crucial second decade of South African democratic consolidation. (Ndlovu-Gatsheni 2007: 5)

Since then, significant political events have occurred: first, the expulsion of ANCYL leader Julius Malema led to the formation of the EFF and, second, the expulsion of the National Union of Miners in South Africa (NUMSA) from the Congress of South African Trade Unions (COSATU) has brought to the fore questions of whether the historical alliance between the ANC (as a political power) and COSATU (as a working-class power) will survive. While in power, the ANC has attempted to chip away slowly at the formidable apartheid economy dominated by whites and has halfheartedly attempted a land reform programme, which has been slow. The ANC, like ZANU (PF), has become a breeding ground for a parasitic and very consumptive black 'capitalist class', which is dependent on liberation credentials to muscle into BBBEE deals and, when this fails, access to state tenders has created another avenue for decadent accumulation. The ANC has left room for the EFF to emerge with a radical demagoguery, which the EFF claims is historically rooted in the tradition of the Freedom Charter – this is a distinguishing feature from the MDC in Zimbabwe that was burdened by 'neoliberal triumphalism', and its policies were largely focused on economic growth and less on the need for 'asset redistribution' (like radical land reform).

From Kliptown Charter to Black Economic Empowerment: The Unfinished NDR

The Kliptown Charter, popularly known as the Freedom Charter, lays the basis upon which the need for BBBEE arises in an attempt to address the vestiges of 350 years of apartheid economics and politics in South Africa. The Freedom Charter notes that:

> The national wealth of our country, the heritage of South Africans, shall be restored to the people; the mineral wealth beneath the soil, the banks and monopoly industry shall be transferred to the ownership of the people as a whole; all other industry and trade shall be controlled to assist the well-being of the people; all people shall have equal rights to trade where they choose, to manufacture and to enter all trades, crafts and professions. (African National Congress 1955)

Essentially, it became necessary for the ANC to institute BBBEE as part of its nationalist agenda to decolonise the economic sphere – a historical necessity, which saw the ANC revisiting the NDR theory as a spirited intellectual effort on the debates on social and economic transformation in post-apartheid South Africa. In this case, the NDR became a basis upon which the ANC sought to transform property relations and thus called for the state to act. Southall (2000: 3) points out that the NDR is fashioned to achieve 'internal decolonization' and also the following: overcoming the legacy of racial oppression of the black majority; achieving democratisation; and transforming power relations as a basis for societal equality. In addition, the ANC went further and defined the NDR as:

> in essence ... the liberation of Africans in particular and Black people in general from political and economic bondage ... the deracialisation of ownership and control of wealth, including land ... the elimination of the legacy of apartheid super-exploitation and inequality, and the redistribution of wealth and income to benefit society as a whole, especially the poor. (Turok 2005: 6)

Therefore, BBBEE has to be interpreted within the historical context of the Freedom Charter and liberation theory, and finally as an attempt by the ANC to fulfil the completion of the unfinished business of the NDR. We are aware here that South Africa is not on any path to a socialist revolution, as its economic policies are largely driven and informed by a pro-market logic, as noted by the shifts from the Reconstruction and Development Programme (RDP) to Growth Employment and Redistribution (GEAR), Accelerated and Shared Growth Initiative-South Africa (ASGISA) and the NDP. We include the concept of the NDR because it was an influential liberation theoretical framework for the 'mass movements' fighting for decolonisation in Africa. It is imperative to understand BBBEE as a policy response to reverse systematic processes of dispossession and oppression of African people by colonialism and apartheid. It is within this context that the adoption of the NDR by liberation movements was principally to deal with the lingering questions of colonialism, apartheid and uneven development. Southall points out that the NDR was put forward to essentially achieve four things:

- legitimate the 'historic' role of the ANC in leading South Africa;
- validate the need for an interventionist state to radically transform society;
- justify the existence, expansion, wealth and function of a black bourgeoisie and middle class so long as they play by the rules laid down by the party; and

- endorse the need for cooperation with white capitalists whose objective interests may eventually lead to their incorporation into the 'patriotic bourgeoisie'. (2000: 4)

However, beyond the ideological framework of the Freedom Charter and NDR is the question as to whether BBBEE as a continuation of these ideologies has managed to alter economic relations and create inclusive and just societies. Leys and Berman pose these questions in their discussion of the role and nature of local capitalists in a capitalist development framework:

> Given that the only kind of development that appears immediately practicable is capitalist development – within the framework of world markets and, at best up till now, within the constraints of the IMF/World Bank regulation of African macro-economic policy – the key questions have still to be asked: what are the specific problems that must be solved for such development to take place? What are the functions that local capitalists are called [upon] to perform? And what are the most significant characteristics of African capitalist classes for achieving whatever can be achieved within this framework? (Leys and Berman 1994: 3)

The next section attempts to answer these questions by analysing the policy and practice of BBBEE and arguing that in its current form, the BBBEE remains theoretically and practically limited to extensively dealing with questions of poverty and inequality in South Africa. While others like Southall (2006) have argued that BBBEE has been broader than its critics have claimed, they have recognised that this argument loses strength when one considers the scale and number of people excluded from these 'empowerment deals'.

BBBEE Policy and Practice: Feasting on Behalf of the Poor

The objective of BBBEE has been to transform the South African economy and make it inclusive, in particular for the non-white population that had faced centuries of systematic social and economic exclusion. Elibiary observes that:

> It is expected that by transforming the economy through BEE, the outcome would be a reduction in inequality (which has an impact on poverty levels), an increase in job creation and, ultimately, economic growth. Therefore, [BB]BEE policy is perceived as the solution to all of South Africa's social and economic problems; not only is it to contribute to the racial transformation of the economy but it is also to stimulate economic growth, create jobs and eradicate poverty. (Elibiary 2010: 2)

However, the practice of BBBEE has cast questions on South Africa's decolonisation and economic empowerment of the majority poor black population, as poverty and inequality continue to dash the aspirations of many poor people. Mbeki (2009: 67) chronicles how BBBEE was 'invented by South Africa's economic oligarchs, that handful of white businessmen and their families who control the commanding heights of the country's economy, that is mining and its associated chemical and engineering industries and finance' and how its key objective 'was to co-opt leaders of the black resistance movement by literally buying them off with what looked like a transfer to them of massive assets at no cost. To the oligarchs, of course, these assets were small change'. Therefore, this led to the overnight transformation of politicians into millionaires without any production taking place and consequently the toning down of the radicalisation of ANC economic policy, as well as creating a comprador bourgeoisie to act as a buffer against the majority poor, thereby creating an impression that all black South Africans would benefit through BBBEE (Mbeki 2009). It may therefore be argued that since its inception, the underlying objectives of BBBEE were not to transform the economies as claimed by the ANC and some nationalists, but to create a comprador class that would play an intermediary role on behalf of capital.

The controversial role of the ANC and the role of South African State Deputy President Cyril Ramaphosa in the Marikana massacre of mineworkers lends credence to Mbeki's claims, a warning that Fanon (1963) had already given years earlier about the African elite not being transformative, but seeking accommodation with capital. Hence, BBBEE has managed to create a few elites, leading to resentment even amongst its supposed beneficiaries, a point that Elibiary (2010: 3) observes: 'some blacks have become critical of its intentions as they see a select, politically connected few benefiting while the majority of blacks (especially Africans) remain "underpowered". Some argue that it is in fact that BBBEE policy that is creating greater inequalities – especially within the African (black) community'. Therefore, issues of poverty and inequality remain a big challenge in South African society as BBBEE fails to transform the economy and society to empower and include previously disadvantaged individuals. In an attempt to account for this widening wealth gap and the exclusive nature of South African society, Zulu (2013) advances two theories to explain this phenomenon: first, the redistributive regime favours elite rewards in both private and public at the expense of workers and the general welfare of the public; second, BBBEE has advantaged new political and economic elites either because of their skills gained from education or because of their connectedness to the political centre of power – attributes that the workers and the general public lack, thus diminishing their eligibility for or excluding them completely from these rewards. There is a tendency to attempt to address the historical questions of poverty and inequality in South Africa through an overemphasis on BEE, as much attention is paid to questions of equity/shareholding transfer without critically thinking about how this will improve the livelihoods of many poor black South Africans. Cargill (2010) questions the overemphasis of corporate shareholding at the expense of other ideas and initiatives that may possibly address the marginalisation of black South Africans from the mainstream economy. BBBEE as a development and economic empowerment policy has been narrowly conceptualised and ends up benefiting a few educated and politically connected elites in the 'name of the poor' or what Onslow (2012: 2) characterises as an 'improvident and greedy narrow clique of new BEEBEE oligarchs, behind the facade of national empowerment'. Others like Zulu (2013) have argued that BBBEE is not liberatory or transformative, but leads the development of an almost decadent elite displaying extreme consumptive patterns.

'Jobless' and 'Comprador' BBBEE Transactions

BBBEE has become widely known for creating jobless transactions, as shares have exchanged hands and the politically connected elites accumulate wealth without any *new* production taking place. In this instance, the 'major' empowerment deals' involving what has been called the 'Fab 4' (Cyril Ramaphosa, Saki Macozoma, Patrice Motsepe and Tokyo Sexwale) has not created any new industries, but has merely redistributed what already existed. By the stroke of a pen, a new breed of entrepreneurs has emerged and they are classified as follows: *tenderpreneurs* – these are composed of briefcase companies that are solely formed in order to target government tenders, yet these companies do not have any record of trade and commerce before the advertising of tenders; *front men* – these include persons co-opted by business to provide a front/figurehead for a company with a perceived politically correct racial profile for a fee, yet these persons will have no power or control within the business, as they are mere placeholders; *bureaupreneurs* – this involves government bureaucrats who have developed intricate networks and systems to influence tendering processes in return for a fee; and *acquirers* (MacGaffey 1987) – these are modelled along the line of Mobutu's acquirers in Zaire (now the DRC) and they are either public officials or persons related to political office who through a mix of manipulation of the law and the flexing of political power acquire assets or companies without any form of payment taking place. This in turn has seen fierce contestations for public office as it has become a vehicle for accumulation or what Breytenbach (cited in *Mail & Guardian*, 4 April 2008) calls an exercise of 'scavenging'.

The NDR Revisited: What Are the Prospects for Inclusive Development?

We have pointed out elsewhere that Africa's postcolonial civil society and some 'postnationalist' political formations like the MDC in Zimbabwe were weakened by an *ahistorical* approach to resolving the postcolonial crisis of underdevelopment, and this loaded these movements with what we called 'the neoliberal burden' (Chirimambowa and Chimedza 2014). This particular limited conception of democracy was associated at a global level with the 'end of history triumphalism' and the collapse of what had been presented as the 'socialist alternative'. In the case of Zimbabwe, the national policy shift from Growth with Equity in 1981 to the infamous Economic Structural Adjustment Program (ESAP) in 1991 triggered deindustrialisation, which by the late 1990s had caused the intensified contestation over state power with the emergence of the MDC in 1999. In South Africa, the movement from the RDP to GEAR achieved similar results. Within the global political economy, this shift was characterised by the 'free market' onslaught on all things *state*. The emerging 'native revolution' led by ZANU (PF) in Zimbabwe and the EFF in South Africa has been led by demagogues. Yet, when this demagoguery is put aside, and in Zimbabwe when 'radical nationalism' (Moyo and Chambati 2013) is also stripped of violence and coercion, there is a simmering historical discontent with the postcolonial political economy insofar as it remained structured and dominated by the same social forces that benefited immensely from colonial and apartheid dispossession. Yet in the process of reconfiguring the postcolonial political economy, the former liberation movements quickly discarded a wider conception of *democracy* as envisaged in the NDR and there was therefore a need for those outside the 'party-state' to reconceptualise democratisation in the historical sense where more social groups win power (Moore 2003).

In this section, we will give an overall assessment of how this 'nativism' ideology and the attendant black economic empowerment policies have fared in both Zimbabwe and South Africa. We will look at three areas: (i) the evolving 'ideology and policy practice'; the nature of 'state structures'; and (iii) the emerging 'state–society' relations. First, a close analysis of the economic policy and practice in both countries reveals that the ideology and policies in practice are more designed to cement political power and also to expand the networks of businesspeople associated with the political class that Mbeki called 'architects of poverty' (2009). In Zimbabwe, the 'nativist revolution' has resulted in 'distribution *without* growth' and the network of 'black businesses' benefiting are not industrialists interested in accumulating and reinvesting capital. In this case, the indigenisation policy has also been characterised by extensive inconsistencies and contradictions, and state bureaucrats and ministers openly differ on which policy direction should be followed. In terms of agrarian relations, while the 'white-settler' class has all but disappeared the reconfigured agrarian relations are very unstable as there is no tenure, and support given to small-scale farmers has been limited. Effectively this unstable land ownership structure favours the party-state as the beneficiaries continued to be subordinated into the party-state for protection and 'largesse'. The indigenisation 'deals' like Community Share Ownership Trusts have not been fully implemented and have often been tainted by corruption, while the celebrated 'empowerment deals' were reported to be collapsing (Mbiba 2014). As Kanyenze et al. (2011) have pointed out, the postcolonial economy in Zimbabwe is still dominated by 'dualism' and 'enclavity', as evidenced by the high level of unemployment and a highly informal economy that exploits, dispossesses and negatively impacts women more than men.

In the case of South Africa, we also pointed out that the BBBEE transactions have been dominated by a typical 'comprador black class', resulting in 'jobless' transactions that only benefit a select few. In South Africa specifically, there is no evidence that the 'mineral-energy' complex, which was the hallmark of the apartheid state's exclusionary political economy, is being transformed into a more 'even' and inclusive economy. In both Zimbabwe and South Africa, there is no evidence that there has been the creation of a black industrialist class like the one created by what Evans (1995) called 'embedded autonomy' in countries like Japan, South Korea, Taiwan, Malaysia and Singapore. While South Africa has a far-advanced 'social policy' system, which can be a basis of expanding what Sen (1999) called 'capabilities', the social protection system has often been designed to meet short-term goals than a long-term transformative social system that can increase social mobility. In terms of education, for example, Statistics South Africa (2015: vi) reported that black people are generally less likely to have an education beyond matriculation and even less so a university degree. In Zimbabwe, social policy has virtually collapsed, with the Minister of Higher Education announcing that universities must be 'self-sustaining'. The result is that while on the one hand there is increased radicalisation of political ideology around the NDR in South Africa and the *Third Chimurenga* (war for economic liberation) in Zimbabwe, policy practices like the NDP and the much-celebrated

Zimbabwe Agenda for Sustainable Social Economic Transformation (ZIMASSET) are failing to meet the decolonisation project of building a more even, inclusive and growing economy.

The evolution of *state structures* in both countries reveals that the political parties in power (ZANU (PF) and the ANC) are increasingly using state institutions to consolidate their political hegemony. In both countries, the bureaucracy has been heavily dominated by the presence of 'party cadres' that are more focused on advancing party interests than developmental projects. In Zimbabwe, this has also meant the increase of bureaucratic positions being dominated by men and women from the military who regard loyalty to the president and the party as more important. In South Africa, there has been overwhelming criticism of the ANC's 'deployment' policy, which has often placed unqualified and inexperienced political appointees at the helm of state-owned enterprises (for example, South African Broadcasting Corporation (SABC, Eskom, PetroSA and so on). Effectively, this has meant that the ANC's project of achieving a democratic developmental state is weakened as state institutions, which can play an important role in national accumulation, become ineffective.

There is also a growing evidence of authoritarianism, especially in Zimbabwe, where state institutions are leveraged against perceived opponents, and political space, which could facilitate deliberative policy-making, is closed out. In the case of South Africa, the State Security Agency (SSA) was reported to be 'investigating' the EFF leader Julius Malema, the Public Protector Thuli Madonsela and former DA leader in Parliament Lindiwe Mazibuko for 'spying' (*Mail & Guardian*, 6 March 2015). The National Development Commission in South Africa, which is supposed to play a central role, has not really lived up to its hype.

Finally, in terms of 'state–society' relations, Edigheji (2010: 2) warned that in order for a developmental state to function well, it has to be able to act 'authoritatively, credibly, legitimately in a binding manner to formulate and implement its policy and programmes'. Zimbabwe perhaps is worse off than South Africa in this respect, especially considering the violence and level of intimidation that Zimbabwe's state institutions have used against political opponents. A common vehicle for implementing Zimbabwe's public policy, often in a very authoritarian manner, is what has been called 'government by operations', and examples have included *Operation Chipo Chiroorwa* (Chipo get married), *Operation Murambatsvina* (clear out the filth), *Operation Chimumumu* (keep quiet) and *Operation Mavhoterapapi* (who did you vote for ?). Interestingly, the South African government also initiated *Operation Fiela* (sweeping clean) in response to the 'problem' of illegal migrants in South African urban areas. A distinctive feature of this 'government by operations' is the reliance on security services as a tool of public policy implementation. While 'state–society' relations are generally better in South Africa than in Zimbabwe, the response of security services to social services delivery protests have revealed a certain level of authoritarianism. The steady increases in the number of votes for the Democratic Alliance, the rise of the EFF and also the splits in COSATU are evidence of growing disillusionment with the post-apartheid political economy. The increasing levels of authoritarianism weaken the *popular* legitimacy of a party or the state to implement developmental projects.

Conclusion: Any Prospects for the Democratic Development State?

In the case of South Africa, Edigheji (2010) has recently assessed the possibility of constructing a developmental state, and the ANC has also committed to developing such a state. In the case of Zimbabwe, the opposition MDC, in its election manifesto for the 2013 election, advanced the need for a democratic developmental state. First, we agree that there is a need for postcolonial states in general and especially in Africa to develop developmental states, particularly because they are capable of being the mythical *Janus*: on the one hand, such a state engages in 'redistribution', yet it also focuses on growing a more even economy. The aftermath of the global financial crisis has resulted in the partial retreat of neoliberalism and on changing global political economic relations in which Chinese influence is rising. The intense development of information technology services, rising commodity prices and the increased remittances flowing into Southern Africa enable the development of dynamic economies, and the nature of the *state* facilitating that process will be central. The radicalisation of political ideology in the form of 'nativism' and/or 'indigenisation' will remain perilous to Southern Africa's development prospects if the focus is on *distribution without growth*.

Tamuka Charles Chirimambowa is a fellow at the University of Johannesburg. He has worked extensively on the subjects of civil society in Zimbabwe and the Southern African region, issues of human rights, governance and democracy, migrants' rights, economic policy and social justice. His main interest is in the political economy of transformation in postcolonial Africa. He is currently undertaking research on economic indigenisation (Zimbabwe) and black economic empowerment (South Africa), business–state relations and economic reform within the

Southern African Development Community region, migration and remittances in Africa, and the possibility of 'democratic developmental states' in Southern Africa.

Tinashe Lukas Chimedza studied Social Inquiry at the University of Technology Sydney. He is interested in the political economy of development in Africa. He is also a cofounder of the Institute for Public Affairs in Zimbabwe.

Notes

1. We are aware here that while the concept of the NDR was prevalent in South African 'liberation' theory, this was not particularly the case in Zimbabwe. However, the concept remains relevant as a framework of assessing the fate of the liberation revolutions. Former President Thabo Mbeki applied the concept of the NDR in assessing the trajectory of the 'Zimbabwe revolution'.
2. In Zambia, the cheer was contested, as some activists rallied at a hotel, chanting 'Mugabe must go'. See *The Standard* (2015).
3. The list includes the following banks: United Merchant Bank (UMB), Allied Bank, Tetrad Bank, Genesis Investment Bank, Trust Bank, AfriAsia (formerly Kingdom Bank), Interfin, Royal Bank, CFX, Barbican Bank and Capital Bank.
4. These reports were commissioned by the Zimbabwean government and were later withheld from public release, but a common thread within them was the case of multiple farm ownership by the politically-connected elites. Interestingly, most of these farms have become idle and have turned into some family holiday and weekend picnic spots. Some have been stripped of assets and equipment.
5. Temba Mliswa Press Conference. Retrieved 18 September 2018 from http://www.newsdzezimbabwe.co.uk/2015/04/watch-ousted-mliswa-speaks.html.

References

African National Congress (ANC). 1955. 'The Freedom Charter'. Retrieved 20 June 2015 from http://www.historicalpapers.wits.ac.za/inventories/inv_pdfo/AD1137/AD1137-Ea6-1-001-jpeg.pdf.
Alexander, J., and J. McGregor. 2013. 'Introduction: Politics, Patronage and Violence in Zimbabwe', *Journal of Southern African Studies*, 39(4): 749–63.
Andreasson, S. 2010. *Africa's Development Impasse: Rethinking the Political Economy of Transformation*. London: Zed Books.
Bond, P. 2000. *Elite Transition: From Apartheid to Neo-liberalism in South Africa*. Pietermaritzburg: University of Natal Press.

———. 2002. *Unsustainable South Africa: Environment, Development and Social Protest.* Pietermaritzburg and London: University of KwaZulu Natal Press and Merlin Press.
———. 2006. *Looting Africa: The Economics of Exploitation.* Pietermaritzburg: University of KwaZulu Natal Press.
Bond, P., and M. Manyanya. 2002. *Zimbabwe Plunge: Exhausted Nationalism, Neoliberalism and the Search for Social Justice.* Harare: Weaver Press.
Cargill, J. 2010. *Trick or Treat: Rethinking Black Economic Empowerment.* Johannesburg: Jacana Media.
Chawafambira, K. 2015. 'Brainworks Roasted in Parliament', *Daily News*, 19 June.
Chirimambowa, C.T. 2007. 'The Rise and Fall of the Indigenous Business Development Centre', Honours thesis. Durban: University of KwaZulu Natal.
Chirimambowa, C.T., and T.L. Chimedza. 2014. 'Civil Society's Contested Role in the 2013 Elections in Zimbabwe: A Historical Perspective', *Journal of African Elections* 13(2): 71–93.
EFF Manifesto. 2014. 'Now is the Time for Economic Freedom'.
Edigheji, O. (ed.). 2010. *Constructing a Developmental State in South Africa: Potentials and Constraints.* Cape Town: HSRC Press.
Elibiary, A. 2010. 'The Pitfalls of Addressing Historic Racial Injustice: An Assessment of South Africa's Black Economic Empowerment (BEE) Policies', Friedrich-Naumann-Stiftung für die Freiheit, Regional Office Africa.
Evans, B.P. 1995. *Embedded Autonomy: States and Industrial Transformation.* Princeton: Princeton University Press.
Fanon, F. 1963. *The Wretched of the Earth.* Trans. Constance Farrington. New York: Grove Weidenfeld.
———. 1968. *The Wretched of the Earth.* New York: Grove Press.
———. 969 *Toward the African Revolution.* Trans. Haakon Chevalier. New York: Grove Press.
Hammar, A.J., B. Raftopoulos and S. Jensen (eds). 2003. *Zimbabwe's Unfinished business: Rethinking Land, State and Nation in the Context of Crisis.* Harare: Weaver Press.
Hansard, 29 May 1998, Col. 3378.
Jauch, H., and D. Muchena (eds). 2011. *Tearing Us Apart: Inequalities in Southern Africa.* Johannesburg: OSISA.
Kanyenze, G., T. Kondo, P. Chitambara and J.M. Jose (eds). 2011. *Beyond the Enclave: Towards a Pro-poor and Inclusive Development Strategy for Zimbabwe.* Harare: Weaver Press.
Levitsky, S., and L. Way. 2013. 'The Durability of Revolutionary Regimes', *Journal of Democracy* 24(3): 5–17.
Leys, C. and B. Berman (eds). 1994. *African Capitalists in African Development.* Boulder: Lynne Rienner Publishers.
MacGaffey, J. 1987. *Entrepreneurs and Parasites: The Struggle for Indigenous Capitalism in Zaire.* Cambridge: Cambridge University Press.
Mail & Guardian. 2015. 'Madonsela, Malema and Others Rubbish Spy Claims'. 6 March.

Mambondiani, L.S. 2011. 'Corporate Governance in Zimbabwe: Evidence from Zimbabwe's Banking Sector', Ph.D. thesis. Manchester: University of Manchester.

Mangongera, C. 2014. '"A New Twilight in Zimbabwe": The Military vs Democracy', *Journal of Democracy* 25(2): 67–76.

Masunungure, E.V. (ed.). 2009. *Defying the Winds of Change: Zimbabwe's 2008 Elections*. Harare: Weaver Press and Konrad Adenaeuer Foundation.

Masunungure, E.V., and J.M. Shumba. 2013. *Zimbabwe: Mired in Transition*. Harare: Weaver Press and IDAZIM.

Matombo, L., and L.M. Sachikonye. 2010. 'The Labour Movement and Democratization in Zimbabwe', in B. Beckman, S. Buhlungu and L. Sachikonye (eds), *Trade Unions and Politics: Labour Movements in Africa*. Cape Town: HSRC Press, pp. 109–30.

Matyszak, D. 2011. 'Everything You Wanted to Know about Zimbabwe's Indigenization and Economic Empowerment Legislation But were Too Afraid to Ask', Research Advocacy Unit (RAU). Retrieved 18 September 2018 from http://archive.kubatana.net/docs/econ/rau_indeg_econ_analysis_2_110616.pdf.

Mawowa, S. 2007. 'Tapping into the Chaos: Crisis, State and Accumulation in Zimbabwe', MA thesis. Durban: University of KwaZulu Natal.

_____. 2011. 'Zimbabwe's Political Economy and the Marange Diamonds' in *Perspectives' Journal* publication series, Heinrich Böll Stiftung, 4–8.

_____. 2013. 'Political Economy of Mining, Crisis and Accumulation: Evidence from Chegutu Mhondoro Area', PhD thesis. Durban: University of KwaZulu Natal.

Mbeki, M. 2009. *Architects of Poverty: Why African Capitalism Needs Changing*. Johannesburg: Picador Africa.

Mbeki, T. 2003. 'Letter from the President: Bold Steps to End the "Two Nations" Divide', *ANC Today* 3(33).

Mbiba, L. 2014. 'Community Share Trusts Probe Underway'. *Dailynews live*, 26 August. Retrieved 18 September 2018 from https://www.dailynews.co.zw/articles/2014/08/26/community-share-trusts-probe-underway.

Movement for Democratic Change (MDC). 2013. 'Jobs, Upliftment and Investment Capital and Environment: A Comprehensive Approach to Sustainable and People Centred Development'. Retrieved 18 September 2018 from https://mdctsa.files.wordpress.com/2012/11/jobs-upliftment-investment-capital-and-the-environment-juice.pdf.

Mhone, G. 2000. 'Enclavity and Constrained Labor Absorptive Capacity in Southern African Countries'. *ILO/SAMAT Discussion Paper* Number 12. Retrieved 18 September 2018 from http://adapt.it/adapt-indice-a-z/wp-content/uploads/2014/08/mhones_enclavity_2000.pdf.

Moore, D. 2003. 'Zimbabwe's Triple Crisis: Primitive Accumulation, Nation-State Formation and Democratisation in the Age of Neo-liberal Globalisation', *Africa Studies Quarterly* 7(2–3): 35–51.

Moore, D., and S. Mawowa. 2010. 'Mbimbos, Zwipamuzis and "Primitive Accumulation" in Zimbabwe's Violent Mineral Economy: Crisis, Chaos, and the State', in V. Padayachee (ed.), *The Political Economy of Africa*. London and New York: Routledge, pp. 317–338.

Moyo, S., and W. Chambati. 2013. *Land and Agrarian Reform in Zimbabwe: Beyond White Settler Capitalism*. Dakar and Harare: CODESRIA and AIAS.

Moyo, S., and P. Yeros. 2007. 'The Radicalised State: Zimbabwe's Interrupted Revolution', *Review of African Political Economy* 34(111): 103–21.

National Planning Commssion. 2013. *National Development Plan 2030: Our Future-Make It Work*. Department: The Presidency, Republic of South Africa. Retrieved 20 July 2016 from http://www.dac.gov.za/sites/default/files/NDP%202030%20-%20Our%20future%20-%20make%20it%20work_0.pdf.

Ndlovu-Gatsheni, S.J. 2007. *Tracking the Historical Roots of Post-apartheid Citizenship Problems: The Native Club, Restless Natives, Panicking Settlers and the Politics of Nativism in South Africa*. ASC Working Paper Number 72. Leiden: Africa Studies Centre.

———. 2009, 'Africa for Africans or Africa for "Natives" Only? "New Nationalism" and Nativism in Zimbabwe and South Africa', *Africa Spectrum* 44(1): 61–78.

Ndlovu-Gatsheni, S.J., and J. Muzondidya (eds). 2011. *Redemptive or Grotesque Nationalism: Rethinking Nationalism in Contemporary Zimbabwe*. Oxford: Peter Lang.

Onslow, S. 2012. 'Book Review: Who Rules South Africa?' Retrieved 20 June 2015 from http://eprints.lse.ac.uk/50556/1/blogs.lse.ac.uk-Book_Review_Who_Rules_South_Africa.pdf.

Raftopolous, B. 2003. 'The State in Crisis: Authoritarian Nationalism, Selective Ciotizenship and Distortions of Democracy in Zimbabwe', in A. Hammar, B. Raftopolous and S. Jensen (eds), *Zimbabwe's Unfinished Business: Rethinking Land, State and Nationalism in the Context of Crisis*. Harare: Weaver Press, pp. 217–241.

Reno, W. 1995. *Corruption and State Politics in Sierra Leone*. Cambridge: Cambridge University Press.

———. 1999. *Warlord Politics and African States*. Boulder: Lynne Rienner Publishers.

Reserve Bank of Zimbabwe. 2013. 'Consequences of Implementing the Current Indigenization Framework on the Banking Sector'.

Sachikonye, L. 2011. *Zimbabwe's Lost Decade: Politics, Development and Society*. Harare: Weaver Press.

Sadomba, Z.W. 2009. *War Veterans in Zimbabwe's Revolution: Challenging Neo-colonialism and Settler and International Capitalism*. Woodbridge and Harare: James Currey and Weaver Press.

Sen, A. 1999. *Development as Freedom*. Oxford: Oxford University Press.

Southall, R. 2000. 'The ANC and Black Capitalism in South Africa'. Paper presented at the RAU Seminar for Anthropology and Development.

———. 2006. 'Ten Propositions about Black Economic Empowerment in South Africa', *Review of African Political Economy* 34(111): 67–84.

The Standard. 2015. '"Mugabe Must Go" Demos Rock Zambian Capital', 25 January. Retrieved 18 September 2018 from http://www.thestandard.co.zw/2015/01/25/mugabe-must-go-demos-rock-zambian-capital/

Statistics South Africa. 2015. 'Quarterly Labour Force Survey', Statistical Release P2011. South Africa. Retrieved 18 September 2018 from http://www.statssa.gov.za/publications/P0211/P02111stQuarter2015.pdf.

Turok, B. 2005. 'The Prospects of a National Democratic Revolution in South Africa'. Paper presented at the Reggen 2005 International Seminar.
UNECA. 2011. *Economic Report on Africa 2011: Governing Development in Africa – The Role of the State in Economic Transformation*. Addis Ababa: UNECA.
ZANU (PF) Manifesto. 2013. 'The People's Manifesto: Taking Back the Economy: Indigenise, Empower, Develop and Create Employment'.
Zulu, P. 2013. *A Nation in Crisis: An Appeal for Morality*. Cape Town: Tafelberg.

Chapter 7

Ethnopolitics and Regionalism, Discipline and Punishment
The Matabeleland Development Question in Postcrisis Zimbabwe

Vusilizwe Thebe

Introduction

Ethnopolitics and regionalism have characterised Zimbabwe's development trajectory since it gained independence in 1980. After a protracted war of liberation, a complex negotiated settlement and an election victory for ZANU (PF), the postcolonial state embarked on nation-state construction. This was a 'struggle to create 'imagined communities' out of regionally, ethnically and racially dispersed 'communities' (Moore 2003: 34) – however fragile it was, and the ease at which such fragility was abrogated with regard to certain sections of society in the context of the state-society complex. In a tale reminiscent of the situation in the rest of postcolonial Africa, the new Zimbabwe became one of the countries in Roe's (1995) continent of 'Except Africa', where nothing appears to work normally.

It turned on those citizens who apparently stood on the way of its designs, using the full weight of its coercive power as an instrument of both discipline and co-option into what Ndlovu-Gatsheni (2008: 34, 47) has labelled a 'Shona-imagined nation'. The disciplinary strategies deployed by the state left certain regions politically and economically disenfranchised and underdeveloped. This was particularly true in the Matabeleland region, where retributive violence and a development embargo left legacies that continue to shape the region's sociopolitical and economic landscape today.

The Matabeleland development question – understood here as perceptions and realities of neglect and disenfranchisement, and the quest for development by people in the region – is by now a reality that presents a complex development problem. This has been worsened by the fact that the local economy was emerging from more than two decades of crisis, and a global economic environment still smarting from the 2008 financial crisis. But still, the Matabeleland development question and its composite elements have received relatively little academic attention, particularly in comparison with the extensive interest in the *Gukurahundi* and post-2000 events.

This chapter explores the elements of the development question, highlighting in particular the historical and political elements. I also emphasise the ethnic and regional dimension and its manifestation in both development politics and demands for development redress. These are illuminated by drawing on Michel Foucault's model of the disciplinary regime. Following Foucault, I see discipline as working through coercion in an attempt to arrange the 'individual's movements and his experience of space and time'.[1] Below I will set out the historical context for discipline and punishment before engaging with the disciplinary strategies and their development implications for a perceived 'dissident region'. The conclusion suggests that post-independence development in Zimbabwe should be understood from the ethnic and regional perspectives and the disciplinary tendencies of an authoritative state.

A Nation Divided by Geography, Ethnicity and Politics

The inequity in development that is currently witnessed in Zimbabwe and what is referred to here as the Matabeleland development question has a complex history. This is often linked to regional/ethnic politics and the unfortunate historical incidents of the nineteenth and twentieth centuries. A detailed discussion of ethnic and regional identity is always a tempting and necessary first step in understanding the state-society complex in Zimbabwe in the immediate aftermath of independence. Not only does ethnicity feature prominently in the analysis of the events between 1982 and 1987, but many elements are also shared with the political (party and election politics) and the socioeconomic (drought relief and land reform and development in general) (see e.g. Alexander 1991, 2006a; Alexander et al. 2000; Herbst 1990; Sachikonye 2011).

In trying to explain how ethnic and regional differences played out in Zimbabwean politics, I begin with the nineteenth-century arrival of the Ndebele in the southwestern parts of Zimbabwe. The literature has shown that the Ndebele embarked on a nation-building process, creating Ndebele ethnic identity through the assimilation of different ethnic groups into the Ndebele nation, and that complex relations soon developed with numerous decentralised Shona dynasties (Ndlovu-Gatsheni 2008; Worby 2001). Despite the complexity of the relations that developed, 'it was common for scholars to highlight only tension, war and destruction' (Alao 2012: 14). While recent scholarship disputes this narrative of Ndebele savagery and aggression, and Shona victimisation, this certainly played a major role in ethnic consciousness (see e.g. Alao 2012; Muzondidya and Ndlovu-Gatsheni 2007; Ranger 1967). In their work '"Echoing Silences": Ethnicity in Post-colonial Zimbabwe, 1980–2007', Muzondidya and Ndlovu-Gatsheni bluntly noted that 'ethnicity has continued to shape and influence the economic, social, and political life of Zimbabwe since the achievement of independence in 1980' (2007: 276).

Second, the colonial conquest and its subsequent consolidation by the British South African Company led to the drawing of national boundaries, bringing together a mix of 'natives' in a single country called Southern Rhodesia (Muzondidya and Ndlovu-Gatsheni 2007). However, this did not bring the two broad ethnic groups together. Rather, through a variety of statutes, the geographical worlds of 'natives' were created miles apart, as the colonial administration created seven provinces, which virtually became regions dominated by different ethnic groups (du Toit 1995). Thus, the Shangani/Tsonga occupied the southeast; the Venda remained in the south of Matabeleland, along the Limpopo Valley; the Tonga settled on the Zambezi escarpment in the northern parts of Matabeleland; the Kalanga and the Ndebele remained in the southwest (Matabeleland); the Karanga occupied the southern parts of the plateau (Masvingo Province); the Zezuru and the Korekore occupied the northern and central parts of Mashonaland (the West, East and Central Provinces) respectively; and the Manyika and Ndau remained in the east (Manyika Province) (Beach 1994; Ranger 1989). While this served to polarise existing ethnic identities, the colonial administrators certainly politicised ethnicity as a strategy of divide and rule, and played one group off against the other. They propagated a powerful narrative that portrayed Shona people as victims of Ndebele aggression, and the white settlers as arbitrators and saviours (Barnes 2004; Muzondidya and Ndlovu-Gatsheni 2007; Ranger 1985). This version of Shona–Ndebele relations was spread through the history curriculum well into the era of independence (Barnes 2004).

The third incident took place in 1963, when a core group of Shona-speaking nationalists engineered a political split from the Zimbabwe African People's Union (ZAPU) to form the *Zimbabwe African National Union* (ZANU). While a number of ethnic Shona nationalists had remained within the ZAPU formation, the split is often seen as an ethnic revolt against the leadership of Joshua Nkomo, who by origin was from the minority Ndebele tribe (Ndlovu-Gatsheni 2008; Nkomo 2001). Augmenting this perspective is the fact that the Ndebele–Shona impasse in ZAPU later led to a second split and formation of the Front for the Liberation of Zimbabwe (FROLIZI) in exile in the 1970s. Although the political split and the post-independence events took place decades apart, one would argue that it became an important contributor to ethnic consciousness and conflict (Alexander 1998; Bhebe 2004; Muzondidya and Ndlovu-Gatsheni 2007; Sachikonye 2011).

The animosity between the two movements spread to the respective military wings, the Zimbabwe People's Revolutionary Army (ZIPRA) and the Zimbabwe African National Liberation Army (ZANLA); and the ordinary supporters on the ground (Alao 1994; Alexander 1998; Bhebe 2004; Sachikonye 2011). What the formation of ZANU in 1963 did was to break the thin façade and expose the ethnic fissures within the nationalist movement and the ordinary people. As others have highlighted, the two groups simply could not coexist, and when they came together, there was often loss of life – they killed each other in Mboroma and in Libya, and the ZIPA experiment failed after ZIPRA cadres were massacred in Tanzania and Mozambique (see e.g. Bhebe 2004: 256; Sachikonye 2011). In common war zones including some parts of Matabeleland South and Mashonaland West, ZIPRA and ZANLA guerrillas were often engaged in fatal skirmishes.

The fourth incident, and rather related to the third, was what Jocelyn Alexander calls the historical accidents of recruitment patterns during the liberation war, including the development of regional areas of recruitment, operations and support, which tribalised both ZIPRA and ZANLA, and their support base (Alexander 1998). After the formation of ZANU and ZANLA, and the independence of Mozambique in 1975, this was hardly surprising. ZANLA had base camps in Mozambique and operated mainly in the Shona-dominated eastern front, while due to the support of Botswana, Zambia and Angola, and a network of rural committees and highly organised party structures together with a long history of nationalist activism in Matabeleland, ZIPRA had more men at the northern front (Brickhill 1995; McGregor 2004; Sibanda 2005). The extent of the damage on Shona–Ndebele relations caused by these incidents cannot be easily underestimated. By the time of Zimbabwe's independence, ethnicity and regionalism were a deep-rooted factor in Zimbabwean society.

Given the context, it is not surprising that ethnic motivated hostilities and distrust were carried over at independence, and the two military wings clashed at Assembly Points (APs) and within the newly integrated units of the Zimbabwe National Army in 1980 and 1981 (Alexander 1998; Sachikonye 2011). In fact, the two guerrilla armies clashed whenever they came into close proximity: Entumbane, Connemara, Ntabazinduna and Glenville (Alexander 1998). It would also be foolhardy to think that Mugabe and ZANU's decision to go it alone during the first democratic elections in 1980, despite attending and signing the Lancaster House Agreement as a combined Patriotic Front, was not an ethnic snub of ZAPU and Nkomo (Laasko 2003; Nkomo 2001). Since these incidents appear to have influenced events in the Matabeleland and Midlands regions after independence, I will now turn to the ethnic or regionally motivated voting trends after independence.

Ethnicity, Political Parties and the Precious Vote

While ZAPU had continued to portray itself as a national party and reflected this in its leadership, which included nationalists of Shona origin like Vice President Josiah Chinamano, Amon Jirira, Joseph Msika, Daniel Nziramasanga and Ariston Chambati, among others, its support became increasingly confined to Matabeleland, parts of the Midlands and a few areas in Mashonaland West (Alexander et al. 2000). This was carried over during the 1980 elections, as voting followed mostly ethnic lines (Cliffe et al. 1980). For example, ZAPU's twenty seats mostly came from Ndebele votes. While ZANLA operations had extended to Matabeleland South during the later stages of the war, and despite incidents of intimidation by ZANLA operatives in areas where both ZANLA and ZIPRA operated, and the threat of a return to war in the event of failure in the elections, ZANU – which contested the elections as ZANU (PF) – won its fifty-seven seats in Shona areas (Alexander et al. 2000; Laasko 2003).

The 1980 elections were certainly a precursor of what followed in future elections. Similar trends followed in the 1984 municipal elections in Bulawayo and the 1985 national elections, where ZAPU recorded impressive victories. In the 1985 national elections, ZAPU had fielded candidates in all constituencies in a new first-past-the-post system rather than the provincial level proportional system of 1980. While it won all the seats in Matabeleland, its total vote dropped significantly after the loss of Shona votes (Kriger 2003; Laasko 2003). What was significant about the outcomes of the 1984 and 1985 elections was the Ndebele position despite the violent military campaign in the region, the leadership vacuum after Nkomo's self-imposed exile and the persecution of ZAPU leaders within Zimbabwe, continued intimidation by state security operatives and ZANU (PF) youth, and ZANU (PF)'s drive for a one-party state (Laasko 2003). The elections certainly polarised Zimbabwean politics into three distinct ethnic/regional groupings and political formations. Laasko (2003: 123) noted that:

> Most of the constituencies, especially in the rural areas, were de facto one-party constituencies whether for ZANU, ZAPU or Sithole's party. Only in cities was there pluralism in terms of more equal voter support between the winning and losing candidates.

While ZANU (PF) won the elections convincingly, the results presented a challenge to the one-party ideology. Thus, the lure of the Ndebele votes and the political hegemony associated with a one-party state forced ZANU (PF) to engage ZAPU in dialogue. It was assisted in this by ZAPU's desire to end the conflict and suffering in Matabeleland, and the hope that development would finally return to the region (Alexander 2006b). Thus, a Unity Accord that integrated ZAPU into the ZANU (PF) party was signed in 1987 after protracted negotiations, which were often punctuated by intimidation, raids and arrests, and a ban of ZAPU, to push the agreement through despite some key issues of concern (Bilin and Andrew 1999; Laasko 2003). After the Accord, ZAPU officials were included in the cabinet, the *politburo* and the central committee.

While the post-Unity Accord period coincided with the new opposition from Tekere's Zimbabwe Unity Movement (ZUM), ZANU could now count on Ndebele votes. Indeed, the Ndebele threw their weight behind former ZAPU officials who were now part of the ZANU (PF) formation (Alexander and McGregor 2001). Even then, people still demonstrated their dissatisfaction and disapproval of ZANU (PF) through apathy and an exceptionally high number of spoilt votes (Laasko 2003). If this was a passive resistance to being co-opted into ZANU (PF), it transformed into an outright rejection after the formation of the Movement for Democratic Change (MDC), and manifested itself through the embarrassing defeat suffered by ZANU (PF) and its former ZAPU officials in Matabeleland and significant parts of the Midlands (Alexander and McGregor 2001; Laasko 2003; Alexander 2006b). In Matabeleland, the MDC won twenty-one of the twenty-three parliamentary seats including a clean sweep in Bulawayo, where former ZAPU stalwarts like Joseph Musika, John Nkomo and Dumiso Dabengwa, who once enjoyed godly status, lost by wide margins (Alexander and McGregor 2001; Alexander 2006b).[2] Dabengwa summed up his defeat better when he told the press that even if he had stood against a donkey, he was still going to lose (Alexander and McGregor 2001; Alexander 2006b).

Disciplining a 'Dissident Region'

It would be ridiculous to pretend that the election results in 1980 and the post-1980 period had no relevance in relation to the catalogue of events that were set in motion immediately after independence, though of course some happened independently. The general consensus among the Ndebele is that ZANU (PF) saw the Ndebele defiance (first in 1980, then in the 1984 municipality elections in Bulawayo and finally the 1985 national elections) as a serious challenge to its hegemony. Musemwa (2006) noted sinister motives by the government to postpone municipality elections in Bulawayo and not in other cities or towns. Accordingly, President Mugabe had issued a stern warning about the dangers of voting for a 'dissident party', and had given people the 'last chance' to vote 'right' (cf. Musemwa 2006: 242). In disciplinary regimes, the deployment of mechanisms of power as an instrument of subjugation is a common phenomenon. In the context of ZANU (PF)'s revolutionary image – often played through intimidation campaign tactics by its cadres and careless talk of 'returning to war' by its leadership – when the postcolonial state fell back on its coercive powers to accelerate the subjectivity of the Ndebele regions, nothing was surprising (Laasko 2003; Sachikonye 2011). In all probability, by voting ZANU (PF) into office, the future pathway was determinedly clear – that the party would doubtless fall back on coercive strategies to rid itself of obstacles in its way.

As Drinkwater (1989: 128–34) noted, 'ZANU (PF)'s ideology was constituted by a populist endorsement of pragmatism and nationalism'. Thus, it was forced into an uneasy policy of moderation and reconciliation towards ZAPU and whites who were willing to work with the government (Alexander 1994). It invited ZAPU to form part of a Government of National Unity as a junior partner and allocated ZAPU only five posts in a 36-seat cabinet, but failed to nature the reconciliation process by withdrawing the five posts at the first sign of conflict (Laasko 2003). As Alexander (1998: 155) noted, 'this certainly worried ZAPU and ZIPRA cadres'. This was not helped by certain developments within the integrated army and the incarceration of ZIPRA commanders (Alao 1994; Alexander 1998; Laasko 2003). While, in all fairness, not all ZIPRA cadres disserted from the army and not all deserters took up arms, incidents of dissidence increased in Matabeleland (Alao 1994; Alexander 1998; Laasko 2003).

Getting Rid of a 'Filthy Obstacle'

The state's response was unprecedented. It deployed its coercive instruments – the infantry (ZNA), the Police Support Unit (PSU), the Central Intelligence Organisation (CIO) and the Paratroopers in Matabeleland and the Midlands between 1982 and 1987 (Catholic Commission for Justice and Peace and the Legal Resources Foundation (CCJP and LRF 1997; Alexander 1998; Kriger 2003). Alongside these conventional security instruments, it also unleashed a special North Korean-trained military unit (the 5th Brigade) on civilians (Alao 1994; Alexander 1998; Kriger 2003). The operation was code-named 'Gukurahundi', in reference to the first summer rains that wash away the filth, and was ostensibly targeted at renegade former ZIPRA guerrillas, but the casualties were overwhelmingly ordinary civilians. The trail of human rights violations, when they were finally exposed, shocked the world: starvation, murder, rape, abduction, torture and beatings, disappearances and mass detentions (Alexander 1998, CCJP and LRF 1997; Kriger 2003: 31). People were forced to speak the Shona language, attend night gatherings known as *pungwes*, sing and dance, and denounce Nkomo and being Ndebele in what some saw as cultural indoctrination (Mozondidya and Ndlovu-Gatsheni, 2007; Ndlovu-Gatsheni 2008). As the CCJP (2008) noted, the dance was forced, the songs were in an unfamiliar language and these were often spiced with physical torture (see excerpts from the CCJP and LRF below). These are the excerpts from '*Breaking the Silence: Report on the 1980s Disturbances in Matabeleland and the Midlands*', which was compiled by the Catholic Commission for Justice and Peace in Zimbabwe, March 1997.

Besides the loss of life and dignity, people also lost rural homes and assets, and thousands were displaced to Bulawayo and neighbouring states (Herbst 1990; Musemwa 2006). The postcolonial Zimbabwean rulers perceived the military campaign in the Matabeleland and Midlands regions as necessary after 1982. In the words of a leading Ndebele scholar, 'the violence was in a way symptomatic of the failure of a smooth blending of major ethnicities into a new national identity called Zimbabwe ... Matabeleland had to be conquered and forced into part of Zimbabwe' (Ndlovu-Gatsheni 2008: 47).

In his analysis of the post-independence events in Matabeleland and the Midlands, Ngwabi Bhebe places emphasis on historical occurrences and expresses reservations as to whether ZAPU would have behaved differently had it won the elections or whether a ZIPRA-dominated army would have fought the war differently in Mashonaland (Bhebe 2004; cf. Ndlovu-Gatsheni 2008). But the *Gukuharundi* has remained a reality and living reminder to survivors, and is visible in every facet of life in

1. 5 Brigade was destined to become the most controversial army unit ever formed in Zimbabwe. Within weeks of being mobilised at the end of January 1993 under Colonel Perence Shiri, 5 Brigade was responsible for mass murders, beatings and property burnings in the communal living areas of Northern Matabeleland, where hundreds of thousands of ZAPU supporters lived.

2. Within the space of six weeks, more than 2000 civilians had died, hundreds of homesteads had been burnt, and thousands of civilians had been beaten. Most of the dead were killed in public executions, involving between 1 and 12 people at a time. The largest number of dead in a single incident so far on record was in Lupane, where 62 men and women were shot on the banks of the Cewale River on 5 March.

3. [In Matabeleland South], in addition to the food embargo, mass detentions became a deliberate strategy of 5 Brigade activity. At least 2000 men and women, including adolescents, could be held at one time in Bhalagwe Camp, near Maphisa (Antelope) in Matobo. People were detained for several days or weeks, in appalling conditions. Many people died, and others suffered permanent injuries. It is likely that around 8,000 civilians were detained during these few months, possibly many more. Once more, it was mainly innocent civilians who suffered.

4. The strategy of 5 Brigade varied in the two regions of Matabeleland, with Matabeleland North experiencing more public executions, and Matabeleland South experiencing more wide-spread detention, beatings and deaths at Bhalagwe camp: both areas experienced mass beatings in the village setting.

5. Victims from most areas report that 5 Brigade would forbid people who were badly injured by them from seeking medical attention. In some cases 5 Brigade would return the day after they had been in an area, to "execute" badly injured victims. Other interviews report victims who spend several days with agonising injuries, too afraid to leave their huts, before finally they were helped by fellow villagers to make harrowing journeys on back paths, with the victim in a wheelbarrow or scotch cart, to get medical attention.

Figure 7.1 Excerpts from the CCJP and LRF report. Source: Witherell (1997).

Matabeleland – family reunions, crumbling school buildings, the kraal, the roads, the veld, the widows and orphans, the song and dance by innocent schoolchildren – and, more importantly, opposition political parties often use the *Gukurahundi* conflict as a draw card to win the coveted Ndebele vote.[3]

Covert Strategies: Starving Dissidents

The *Gukurahundi* was finally withdrawn from Matabeleland after a publicity campaign by civil society organisations in 1984 (Alexander 1998; Aloa 2012). Instead of a *Gukurahundi*, people in the region were now served with yet another policy menu, centred on discrimination and marginalisation. While some within the ruling party in Matabeleland remain in denial about the state neglect of Ndebele-occupied areas (for example, Cain Mathema), there is evidence that Matabeleland lags behind other provinces in terms of development (Mathema 2013). The interaction between ethnicity/regionalism and state resources in post-independence Zimbabwe deserves particular mention. Large chunks of investment and development funding continue to be directed towards Mashonaland regions, while the needs of minority populations in Matabeleland are ignored by the state (Fisher 2010: 148).

While it is important not to overgeneralise, perceptions about the *shonaisation* of the country's wealth are dominant and have subsequently led to the radicalisation of demands for political and administrative redress. The people of Matabeleland feel neglected, excluded, marginalised, dominated and more like second-class citizens (see Alexander et al. 2000; Alexander 2006b; Ndlovu-Gatsheni 2011). Frustrations with government policy towards Matabeleland climaxed in the 1990s, when senior politicians who had signed the Unity Accord openly criticised the government for discriminatory treatment, and Ndebele diaspora online communities emerged alongside cultural groups in Matabeleland to lobby for change (Ndlovu-Gatsheni 2008; Peel 2010).

Infrastructural Development

In the context of conflict and a security risk due to the military campaign and South African destabilisation strategies, development projects dried up in Matabeleland after 1982 (Bilin and Andrew 1999; Musemwa 2006). Similarly, expectations after the signing of the Unity Accord in 1987 were frustrated as little resulted in the form of postconflict reconstruction or payback for agreeing to the union with ZANU (PF) (Alexander et al. 2000; Alexander and McGregor 2001; Musemwa 2006).

Despite the unveiling of capital projects like road development, rural growth centres, agricultural markets, irrigation systems and health centres nationwide, as the country reaped the fruits of independence, Matabeleland was left out (Alexander and McGregor 2001; Fisher 2010). While new schools were built and others were upgraded immediately after independence, when the infrastructural provision through the reconstruction programme expanded throughout the country, but people in Matabeleland would struggle to identify any road infrastructure developed after independence (Eppel 2013: 228).

The colonial government developed the available road infrastructure. Roads often terminated at district administration centres, while all roads connecting to communal areas were untarred. These developments were geared at catering for the needs of white colonial officials. More than thirty years after independence, rural communities are still connected by untarred roads, but more importantly, the colonial roads have not been upgraded and are in pretty bad shape. For example, the colonial state left a strip of tarred road to the Kezi District offices in Matabeleland South, and this has not been upgraded. The single-lane road Nkayi Road in Matabeleland North has not been upgraded, despite numerous accidents and fatalities. The two single-lane roads connecting Bulawayo to Tsholotsho in Matabeleland North Province are now in a state of disrepair, while the construction of the 40 km section of the Beitbridge/Bulawayo Highway took over fifteen years to complete. Lupane, now the provincial capital of Matabeleland North, Gwanda, the provincial capital of Matabeleland South, and the border town of Plumtree have a little more fortunate due to access through the A8, A7 and A6 Highways, respectively. Even luckier was the poor and neglected Binga District, which was rewarded with a road connection from the A8 Highway. This was mainly because the first Governor of Matabeleland North, Mr Jacob Mudenda, was of Tongan origin, and until his involvement in corruption scandal that came to be known as *Willowgate* was central to ZANU (PF)'s strategy to attract Tongan votes.[4]

Disparities in development between Matabeleland and the rest of the country continue to dominate political debates and become politically significant points in every election. More recently, Dumiso Dabengwa, the President of ZAPU, told the country: 'ZAPU is convinced the people of Matabeleland and some parts of the Midlands have genuine grievances against the current governance system that has disadvantaged them' (Dabengwa 2011).

Land Reform and Redistribution

One area of development concern, which has led to clamours for redress, is land redistribution and resettlement. Despite well-documented past land alienations, the Ndebele did not benefit from the post-independence land reform process. First, the restrictions that accompanied the land acquisition process during the first phase of land reform meant that land acquired for resettlement in Matabeleland was marginal for farming. Second, land that was acquired was mostly leased to commercial ranchers, civil servants and parastatals (Alexander 1991). During the Fast Track Land Reform and Resettlement process, land mainly went to ex-combatants, ZANU (PF) members and their relatives (Sithole et al. 2003; Thebe 2018). Even then, good land was allocated as commercial A2 plots, while the ordinary person could only access A1 category land, often on former ranches.

While the land reform exercise has been hailed as a success (e.g. Scoones et al. 2010; Moyo 2011), in the Matabeleland regions, the majority of the needy population was left out due to the inherent politics. Those who helped themselves to a piece of former ranch land found themselves holding on to land with very little livelihood value, with virtually no support from the state in a changing climatic environment and a new farming system (Thebe 2018). Even in the context of landing the economy, land reform for crop production in Matabeleland was tantamount to the betrayal of the very objectives of land reform and redistribution.

The Politics of Water for Bulawayo: Disciplining a Dissident City

Perhaps the postcolonial state's most controversial policy towards Matabeleland was the failure to find a lasting solution to Bulawayo's water problems, despite the situation degenerating into a humanitarian disaster. While the availability of water is dependent on environmental factors (precipitation, runoff and temperatures) and Bulawayo is prone to drought, mainly due to its location in the semi-arid zone, I agree with Musemwa (2006: 240) that it 'has as much to do with the command over the distribution of scarce resources as with the environment' (see also Gunby et al. 2001). The postcolonial state failed to improve and expand the city's water delivery system, despite the massive growth of the city since independence. The city has five supply dams, all situated in a region with low precipitation and on rivers with poor catchment, and since 1976 the government has not developed a single dam for Bulawayo

(Gunby et al. 2001; Musemwa 2006). In part, this reflects the complexities of Zimbabwe's ethnic and electoral politics since 1980, particularly what we may term postelection reprisal.

The first post-independence water crisis started in 1983 and up to 1993, the city experienced three water shedding regimes due to a series of droughts (1984–85, 1987–88 and 1991–93), yet the central government could not assist the city council in finding a lasting water solution. It is interesting that short, medium and long-term solutions to the water problems are known, and have been debated and documented in various forums (Gunby et al. 2001). Only the short-term solution, which central government was prepared to back, was implemented. The central government preferred that 'potential water sources near Bulawayo should be exhaustively exploited' before exploring other solutions *(Musemwa 2006: 245)*. This was achieved through the development of the *Nyamandlovu aquifer*. The medium-term solution included the damming of the Mshabezi and Glassblock Rivers, and the duplication of the Insiza pipeline. Although the Mtshabezi Dam was developed, its water only managed to reach the people of Bulawayo in December 2012.[5]

The Zambezi Water Project, long seen not only as a long-term solution to the water crisis but also as a region-wide livelihood programme, remains in a state of limbo (Gunby et al. 2001; Musemwa 2006). While good progress has been made in terms of initiating the Gwayi/Shangani Dam, construction works have stalled. After much dilly-dallying and politicking, central government awarded the project to a Chinese construction company. The company conducted surveys and then set about the task of dam construction, only to stop again. While this is happening, water woes have deepened, forcing a water rationing regime of up to 96 hours a week as the city has struggled to keep the taps flowing due to dwindling water levels in the five supply dams.

The idea of diverting water from the Zambezi River to Bulawayo via a pipeline is not new. It has been part of the agenda of various colonial administrations since 1902, but never took off due to the costs involved (Musemwa 2006). It was resuscitated after the 1991 water crisis, when various stakeholders in Matabeleland formed the Matabeleland Zambezi Water Project (MZWP) to manage, fundraise and implement the project (Gunby et al. 2001; Musemwa 2006). However, even before the MZWP had started its task, the government created the Matabeleland Zambezi Water Trust (MZWT) as a parallel lobby, which ultimately incapacitated the MZWP. As leading Bulawayo economist Eric Bloc (2004) noted: 'The project was hijacked from the city years ago, and there has been no substantive progress other than for repeated promises and press statements (and especially so ahead of each parliamentary and presidential election.'

The issue of cost aside, people had their eyes set on larger things, which included water for Bulawayo and an agricultural green belt in Matabeleland, and they saw the failure by the government to sanction the project as a punitive strategy. It was envisaged that water would be diverted to irrigate as much as 60,000 ha of land; that Bulawayo supply dams would be released for irrigation in Matabeleland South; and that the project would create between 150,000 and 300,000 jobs, and would contribute 2–6 per cent to the country's gross domestic product (GDP) (Gunby et al. 2001).

Deindustrialisation in Bulawayo

It is tempting to attribute deindustrialisation in Bulawayo (the collapse of some enterprises and relocation of some to the capital) to the general lack of response to the region's development needs by the state. However, it seems more likely that deindustrialisation was a result of the economic downturn since 1993, when the country signed into Economic Structural Adjustment Programme (ESAP) (Saunders 1996; Carmody and Taylor 2003). This certainly affected Bulawayo and the Matabeleland region as a whole. In the context of colonial evictions and the development of capitalism in Zimbabwe, Bulawayo had become the main livelihood centre for worker-peasant Ndebele communities in areas of restricted agricultural potential. It was the industrial capital of Zimbabwe, with a broad industrial sector, surrounded by mining establishments. It also housed the headquarters of parastatals like the National Railways of Zimbabwe and the Cold Storage Commission. Large companies like the Treger Group, National Blankets, the Zimbabwe Engineering Company (ZECO), Merlin, G & D Shoes, Hunyani Holdings, Radar Metals and Dunlop provided employment to thousands of people and funded the operations of Bulawayo City Council. However, these are now outdated in a city that former President Mugabe once labelled a 'Ghost City'.

While giant industrial companies like Zeco, More Steel, More Wear and General Steel remain closed, others continue to operate at minimum capacity, a situation that has thrown the livelihoods of over 20,000 workers into jeopardy (Ndou 2011; Mwase 2012). A 2009 study commissioned by the Ministry of Industry and Commerce showed that one hundred companies had closed shop. In 2012 alone, one hundred companies had wound up operations, while several others were reportedly in distress (Bhebhe 2012). Quiet obviously, the continuing deindustrialisation in Bulawayo, despite the relative stabilisation of the country's economy after the Government of National Unity, has been cause for concern for all actors. Thus, the *Distressed and Marginalised Area Fund* (Dimaf), a fund that was established by the government and Old Mutual to fund business activities in formerly neglected areas like Matabeleland, gave people much-needed hope.

However, the fund has not reached the majority of companies due to a failure by the government to honour its side of the bargain, as well as bureaucratic bundling. There are also growing concerns that the funds were being diverted to companies in Harare (Karimakwenda 2012). People in the region note sinister motives and a plan to sabotage the rescue mission. Augmenting people's suspicions is the fact that the man who controlled the national purse at the time (between 2009 and 2013), former Finance Minister Tendai Biti, originates from the Mashonaland region. It is no coincidence that the then Minister of Industry and Commerce, Professor Welshman Ncube, recently called for Matabeleland to have an independent financial sector to provide capitalisation for industry and commerce in the region.

Food Aid and Relief

The other major area in which people felt hard done by was food and humanitarian assistance. The early years of Zimbabwe's independence are often remembered for what came to be called an 'agricultural miracle', but the country also experienced four severe droughts in 1982/84, 1986/87, 1991/92 and 1994/95 (Bird and Shepherd 2003; Musemwa 2006). The impact of these droughts was particularly severe in Natural Agro-regions IV and V, where droughts are recurrent, and occur even during years of moderate to good rainfall nationally. In short, droughts affected maize output and increased the demand for humanitarian assistance. While state and nongovernmental organisations (NGO) drought-relief schemes were launched nationally during three of the four droughts, in some regions drought relief for some households were perennial (Kinsey et al. 1998).

Although these schemes were extended to Matabeleland, there was political pressure on ZANU (PF) officials on the ground to engage on patronage politics (Alexander 2006a). Also, the government failed to maintain a sustained response to Matabeleland during years when other regions had a good harvest. This put pressure on households to provide for their own food security. This in turn led to increased cross-border movements and the movement of goods to Matabeleland (Maphosa 2010; Thebe 2011a). While recent Ndebele scholarship associates these manifestations with a wider process of reciprocal disengagement by citizens (e.g.

Thebe 2013; see also Ndlovu-Gatsheni 2008), the Matabeleland problem and its composite development question continue to have a bearing on the politics of postcrisis Zimbabwe.

Conclusion

The historiography on Zimbabwe's national politics, from the eighteenth-century arrival of the Ndebele to the postcolonial period, and the post-independence state–Ndebele relations open up a number of avenues for thinking about development, inequality and poverty in postcolonial Zimbabwe, and in making sense of the development demands in the twenty-first century. One avenue that enjoys regional consensus and one that is reinforced by evidence of glaring disparities between two regions, the dominions of two major ethnic groups, is the deployment of the ethnic and regional dice. In their popular book *Violence and Memory: One Hundred Years in the 'Dark Forests' of Matabeleland*, Alexander et al. (2000) offered a typology of overt and covert violations on the Ndebele. These ranged from violence by the 5th Brigade to the withdrawal and diversion of resources from Matabeleland, which when aligned with 'historical memories, reinforced the widely held belief that Matabeleland was being discriminated against on ethnic grounds' (Gewald 2001: 124).

The state did not intend to achieve security and stability in Matabeleland and the Midlands through a political and military solution, and lack of development; rather, these should be seen in the context of the region's threat to ZANU (PF)'s imagined nation-state. This also built on existing political and ethnic tensions, built over decades of interaction. Drawing upon Michel Foucault's model of the disciplinary regime, I view ZANU (PF)'s deployment of the instruments of the state both as a disciplinary move and as punishment. Following on from earlier Ndebele scholarship, violence and starvation served as a reminder to the people in Matabeleland of the power of the state to determine their destiny (see e.g. Ndlovu-Gatsheni 2008). In a dark irony of history, the retributive actions, which were wielded by the postcolonial state on a region perceived to be dissident, continue to haunt future governments as the Matabeleland problem and its composite development question increasingly assumes relevance in twenty-first century Zimbabwe.

Vusilizwe Thebe is Associate Professor in Development Studies and Coordinator of the Development Studies programme at the University of Pretoria. His research interests focus on migrant labour societies and their transformation: the worker-peasantry and its dynamics, the context of its existence, its relationship to land and labour, its transition over time, and its interaction with state institutions and policy, gender dynamics and agrarian transformation.

Notes

1. Cited from https://www.sparknotes.com/philosophy/disciplinepunish/summary/.
2. Dumiso Dabengwa was the former ZIPRA intelligence Chief who was incarcerated for four years by the ZANU (PF) government. Upon his release, he was co-opted into the government and became a member of ZANU (PF)'s *politiburo*. After the troubled 2008 election, he initiated the official divorce of ZAPU from ZANU (PF) and was later elected President.
3. The kraal is a significant part to the *gukurahundi* violence since the violence and murders were committed using the huge poles used to house the cattle in the kraal at night (*umgoqo*), while due to the deployment of Shona teachers even at the primary level in Matabeleland, children are now familiar with Shona songs and dancing routines.
4. 'Willowgate' was a Zimbabwean political scandal that occurred in 1988–89, in which government officials purchased discounted cars from a government-owned car assembly plant and then sold them at exorbitant prices.
5. While the pipeline connecting the dam to Umzingwane was completed, the dam pumping capacity restricted water supply to an average of 3,000 cubic metres of water to the city daily, compared to an expected 17,000.

References

Alao, A.M. 1994. *Brothers at War: Dissidence and Rebellion in Southern Africa*. London: British Academy Press.
_____. 2012. *Mugabe and the Politics of Security in Zimbabwe*. Montreal: McGill-Queen's Press.
Alexander, J. 1991. 'The Unsettled Land: The Politics of Land Distribution in Matabeleland, 1980–1990', *Journal of Southern African Studies* 17(4): 581–610.
_____. 1994. 'State, Peasantry and Resettlement in Zimbabwe', *Review of African Political Economy* 21(61): 325–45.
_____. 1998. 'Dissidents Perspectives on Zimbabwe's Post-independence War', *Africa* 68(2): 152–82.
_____. 2006a. *The Unsettled Land: State-Making and the Politics of Land in Zimbabwe, 1893–2003*. Oxford: James Currey.
_____. 2006b. 'Legacies of Violence in Matabeleland, Zimbabwe', in P. Kaarsholm (ed.), *Violence, Political Culture and Development in Africa*. Oxford: James Currey, pp. 105–21.
Alexander, J., and J. McGregor. 2001. 'Elections, Land and Politics of Opposition in Matabeleland', *Journal of Agrarian Change* 1(4): 510–33.

Alexander, J., J. McGregor and T. Ranger (eds). 2000. *Violence and Memory: One Hundred Years in the 'Dark Forests' of Matabeleland.* Oxford: James Currey.

Barnes, T. 2004. 'Reconciliation, Ethnicity and School History in Zimbabwe', in B. Raftopoulous and T. Savage. (eds.), *Zimbabwe: Injustice and Political Reconciliation 1980–2002.* Cape Town: Institute for Justice and Peace, pp. 140–59.

Beach, D. 1994. *The Shona and Their Neighbours.* Oxford: Blackwell.

Bhebe, N. 2004. *Simon Vengayi Muzenda and the Struggle for and Liberation of Zimbabwe.* Gweru: Mambo Press.

Bhebhe, N. 2012. 'Bulawayo's Dying Industry: Is there Hope for Revival?', *Newsday,* 22 November. Retrieved 3 October 2018 from: https://www.newsday.co.zw/2012/11/bulawayos-dying-industry-is-there-hope-for-revival/.

Bilin, N., and G. Andrew. 1999. *Development Centre Studies Conflict and Growth in Africa: Southern Africa, Volume 3.* Paris: OECD Press.

Bloc, E. 2004. 'Unfounded Rumours of Bulawayo's Death', *The Independent,* 29 October.

Brickhill, J. 1995. 'Daring to Storm the Heavens: The Military Strategies of ZAPU, 1976 –79', in N. Bhebe and T. Ranger (eds), *Soldiers in the Zimbabwe's Liberation War.* London: James Currey, pp. 48–72.

Carmody, P., and S. Taylor. 2003. 'Industry and the Urban Sector in Zimbabwe's Political Economy', *African Studies Quarterly* 7(2–3): 53–80.

CCJP. 2008. *Gukurahundi in Zimbabwe: A Report on the Disturbances in Matabeleland and Midlands, 1980–1988.* New York: Columbia University Press.

CCJP and LRF. 1997. *Breaking the Silence, Building True Peace: A Report on the Disturbances in Matabeleland and the Midlands, 1980–1989.* Harare: Catholic Commission for Justice and Peace (CCJP) & Legal Resources Foundation (LRF).

Cliffe, L., J. Mpofu and B. Munslow. 1980. 'Nationalist Politics in Zimbabwe: The 1980 Elections and beyond', *Review of African Political Economy* 7(18): 44–67.

Dabengwa, D. 2011. 'Zapu against Secession of Matabeleland', *The Herald,* 4 May. Retrieved 19 June 2015 from https://www.herald.co.zw/zapu-against-secession-of-matabeleland/.

Drinkwater, M. 1989. 'Technical Development and Peasant Impoverishment: Land Use Policy in Zimbabwe's Midlands Province', *Journal of Southern African Studies* 15: 287–305.

du Toit, P. 1995. *State Building and Democracy in Southern Africa: Botswana, Zimbabwe, and South Africa.* Washington DC: United States Institute of Peace.

Eppel, S. 2013. 'Repairing a Fractured Nation: Challenges and Opportunities in Post-GPA Zimbabwe', in B. Raftopolos (ed.), *The Hard Road to Reform: The Politics of Zimbabwe's Global Political Agreement.* Harare: Weaver Press, pp. 211–50.

Fisher, J.L. 2010. *Pioneers, Settlers, Aliens, Exiles: The Decolonisation of White Identity in Zimbabwe.* Canberra: ANU Press.

Foucault, M. (n.d.). 'Discipline and Punishment Summary', *Sparknotes.* Retrieved 3 October 2018 from https://www.sparknotes.com/philosophy/disciplinepunish/summary/.

Gewald, J. 2001. 'Violence and Memory: One Hundred Years in the 'Dark Forests' of Matabeleland by Jocelyn Alexander, Joanne McGregor and Terence Ranger, Portmouth: N. H. Heinemann, 2000. Book Review', *African Studies Review* 44(3): 122–25.

Gunby, D., R. Mpande and A. Thomas. 2001. 'The Campaign for Water from the Zambezi for Bulawayo', in Susan Carr, David Humphreys and Alan Thomas (eds), *Environmental Policies and NGO Influence: Land Degradation and Sustainable Resource Management in Sub-Saharan Africa*. Abingdon: Routledge, pp. 72–93.

Herbst, J. 1990. *State Politics in Zimbabwe*. Berkeley: University of California Press.

Karimakwenda, T. 2012. 'Government Breaks Promise to Fund Companies in Bulawayo', *SW Radio Africa*, 11 May. Retrieved 19 June 2015 from https://allafrica.com/stories/201205140162.html.

Kinsey, B.H., K. Burger and J.H. Gunning. 1998. 'Coping with Drought in Zimbabwe: Survey Evidence on Responses of Rural Households to Risk', *World Development* 26(1): 89–110.

Kriger, J.N. 2003. *Guerrilla Veterans in Post-war Zimbabwe*. Cambridge: Cambridge University Press.

Laasko, L. 2003. 'Opposition Politics in Independent Zimbabwe', *African Studies Quarterly* 7(2–3): 119–37.

Maphosa, F. 2010. 'Transnationalism and Undocumented Migration between Zimbabwe and South Africa', in J. Crush, and D. Tevera (eds), *Zimbabwe's Exodus: Crisis, Migration, Survival*. Cape Town: SAMP/Ottawa: IDRC, pp. 346–62.

Mathema, C. 2013. 'Myth About the President Not Developing Matabeleland', *The Chronicle*, 09 July. Retrieved 3 October 2018 from: https://www.chronicle.co.zw/myth-about-the-president-not-developing-matabeleland/.

McGregor, J. 2004. 'Containing Violence: Poisoning and Guerrilla/Civilian Relations in Memories of Zimbabwe's Liberation War', in K.L. Rogers, S. Leydesdorff and G. Dawson (eds), *Trauma: Life Stories of Survivors*. New York: Routledge, pp. 131–59.

Moore, D. 2003. 'Zimbabwe's Triple Crisis: Primitive Accumulation, Nation-State formation and Democratisation in the Age of Neo-liberal Globalization', *African Studies Quarterly* 7(2–3): 33–51.

Musemwa, M. 2006. 'Disciplining a "Dissident" City: Hydropolitics in the City of Bulawayo, Matabeleland, Zimbabwe, 1980–1994', *Journal of Southern African Studies* 32(2): 239–54.

Muzondidya, J., and S.J. Ndlovu-Gatsheni. 2007. '"Echoing Silences": Ethnicity in Post-colonial Zimbabwe, 1980–2007', *African Journal on Conflict Resolution* 7(2): 275–97.

Mwase, E. 2012. 'Death of Zimbabwe's Industrial Hub', *Sunday Mail*, 12 May. Retrieved 18 September 2018 from http://www.sundaymail.co.zw/index.php?option=com_content&view=article&id=28657:death-of-zi..#.UcAUt9iTXTM.

Ndlovu, R. 2012. 'Bulawayo's Taps Tightened as Water Shortage Bites', *Mail & Guardian*, 12 October. Retrieved 15 June 2015 from https://mg.co.za/article/2012-10-12-00-bulawayos-taps-tightened-as-water-shortage-bites.

Ndlovu-Gatsheni, S.J. 2008. 'Nation Building in Zimbabwe and the Challenge of Ndebele Particularism', *African Journal of Conflict Resolution* 8(3): 27–55.

———. 2011. 'The Changing Politics of Matebeleland since 1980', Solidarity Peace Trust. Retrieved 19 September 2018 from http://www.solidaritypeacetrust. org/994/the-changing-politics-of-matebeleland-since-1980.

Ndou, P. 2011. '20 000 Workers Lost their Jobs in Bulawayo', *Bulawayo 24 News*, 06 June. Retrieved 03 October 2019 from https://bulawayo24.com/index-id-news-sc-local-byo-3841-article-20+000+workers+lost+their+jobs+in+bulawayo.html.

Nkomo J.M. 2001. *The Story of My Life*. Harare: SAPES.

Peel, C. 2010. 'Exile and the Internet: Ndebele and Mixed-Race Online Diaspora', in J. MacGregor and R. Primorac (eds), *Zimbabwe's New Diaspora: Displacement and the Cultural Politics of Survival*. New York: Berghahn Books, pp. 229–45.

Ranger, T.O. 1967. *Revolt in Southern Rhodesia*. London: James Currey.

———. 1985. *The Invention of tribalism in Zimbabwe*. Gweru: Mambo Press.

———. 1989. 'Missionaries, Migrants and the Manyika: The Invention of Ethnicity in Zimbabwe', in L. Vail (ed.), *The Creation of Tribalism in Southern Africa*. London: James Currey, pp. 118–50.

Roe, E.M. 1995. 'Except-Africa: Postscript to a Special Section on Development Narratives', *World Development* 23(6): 1065–1069.

Sachikonye, L.M. 2011. *When a State Turns on its Citizens: 60 Years of Institutionalised Violence and Political Culture*. Harare: Weaver Press.

Saunders, R. 1996. 'Zimbabwe: ESAP's Fables', *Southern Africa Report Archive* 1 (2): 8. Retrieved 19 September 2018 from http://www.africafiles.org/article.asp?ID=3894.

Scoones, I., N. Marongwe, B. Mavedzenge, F. Murimbarimba, J. Mahenehene and C. Sukume. 2010. *Zimbabwe's Land Reform: Myths and Realities*. Oxford: James Currey.

Sibanda, E. 2005. *The Zimbabwe African People's Union, 1961–87: A Political History of Insurgency in Southern Rhodesia*. Trenton, NJ: Africa World Press.

Sibanda, T. 2011. 'Bureaucracy Delays Resuscitation of Bulawayo Industries', *The Zimbabwean*, 18 November. Retrieved 19 June 2015 from https://www.thezimbabwean.co/2011/11/bureaucracy-delays-resuscitation-of-bulawayo/.

Sithole, B., B. Campbell, D. Doré and W. Kozanyi. 2003. 'Narratives on Land: State–Peasant Relations over Fast Track Land Reform in Zimbabwe', *African Studies Quarterly* 7(2–3): 81–95.

Taylor, I. 2006. *China and Africa: Engagement and Compromise*. New York: Routledge.

Thebe, V. 2011. 'From South Africa with Love: The "Malayisha" System and Ndebele Households' Quest for Livelihood Reconstruction in South-Western Zimbabwe', *Journal of Modern African Studies* 49(4): 647–70.

———. 2013. '"Discipline and Disengagement": Cross-border Migration and the Quest for Identity among the Ndebele of South-Western Zimbabwe', in S.J. Ndlovu-Gatsheni and B. Mhlanga (eds), *Bondage of Boundaries and 'the Toxic Other' in Post-colonial Africa: The 'Northern Problem' and Identity Politics in the 21st Century*. Pretoria: Africa Institute of South Africa (AISA), pp. 205–221.

———. 2018. 'Youth, Agriculture and Land Reform in Zimbabwe: Experiences from a Communal Area and Resettlement Scheme in Semi-arid Matabeleland, Zimbabwe, *African Studies* 77(3): 336–353.

Wetherell, I. 1997. 'The Matabeleland Report: A Lot to Hide'. Southern African Report (SAR)12(3), June 1997. Retrieved 3 October 2018 from http://www.africafiles.org/printableversion.asp?id=3843.

Worby, E.L. 2001. 'A Redivided Land? New Agrarian Conflicts and Questions in Zimbabwe', *Journal of Agrarian Change* 1(4): 475–509.

Chapter 8

The Politics of Land Ownership in South Africa
Self-Perceptions and Identities of Backyard Dwellers within the Coloured Community

Wendy Isaacs-Martin

Introduction

Backyard dwellers form part of an increasing population of informal settlements across South Africa. At present, even with legislative changes such as the Breaking New Ground (BNG) Policy Housing Strategy, a large proportion of the population remain without formal permanent housing (Govender et al. 2011b). This has created an environment of competition amongst communities for access to resources and a distrust of government structures, and it has incited incidences of ethnic racial confrontation (Hweshe 2009). Further, this is complicated by the lack of communication between leadership structures and populations who feel that they are being ignored, marginalised or excluded from certain processes (Bank 2007; Radebe 2014). The question posed in this chapter is: do backyard dwellers perceive that racial identifiers are linked to spatial planning and (re)distribution?

The issues of land, housing and spatial development are complex issues in South Africa. The historical legacy of segregation, discrimination and marginalisation resulted in a population that existed on the periphery of towns and cities with little invested in property ownership. Since 1994, many informal settlement residents and backyard dwellers believed that they would receive free houses from the African National Congress (ANC)-led government. However, slow rollout, corruption and the rapid increase of urban populations has impeded the successful delivery of houses and thus limited the number of homeowners. Communities have responded to the lack of housing with accusations of government apathy and racism (Johns 2009). Due to the construction of communities before and during apartheid, there is a concentration of single ethnic racial groups in a particular location. This pattern of suburbs for black South Africans, notably Coloured (classification for racial mixture) and black Africans was to create dormitory suburbs of municipal-owned houses for urban labour purposes (Bähre 2007). When the National Party (NP)-led government stopped building municipal-owned houses in the Coloured areas, the number of yard dwellings grew (Benit 2002). With the end of apartheid, the number of yard dwellings exploded, demands for housing were immediate and those located in the former Coloured townships, and therefore predominantly Coloured in identity, accused the government of favouritism and marginalisation.

The issues of housing are complex and compounded by self-interested, self-promoting and self-enriching associations, organisations and role players that are beyond the scope of this chapter. Instead, the argument is limited to the experiences of yard dwellers, but this is not to oversimplify what is a very complex issue where market forces, social trends, population growth and movement have replaced racialised legislation.

This chapter is divided into two sections. The first provides a background of Coloured backyard dwellers in the Western and Eastern Cape Provinces of South Africa. It describes the process of identity structure within a legislated racial classification (Population Registration Act 30 Of 1950) and the creation of racially homogeneous suburbs and communities (Group Areas Act 41 of 1950). Furthermore, the section demonstrates the manner in which backyard dwellers came into being and how its proliferation (there were two phases) was a response to government decisions and actions taken under the NP-led and ANC-led governments. The second section examines the self-perception of Coloured yard dwellers. Through newspaper articles, the identities, perceptions and emotions of the yard dwellers are revealed. The themes extracted from the articles highlight the different reactions and responses of yard dwellers through print media.

The lack of communication and information between officials and yard dwellers escalates concerns of marginalisation and discrimination. Coloured yard dwellers apply their identity to explain their reality, their experience and their expectations. The collective sentiment expressed by Coloured yard dwellers is that officials and government ignore them in general because of their racial identity.

The Proliferation of Backyard Dwellers

South African cities remain fragmented due to social segregation (Wilkinson 2000; Turok 2001; Lizzaralde and Massyn 2008; Petrus and Isaacs-Martin 2012). Land remains contested and contentious. With the repeal of discriminatory laws and the 1994 inclusive national election, many black South Africans believed that their lives would improve dramatically (Morange 2002). The expectation was that a new government would institute changes to (re)distribute resources to all black South Africans. One of these resources was, and continues to be, access to formal housing. The historical legacy of housing in South Africa must be taken into account in order to understand the present dynamics.

This study is restricted to the Coloured population in South Africa, who perceive that their social, political and economic positions and interests are marginal to all other groups. As an indigenous minority comprising 9 per cent of the national population, the group is classified as mixed racial ancestry and under apartheid occupied a position of relative privilege (Adhikari 2005). This privilege resulted in their economic position being significantly better than that of black Africans, but significantly worse and declining exponentially in comparison to that of whites. Like all black South Africans, the Coloured population was subject to the Group Areas Act and was forcefully relocated to suburbs far from transport networks, commercial districts, sporting facilities, places of worship and entertainment (Kamish 2008). Established communities were evicted forcibly from suburbs they had resided in for generations and many, through lack of alternate accommodation, were moved into distant townships composed of small council-owned houses (Posel 2001; Turok 2001; Ruiters 2009; Isaacs-Martin 2014).

Others, predominantly from the rural areas, were confined to shanty towns on the periphery of these segregated townships. Later, these informal settlements were destroyed and replaced with walk-up tenements. The municipal-owned houses and tenements together formed dormitory suburbs. These suburbs were isolated zones of racialised and economically depressed areas characterised by high unemployment, lack of or poor infrastructure and high criminality. The rationale behind these dormitory suburbs for the apartheid government was to create an urban labour source for white-owned industry. The Coloured townships were not areas of family development, stability and security, but labour pens for the urbanised working poor.

To further isolate the Coloured population from the 'white' urban spaces, officials attempted to create a Coloured ethno-city a significant distance from the city of Cape Town. In 1974, Atlantis, a Coloured ethnosuburb, was built on the west coast of the Western Cape as part of the Industrial Decentralisation Policy (IDP) (Gottschalk 1977). This policy was to incentivise white-owned businesses to (re)locate their factories and to create greater physical difference and physical boundaries between white residential suburbs and Coloured dormitory suburbs. The landscape of the racialised suburbs was, and remains, visibly apparent. Instead of laws and play areas, Coloured townships were dusty sandy areas of small tenements and congestion. These IDP incentives included a cheap labour source, subsidised rates and lower taxes. The policy disadvantaged black African artisans and favoured Coloured artisans in particular industries.

This preference for Coloured artisans, and the increased employment opportunities, resulted in a wave of migration from the rural areas. In the 1970s, the NP-led government stopped building municipal-owned houses in the dormitory suburbs and informal backyard dwellings proliferated (Turok 2001; Bank 2007; Govender et al. 2011a, 2011b). Apart from expanding families that could no longer be accommodated in the main house, migrants from the rural areas were left with few options other than becoming yard dwellers.

Those fortunate enough to receive municipal-owned homes often had limited financial resources. The only other resources available to them were space and water, and they capitalised on these as home owners, by renting out the space to desperate tenants who would surround the main house and then additionally sold them water and electricity. This practice generated income for the main houses, but it led to overcrowding within these communities, placing strain on already strained limited infrastructures (Govender et al. 2011a, 2011b).

Backyard dwellers are symptomatic of policies and public expectation. During apartheid, the desire to create dormitory suburbs of urbanised workers increased rural migration to the urban areas. Ironically, under the ANC-led government, the building of formal houses and the presumption of economic growth has once again escalated rural migration. There are many reasons why tenants choose to live in yards, but there is a common perception that there is less vulnerability to criminals and gangs that tenants would otherwise be exposed to in freestanding informal settlements.

Realities Confronting and Expectations amongst Yard Dwellers

The majority of the Coloured population in the Western and Eastern Cape Provinces are confined to townships and informal settlements. The group is also subject to high unemployment and crime. The municipal-owned low-cost housing communities, due to the racial spatial planning, were and remain predominantly represented by a single ethnic racial group. It is argued that as an ethnic minority the Coloured population, in lacking access to proper housing further undermines their ability to achieve social and financial equality or to access the corollary opportunities to improve their lives (Anthony Downs in Schuetz 2009: 296).

Yard dwellers are not a homogeneous group in the Coloured community. The reasons why yard dwellers remain in the locations are varied (Lemanski 2009). Depending on the township, many yard tenants are relatives of those in the main house, while others are complete strangers (as argued by Reader 1960; Crankshaw et al. 2000; Govender et al. 2011a, 2011b). Some aspire to eventual homeownership by waiting for the housing subsidy grant (names are placed on waiting lists), but for others the shack simply serves as temporary accommodation away from their main homes located in other locations, towns or countries. For a large proportion of those who are yard dwellers, it is the proximity to transport networks, their jobs or potential employment that forces them to accept these living conditions (Turok 2001).

Often without alternatives, the increase in families renting in yards of municipal homes and ground-floor walk-ups is at saturation point. Almost half of the formal houses in the townships in South Africa have yard tenants (Bank 2007). In South Africa, more than 25 per cent of rented dwellings are shacks and 66 per cent of these are in backyards (Lemanski 2009). Tenants, but often homeowners too, erect a wooden structure, incorporating corrugated iron, hardboard and plastic, often the size of a garden shed popularly referred to as Wendy houses. These crude structures consist of a single room in which tenants eat, sleep, wash and live. These structures leak and are prone to draughts due to the holes in the corrugated iron and wood. There is little to no ventilation or insulation in these structures, so mould, rot and damp are common (Lemanski 2009). Poor ventilation means that the temperature inside is extreme – either very hot or very cold. Without internal plumbing and direct access to water, it is difficult to dispose of household and solid waste, or to maintain any standard of hygiene. Although few owners of council houses pay for water usage, yard dwellers are charged for water by the bucket (Govender et al. 2011b). Where the main homeowners are cash-poor and unemployed, backyard dwellers are a source of stable income. Therefore, several structures can be found in a single yard.

These communities face a socioeconomic depressed environment coupled with (mis)education and (mis)information. Entire families (both nuclear and extended) and migrants who are unemployed, unskilled and possess little formal education live in these tiny structures. The reality for yard dwellers in these areas is criminal activity attributed to boredom, unemployment, drug and alcohol availability, and gangsterism. Frustrated males with little access to opportunities resort to criminal activity, and many are forced into gang structures that offer protection and minimal access to financial reward. Often this assists economically poor families. Young females often resort to prostitution, reneging on education, to assist their families. These environments are plagued by delinquency, single-parented households and high numbers of family members imprisoned, who on their release return to criminal activity and compound social ills within the home (Okecha 2011). This is further complicated by the underresourced health, educational and social infrastructure such as clinics, schools and sports facilities. What little resources exist are often subject to vandalism and theft.

Yard dwellers want their state-subsidised houses to be built near their existing homes. However, rollout is slow, as evidenced by the backlog characterised by the infamous waiting lists. Yet people who applied for the housing subsidy grant back in 1988 have yet to receive their homes (Samodien 2012). Such delays create perceptions amongst the Coloured yard dwellers, also exacerbated by misinformation, that lead to conclusions of racism and marginalisation.

Exclusion, Marginalisation and Identity

Backyard dwellers form a significant proportion of the population without access to permanent housing (Lemanski 2009). Expectations of yard dwellers and those of municipality officials and the national government vision of housing differ. Municipal official and government policy is to eradicate informal structures and provide private property ownership. The perception was that informal homes will disappear when all tenants become homeowners (Okecha 2011). The state approach is to simply eradicate backyard dwellings as illegitimate structures and replace them with legitimate state-subsidised housing; yet, many yard dwellers prefer to rent. However, the vacancies created by those allocated formal housing is simply filled by new tenants who are often returning new homeowners who wish to remain close to work, transport networks and commercial centres (Crankshaw et al. 2000; Morange 2002).

Controversially, Lizzaralde and Massyn (2008) argue that amongst the low-income communities, housing is not a priority. The desire for cash within these communities, particularly around the festive season, is to sell their allocated RDP homes and plots of land given to them by the provincial government, often at a fraction of the value or replacement cost. Such impressions add another element to yard dwellers and informal settlements.

Municipal officials assume that backyard dwellers have access to the same infrastructure as the main houses. It is assumed that the backyard dweller will through proximity and rental agreement have access to sanitation, electricity, water and refuse collection. According to the BNG Policy Housing Strategy, backyard dwellings are considered 'an important component of the overall private rental sector' that severely problematises the issue of informal housing. The policy states that backyard structures form part of the 'residential property market' and that 'private renting is the fastest growing form of accommodation for low-income households' (BNG 2004: 28–29). Lemanski (2009: 475) argues that 'poor tenants are most likely to rent from poor landlords'.

The BNG policy raises concerns in terms of its interpretation of yard dwellers. The implication is that yard dwellers form part of a rental cycle, so their needs are secondary to those of freestanding informal settlements. The yard dweller segment is growing faster than the proportion in informal settlements. Twice as many backyard dwellers paid rent as opposed to informal houses not located in a yard (General Household Survey, StatsSA 2013).

The Community Residential Units Programme (CRU) is geared towards private ownership of these yard dwellings, but there is no little communication between shareholders on the matter. This programme raises concerns relating to private property and the number of informal dwellings on a particular plot. Not all dwellings are the same size and certain yards have several dwellings, while others have only one. These issues need to be communicated to communities. Instead, misinformation is spread and residents become angry.

Yard dwellers complain of an inability to communicate with municipal officials regarding housing concerns. However, the lack of community leadership is due in part to their disorganisation (Morange 2002). From the perspective of yard dwellers, consensus is group-determined. This lack of communication is perceived by the Coloured yard dwellers as exclusion and therefore must be racist, particularly with regard to proximity housing.

The reality is that officials do not consider the proximity of yard dwellers when allocating housing on neighbouring vacant land. In Cape Town, the Development Planning Committee (DPC), later incorporated into the state-driven national Reconstruction and Development Plan and now referred to as the BNG policy, intended to provide houses to backyard dwellers and residents in informal settlements (Bähre 2007). While yard dwellers are identified as being in need of formal housing, the indications are that yard dwellers have advantages in the form of security and access to infrastructure, although limited and dependent on the homeowner. As a large proportion of yard dwellers in the two provinces are Coloureds, communities skew such interpretations regarding housing policy.

Tensions are exacerbated by the interpretation of informal housing. In terms of policy, it appears that informal settlements take precedence over backyard dwellers (Lemanski 2009). This was most apparent in the 2007 N2 Gateway Project, in which backyard dwellers (who were predominantly Coloured) perceived that the informal settlement occupiers (who were predominantly black African) were being favoured in terms of allocation. Backyard dwellers felt marginalised and that their needs were being overlooked.

The Notion of Identity and Exclusion

The Coloured population, for the most part, is an impoverished low-economic segment of the South African society. A group defined by their racial 'inferiority' and 'mixture' in the South African racist lexicon, even with the advantage of relative privilege during apartheid, are as impoverished and economically deprived as the black African population. It is difficult to comprehend the enormity of losing property, or being evicted from areas that served as communities with the accompanying sentiment, symbols and boundaries. Forceful evictions led to the disintegration of established communities. These memories, narratives and shared experiences are central to the notion of Coloured identity.

The Coloured identity is characterised and typified by exclusion and marginalisation (Isaacs-Martin 2011). Perceptions amongst the group are that a few are beneficiaries of government policies, but that the majority are excluded from housing allocations under the NP-led and ANC-led governments. Those who experienced forced removals were linked together by the nostalgia of their former communities. These shared memories were mainly confined to the group and were seldom shared with other racial groups. For many Coloured communities, their historical legacy remains in the city centres in the Eastern and Western Cape.

The lack of access to residential land is an inherited issue enmeshed with aspects of identity. Land issues pertaining to Coloureds in the two Cape provinces are confined primarily to the urban areas. The adage of 'first not being white enough and now not being black enough' is often uttered throngs of Coloureds protesting against their lack of access to services that include lack of access to housing (Adhikari 2005). The belief is that black Africans are recipients of state generosity as whites were recipients under the previous regime. Therefore, it is assumed that the Coloured experience remains constant and not beneficial to the group. Amongst the Coloured population in townships, there is a belief that the quality of their lives have deteriorated since apartheid.

Many backyard dwellers were often born during apartheid. Therefore, the only socialisation they have experienced was within townships that were congested and far from employment opportunities, being limited to low-paying wages, and access to education. Their parents and families would have been informed of life before apartheid, before forced removals and relocations. Their experience of township life, with its limitations, was the structure of a community with boundaries located in race classification and therefore racial experience. Without the resources and opportunities to improve their social realities, many resort to living in yards belonging to their parents, their extended family or strangers. However, these communities of backyard dwellers, particularly Coloureds, believe that there has been little or no change in their lives (Johns 2009). Many who supported the ANC perceive that the government has ignored them and they believe that they have been subjected to reverse racism. Their options are limited and they feel compelled to claim space before it is allocated to others.

Land invasions have become commonplace amongst the Coloured community for those unfortunate enough not to have access to backyard dwellings. In Cape Town, the Mayor has implemented the Backyard Essential Services Improvement Programme, in which backyard dwellers were to receive toilets, running water, electricity and wheelie bins. This programme is limited to municipal-owned houses and the accompanying stands. Many such programmes indicate that formal housing will not be provided to existing yard tenants. Many others who have lived in these structures for years consider it an improvement. Regardless of the processes put in place by municipalities and government institutions to assist with the allocation of housing, yard dwellers will remain in the foreseeable future.

Methodology

This study uses the data and content analysis to contextualise the story within the paradigm of importance and value. Both offer insight into the analysis of data material and text interpretation. The aim is to determine the self-perceptions and identities of Coloured backyard dwellers during periods of land invasions and home allocations in the Eastern and Western Cape Provinces. Thus, the scope is very narrow, although the realities of backyard dwellers are a complex social phenomenon. The case studies are located in newspaper articles as this source represents the most current topical events.

Of the 706 articles located in the NewsBank Access South Africa database, n=25 of those contained the word 'Coloured' in the text, representing 4 per cent of the total. The Coloured population represents less than 10 per cent of the national population and is mainly resident in the Western and Eastern Cape provinces. The IOL (independent newspapers) database consists of fifteen national and regional newspapers as well as Cape-based community newspapers. Of the 406 articles, a sample of n=25, representing 6 per cent of the 'Coloured' articles (N), was used. In both databases, only the newspapers that covered the Western and Eastern Cape provinces were included.

The equation used to establish sample is $y = 2x+1$ if the variable substituted begins at 1,2,3…25. The equation is applied anew for each database sample. The focus was on newspaper articles on the NewsBank Access South Africa database published on backyard dwellers after 1997. The IOL database is only used from 2005 due to the nature of e-newspapers. The papers are also divided into years so that equal representation for each year can be established. The following step is to read all the articles (n=50) and then assign them in a content analysis structure format (see Figure 8.1).

First, each relevant article is assigned a story ID (that contains an eight-digit date, the database coded as X1 or X2 and finally the number of the article is each database ranging from 1 to 25) and what the placement of the article was (front section or a story jump). Other factors include photographs and what the photo diversity depicts. The format also records the geographical focus and the treatment the article receives, and whether it is general news, a feature or a commentary. The final aspect of the analysis is to determine the theme and subtheme contained within each article.

Results and Discussion

The articles selected were reliant on local issues with an emphasis on the informal backyard dwellers in the Western and Eastern Cape. There were few reports outside the Western Cape Province; there were four articles that highlighted backyard dwellers in Gauteng. The coverage of backyard dwellers appears to be an overwhelmingly local issue (80 per cent). Most newspapers only covered issues relating to the provinces and particularly those concentrated in the main metropole areas.

Story ID	.... (Date/Article X1')
Front page of Newspaper	.... Yes =1; No = 2
Story jump	.... Yes = 1; No = 2.
Photos	.... Yes =1; No = 2

Photo Diversity

.... with visible faces

.... with Coloured faces

.... with black African faces

.... with Coloured and black African faces

.... with scenes of confrontation

Geographical focus

.... Local

.... Regional

.... National

.... None

Treatment

.... with visible faces

.... General news

.... Feature

.... Commentary

.... Other

Theme:

Figure 8.1 Content analysis format.

Photos were evident in 50 per cent of the articles and of those, 25 per cent depicted scenes of violence, confrontation or anger. Print media interest on backyard dwellers has increased year on year since 1998. A possible reason could be due to the increased violence surrounding the issue of housing and spatial allocation, as well as popular knowledge of housing subsidy grants. These violent episodes include the invasion of vacant municipal-owned land, the confrontation between squatters and existing homeowners, confrontations between yard dwellers and those to be allocated new houses, and lastly between squatters and the police.

None of the stories consulted were featured on the front page and there were no feature stories or commentaries on backyard dwellers. Eight themes could be extracted from the material. These include waiting lists, issues of proximity, timelines and land invasions, the afterthought of backyard dwellers with regard to housing allocations, lack of communication between municipal officials and backyard dwellers, illegitimate and legitimate housing, withholding political support and competition, and feelings of hopelessness. In all the themes, the element of racial identity was apparent.

The issue of the waiting lists, housing subsidy grants provided by the government, seem to be central to the housing concerns of many backyard dwellers. When houses are being constructed, it raises tensions within the backyard dweller community as many claim to have been on these lists since 1988 (Samodien 2012). Amongst these individuals, there is a sense that they should be considered for housing allocation before anyone else. Those living in informal settlements are considered to be latecomers, pretenders and opportunists:

> as contractors clear the fire-damaged site, long-term residents of areas such as Ravensmead, Bokmakierie and Epping Industria [formerly Coloured-only areas] are unhappy that thousands of people from Joe Slovo are to be temporarily housed among them. Other Langa residents [a Xhosa-only area] living in backyard shacks are also angry that Joe Slovo fire victims are seemingly getting preferential treatment. In the Masiphumelele settlement, near Fish Hoek, people blockaded the Kommetjie road after a fire there a fortnight ago, complaining that while Joe Slovo fire victims were to get brick houses, they were merely being given starter kits to rebuild their shacks. There have also been allegations that many of the Joe Slovo residents only recently settled in the Western Cape and if they were on the housing list, they came on to it late. (Essop et al. 2005)

In the Western Cape, he cautioned, people should not jump on the racism bandwagon too quickly just because of the angry exchanges between Coloured and black people in Bokmakierie and Ravensmead: 'Both these groups are poor. They have been promised houses, services and jobs, they did not clash with each other out of the blue. We have one group that has been waiting for houses for years, while another is seen as jumping the housing queue. The competition for housing is intense and emotions are already running high. This led to the dissatisfaction with delivery expressing itself as racism.' (Essop 2005)

The issue is primarily competition for resources as all those affected are either lower-earning homeowners, backyard dwellers or squatters. The issue of racial identity often surfaces in these conflicts and becomes intertwined with accessing resources such as housing. The tensions between the various communities highlight the enormity of the poverty in specific areas in Cape Town in the Western Cape and Port Elizabeth in the Eastern Cape.

The waiting lists are often linked with overcrowding, which inhabitants infer is a result of their lack of choice. Yard dwellers contribute their living conditions to the lack, or slow rollout, of housing subsidy grants. The perception that they lack alternatives forces them into conditions of overcrowding and lowers their dignity. Another is the appeal to the longevity of their being subjected as backyard dwellers:

> Thirty-four people share a one-bedroomed council house in Hanover Park – the majority living in makeshift shacks in the back yard … seven people share the main house and 27 live in four backyard structures which cover the plot, leaving only a tiny outside area … All 34 share a single toilet and bath. And if the house is locked, they must use a bucket. Just one person among the four families sharing the plot has a job. (Lewis 2010)

> The residents said they had been backyard dwellers for more than 20 years, sharing yards with more than 25 people. (Radebe 2014)

Overcrowding in the yards is common and tenants often complain of their poor health due to their living conditions. However, tenants blame the municipality, and usually the national government, for their predicament. The common interpretation is that housing issues are politicised against the Coloured population:

> A backyarder trying to get a house for the past five years [stated:] 'I have written to our councillor, the mayor and Human Settlements MEC. How can people from out of nowhere just get houses on land we were told is not for houses?' (Felix 2014)

Racist accusations of preference seemed to be common in black African and Coloured communities. Due to levels of frustration amongst those awaiting houses and their lack of insight into bureaucratic processes, the common shared sentiment is to contribute all decisions made to race. This is further exacerbated by the notion that yard dwellers wish to stay in the area in which they currently reside. Due to the segregated arrangement of townships because of a longstanding racist legacy, the stance taken by yard dwellers reinforces segregation amongst residents:

> [The houses] were occupied last month by local residents [Coloureds], including backyard dwellers, who defeated a bid to evict them. They said they did not see why the homes should go to residents of the Joe Slovo [Xhosa] informal settlement, when some of them had been on council waiting lists for decades. (South African Press Association (SAPA) 2008a)

> 'It's a race thing', explains resident Aziza Rhoda, as she washes sand from her crockery for the sixth time that day. Like many other members of the tight-knit community, she believes she is being sidelined because she is 'coloured and not black'. 'The African people from Joe Slovo don't want to move here because it's too far. If they don't want it, why should we, as the people of Delft, not get it? The government only cares about the coloured people when it's time to vote.' (SAPA 2008b)

Issues of proximity are the sites of racial tension. The issue of spatial development and the building of housing have racial implications. Due to the continuing segregation in areas, now not as a result of racist divisive legislation, but economics there is a concentration of single racial and ethnic groups in particular areas. Therefore, people located in these areas, particularly those renting as backyard dwellers, perceive that if there is development in the locale, then they should benefit first. This was a shared sentiment within the stories, namely proximity and its link to entitlement. Clashes between communities, often of different racial groups, are raised when the new inhabitants for the open land or new houses arrive, often in droves. These events reveal the *realpolitik* often played out through national, regional and local political agendas. A common theme amongst the communities involved is typically the resident community who are opposed to the arrival of outsiders. Legislation creates a community of tenants as well as a community of beneficiaries who often have opposing interests, causing tensions between the two (Benit 2002).

Another theme extracted from the articles was that of competition between those who have applied for the housing subsidy grants, or commonly known as the waiting lists, the migration of the rural poor, slow rollout and a lack of correct information, which create unnecessary tensions between communities seeking access to the same resources:

> It is about the allocation of N2 Gateway houses in Delft. The 70/30 split between squatters, mainly African people from Joe Slovo, and backyard dwellers, mainly coloured people, is pitting amaXhosa and the coloured Khoi people against each other. (Hartley 2008)

There is resentment against individuals who are not part of an existing community who move into an area of newly built state-subsidised homes. This suggests that there is an unwillingness to incorporate new people into an area. This does not suggest racism, but it does imply that residents wish to maintain racial homogeneity. Perhaps the housing list needs to be changed and augmented not to represent people of a particular community, but rather to disperse it:

> The residents also expressed unhappiness over outsiders from Gugulethu ... getting 'first preference' in the allocation of housing units in Mandela Park, 'while we are getting nothing' ... 'Our children should occupy these houses', said a mother of three, a backyarder there for about 20 years. (Hweshe 2009)

Yet this is the same pattern applied by both racial groups. The issue is competition for land in areas where they are already located. Those who are forced, due to overcrowding, to move do so to vacant land closest to their existing homes. As an example, the Zola squatters moved to SANRAL land in Lwandle in the Strand. The Strand is several kilometres outside of Cape Town Central. When these squatters then moved to Gaylee, tensions rose between the new arrivals and the yard dwellers. In order to give legitimacy to their complaints, both sides opted to use racist language against each other. Each perceived it as their right to occupy the land. The Coloured community felt that as the area was dominated by their group, this should be the logical continuation in terms of spatial distribution: 'Nothing is happening for the coloured community. This is not a political thing but a community struggle' (Radebe 2014).

Authorities admit that they do not consult backyard dwellers, and this is attributed to the issue of prioritising informal settlements and assuming that backyard dwellers are already a fixture. This demonstrates a bifurcated view in terms not only of policy but also of implementation. One of the residents in Langa, the first Xhosa suburb in Cape Town, remarked: 'I am now 45 years old and I still don't have a house. Government is too slow. These houses are not enough and now people from other areas [Coloured areas] are going to apply' (Hawker 2006).

A common theme of frustration exists amongst yard dwellers concerning the use of vacant land that lies adjacent to townships and locations. There is a common perception that the land has been vacant for many years (often decades) and therefore the municipality has no plans to use the land. In addition, the defence used for occupying the land is that it is used for criminal activity. The racial issue becomes salient for Coloured people because they believe that black African people are being allocated houses before them; 'Outraged residents of the largely coloured community of Gaylee in Blackheath said they had no idea Africans would be moved to the piece of land on Albert Philander Way' (Felix 2014).

The reality is that informal settlements are prioritised over backyard dwellers and this has been compounded by the BNG housing policy. While the policy acknowledges the yard dwellers, the claims to private rental markets hinder progress for those who continue to live in these informal structures: 'I've lived in Pelican Park for 37 years. We've been squatting in this area for two years now. I built this camp, and I won't move until I see that everyone who's lived with me all these years has their own houses', said Brian Collins, a 54-year-old settler (www.dailymaverick.co.za).

The themes extracted demonstrate that backyard dwellers have concerns, priorities and viewpoints regarding their socioeconomic and political circumstances. Rather than perceiving yard dwellers as simply individuals, they can be regarded as a community connected not only through their experiences but also their identity. Coloured backyard dwellers are found predominantly in the former Coloured townships and therefore the issue of racial identity becomes salient with regard to resources. The waiting lists play a central role in the desire for home-ownership and it adds to the resentment and frustrations experienced by these communities. Lack of communication between officials and the yard dwellers exacerbates the tensions and elevates the land invasions, the competition and racial tensions between groups seeking access to housing. Racial identities in South Africa is the constant in citizens' lives, and particularly for the Coloured experience, where their history and its narrative is defined in terms of forced removals, the lack of formal housing has a greater appeal to that identity and experience of marginalisation.

Conclusion

The backyard dweller existed before enforced legislated segregation, but it is the legacy of racialised South Africa and the obsession of keeping black people out of the cities and away from white suburbs. However, as black South Africans were a cheap labour source, the proliferation of shanties was permitted on the periphery of towns and cities. During apartheid, yard dwellings increased due to rural migration by people searching for employment in the urban areas. When the government stopped building municipal-owned houses in the 1970s, the lack of new houses and high unemployment that forced generations to remain in these dormitory suburbs, coupled with migrants, led to an explosion in backyard structures. Tenants were then – and often remain today – the only source of income for homeowners.

The national housing subsidy scheme was meant to assist the yard dwellers. The inability of the scheme to keep pace with ever increasing population, along with its slow application and corruption, keeps tenants reliant on informal housing. Many choose to remain in these structures due to close proximity to employment opportunities as well as access to infrastructure such as water, sanitation, electricity and waste removal. For homeowners, it is an issue of financial assistance.

For those who are struggling to establish homes, it appears that little has changed since apartheid structures were dismantled. Generations were born in these townships in the municipal-owned houses and were forced to move into these informal structures with their families. For many, their perceptions of marginalisation are racially constructed. Their racial identity gives them a shared sense of suffering with other Coloured yard dwellers and reinforces the notion that they are not alone in their misfortune or inability to secure state-funded housing.

Yard dwellers perceive the waiting list, a continuation of apartheid spatial planning, as a marker of their right to receive state-subsidised homes. Homeownership is seen as an ideal. Many have been on these lists for decades without a change in their residential predicament. Although the government and municipalities had a common agenda of ensuring that all informal dwellers became homeowners, no consideration was given to whether that was the goal of all yard dwellers or whether all could afford to maintain and service homes. This has led to the proliferation of informal structures in these yards as a source of income for many unemployed homeowners. Often many new homeowners return or remain as yard dwellers as the cost of transport is lower and there is closer proximity to services.

Land invasions amongst the Coloured yard dwellers often occurred on land adjacent or in close proximity to the existing predominantly Coloured townships. The perception of yard dwellers is that vacant land, owned by the municipalities, is not being used, and invaders justify their behaviour as a result of marginalisation and exclusion. These perceptions are reinforced as officials do not engage or communicate with yard dwellers, as they do not recognise or acknowledge their representatives. This creates distrust of government and reinforces racist notions of preference and exclusion.

Backyard dwellers are not a homogeneous group as their reasons for remaining in this situation vary. For some, it is the lack of a home and desperation, while for others, it is merely a temporary space to earn enough to send home to families in distant towns and countries. Many others are homeowners elsewhere, but choose to live in the yards because it is closer to their employment and reduces the cost of travelling. However, all are eager to accept the opportunity to own a state-subsidised home, whether this is a permanent residence, a rental opportunity or simply an asset that can be sold – the reasons are varied.

These variations are not taken into account by municipalities or government officials, who simply perceive backyard dwellings as illegitimate structures that must be replaced with houses (legitimate structures). With the BNG policy, there is a realisation that the backyard dwellers are an income source for homeowners who are often old, female and unemployed. The yard dweller is being redefined as a contributor to the private rental establishment rather than as a yard squatter. However, this could have an impact on house allocation to yard dwellers as the number of people seeking state-subsidised houses continues to increase. As municipalities consider providing yard dwellers with sanitation, water and waste removal services, many yard dwellers believe that they will not receive houses.

For many yard dwellers, living in these structures are dehumanising. Common complaints include declining health and overcrowding. The poor fabrication of their homes exposes tenants to water, wind, vermin and sand. Such circumstances lead tenants (particularly those who have been on waiting lists for years) to believe that political structures are dismissive of their experiences, and racial identity often becomes salient due to these developments.

The Coloured backyard dweller perceives their position as one of dependence on others and hopelessness. Their response is primarily based in anger towards government and hostility towards 'invading' squatters who are often black Africans. Rather than creating communities of common experience, racial identities and its divisions are held to be salient, thereby repeating the perceptions and antagonisms of the past.

Wendy Isaacs-Martin is Associate Professor in the Archie Mafeje Research Institute (AMRI) at the University of South Africa (Unisa). Her research focuses on identities – national, ethnic and racial – and scapegoating violence. She is currently conducting research that connects escalating conflict to the (re-)enforcement of singular salient identifiers and the (de)construction and self-imposed marginalisation of communities in homogeneous societies.

References

Adhikari, M. 2005. *Not White Enough, Not Black Enough: Racial Identity in the South African Coloured Community.* Cape Town: Double Storey Books.

Bähre, E. 2007. 'Beyond Legibility: Violence, Conflict and Development in a South African Township', *African Studies* 66(1): 79–102.

Bank, L. 2007. 'The Rhythms of the Yards: Urbanism, Backyards and Housing Policy in South Africa', *Journal of Contemporary African Studies* 25(2): 205–28.

Benit, C. 2002. 'The Rise or Fall of the "Community"? Post-apartheid Housing Policy in Diepsloot, Johannesburg', *Urban Forum* 13(2): 47–66.

BNG – Breaking New Ground. 2004. 'A Comprehensive Plan for the Development of Sustainable Human Settlements'. Retrieved August 2012 from http://abahlali.org/files/Breaking%20new%20ground%20New_Housing_Plan_Cabinet_approved_version.pdf.

Crankshaw, O., A. Gilbert and A. Morris. 2000. 'Backyard Soweto', *International Journal of Urban and Regional Research* 24(4): 841–57.

Daily Maverick. 2014. 'Pelican Park: Still Waiting for Change: After all These Years.' Retrieved 9 September 2014 from https://www.dailymaverick.co.za/article/2014-05-06-pelican-park-still-waiting-for-change-after-all-these-years/.

Essop, P. 2005. 'Poor Delivery Causing Tension on Cape Flats'. Retrieved 9 September 2014 from https://www.iol.co.za/news/politics/poor-delivery-causing-tension-on-cape-flats-235660.

Essop, P., Z. Khoisan and A. Smith. 2005. 'Fury as Fire Victims Jump Housing Queue'. Retrieved 9 September 2014 from https://www.iol.co.za/news/south-africa/fury-as-fire-victims-jump-housing-queue-234028.

Felix, J. 2014. 'Go Back to Eastern Cape – Residents'. Retrieved 10 September 2014 from https://www.iol.co.za/capetimes/news/go-back-to-eastern-cape-residents-1701056.

General Household Survey (GHS). 2013. Statistics South Africa (StatsSA).

Gottschalk, K. 1977. 'Industrial Decentralisation, Jobs and Wages'. Retrieved 9 September 2014 http://www.disa.ukzn.ac.za/webpages.

Govender, T., J.M. Barnes and C.H. Pieper. 2011a. 'Contribution of Water Pollution from Inadequate Sanitation and Housing Quality to Diarrheal Disease in Low-Cost Housing Settlements of Cape Town, South Africa', *American Journal of Public Health* 101(7): e4–e9.

———. 2011b. 'The Impact of Densification by Means of Informal Shacks in the Backyards of Low-Cost Houses on the Environment and Service Delivery in Cape Town, South Africa', *Environmental Health Insights* 5: 23–52.

Hartley, A. 2008. 'SAHRC to Probe Rights Abuse in Delft Eviction'. Retrieved 10 September 2014 from https://www.iol.co.za/news/south-africa/sahrc-to-probe-rights-abuse-in-delft-eviction-390233.

Hawker, D. 2006. 'Langa Outrage about Gateway Integration'. Retrieved 12 September 2014 from https://www.iol.co.za/news/south-africa/langa-outrage-about-gateway-integration-282832.

Hweshe, F. 2009. 'Backyard Dwellers Demand Change'. Retrieved 10 September 2014 https://www.iol.co.za/news/south-africa/backyard-dwellers-demand-change-454708.

Isaacs-Martin, W. 2011. 'National Identity and Distinctiveness: Developing a Common Identity in a Nation State', *Africa Insight* 41(1): 59–70.

———. 2014. 'National and Ethnic Identities: Dual and Extreme Identities amongst the Coloured Population of Port Elizabeth, South Africa', *Studies in Ethnicity and Nationalism* 14(1): 55–73.

Johns, L. 2009. 'Hope Springs Eternal? Not in This Town'. Retrieved 9 September 2014 from https://www.iol.co.za/news/politics/hope-springs-eternal-not-in-this-town-438516.

Jooste, B., and C. Barnes, 2011. 'Service Plan for Backyard Dwellers'. Retrieved 10 August 2014 from https://www.iol.co.za/capeargus/services-plan-for-backyard-dwellers-1132867.

Kamish, A. 2009. 'Coloured and Black Identities of Residents Forcibly Removed from Blouvlei', *South African Historical Journal* 60(2): 242–257.

Lemanski, C. 2009. 'Augmented Informality: South Africa's Backyard Dwellings as a By-product of Formal Housing Policies', *Habitat International* 33(4): 472–84.

Lewis, E. 2010. 'Living Like This is Making Us Sick'. Retrieved 12 September 2014 from https://www.iol.co.za/news/south-africa/western-cape/living-like-this-is-making-us-sick-686500.

Lizzaralde, G., and M. Massyn. 2008. 'Unexpected Negative Outcomes of Community Participation in Low-Cost Housing Projects in South Africa', *Habitat International* 32(1): 1–14.

Morange, M. 2002. 'Backyard Shacks: The Relative Success of This Housing Option in Port Elizabeth', *Urban Forum* 13(2): 3–25.

Okecha, K. 2011. 'Regime Politics and Service Delivery in the Cape Town Unicity Council area', *Urban Forum* 22(1): 95–110.

Petrus, T., and W. Isaacs-Martin. 2012. 'The Multiple Meanings of Coloured Identity in South Africa', *Africa Insight* 42(1): 87–102.

Posel, D. 2001. 'What's in a Name? Racial Categorisations under Apartheid and Their Afterlife'. Retrieved 18 September 2018 from http://www.academia.edu/1012471.

Radebe, P. 2014. 'Ennerdale Residents Seize Land'. Retrieved 10 September 2014 from http://www.iol.co.za/news/crime-courts.

Reader, D. 1960. *The Black Man's Portion: History, Demography and Living Conditions in the Native Locations of East London*. Cape Town: Oxford University Press.

Ruiters, M. 2009. 'Collaboration, Assimilation and Contestation: Emerging Constructions of Coloured Identity in Post-apartheid South Africa', in Mohamed Adhikari (ed.), *Burdened by Race: Coloured Identities in South Africa*. Cape Town: UCT Press, pp. 104–33.

Samodien, L. 2012. 'Housing Backlog Stretches back 24 years, Court Told'. Retrieved 10 August 2014 from https://www.iol.co.za/capetimes/news/housing-backlog-stretches-back-24-years-court-told-1216913.

South African Press Association (SAPA). 2008a. 'Thubelisha Calls on Zille to Speak out'. Retrieved 12 September 2014 from https://www.iol.co.za/news/politics/thubelisha-calls-on-zille-to-speak-out-385388.

―――. 2008b. 'Delft Squatters Banish Memory of Evil'. Retrieved 10 September 2014 from https://allafrica.com/stories/200804090211.html.
Schuetz, J. 2009. 'No Renters in My Suburban Backyard: Land Use Regulation and Rental Housing', *Journal of Policy Analysis and Management* 28(2): 296–320.
Turok, I. 2001. 'Persistant Polarisation Post-apartheid? Progress towards Urban Integration in Cape Town', *Urban Studies* 38(13): 2349–77.
Wilkinson, P. 2000. 'City Profile: Cape Town', *Cities* 17(3): 195–205.

Part IV

Development, Social Policy and African Families

Chapter 9

Understanding the Conceptualisation of African Families
A Social Policy Development Poser in South Africa

Busani Mpofu

Introduction

This chapter is an introductory study to the ongoing research on the conceptualisation of a family policy in South Africa. It seeks to understand the conceptualisation of an African family from an African perspective using case studies of families in the KwaZulu-Natal, Eastern Cape and Limpopo Provinces. Before 1994, people from different races were treated differently by social policies in South Africa. The apartheid government, with its policies of separate development, deliberately excluded black African families from welfare service provision (Sunde and Bozalek 1995: 63). South Africa does not have an explicit family policy. While not usually acknowledged as part of family policy, social, health, housing and economic policies impact on relationships within families and between families and the state (Sunde and Bozalek 1995: 64). However, from the outset, it is also crucial to understand that it is a complex challenge to conceptualise and assess family-related policies (Hantrais 1994; Anttonen and Sipila 1996; Neyer 2003). This is because in many countries, policies that impact family life are included in several different legislation documents. While those family related policies usually relate to many features of family life, they are rarely combined to constitute one overarching family policy. Yet, countries that have made great strides towards social development, that is, in improving the social security and empowerment of their citizens, have done so through the avenue of family-related policy (Smit 2011: 15).

In South Africa, Holborn and Eddy (2011: 1) argued that family life has never been simple to describe or understand. However, what is clear is that the concept of a nuclear family has never accurately captured the norm of all families in a country with extended families, caregivers and guardians. The country's history of apartheid, especially the migrant labour system, is one unique circumstance that affected the structure and situation of families, especially black African families. This gave rise to the prominence of single-parent (particularly mothers) households. Law (2013: 3) argued that there is no typical South African family as most families are fluid, with members moving in and out of them, and often across the rural and urban divide. The HIV/AIDS pandemic also left many households headed by children and grandparents. While the *White Paper* acknowledged that various kinds of families exist in the country, it concluded that the nuclear family is the most common type in South Africa (Department of Social Development, Republic of South Africa (DoSD) 2012: 15). This is the subject of analysis in this study. This conceptualisation of black South African families needs further interrogation. This was therefore the thrust of this research, that is, to conduct ethnographic research (oral interviews) in order to understand the conceptualisation of African families. This is necessary because it may have massive, positive implications for social policy vis-à-vis the African family in South Africa. It is argued that living in nuclear households does not equate to having a nuclear family.

Therefore, in an attempt to come up with a conceptualisation of families that could enhance social policy provisions in the country, this study seeks to address the following issues, among others: the concept of 'family', definitions of 'family' and different forms of family and major forms of African families in South Africa. The second major question asked by this study seeks to establish problems that are faced by African families today (for example, unemployment, poverty, child poverty, orphans, substance/drug abuse, diseases, separation of families (due to labour migration), absent fathers (absent physically and not supporting their dependants) and so on. Since the end of apartheid, the South African government has endeavoured to design and implement new forms of social policy to address some of the problems stated above. These social policies include a number of cash grants to support vulnerable individuals, including the following: the State Old Age Pension (for older persons without sufficient means to support themselves), the Disability Grant (for people with disabilities aged eighteen and over, the Child Support Grant (for children), the Foster Care Grant (for the support of children by nonkin parents) and the Care Dependent Grant (for caregivers of children with physical and mental impairments).

These grants are a form of social protection. According to Law (2013: 4), social protection refers to those 'policies and programmes that protect people against risk and vulnerability, mitigate the impact of shocks, and support people from chronic incapacities to secure basic livelihoods'. Another question in this study related to the giving of grants was whether or not cash transfers/grants to individuals promote/enhance family cohesion/unity in the country and how best these social welfare grants can be disbursed to promote family cohesion. I will examine whether these social grants can be regarded as part of the Family Preservation Services that the White Paper spoke of. Family Preservation Services were defined as 'services to families that focus on family resilience in order to strengthen families, so as to keep families together as far as possible'. The purpose is to ensure that the family withstands and survives life challenges that tend to disrupt or destroy families (see Law 2013: 4). Effective policies, institutions and processes need to be adopted that can respond to the circumstances, activities and requirements of the poor. The increasing recognition that is not static among individuals, households or communities, but that varies in space and time in terms of its conditions, effects and causes, necessitates the need for more nuances and tailor-made approaches (May 2008: 43).

Why Family Policy in South Africa?

The White Paper views family policy as 'any policy that has any direct or indirect influence on the well-being of the family' (Law 2013: 4). Developing an African family policy from an African perspective is even more crucial now because black African families in South Africa are in a state of crisis, which manifests itself in the form of escalating family breakdowns and very negative effects on children and the youth. For example, in 2011, the South African Institute of Race Relations highlighted that the 'typical' child is raised by their mother in a single-parent household and that most children also live in households with unemployed adults (see Holborn and Eddy 2011). Before 1994, the history of apartheid and the migrant labour system were cited as some of the major reasons that greatly affected the structure and situations of many black African families, contributing to misery and separations of married couples, exacerbating poverty circumstances. Apartheid policies of residential segregation and the migrant labour system damaged South African family life through the imposition of family separation, and this legacy of fractured families remains. The Africa Centre's demographic surveillance area in KwaZulu-Natal province reported that 52 per cent of children receiving grants had fathers reported as missing or their whereabouts not known at all, as compared to those reported as resident, non-resident or dead (Lund 2006: 166).

Since 1994, the disintegration of African families seems to have been escalating, which is a source of concern. Added to this, since the 1990s, the HIV/AIDS pandemic has also profoundly affected the health and wellbeing of family members, and has consequently placed an added burden on children. The HIV/AIDS pandemic put additional pressures on the sustainability of families and households. High poverty levels experienced by many African families mean that they have to be supported in one way or another in order to flourish and function optimally. It was in recognition of this problem that the DoSD in 2011 valiantly came up with a *Green Paper* to promote family life and strengthen the family in the country (DoSD 2011). This was after the realisation of the existence of weak family systems or nonexistent families altogether. The *Green Paper* stated that the problem with the family was its inability to play its critical roles of socialisation, nurturing, care and protection effectively due to failures in the political economy and the legacy of colonialism and apartheid. The *Green Paper* thus sought well-functioning, resourced, viable and prosperous families, which would play pivotal roles in the country's human, social and economic development (DoSD 2011: 16).

In September 2012, the DoSD took a step further in the national government's endeavour to promote family life and strengthen the family in the country by producing a *White Paper on Families in South Africa*. This was after policy makers, academics and civil society members among others had voiced serious concerns over the absence of a policy framework on the family in South Africa, given the detrimental effects of the policies of the colonial apartheid on the family, for example, land dispossessions, migrant labour and homeland systems and their impact in contemporary South Africa (DoSD 2012: 6). The DoSD noted that since 1994, various national policy and legislative reforms did not explicitly address the concerns of the family. As a result, most of the socioeconomic benefits filtered to the family only indirectly because the measures did not target the family in the first place. The country's national socioeconomic development policies tend to target individuals or specific categories and rarely place them in the family context. For example, the five major social assistance policies in the country focus on specific individuals, that is: older persons (the State Old Age Pension), people with disabilities (the Disability Grant) and children (the Child Support Grant, the Foster Care Grant and the Care Dependent Grant). The DoSD argued that the needs of such individuals may not align with those of the family. It also argued that past and present poverty analyses and strategies of intervention primarily concentrated on households, as opposed to families, thereby overlooking intra-family dynamics in the country.

The *White Paper* was therefore a welcome attempt to promote family life and strengthen families in South Africa. It was developed through a consultative process, which involved provincial and national stakeholder workshops attended by a range of participants, including representatives from the national, provincial and district departments of the DoSD, representatives from other government departments and civil society organisations, including the faith-based sector and community-based organisations (DoSD 2012: 7). However, while the *White Paper* acknowledged that various kinds of families existed in the country, it concluded that the nuclear family was the most common type in South Africa (DoSD 2012: 15). This is the source of concern for this chapter. This conceptualisation of black South African family policy needs further interrogation. The problem with this assumption is that, in the end, the Western nuclear family, which is regarded as the norm due to the hegemony of Western imperialism, continues to be the basis of many social policies despite the fact that this family form is not a reality (Sunde and Bozalek 1995: 65).

While the *White Paper* is certainly a valuable document that goes a long way in terms of the search for a policy framework for families in South Africa, it is important to gain an ethnographic understanding of which family type black African families think is the most common. This is therefore the thrust of this study, that is, to conduct ethnographic research (oral interviews) in the KwaZulu-Natal, Eastern Cape and Limpopo Provinces in order to come up with a conceptualisation of families that may have massive, positive implications for social policy vis-à-vis the African family in South Africa. The aim of this study has been to engage with the African communities and produce research that can influence or compliment the national government policy for the benefit of disadvantaged African families in South Africa.

Respondents were selected from urban communities of the KwaZulu-Natal, Eastern Cape and Limpopo Provinces, mostly in townships markets and transport ranks where African families from the low-income bracket work, and most of them can be classified as members of poor families. This first phase of this ethnographic research was conducted in KwaZulu-Natal Province in 2013. In this province, interviews were conducted in the cities and towns of Durban, Ladysmith, Pietermaritzburg, Empangeni and Newcastle. African townships visited in Durban included Umlazi. Most of the respondents interviewed had links with the rural communities surrounding these urban areas. According to Julian May (2008: 42), families who are poor are vulnerable to change and sudden shocks, experience ill-health, live in crowded conditions, find it difficult to feed, educate and care for their children, and are deeply worried about their future. Some of their members can be said to be part of the working poor. The working poor may comprise the unemployed (or self-employed, like informal traders or street vendors), underemployed, engaging in work that is arduous, insecure and frequently unsafe. Poor children are usually malnourished and frequently fall behind at school, are often improperly parented and are at risk of sexual predation, early pregnancy and HIV infection (May 2008: 42). A historical understanding of the conceptualisation of an African family is necessary before we can think of conceptualising a family policy.

Historical Understanding of the Conceptualisation of an African Family in South Africa

Writing in 1998, Siqwana-Ndulo argued that there has been no systematic documentation of the African family and household structure in South Africa by sociologists, leading to the perpetuation of generalisations and assumptions about them made decades ago (Russell 1994: 64, cited in Siqwana-Ndulo 1998: 407). In Western societies, 'family' is understood to refer to the conjugal pair who maintain a household with their offspring or adopted children. Anyone else outside this circle is regarded as 'extended family'. In African societies generally – for example, among the Xhosa – 'family' refers to a much wider circle, even though marriage is the basis for family as in Western society (Siqwana-Ndulo 1998: 407). The *White Paper* defined an extended family as 'a multigenerational family that may or may not share the same household' (DoSD 2012: 3). An extended family usually consists of a three-generational structure made up of genealogically related kin comprising grandparents, parents, grandchildren and sometimes a fourth generation, if it still exists (Singh 2008: 453). While some present-day African marriages may not involve a plurality of wives as had been the case in some instances in the past, the fundamental principles of family life have not been altered. The basic difference is that, while Western marriage is based on individualism and independence, African marriage is based on the principle of collectivity and interdependence. In spite of this, African households have been and continue to be compared uncritically to Western households (Siqwana-Ndulo 1998: 407).

Prevalent approaches to African family ignore the fact that African social reality is determined by a particular philosophical view of life, which defines society and the individual's place in it and the world. Individuals see themselves and their roles in society only in relation to the community in which they belong (Mbiti 1969: 108–9, cited in Siqwana-Ndulo 1998: 411). In traditional life, the individual does not and cannot exist alone, except corporately (Mbiti 1969: 108–9; Menkiti 1984: 171; Ruch and Anyanwu 1981: 371–72). As such, more research needs to be done on the African family and household structure in both rural and urban areas in order to determine how families are changing in response to social and economic conditions, based on the principles of social organisation of these groups rather than on some imagined 'universal' household structure (Siqwana-Ndulo 1998: 415). Sihlongonyane (2000: 5) argued that the nuclear form of family does not reflect the true conditions of African societies.

One of the challenges in doing sociological research on families in South Africa has always been that the works of early anthropologists still have a tremendous influence on the way in which African households are viewed in the country today. An example is that of Philips (1953), who implied that African families were in linear progression towards the supposedly superior, most advanced Western-style nuclear family. Russell (1994: 64) also revealed a similar approach. However, adherents of this viewpoint fail to recognise that even the Western nuclear family form is undergoing changes (Siqwana-Ndulo 1998: 409).

Early literature on African families claimed that the African family was disintegrating and becoming increasingly disorganised because of Western influence, with increasing preference for Western-style marriages. As a result, it was claimed that obligations and responsibilities to each other and to society, which were enshrined in African marriage procedures, were also disappearing (Siqwana-Ndulo 1998: 408). Later, the evolutionary view of polygyny as a marriage view predicted that this family form would eventually disappear as 'part of the universal progression toward a nuclear and conjugal family' (Siqwana-Ndulo 1998: 408). This view implicitly assumed that the Western family form was 'rational'. While there was some merit in this view, Siqwana-Ndulo argued that it was problematic because of its Eurocentric assumption about the family (1998: 408).

Another Eurocentric view by Krige (1936) claimed that changes and adjustments to black families such as out-of-wedlock births, loss of parental control over children and preference for Western-style marriage were to 'gain equilibrium'. This assumed that families had no control or influence on changes in their lives, but were being caught up in a powerful current of change facilitating the singular progression from 'primitive to modern' family forms (Siqwana-Ndulo 1998: 409). It was also claimed that the drive towards nuclear families was gaining ground among families of Indian descent in South Africa. However, Singh also discovered that among people of Indian origin, there are still entrenched philosophical principles, especially in Hinduism, that the joint or extended family system continues to show prevalence. This was in spite of the numerous publications in the 1980s and 1990s claiming that the idea of extended families have all but broken down among people of Indian origin (Singh 2008). Such ideas, according to Singh, failed to take into consideration how municipality-built houses and living arrangements that favoured nuclear-type household arrangements were not a sufficient indication of people's real attitudes towards conventional patterns of living (Singh 2008: 468).

Generally, the inferred drive towards nuclear families is because naturally, the expansion of education, healthcare, employment and immigration (socioeconomic positions) has tended to alter the structure of the family away from traditional patterns to new ones. However, according to Bigombe and Khadiagala, the same forces have also produced multiple constraints on the family. African families are thus embedded in political and socioeconomic circumstances that are characterised by longstanding domestic dynamics of economic fragility, debilitating poverty, poor governance and civil conflicts. While forces of globalisation also offer families new opportunities, the same forces heighten their vulnerability to these forces. As a result, the state of African families is clouded in competing strains of social regeneration and economic constraints (Bigombe and Khadiagala 2004: 1). According to Sihlongonyane, the presentation of human development as a unilinear change from 'primitive' societies to complex 'modern' communities was a diffusionist effort to submerge African societies into dependency on Eurocentric values (2000: 4).

However, Bigombe and Khadiagala argued that in a country such as South Africa, with a population of more than 60 million people and with a considerable percentage still residing in nonurban areas, it may be too early to conclude that the majority of families in the country are nuclear. As such, changes in the structure of African families may still reflect enduring tensions between traditional and modern values and structures. But the trend remains the creation of systems of marriage and family organisation that draw on both traditional and modern norms – 'that ability to make new things out of the old' – and to draw forth new solutions from the traditional resources of family institutions. The country may still be stark in adaptations of family organisations that are currently an 'uneasy amalgam' that is yet to crystallise into a dominant pattern (Bigombe and Khadiagala 2004: 2). Some families have actually abandoned traditional practices in favour of modern ones. Furthermore, one has to understand that the study of African family forms, both in Africa and the diaspora, requires recognition of the fact that the family or household organisation is part of a social system with a cultural heritage based on a value system quite distinct from the Western one (Siqwana-Ndulo 1998: 410). According to Russell:

> if it was correct that blacks were experiencing a trend towards nuclear family households as a consequence of their participation in the commercial industrial capitalist economy, we would expect this to manifest itself in smaller families in the urban areas where the pressure to individuation, competition, consumption and display are greatest. We would expect some convergence of black and white urban family distributions. (Russell 1994: 62, cited in Siqwana-Ndulo 1998: 410)

Siqwana-Ndulo argued that the African perspective therefore provides a basis for understanding the practices of African family and household arrangements. Their cultural values have great influence in terms of the ways in which African households organise themselves and make their choices. African marriage and family have always been at the core of a unique and complex social organisation underpinned by the value system unique to African societies. In South Africa's Eastern Cape Province, for example, the institution of marriage, family, household and the entire social organisation from the early days of polygyny have been geared towards the community interest and to ensure that everyone's needs are taken care of. There was a well-defined code of behaviour, with everyone's place, responsibilities and obligations in the family and society clearly defined. Some families and households today still strive to fulfil those obligations to one another (Siqwana-Ndulo 1998: 411–12).

However, the fact that many males have been displaced by migration means that the responsibilities have now shifted to those who remain as resident heads of households, who in most instances happen to be the elderly widowed women and other women left behind by the migrants. Female migration has tended to occur at a much slower rate. The families left behind had to adapt to living without the males (Siqwana-Ndulo 1998: 412).

In 1992, Siqwana Ndulo's survey of the family structure in the Ngcingwane village, Idutywa, Eastern Cape revealed thirty-three husband-and-wife households, with a variety of dependants, ranging from the couple's children to a variety of relatives and nonrelatives. Only in five of the households did the couples only live with their children, but these households could not be classified as 'nuclear' families in the Western sense as they anticipated being joined by relatives sooner or later (Siqwana Ndulo 1998: 413).

Of the ninety-six households that Siqwana-Ndulo surveyed, sixty (62.5 per cent) were headed by women, widows, never-married women and wives of migrants. Absent husbands acted as heads of families in decision making, except in cases where never-married women were heads. As such, African households have never been exclusively for the man and his wife or wives and their children. What Westerners call 'extended family' among Africans refers to a collectivity of people who live together, whose relationship could be traced through kinship or marriage, and who considered themselves family. The term 'extended family' assumes that households comprise the core family of a husband, his wife and children. All others are viewed as extensions of this core family. But among the patrilineal Xhosa, if one can trace a relationship through the father's side, they are entitled to call the household 'home' – they are family. Relations from the mother's side are also present (Siqwana-Ndulo 1998: 415). So, in this sense, the idea of the 'extended family' is alien to the African household structure. The household is viewed as home to a collective, the members of which may or may not be present at the time. Data also showed that African families in this area are not likely to evolve into nuclear families as has been predicted. The census data also indicated that even urban blacks were not experiencing a trend towards nuclear family households because of their participation in the capitalist economy (Russell 1994: 62).

Bigombe and Khadiagala argued that the trend towards modernity has been captured in the gradual transformations of African marriage and family organisations away from corporate kinship and extended families towards nuclear households. This is partly due to the breakdown of collective, kinship-oriented systems of production and reproduction. Where nuclear households have solidified, there have equally been significant shifts from high to low fertility rates in African families (Bigombe and Khadiagala 2004: 2). The rapid expansion of educational opportunities and the availability of contraceptive methods have contributed to the emerging perception that large families are an economic burden. Slow rates of economic growth and the mismatch between educational outcomes and labour opportunities have compelled small family sizes (Bigombe and Khadiagala 2004: 2). In urban areas, factors such as wage labour, the monetised economy and the cost of living have altered the value of children. In addition, while family networks previously mediated the negative effects of large families, resource constraints have contributed to the reduction of family sizes and denuded the institutional structures of the extended family (Bigombe and Khadiagala 2004: 2–3).

A critical continuity in African family patterns relates to the persistence of polygynous practices. As such, the much-anticipated decline in polygynous households is still far from a social reality in most African countries. According to Bigombe and Khadiagala, the situation is still more prevalent in rural areas because of the imperatives of the sexual division of labour in agriculture, where wives and many children are considered an asset. Increasing education, urban migration and employment have created new courtship patterns that emphasise individual choice, thus providing women with relative equality in the arena of sexuality and male selection (Bigombe and Khadiagala 2004: 7).

Another factor that is undermining kinship-based family structures in the prevalence of single parenthood, especially among young urban females. With more women joining the labour force, single and female-headed households are becoming a discernible pattern in the African social landscape. According to Bigombe and Khadiagala, this is a result of secular changes in educational status, employment and occupational mobility, and, in some cases, the decline of marriageable men. Studies in African cities also show a high representation of female-headed households among the poor who fail to overcome dislocation, migration and deprivation, especially in unplanned urban settlements (Bigombe and Khadiagala 2004: 8).

Bigombe and Khadiagala noted that in South Africa, apartheid policies in many ways directly impacted family cohesion and reinforced the destructive influences that urbanisation and industrialisation had on the family. This left a high number of single-parent families, resulting largely from pregnancy outside marriage and divorce. As such, a large proportion of the nation's children grow up in female-headed households with little financial support, and the African family in South Africa continues to suffer considerably greater disintegration than families in the rest of Africa. This has led to cases of illegitimacy and poverty, inadequate childcare and psychological difficulties, with enormous consequences on the downward spiral of family disintegration in South Africa (Bigombe and Khadiagala 2004: 8).

In order to cope with issues of family disruption in most African countries in general, Bigombe and Khadiagala noted that single-parent families among lower income groups take their children to live with relatives, especially the children's grandparents. In South Africa, this was strengthened by childcare problems and restrictions by many employers on children of their workers residing on their premises. This was also strengthened by customary practices of multigeneration guarantees of the wellbeing of a person born into African families throughout their life cycles. In the 1990s, some national surveys in South Africa indicated that the proportion of older black South Africans living in two, three and four-generation households has remained stable since the early 1990s. According to Bigombe and Khadiagala, a study of 300 three generational households in two urban areas of the country revealed that about nine in ten African elders live in multigenerational households and that the ethos of the African extended family appeared to be intact even in the urban settings, with over 80 per cent of the top, middle and bottom generations of these families studied reporting harmonious relations between generations (Bigombe and Khadiagala 2004: 8–9).

In KwaZulu Natal Province, some grandmothers regarded themselves as important in building families, educating younger generations and providing generational continuity. For example, a survey of rural women aged around fifty-one indicated that most of them felt empowered when they took responsibility for important family decisions, including the education of grandchildren. In addition to being homemakers, the women were proud of adopting the 'traditional male' role as providers of the family if their men were unemployed (Sotshongaye and Moller 1996, cited in Bigombe and Khadiagala 2004: 9). Since the major source of funds for multigenerational support for grandchildren are pensions from grandparents, the post-1994 government continued with the transfers of the State Old Age Pension to extended families. The pensions have thus enhanced the status of the elderly household members as income earners and have provided lifelines to poorer older households. The pensions and grants are intended as a mechanism of redistribution to address racial and spatial patterns of poverty and inequality, but Lund questioned how many of those entitled to receive benefits actually do so (Lund 2006: 163).

Since the beginning of the democratic dispensation in South Africa in 1994, there has been interest in establishing what distributive gains have been made to the poorer people in the country, with the state's social assistance being a major focus of attention. State pensions and grants attract a lot of interest (Lund 2006: 160). Patterns of poverty are deeply gendered and racial in South Africa, with women generally poorer than men, girls more vulnerable than boys, old widows more vulnerable than older widowers and blacks poorer than whites because of the racial distribution of resources and opportunities under colonialism and apartheid. Just like in Britain, social security in pre-1994 South Africa was based on the 'male breadwinner model', which contained assumptions of a nuclear family in which the male head would be in full employment, and the mother's primary role would be homemaker and childrearer (Lund 2006: 161). According to Meth, while millions of South Africans directly receive state social assistance, many millions who are even poorer do not receive it (cited in Hunter et al. 2004; Lund 2006: 165). A popular legend or myth in the country is that grants for children would encourage women to get pregnant, especially teenage pregnancy (Lund 2006: 165).

The South African case thus indicates that the multigenerational African family is not in decline. It is only the economic downtowns and increased urban poverty that have undermined the institution of fosterage that had for long been part of the trend where the welfare of rural families depended on their solidarity ties with urban kin families. The mobility of children in rural areas tended to be enhanced by the financial and educational support of their urban kin (Bigombe and Khadiagala 2004: 9).

Conclusion

This chapter is an introduction to the ongoing research on the conceptualisation of a family policy in South Africa. It has argued that developing an African family policy from an African perspective is even more crucial now because black African families in South Africa are in a state of crisis, which manifests itself in the form of escalating family breakdowns and very negative effects on children and the youth (see Holborn and Eddy 2011). However, before attempting to come up with a family policy, it is also crucial to understand that it is a complex challenge to conceptualise and assess family-related policies (Anttonen and Sipila 1996; Hantrais 1994; Neyer 2003). The major source of concern to this ongoing study is that while the *White Paper* acknowledged that various kinds of families exist in the country, it concluded that the nuclear family is the most common type in South Africa (DoSD 2012: 15). The problem with this assumption is that, in the end, the Western nuclear family, which is regarded as the norm due to the hegemony of Western imperialism, continues to be the basis of many social policies despite the fact that this family form is not a reality for many black African families (Sunde and Bozalek 1995: 65). Living in nuclear households in urban or semi-urban areas should not be conflated with having a nuclear family. A historical understanding of the conceptualisation of a black African family, which was incorrect at certain levels, is necessary before we can think of conceptualising about a family policy.

Busani Mpofu is a senior researcher at AMRI, College of Graduate Studies. His main research interests include Third World urbanisation and the history of African cities, urban poverty, inclusive development, development discourse and theory. His publications include 'The Urban Land Question, Land Reform and the Spectre of Extrajudicial Land Occupations in South Africa', *Africa Insight* (2017); and 'The Land Question, Agriculture, Industrialisation and the Economy in Zimbabwe: A Critical Reflection', in O. Akanle and J.O.T. Adesisa (eds), *Development of Africa: Issues, Diagnoses and Prognoses* (2018).

References

Anttonen, A., and Sipila, J. 1996. 'European Social Care Services: Is it Possible to Identify Models?', *Journal of European Social Policy* 6: 87–100.

Bigombe, B., and G.M. Khadiagala, 2004. 'Major Trends Affecting Families in Sub-Saharan Africa'. Retrieved *20 September 2018* from http://www.un.org/esa/socdev/family/Publications/mtbigombe.pdf.

Cattell, M.G. 1997. 'Zulu Grandmother's Socialization of Granddaughters', *Southern African Journal of Gerontology* 6(1): 14–16.

Department of Social Development, Republic of South Africa (DoSD). 2008. *Quantitative Assessment of Families in South Africa*. Pretoria: DoSD.

_____. 2011. *Green Paper on Families: Promoting Family Life and Strengthening Families in South Africa*. Pretoria: DoSD.

_____. 2012. *White Paper on Families in South Africa*. Pretoria: DoSD.

Ferreira, M. 1997. 'Of Pensions, Caters, and Homes for the Aged', *Southern African Journal of Gerontology* 7(1): 1–2.

Hantrais, L. 1994. 'Comparing Family Policy in Britain, France and Germany', *Journal of Social Policy* 23: 135–60.

Holborn, L., and G. Eddy. 2011. 'First Steps to Healing the South African Family', Research Paper. Johannesburg: South African Institute of Race Relations sponsored by the Donaldson Trust.

Hunter, N., I Hyman, D. Krige and M. Olivier, with A. Dekker, M. Khandlela and J. May. 2004. *South Africa Social Protection and Expenditure Review*. Durban/Johannesburg: School of Development Studies, UKZN/Centre for International and Comparative Labour and Social Security Law, RAU.

Krige, E.J. 1936. 'Changing Conditions in Marital Relations and Parental Duties among Urbanized Natives', *Africa: Journal of the International Institute of African Languages and Cultures* 9(1): 1–23.

Law, L. 2013. *The White Paper on the Family: Briefing Paper 317*, March, Southern African Catholic Bishops' Conference, Parliamentary Liaison Office.

Lund, F. 2006. 'Gender and Social Security in South Africa', in V. Padayachee (ed.), *The Development Decade: Economic and Social Change in South Africa, 1994–2004*. Cape Town: HSRC Press, pp. 160–82.

May, J. 2006. 'Constructing the Social Policy Agenda: Conceptual Debates around Poverty and Inequality', in V. Padayachee. (ed.). *The Development Decade: Economic and Social Change in South Africa, 1994–2004*. Cape Town: HSRC Press, pp. 143–59.

_____. 2008. 'Conceptualising and Measuring Poverty in the SADC Region: Debates and Implications', in M. Pressend and M. Ruiters (eds), *Dilemmas of Poverty and Development: A Proposed Policy Framework for Southern Africa Development*. Braamfontein: Institute of Global Dialogue, pp. 27–47.

Mbiti, J.S. 1969. *African Religions and Philosophy*. London: Richard Clay (The Chaucer Press) Ltd.

Menkiti, I.A. 1984. 'Person and Community in African Traditional Thought', in A.R. Wright (ed.), *Africa Philosophy: An Introduction*, 3rd ed. Lanham: University Press of America, pp. 171–91.

Moller, V., and R. Devey. 1995. 'Black South African Families with Older Members: Opportunities and Constraints', *Southern African Journal of Gerontology*, 4(2): 3–10.

Neyer, G. 2003. 'Family Policies and Low Fertility in Western Europe', MPIDR Working Paper WP 2003-21 July. Rostock: Max Planck Institute for Demographic Research.

Phillips, A. (ed). 1953. *Survey of African Marriage and Family Life*. London: Oxford University Press.

Preston-Whyte, E. 1993. 'Women Who are Not Married: Fertility, Illegitimacy and the Nature of the Households and Domestic Groups among Single African Women in Durban', *South African Journal of Sociology* 24(3): 63–71.

Ruch, E.A., and K.C. Anyanwu. 1981. *African Philosophy: An Introduction to Main Philosophical Trends in Contemporary Africa*. Rome: Catholic Book Agency.

Russell, M. 1994. 'Do Blacks Live in Nuclear Family Households? An Appraisal of Steyn's Work on Urban Family Structure in South Africa', *South African Sociological Review* 6(2): 56–63.

Sihlongonyane, M. 2000. 'The Invisible Hand of the Family in the Underdevelopment of African Societies: An African Perspective'. Retrieved 20 September 2018 from http://hdl.handle.net/10539/12673.

Singh, A. 2008. 'A Critical Evaluation of Attitudes towards Nuclear, Joint and Extended Family Structures among People of Indian Origin in Durban, South Africa', *Journal of Comparative Family Studies* 39(4): 453–70.

Siqwana-Ndulo, N. 1998. 'Rural African Family Structure in the Eastern Cape Province, South Africa', *Journal of Comparative Family Studies* 29(2): 407–17.

Smit, R. 2011. 'Family-Related Policies in Southern African Countries: Are Working Parents Reaping Any Benefits?', *Journal of Comparative Family Studies* 42(1): 1–36.

Sotshongaye, A., and V. Moller. 1996. 'My Family Eats This Money Too: Pension Sharing and Self-Respect among Zulu Grandmothers', *Southern African Journal of Gerontology* 5(2): 9–19.

Sunde, J., and V. Bozalek, 1995. '(Re)Presenting "the Family": Familist Discourses, Welfare and the State', *Transformation* 26: 63–77.

Chapter 10

Socioeconomic and Cultural Barriers to Marital Unions and HIV Incidence Correlates
A Public Policy Poser for South Africa

Busani Ngcaweni

Introduction

Recent studies have shown that in South Africa, the prevalence of HIV is higher among single and cohabiting people compared to their married counterparts. Citing evidence, Shisana et al. (2016: 238) observe that:

> The results show that the HIV incidence of married individuals who lived with their spouses was lowest at 0.27 per cent compared to all other marital status groups that had significantly higher incidence rates. Those who were in a relationship and going steady with their sexual partners were 6.6 times more likely than the cohabitating married group to acquire HIV. Similarly, those who were either single, widowed or divorced were 7.5 times more likely to acquire HIV than those who were married and live together with their partners. The risk of acquiring HIV was highest in the cohabiting group, which was 10.8 times higher than that of the married and living together group.

This development is attributed to a number of factors, including the propensity for multiple sexual partnerships among single people (Shisana et al. 2014). Research also shows that the risk of HIV transmission is higher among those with multiple sexual partners (Clark et al. 2006) and even greater for those who have concurrent sexual liaisons with these multiple partners (Onoya et al. 2015).

The perceived protective effects of marriage are attributed to married people contracting into a form of sociocultural and economic benefit, which induces the expectation of restricted sexual liaisons or none at all – in relative and comparative terms (Shisana et al. 2014).

Furthermore, there is evidence to suggest that among married people, there are 'social sanctions' that act as a deterrent to extramarital affairs. These include the possible negative impact on their reputations, commitment to the family, the tendency to view monogamy as the foundation for successful family life and broader social relations, and concerns about negative reputation on children if extramarital affairs become public (Zungu 2013; Shisana et al. 2014; Shisana et al. 2016).

While the recent studies show that marriage is protective to some extent, there is also evidence highlighting the higher prevalence of HIV among younger married women (Shisana et al. 2014) who get infected in the course of marriage. Serodiscordancy and the associated risk of infection is well documented. In many cases one partner in a marriage could have been positive before they got married or may be infected outside the marriage by engaging in an extramarital affair, then infecting the marital partner (see Shisana et al. 2016).

The chances of serodiscordancy are higher in countries like South Africa, where multiple sexual partners are common (Onoya et al. 2015), coupled with high levels of domestic violence (Jewkes et al. 2003), low sero-status disclosure (Vu et al. 2012) and partners who rarely test as a couple before engaging in unprotected sex (van Rooyen et al. 2013). There is also evidence of new infection within marriage due to extramarital affairs (Shisana et al. 2014). Domestic violence is a factor as it reduces the women's chances of negotiating safe sex measures like condom use (Jewkes et al. 2003; Kishor and Johnson 2004; Maharaj and Cleland 2005).

While evidence suggests that married couples are at a lower risk of HIV compared to cohabiting and single people, there are other factors that have to be considered before one can conclude that marriage is protective. As we have mentioned, these include domestic violence and multiple sexual partners within marriage (MSP). Where domestic violence in high, so is the risk of HIV as women's ability to negotiate safe sex is diminished (Jewkes et al. 2003). Multiple sexual liaisons are a factor that significantly increases the risk of HIV infection, especially where there is inconsistent or no condom use (Moyo 2008).

This chapter discusses the policy poser arising from evidence presented in Shisana et al. (2015) suggesting that marriage reduces the risk of HIV infection. In discussing these results, the chapter seeks to explore the following question: should the government actively promote marriage as part of public policy responses to the AIDS epidemic and, if so, how far can public policy go in addressing apparent sociocultural determinants of low marriage rates in South Africa?

These questions are complicated by a few factors, namely, there are expressed concerns about the high levels of domestic violence and serodiscordancy as mentioned above. Also, the government will have to balance constitutional values of secularism (the state cannot impose marriage on citizens), whilst including marriage or committed faithful relationships in the basket of intervention designed to contain the HIV epidemic. Further, as we will discuss below, South Africa is experiencing a significant decline in marriage rates (Statistics South Africa 2012; Shisana et al. 2015), especially among black people, who because of their low socioeconomic conditions also happen to carry a higher burden of HIV. The 2012 *South African National HIV Prevalence, Incidence and Behaviour Survey* by the Human Sciences Research Council (HSRC) found that Africans have a greater risk of exposure to HIV compared to other race groups and that they are 'less likely to report being married than the white, Indian or Asian groups. HIV prevalence was found to be higher in the unmarried, co-habiting population than in the married population' (Shisana et al. 2014: xxvi). Recent estimates are recording a similar trend.

It is important to state upfront that the limitation of the current chapter is that it draws much of its main thesis from an article by Shisana et al. (2016) and the earlier study (Shisana et al. 2014), which had reported lower HIV prevalence among married couples (10.5 per cent) compared to those living together (24.3 per cent) and those who are single (14.3 per cent). The Shisana et al. (2016) study deliberately included marital status in a survey of HIV status of the population because previous research by the HSRC had showed the relationship between the two.

Although we will restate this in the conclusion, it is worth observing here that perhaps in the course of future household surveys, there is a need to expand the scope of indicators and test many variables that seem to impact on marriage trends and further establish the attitudes of households to marital and HIV infection dynamics. This might close some of the data gaps that confine the scope of policy discussions like the present project.

Although this chapter goes into some detail to explain why marriage appears to be providing some sort of protection against HIV, it argues that there is scope to expand our understanding of perceptions about marriage, its future and associated dynamics. Before discussing the possible contentious subject of promoting marriage as a possible policy consideration, we will briefly discuss the notion of the protective effect of marriage and then proceed to review the literature on the dynamics of falling marriage rates in South Africa.

Understanding the Protective Effect of Marriage

It has been suggested that the protective effect of marriage might include fidelity, sharing of challenges among couples and some form of behavioural restraint, which imposes itself in formal unions (Shisana et al. 2016). Again, the notion of 'social sanction' associated with engaging in an extramarital affair should also be studied further, alongside exploring whether being in a formal union acts as a form of deterrent to risky sexual behaviour that puts both men and women at risk of being infected with HIV. The questions of HIV and its determinants have increasingly become a matter of public interest. Judging by the media attention given to the results of the 2014 HSRC study, one can conclude that the public is interested in understanding who is at risk of HIV and how this risk arises.

This HSRC survey for an example saw media houses like Independent Newspapers covering it more widely and paying particular attention to the issue of the correlation between marital status and HIV. In one of its titles, the *Sunday Independent* (23 June 2013), Kerry Cullinan and Sibongile Nkosi reported:

> Marriage apparently has a condom effect, with the HIV rate among married South Africans half that of unmarried people. Almost one-fifth (19.2 per cent) of unmarried South Africans are living with HIV, as opposed to 9.8 per cent of married people. In addition, unmarried people are five times more likely to have had more than two sexual partners in the past year. (Cullinan and Nkosi 2013)

In a study conducted among men in Cape Town, Zungu (2013: 213) found that some married men who have extramarital affairs reported that they were more likely to use protection due to concerns about negative consequences on the family, especially their wives. One of respondents in this study was quoted as saying: 'Yes, I know what I am doing is wrong [having multiple partners], but I must know and also make sure that with the other one outside I use *ijazi lasebukhweni* [condom].' Another respondent said:

> Others do these things [have multiple sexual partners] but are still able to do their thing and still make it safe. Even if they are with a person they do not know that well [referring to HIV status and behaviour], they still make it safe and use condoms. There are guys who do that. Of course I know this from what they say; I know they are doing it safe – that is what they say.

Concerned about the impact of multiple sexual partners and the increasing risk of HIV infection on children and the whole family, a male respondent in the same study remarked:

He is married but is still out there having affairs. I want to agree; he is speaking the truth. In many cases where this has happened, men are to blame. In most families where the children are left alone [orphaned], it [is] very rare that it is the mother who brings it [HIV] from outside for her husband, it is very rare. Most of the time it is us men who bring it from outside ... from their *makhwapheni* [roll-on/secret lovers].

Corroborating the phenomenon of protective effects of marriage against HIV, Zungu's (2013: 214) study concluded that 'by emphasising that the sexual encounters outside are protected, married men maintain a sense of control over their risky behaviour, allowing them to achieve two masculine imperatives simultaneously: that of being *isoka* outside (characterised by an uncontrollable sex drive) and a protector at home (mainly to his wife)'. Coma (2014) makes similar findings about the use of condoms by married partners in Kenya, who use protection in order to protect their spouses and families.

Marriage and Divorce Trends in South Africa

As already stated above, there is a concerning trend of decline in marriage or committed partnership trends across racial groups in South Africa. However, the declines are higher among Africans. As the chapter suggests, these declines have implications for the broader HIV response in South Africa, especially taking into account the propensity of unmarried people to have multiple sexual partners and for cohabiting partners to have loose arrangements that do not necessarily mitigate against MSP.

Table 10.1 below shows that whereas 186,522 civil marriages were recorded in 2008, the figure declined to 167,264 in 2011. The latter represents a 2.1 per cent decrease from the figures recorded in 2010 (170,826). In the same Statistics South Africa (2012) report, a significant drop in registered customary marriages is recorded. Whereas 17,283 customary marriages were registered in 2003 and 20,259 were registered in 2007, only 5,084 were registered in 2011. Beyond 2011, these numbers have not changed significantly as fewer marriages continue to be recorded.

This sharp drop between 2008 and 2010 in both civil and customary marriages might be consistent with presuppositions that economic pressures feature prominently among the factors that impact on decisions to marry. It should be noted that between 2008 and 2010, South Africa lost close to one million jobs due to the global economic meltdown, which affected labour market in labour-intensive sectors such as mining, agriculture, domestic service and manufacturing.

As far as divorces are concerned, a further negative trend is recorded in the Statistics South Africa marriage and divorce trends report (2012), especially as far as it affects black people, who are shown by data to be the population group most at risk of HIV. Using data from 42 courts nationwide, the report reveals that the divorce rate for Africans stood at 22.5 per cent in 2002. For the same period, the Coloured (people of mixed race) population recorded 11.4 per cent. Respectively, the numbers rise

Table 10.1 Civil marriages in South Africa between 2002 and 2011.

Year of registration	Number of marriages
2002	177,202
2003	178,689
2004	176,521
2005	180,657
2006	184,860
2007	183,030
2008	186,522
2009	171,989
2010	170,826
2011	167.264

Source: Statistics South Africa
(Marriages and Divorces, December 2012)

Table 10.2 Registered customary marriages between 2003 and 2011.

Year of registration	Number of marriages
2003	17,283
2004	20,301
2005	19,252
2006	14,039
2007	20,259
2008	16,003
2009	13,506
2010	9,996
2011	5,084

Source: Statistics South Africa
(Marriages and Divorces, December 2012)

significantly to 35.8 per cent and 16.6 per cent in 2011. What this suggests is that 'the propensity to marry is lower among South Africans than is the case in more developed society' (Hennon et al. 2011: 187), and the picture is further complicated by arguable high divorce rates.

Sociocultural Determinants of Marriage among Africans

We have seen from the evidence above that marriage rates, as a proportion of the population, are comparatively low in South Africa. They are even lower among Africans – declining from 29.6 per cent in 2001 to 26.8 per cent in 2011. In the same period, the number of those classified as 'never married' increased from 53.8 per cent to 56.2 per cent, yet the proportion of those living together or cohabiting jumped from 8.6 per cent to 10.4 per cent.

Citing evidence from other studies, Moore and Govender (2013: 624) noted that 'cohabitation in South Africa is predominantly a phenomenon of the 20–40 years age group and it has grown by about 50 per cent between 1996 and 2007'.

On its own, this chapter makes no value judgement on cohabitation as a practice. The point being made is that prevention measures are required to address the higher HIV rates among cohabitating partners, as Shisana et al. (2014 and 2016) demonstrate.

Since this negative marriage trend affects mainly black Africans, sociocultural and historical factors are suspected to be the main determinant. These will be discussed in detail below, starting with the sociocultural factors.

In the study by Posel and Rudwick, the cultural practice of lobola featured among the factors influencing marriage decisions:

> In both the quantitative survey data and the qualitative interview data, *ilobolo* is identified as a constraint to marriage. Our interviews suggest that this is linked both to the individualization of the custom, which has increased the responsibility on prospective husbands to save for *ilobolo* through their own earnings, and to what is seen to be a commercialisation of the custom. (2014: 19)

Posel and Rudwick also noted that although there is general concern about perceptions of *lobola* (loosely translated as the bride price and culturally prescribed in pre-marital rites) being commercialised, the option of moderating it is immediately considered by families, who believe that its value is a signifier of respect and some sort of compensation to the family for the costs of raising and educating the bride to be.

The inability to meet *lobola* 'demands' seem to be causing delays in marriage for black Africans relative to other population groups. In this connection, the study by Richter et al. (2010: 86) found that 'marriage may be delayed because of the difficulties of negotiating arrangements between families. Moreover, *lobola*, previously payable in the form of livestock, was monetised and, more recently, commercialised'. This creates challenges for young black men, especially if they are employed in poor-paying jobs, given the high levels of deindustrialisation (Decoteau 2013). By extension, marriage is delayed, which then brings down overall marriage rates among black Africans.

In another study, Posel and Casale (2009: 1) make a direct connection between high unemployment and low marriage rates among black people. They concluded that since 'in many African marriages, bridewealth is paid by the prospective husband to his wife's family to validate the marriage', the prevalence of unemployment impacts black males' ability to meet their premarital cultural obligations. Besides perceptions of excessive *lobola* demands due to women increasingly accessing education and better employment opportunities, the evidence also shows that education and employment impact on fertility, a phenomenon that is consistent with trends from other developing countries (Thomas 1999; Hazelhurst 2010).

For men, better education and work opportunities mean they can rely more on technology and fast-moving consumer products for sustenance (Ngcaweni 2012), which increases self-sufficiency and diminishes the 'traditional' role of a wife (Ngoma 2012). The meaning of manhood in traditional terms has mutated to prioritise material assets. Having a 'wife' or family is no longer a proxy for *ukukhula ube yindoda* (becoming a man), as was the case decades ago. Social mobility pressures (to accumulate assets that mark one's position on the social ladder) also influence marital status choices.

With the advent of democracy in 1994, freedom of choice was also extended to lifestyle and family options. Africans had a choice to embrace certain lifestyles and to renegotiate what their 'own' cultures and traditions mean, especially under colonialism and apartheid, where they were proletarised. The direct influence of other cultures also increased, with institutional barriers of contact being created by the removal of apartheid. Social mobility is also a factor here, as we discuss elsewhere in this chapter. Post-1994, more Africans, especially females who could now participate freely in the labour market, moved away from their close-knit communities where everyone knew each other. This moved them further away from the social support system.

The practice of cohabiting also became more prevalent (there was no longer any cultural stigma associated with this). Two causes are assumed here: first, couples needed to pool their sparse resources to afford the increasing costs of living; and in some instances, it might have had to do with changing perceptions of marriage – away from the predominantly Nguni tradition, which stigmatised cohabitation. With deepening middle-class aspirations and lifestyles, wedding costs (for white/civil/reception and traditional ceremonies) continue to rise today as they did in the mid 1960s, when Mair (1969) wrote that the cost of marriage was further increased by the standard of display that was expected at weddings. This resulted from the idea that a Christian wedding should include all the elements which characterised it in European culture.

Add *lobola* and other premarital cultural ceremonies to the mix, and the costs escalate exponentially compared to the wedding ceremonies of other population groups. Most probably, this explains the low marriage rates among Africans. Even with the legal recognition of African customary marriages as having the same binding effect as other civil unions, the practice of hosting two ceremonies persists within the demographic group that occupies the epicentre of economic deprivation.

The phenomenon of lavish weddings is not unique to South Africa. It appears to be common in postcolonial societies where colonial administrators devalued traditional weddings. With European modernity in the ascendency, marriage unions could only be legitimised or solemnised through Christian rites. For example, in Case et al. (2013), the point is made that expensive weddings involving poor families in India, where the lavishness of the wedding ceremony confers status and respect, increased with European values being imposed by colonial administrators. Lavish weddings in India are a sign of social mobility. Case et al. (2013) continue to draw parallels between expensive weddings and lavish funerals in black communities in South Africa and found striking similarities – Africans spend more than double on funerals compared to other population groups.

As social pressures set in to spend on lavish weddings (and as *lobola* is perceived to be expensive especially for educated women), it is not inconceivable to sympathise with perceptions that marriage is becoming a preserve of those who have better-paying jobs and therefore can afford *lobola*, premarital rituals as well as two wedding ceremonies: the Christian (white wedding) and the traditional wedding ceremonies.

From the evidence discussed above, it is clear that the marriage institution is declining among black Africans, both as new marriages decrease and divorce rates increase. Thus, the protective effect of the marital union is diminished, especially in the context of studies by Shisana et al. (2014 and 2016), which concluded that marriage has a protective effect against HIV infection, with only 0.27 per cent of married people found to have newly acquired HIV in 2012 compared to unmarried people, where rates for those cohabiting stood at 2.91 per cent.

From the marriage-labour market status trends, we can deduce that the poor and un(der)employed are trapped in structural conditions and are less likely to marry, thereby increasing their susceptibility to HIV infection – most end up residing in informal settlements, where infections rates are higher than in formal urban areas. This has the potential of becoming a vicious cycle in that, as Levinsohn et al. (2011: 18–19) found, HIV-positive people in South Africa are 6–7 per cent most likely to be unemployed compared to people who are HIV negative. The latter would most likely work in low-skilled labour shedding sectors like mining, domestic service and agriculture.

Education is another factor, as educated people tend to be at lower risk of HIV infection. A study by Louw et al. (2009) found that HIV rates between female and male educators were not different. This was attributed to relatively similar levels of education – most have matric plus three years of postsecondary school qualifications. In other words, with education, the vulnerability rates reach equilibrium.

A Brief Overview of Marriage in Historical Context

Historical factors also seem to play a role in determining marriage trends. Here we are referring to the painful history of the migrant labour system, which 'normalised' the idea of multiple sexual partners and devalued the meaning of family (Morrell 1997 and 2001; Hunter 2005 and 2007; Cullinan and Nkosi 2013). In this instance, the family institution is defined, in Western terms, as a unit consisting of husband and wife(s).

Because of the migrant labour system, which took men away into mining and production centres, the majority of black workers either kept casual partners or cohabited with other women in the hostels and townships next to their areas of work. They would occasionally visit home during the Easter or Christmas holidays to be with their families and wives. The literature has already established the impact of HIV and tuberculosis (TB) among migrant workers and their families in labour-sending rural villages (see Sonnenberg et al. 2001; Corbett et al. 2004). As already argued, the migrant labour system devalued the family and left many children and women vulnerable to poverty and abuse. With the weakening of African family structures, support systems to help young couples before and after marriage diminished.

Further, the structure of the South African economic geography is such that most young couples tend to stay far away from parents/relatives. Fewer in the black communities readily resort to professionals for therapy and psychosocial support. These observations are relevant to the extent that data points to rising divorce numbers among Africans, as reported in the Statistics South Africa report cited earlier in this chapter.

In their works on the impact of colonialism and apartheid on masculinity among African men, Hunter (2005, 2007) and Morrell (1997, 2001) argue that being a man was defined by one's ability to create wealth, own cows and land, and take a wife, thereby qualifying to be *uMnumzana* (a grown man) with a homestead. Apartheid and migration took this aspect away and resulted in a crisis of masculinity and a slow destruction of the African family. With increasing socioeconomic difficulties and the adverse effect of migration into single-sex hostels and reservations, manifestations of masculinity changed and impacted on the concept of the family. Therefore, current marriage and divorce trends within the African population group might be experiencing the residual effects of the negative consequences of the migrant labour system as well as colonialism, which set the standard for *lobola* (in the Natal colony it was Theophilus Shepstone, the representative of the British Empire, who set the bride price at eleven cows) and two wedding ceremonies. Many working people in South Africa, especially in the agriculture, mining, construction and domestic work sectors, continue to work and stay away from their families. Taking into account that even registered customary marriages are on the decline, as the data presented above demonstrates, there is clearly a need to interrogate the burden of history more closely and find solutions to the structural nature of unemployment among black people.

Linked to earlier reflections on sociocultural determinants of marriage are additional socioeconomic realities facing black people due to the legacy of colonialism and apartheid. Here we are referring to a growing public discourse suggesting that a 'black tax'[1] places a burden on black people's disposable income and overall socioeconomic wellbeing. 'Black tax' refers to remittances and other family responsibilities that the early generations of the post-apartheid black middle class have to pay. These include supporting siblings' education, improving the family (parental) home and paying off study loans. For married couples, perceptions are that the black tax reduces income and increases competition between the partners, as they want their parents/families to benefit equally from their joint income. This obviously requires detailed research in order to validate these public claims about the black tax issue.

The Policy Poser of Promoting Marriage in a Secular Society

Let us now return to the primary concern of this chapter: having established the association between material status and susceptibility to HIV (where married people tend to have lower infections rates) and noting from the Statistics South Africa (2012) data that fewer people are getting married in South Africa (and more are divorcing), should the government add the practice of marriage to the continuum of measures required to manage the AIDS epidemic in South Africa? In a liberal democracy such as South Africa, the government will be cautious not to aggressively promote marriage as a public policy response to HIV, not least because it interferes with cultural, religious and personal choices, but more so because some of the factors that stunt marriage rates cannot easily be regulated. The latter refers to *lobola* and high wedding ceremony costs, as well as the growing choice to remain single, cohabit or delay fertility. There is however room for civil society campaigns that involve conversation with traditional leaders who see themselves as custodians of culture. Because both colonial and apartheid administrations used state apparatus to interfere with the culture of the oppressed black majority, the democratic state would walk a tight rope if it was seen to be either changing or making cultural impositions.

Later marriage (after age 24) was associated with increased odds of HIV infection (Shisana et al. 2015: 1). The evidence has shown that stable marital unions are beneficial in many other ways than simply preventing HIV infection, including ensuring economic and psychosocial benefits not only for men and women, but also largely for children (Wilkins (2012), cited in the Department of Social Development's *White Paper on Families in South Africa* (2013)).

It is also believed that strong families premised on strong marital unions could help resolve many social challenges and, by implication, reduce the burden of social spending by the government (Fagan 2001). In this connection, efforts aimed at promoting some sort of formal unions have the potential to yield many positive spin-offs to the broader society, as some of the evidence in this chapter suggests. Developmental states like Singapore offer valued lessons in this regard.

Owing to the complex nature of the problem and the many factors involved, public policy interventions need to be nuanced, multipronged, multisectoral and sensitive to both sociocultural and constitutional considerations. A few public policy options are discussed below for consideration by the government, practitioners and social partners involved in the field of HIV prevention. The first relates to addressing barriers to marriage for those who wish to get married. With economic pressures cited among the reasons for lower marriage rates, one of the interventions in this entry point should deal with the structural conditions of poverty and unemployment.

Evidence points to poverty or socioeconomic status as one of the key social determinant of AIDS in South Africa, with women-headed households occupying the epicentre (Ngcaweni 2016). Their vulnerability to HIV increases (17.9 per cent versus 13.1 per cent) more than that of their male counterparts (Shisana et al. 2010). The HSRC (2012: 51) study concluded that 'there is an inverse relationship between household economic status and HIV status, with members from lower household economic status having higher HIV prevalence'.

Improving the socioeconomic wellbeing of South Africans, especially through the creation of decent and sustainable jobs, remains one of the most effective policy interventions that should be intensified. This will liberate women to make choices on matters pertaining to fertility and condom use, and will assist those who wish to marry but are prevented from doing so by resource constraints.

Alternative means of earning livelihoods, like self-employment, should also be prioritised, as sustainable small businesses set people on a course of economic freedom (Treat et al. 2012; Treat 2014). Alongside sustainable employment creation measures, the state should accelerate the skills revolution in order to empower poor people to make decisions and to participate in the labour market, thus allowing them the freedom to make choices about fertility, marriage, educating their children and so on.

Alongside the hard real-economy intervention, the government should actively promote wide-ranging and inclusive social dialogue in order to create safer spaces for a national conversation on the sensitive subject of sociocultural determinants of marriage. Given the sensitive nature of the history of colonial and apartheid state involvement in private matters like marriage, fertility and interracial unions, it will be difficult for the democratic state to be seen to be actively involved in measures to regulate *lobola*, although some have quipped that it should be taxed (see 'Tips for Trevor' from the various budget speeches by former Finance Minister Trevor Manuel). Civil society organisations are better placed to debate and raise consciousness about the dangers of the perceived commercialisation of *ilobolo* and the unintended negative consequences of societal expectations of lavish weddings.

Traditional leaders in provinces like KwaZulu-Natal have proven to have a very powerful influence on cultural issues, as evidenced in the recent dramatic uptake of medical male circumcision. Circumcision as a cultural practice had been abandoned among the Zulu cultural adherents since the King Shaka wars of the mid nineteenth century. Already, the data shows that it is not just HIV infection rates that are high in KwaZulu-Natal (where medical male circumcision is being successfully implemented as one of the prevention measures); there are also 'very low marriage rates among Zulu adults' (Posel and Rudwick 2014: 51), who are predominant in KwaZulu-Natal. Posel and Rudwick (2014: 67) concluded that: '*Ilobolo* therefore remains a defining feature of a Zulu marriage, explaining why high *ilobolo* demands are likely to constrain marriage in Zulu society.' If the need arises, policy makers can engage traditional leaders to discuss unintended negative consequences of the perceived commercialisation of *lobola* or high costs of getting married.

Another possible policy option relates to the public provision of support services to people who wish to marry or to remain married. The *White Paper on Families in South Africa* has already signalled the government's commitment in this regard (Department of Social Development 2013). Among the low-hanging fruit is the strengthening of institutions that support young adults contemplating marriage and those already married and requiring psychosocial support. With regard to marriage and its association with a reduced risk of HIV infection, the message should be very clear: marriage is not a condom. It does not prevent HIV infection. However, being in a formal monogamous union tends to reduce the risk. It should be noted that whilst the *White Paper on Families in South Africa* does not issue a clarion call to all citizens to marry, it tacitly promotes formal unions as a basic unit of the family. The policy can be used to encourage stable relationships and to discourage sexual relations outside the union, particularly where there is no adherence to safe-sex messages.

For those residing in rural areas, the government can strengthen the capacity of rural NGOs and traditional authorities to provide support to families, especially young couples who wish to formalise their unions. Some of these proposals are already contained in the *White Paper on Families in South Africa* (Department of Social Development 2013). This should be in addition to accelerating the development of rural areas and creating livelihoods there in order to mitigate migration pressures that see many rural people end up in poorly serviced informal settlements where exposure to HIV is high.

Most importantly, efforts to support family unions should be coupled with those aimed at reducing domestic violence, addressing gender inequality and empowering women to negotiate safe sex and make decisions about fertility. As the evidence demonstrates that cohabiting trends are on the increase and that the cohabiting cohorts have greater HIV infection rates compared to those in legal unions, the government and development partners need to package HIV prevention messages targeted at cohabiting couples. A similar point can be made about other high-risk groups like married adults who live apart. The risk of multiple concurrent sexual partners should form the basis of this communication and behaviour change message.

Conclusion

This chapter does not see marriage as a silver bullet in the fight against the AIDS pandemic in South Africa. To the extent that the literature we have surveyed points to a negative correlation between marital status and the incidence of HIV among married heterosexual couples compared to other cohorts, we are proposing possible policy responses to factors that seem to negatively affect marriage rates, especially among black people, who carry the disproportionate burden of HIV and AIDS in South Africa. It is not a silver bullet because rates of infection continue to be high among young girls, suggesting that they might be infected before most of them marry from their mid twenties onwards. It is also not a silver bullet in any context showing high rates of domestic violence and multiple concurrent partners.

However, public policy can deliberately highlight the risks associated with being single, cohabiting, being married and living apart, and most of all engaging in risky sexual behaviour, such as engaging in multiple concurrent sexual liaisons. For those entering marriage or cohabiting, PreP should be encouraged for serodiscordant partners and consistent condom use should be promoted.

Recommendations about possible policy measures to de-escalate *lobola* from being a barrier to couples who wish to formalise their unions are sensitive policy matters that require delicate handling, since a secular state like South Africa cannot be seen to be actively imposing a value system that might be in conflict with the rights of individuals to choose. The *White Paper on Families in South Africa* recognises this and carefully nuanced earlier drafts that had openly advocated marriage and reduced the definition of a family to a household led by heterosexual individuals in a formal union.

For those who elect to formalise their union but might be deterred by perceived excessive cultural requirements, the policy makers have the authority to engage social actors like traditional leaders and civil society organisations, who can use community engagements to discuss and find organic solutions. This debate is more germane today as the AIDS agenda moves beyond the biomedical into investigating and finding solutions to the social determinants of the epidemic, including but not limited to domestic violence, multiple concurrent sexual relations, low condom use and intergenerational sex. Economic determinants also require coherent policy responses, as poverty, unemployment and inequality increase vulnerability to HIV infection, and as the evidence shows that poor people who reside in informal settlements are at higher risk (HSRC 2012) compared to those in formal jobs and suburbs.

South Africa also has multisectoral policy advice and coordination from structures like the South African National AIDS Council (SANAC), which have proved effective in engaging communities and stakeholders on difficult matters like medical male circumcision. SANAC should therefore actively consider taking up some of the policy posers discussed in this chapter to the extent of advising relevant stakeholders and the government on appropriate responses and social mobilisation campaigns. The successful introduction of medical male circumcision in KwaZulu-Natal presents valuable lessons for future campaigns involving sensitive matters relating to culture and belief systems (Ngcaweni 2016).

This cannot be regarded as the most difficult policy matter that the state has delved into. There are arguably more sensitive matters that the South African government has carefully and successfully negotiated with stakeholders and then implemented; these include same-sex civil unions and abortions. Opportunities abound for a balanced response in the arena of marriage as well.

Busani Ngcaweni is Head of Policy and Research Services in The Presidency, South Africa. He is Non-Resident Research Fellow at the University of Johannesburg where he is registered for doctoral studies in Development Studies. He holds a Master of Science in Urban and Regional Studies from from the University of KwaZulu-Natal.

Note

1. For more discussion on the black tax debate, see http://www.enca.com/south-africa/working-pay-black-tax%E2%80%99; http://www.702.co.za/articles/3451/do-many-black-south-africans-pay-a-silent-yet-crushing-tax-aka-black-tax; and http://www.news24.com/Opinions/Black-tax-is-not-real-20150508 (accessed 20 September 2018).

References

Case, A., A. Garrib, A. Menendez and A. Olgiati. 2013. 'Paying the Piper: The High Cost of Funerals in South Africa', *Economic Development and Cultural Change* 62(1): 1–20.

Coma J.C. 2014. 'HIV Prevention and Marriage: Peer Group Effects on Condom Use Acceptability in Rural Kenya', *Social Science and Medicine* 116: 169–77.

Corbett, E.L., S. Charalambous, V.M. Moloi, K. Fielding, A.D. Grant, C. Dye, M.K. de Cock, H. R. Hayes, B.G. Williams and G.J. Churchyard. 2004. 'Human Immunodeficiency Virus and the Prevalence of Undiagnosed Tuberculosis in African Gold Miners', *American Journal of Respiratory and Critical Care Medicine* 170(6): 673–79.

Cullinan, K., and S. Nkosi. 2013. 'HIV Rate of Married People Half that of Unmarried in SA', *Sunday Independent*, 23 June 2013. Retrieved 20 September 2018 from http://www.iol.co.za/sundayindependent/hiv-rate-of-married-people-half-that-of-unmarried-in-sa-1.1536152#.Vhbga9FzPL8.

Decoteau, C.L. 2013. 'The Crisis of Liberation: Masculinity, Neoliberalism and HIV/AIDS in Post-apartheid South Africa', *Men and Masculinities* 16(2): 139–59.

Department of Social Development. 2013. *White Paper on Families in South Africa*. Pretoria: Government of South Africa.

Fagan, P.F. 2001. *Encouraging Marriage and Discouraging Divorce*. Washington DC: The Heritage Foundation.

Hazelhurst, E. 2010. 'SA's Falling Fertility Rate is a Mixed Blessing', *The Star Business Report*, 25 October. Retrieved 20 September 2018 from http://www.iol.co.za/business/opinion/sa-s-falling-fertility-rate-is-a-mixed-blessing-trading-agenda-1.723470#.VhgHf9FzPL8.

Hennon, C.B., and S.M. Wilson. 2011. *Families in a Global Context*. New York: Routledge

Hunter, M. 2005. 'Cultural Politics and Masculinities: Multiple Partners in Historical Perspective in KwaZulu-Natal', *Culture Health and Sexuality* 7(4): 389–403.

———. 2007. 'The Changing Political Economy of Sex in South Africa: The Significance of Unemployment and Inequalities to the Scale of the AIDS Pandemic', *Social Science and Medicine* 64(3): 689–700.

Human Sciences Research Council (HSRC). 2005. *South African National HIV Prevalence, HIV Incidence, Behaviour and Communication Survey*. Pretoria: HSRC Press.

———. 2012. *South African National HIV, Behaviour and Health Survey 2012*. Pretoria: Human Sciences Research Council.

Jewkes R.K., B.L. Levin, and L.A. Penn-Kekana. 2003. 'Gender Inequalities, Intimate Partner Violence and HIV Preventative Practices: Findings of a South African Cross-sectoral Study', *Social Science and Medicine* 56(1): 125–34.

Louw, J., O. Shisana, K. Peltzer and N. Zungu. 2009. 'Examining the Impact of HIV and AIDS on South African Educators', *South African Journal of Education* 29(2): 205–17.

Levinsohn, J.A., Z. McLaren, O. Shisana and K. Zuma. 2011. 'HIV Status and Labour Market Participation in South Africa', *NBER Working Paper Series*: Working Paper 16901, National Bureau of Economic Research.

Kishor, S., and K. Johnson. 2004. *Profiling Domestic Violence: A Multi-country Study*. Calverton, MD: ORC Macro.
Mair, L.P. 1969. *African Marriage and Social Change*. New York: Routledge.
Maharaj, P., and J. Cleland. 2005. 'Integration of Sexual and Reproductive Health Services in KwaZulu-Natal, South Africa', *Health Policy and Planning* 20(5): 310–18.
Moore, E., and R. Govender. 2013. 'Marriage and Cohabitation in South Africa: An Enriching Explanation?' *Journal of Comparative Family Studies* XLIV(5): 623–39.
Morrell, R. 1997. 'Masculinity in South African History: Towards a Gendered Approach to the Past'. Paper presented at the Colloquium on Masculinities in South Africa. Durban: University of Natal.
_____. (ed.). 2001. *Changing Men in Southern Africa*. London: Zed Books.
Moyo, W., B.A. Levandowski, C. MacPhail, H. Rees and A. Pettifor. 2008. 'Consistent Condom Use in South African Youth's Most Recent Sexual Relationships', *AIDS and Behaviour* 12(3): 431–40.
Ngcaweni, B. 2012. 'Men Marry to Be Cared for', *Sunday Independent*, 6 May.
Ngcaweni, B. (ed.). 2016. *Sizonqoba! Outliving AIDS in Southern Africa*. Pretoria: Africa Institute of South Africa.
Ngoma, L. 2012. 'It's Not about Buying a Woman: A Rejoinder to Busani Ngcaweni', *Sunday Independent*, 14 May.
Onoya, D., K. Zuma, N. Zungu, O. Shisana and V. Mehlomakhulu. 2015. 'Determinants of Multiple Sexual Partnerships in South Africa', *Journal of Public Health* 37(1): 97–106.
Posel, D., and D. Casale. 2009. 'Sex Ratios and Racial Differences in Marriage Rates in South Africa', *Working Paper* No. 153, Durban: University of KwaZulu-Natal.
Posel, D., and S. Rudwick. 2014. 'Marriage and Bridewealth (*Ilobolo*) in Contemporary Zulu Society', *African Studies Review* 57(2): 51–72.
Richter, L., J. Chikovore and T. Makusha. 2010. 'The Status of Fatherhood and Fathering in South Africa', *Childhood Education* 86(6): 360–65.
Shisana, O., K. Rice, N. Zungu and K. Zuma. 2010. 'Gender and Poverty in South Africa in the Era of HIV/AIDS: A Quantitative Study', *Journal of Women's Health* 19(1): 39–46.
Shisana, O., T. Rehle, L.C. Simbayi, K. Zuma, S. Jooste, N. Zungu, D. Labadarios and D. Onoya. 2014. *South African National HIV Prevalence, Incidence and Behaviour Survey, 2012*. Cape Town: HSRC Press.
Shisana, O., K. Risher, D.D. Celentano, N. Zungu, T. Rehle, B. Ngcaweni, and M.G.B. Evans. 2016. 'Does Marital Status Matter in an HIV Hyperendemic Country? Findings from the 2012 South African National HIV Prevalence, Prevalence and Behaviour Survey', *AIDS Care* 28(2): 234–41.
Sonnenberg, P., J. Murray, J.R. Glynn, S. Shearer, B. Kambashi and P. Godfrey-Faussett. 2001. 'HIV-1 and Recurrence, Relapse, and Reinfection of Tuberculosis after Cure: A Cohort Study in South African Mineworkers', *Lancet* 358(9294): 1687–93.
Statistics South Africa. 2012. *Marriage and Divorces Trends in South Africa*. Pretoria: Statistics South Africa.

Thomas, D. 1999. 'Fertility, Education, and Resources in South Africa, in Critical Perspectives on Schooling and Fertility in the Developing World', in C.H. Bledsoe, J.B. Casterline, J.A. Johnson-Kuhn and J.G. Haaga (eds), *Critical Perspectives on Schooling and Fertility in the Developing World*. Washington DC: National Academy Press, pp. 138–80.

Treat, J. 2014. 'On the Use and Abuse of Education: Reflections on Unemployment, the "Skills Gap" and "Zombie Economics"', in S. Vally and E. Motala (eds), *Education, Economy and Society*. Pretoria: UNISA Press, pp. 171–189.

Treat, J., M. Hlatshwayo, M. di Paola, and S. Vally. 2012. *Youth Unemployment: Understanding the Causes and Finding Solutions – Reflections on Education, Skills and Livelihoods*, Booklet. Johannesburg: University of Johannesburg.

Van Rooyen, H.B., J.M. Baeten, Z. Phakathi, P. Joseph, M. Krows, M. Pamela, P.M. Murnane, J. Hughes and C. Celum. 2013. 'High HIV Testing Uptake and Linkage to Care in a Novel Program of Home-Based HIV Counselling and Testing with Facilitated Referral in KwaZulu-Natal – South Africa', *Journal of Acquired Immune Deficiency Syndrome* 64(1): e1–e8.

Vu, L., K. Andrinopoulos, C. Mathews, M. Chopra, C. Kendall and T.P. Eisele. 2012. 'Disclosure of HIV Status to Sex Partners among HIV-infected Men and Women in Cape Town-South Africa', *AIDS and Behaviour* 16(1): 132–38.

Wilkins, R.G. 2012. 'Foreword', in S. Roylance (ed.), *'The Family and the MDGs': Using Family Capital to Achieve the Millennium Development Goals*. Doha: Doha International Institute for Family Studies Development, pp. 5–8.

Zungu, N.P. 2013. 'Social Representations of AIDS and Narratives of Risk among Xhosa Men', Ph.D. thesis. Cape Town: University of Cape Town.

Chapter 11

Old-Age Cash Grant Pay-out Days
How Beneficiaries Become Victims of Abuse in South Africa

Gloria Sauti

Introduction

In South Africa, old-age grants are not utilised solely to benefit senior citizens. While it is government's aim to benefit senior citizens, it is questionable whether it offers the benefit it should. Old-age grants have inevitably evolved to become a financial support for entire families ranging from children to grandchildren and other close relatives. This is primarily because a considerable number of South Africans still live in poverty-stricken conditions in the post-1994 era. As a result, the grant indirectly benefits all household members. This chapter explores the unprecedented attention placed on the old-age grants to senior citizens just before and on pay-out days in South Africa. In addition, it explores the underlying dynamics embedded in the 'celebrations' that have become a regrettable social phenomenon.

The first section of this chapter outlines the methodological approach of the study and defines old-age grants that Gillion (2000: 35–62) suggests 'includes 90 percent of the population who are not covered by a contributory pension scheme'. In addition, it discusses the origins of pension grants and the reasons why the majority of black senior citizens receive them, which Ferreira (2015: 1) statistically indicates had increased markedly by 2015. The next sections describe the scenes that are experienced in communities on pay-out days. Special attention is paid to the unprecedented attention placed on senior citizens by family members just a few days before and on pay-out days. It also explains how the vendors, local stores and nearby towns, as well as minibus taxi drivers, manipulate and abuse senior citizens on their pay day and what stakes they have in the old-age grant. The seventh section deals with a fundamental issue, that is, how senior citizens are compelled to engage in what Collins, Murdoch and Rutherford (2010: 95–132) describe as 'obligatory lending' to close family members and friends. Section eight highlights the conditions under which money is lent to senior citizens. It explains how *mashonisas* or South African loan sharks operate. The ninth section explores who the winners and losers are on grant pay days, and how this severely undermines government and other stakeholders' goals in poverty alleviation and the overall wellbeing of senior citizens. The abusive situations in some senior citizens' own homes are highlighted in the last section. In conclusion, the urgent need for policy frameworks that could help to combat some ills that have become a phenomenon are described. Urgent intervention from stakeholders is required to ensure that old-age pensions indeed principally benefit senior citizens.

Methodological Approach

Qualitative research methods were applied during the study. These included face-to-face interviews with senior citizens, family members of senior citizens, and those who have closely observed the old-age grant dynamics around Gauteng Province. Research was conducted in the following areas around Johannesburg: Randfontein, Snake Park, Dobsonville, Badirile, Brandvlei and Kagiso. Apart from structured and unstructured interviews, surveys and questionnaires were widely distributed in the areas studied. The study also included extensive observations over a three-year period from 2012 to 2015. While the study primarily explored townships, it included an analysis of people who hail from semi-urban and rural areas, who are often considered the poorer, lower-class, less-privileged or severely disadvantaged groups.

In order to understand inequality and poverty in a society such as South Africa, we need to understand the structure of opportunities that individuals and groups of people have in terms of earning wages, profits or income from investments or other forms of income (Seekings and Nattrass 2015: 106). Therefore, it was imperative to explore the old-age grant dynamics through the lenses of middle, upper and higher-income groups. In most urban societies, the aged get paid their pensions at local stores or banks. Therefore, it brings the aged of different classes to the same points on grant pay-out days. Some suffer different forms of abuse both personally and in the process of obtaining their cash pay-outs.

The selected approach was crucial. Pearson Education (2011: 3) suggests that 'because all expressions of human culture are related and interdependent, to gain a real understanding of human society we must have some knowledge of all its major aspects'. If we concentrate on some aspects and neglect others, we will gain a distorted picture. This study probed diverse dimensions of the grant for all races, cultures and classes from a number of communities in Gauteng. While 'the spirit of curiosity motivates social research', according to May and Williams (2002: 7), this study provides an in-depth analysis of the subject and pertinent issues that are a major concern and are often neglected in research.

Defining Old-Age Grants

In the last decade, countries in Southern Africa (including Lesotho and Swaziland), along with countries in other parts of the world, introduced old-age grants for their senior citizens. In these countries, the majority of the population are poor and are not employed in workplaces where they could formally contribute to retirement schemes. As a result, they are dependent on old-age grants provided by the state. These non-contributory grants are 'regular transfers to people, 60 years and older' (Standing 2003). Those who are eligible must earn no more than R64,680 per annum and have assets of no more than R930,600 for a single older person, whereas couples not earning more than R129,360 and having joint assets of no more than R1,861,200 are eligible. No obligatory contributions have to be made prior to qualifying to be a recipient of the old-age grant. The amount the elderly receive ranges between R1,410 per month for those aged between sixty and seventy-five and R1,430 per month for those older than seventy-five (SASSA, South African Social Security Agency; 2015). These grants are funded from general taxation and other state revenue (Pelham 2007: 1). South Africa is one of the few countries that provides non-contributory old-age grants for its elderly population.

Black South Africans were excluded from this scheme from 1928 to 1940. At that time, South Africa was one of only four African states with a well-established non-contributory pension scheme, which differs from the grant, and it was one of the largest in the developing world. Other countries that provided old-age grants for their senior citizens included Namibia, Mauritius and Botswana. The political transition after apartheid resulted in the old-age grant scheme being widened to include both whites and blacks. Gillion (2000: 53–63) affirmed almost a decade ago that 90 per cent of the world's working-age population is not covered by pension schemes capable of providing adequate retirement income.

He suggested that this is due to the 'bad management of many existing schemes, which leaves much of the world's population exposed to the risk of poverty during old age'. This trend includes South Africa. The government aims to reduce poverty among the targeted sectors. Barrientos (2003: 23–24) is of the view that the broader developmental role of social protection in developing countries involves three main functions, which are:

> (i) to help prevent basic levels of consumption among those in poverty or in danger of falling into poverty; (ii) to facilitate investment in human and other productive assets which alone can provide escape routes from persistent and intergenerational poverty; and (iii) to strengthen the agency of those in poverty so that they can overcome their predicament.

What is absent in the case of the aged is their 'agency', which enhances their ability to overcome poverty.

There are several key requirements stipulated by the South African Social Security Agency (SASSA) for senior South Africans or permanent residents to qualify for the old-age grant. Age is the first factor. Beneficiaries must be South African citizens or permanent residents. They must live in South Africa and not receive any other social grant for themselves. The vast majority of South Africa's senior citizens fall within the stipulated categories. They have been employed largely on a minimum wage and are often penniless by the time they reach retirement age. The government's aim to combat poverty and provide financially for the aged is therefore severely undermined by the abuse that has become a South African phenomenon and a focal point of this chapter.

The Origin of Old-Age Grants

From 1928 until 1940, whites were the only beneficiaries of pensions. This grant was only extended to blacks in 1940 (Marock and Soobrayan 2008). But there was a huge disparity in the *amounts* paid to different racial groups. This disparity continued until 1994, when the democratic government eradicated disparities. Since then, approximately 2 million South African senior citizens have been receiving a monthly grant, compared to 5.3 million in Brazil, where the population is four times that of South Africa. Lam, Leibrandt and Ranchod, who focus on statistics as well as disabilities within this age group, suggest (in Cohen and Menken 2006: 9–55) that the number of people in the 70–74 age category in the South African census sample was over 12,800 black men, 2,500 black women, 4,500 white men and 6,000 white women. These numbers have increased significantly to 3 million, as per the *Fact Sheet* statistics of August (Ferreira 2015). In comparative terms, South Africa runs a far more extensive non-contributory state pension than Brazil does.

In recent years, elderly South Africans who retire from more affluent employment with a contributory pension scheme often tend to reach bankruptcy within less than five years of their retirement. Individuals who retired from professional careers, particularly in academic circles, are then compelled to either seek employment from previous employers on a contractual basis at a meagre wage – many companies are becoming aware of the importance of retaining the skills and experience of older workers (Auer and Fortuny 2002: 19) – or to settle for the old-age grant. This emerged and was attested to by participants during the study. Affluent retirees may consider emigration to other countries, but less fortunate South Africans are already poor by the time they retire; therefore, they depend on the old-age grant provided by the state.

A research study funded by the British Department for International Development in 2016 indicates that 'pensioners, particularly those in poor rural areas, did no always enjoy the full benefit of the payment' (Yeng 2016). Another study (Surrender 2010: 203–221) indicates that grants help to perpetuate poverty rather than alleviate it, because they perpetuate dependency on the state. Conversely, this study argues that while social grants do indeed alleviate poverty and benefit senior citizens, they seem to be severely deprived by family members, vendors and others who take their money. Lombard and Kruger (2009: 119–35) observed that for every grandmother receiving a grant, twenty people are being supported. However, this is not the case in all families.

South Africa's approach to social policy must be viewed in the context of the political transition, which aimed to ensure the wellbeing of Africans disadvantaged by apartheid. After coming to power, the African National Congress (ANC) committed itself to poverty reduction, better income distribution, lower unemployment levels and increased social assistance (Ocampo 2010: 150). This is precisely why senior citizens benefit from old-age grants, increased from the previous lower amounts before 2014 to R1,410 and R1,430 per month respectively. However, the government's social policy is undermined through the abuse of senior citizens' grants.

Why Old-Age Grants are Paid to So Many African Senior citizens

It is imperative to discuss briefly, in terms of South Africa's political history, the reason for the number of African seniors receiving a state grant. African in this context includes blacks, whites and Coloureds as segregated by the apartheid dispensations. The why factor on state grants for senior citizens is undoubtedly coupled with colonial occupation and apartheid. It played an extensive role in the vast amount of poverty observed in South Africa, particularly amongst Africans – blacks, Coloureds and Indians who were dispossessed of their land and younger generations were prevented from acquiring land. This severely affected their agricultural independence. Colonial conquest and exploitation weakened the African family on two fronts: first, colonialism enforced labour migration, which compelled African families to live apart; and, second, the policies, laws and practices were aimed at impoverishing African families, and this had dire long-term consequences for them (Boyle et al. 2014: 102). Consequently, the colonial impact is still visible in the poverty-stricken conditions observed amongst the majority of South Africans.

The vast majority of the South African population is black and colonialism played a major role in disadvantaging black South Africans, who could previously sustain their families economically through crops and other exchanges. Although the 'state pension' was extended to blacks in 1940, there were huge disparities that were only eradicated in 1993 and deracialised in 1994. This means that during the pre-democratic dispensation, only white workers were entitled to a 'civilised' standard of living socially, politically and financially. These stringent exclusions had debilitating and far-reaching implications for all 'non-white' inhabitants of South Africa.

The colonial or apartheid state aimed to ensure that Africans remained dependent on the state and it succeeded in accomplishing this. The institutionalisation of apartheid in 1948 intensified racial discrimination and excluded black people from socio-economic activities and other opportunities. According to Surrender (2010: 203–221), social dependency debates have transitioned to issues of rising expenditure, handouts and the language of welfare dependency. Hence, the majority of senior citizens who depended on the state grant were employed in labour work where a contributory pension scheme was non-existent.

Black workers were subjected to separate and restrictive labour relations through laws such as the Industrial Conciliation Act of 1924 (Act No. 11). This law prohibited black workers from becoming members of trade unions and having representation in the workplace. Policies and Acts such as the Labour Policy and the Wages Act (Act No. 27) of 1925 were structured to exclude blacks from benefiting from state programmes designed to raise standards of living. Katzen (1961: 196) suggests that as black labourers were recruited on a migratory basis, the workers did not receive a 'family' wage. They were fed and housed while in the mines, and the low cash wage they received was merely supposed to supplement the earnings from the agriculture of their families in the Native Reserves (Katzen 1961: 196).

The majority of Africans were not employed in jobs where they could accumulate pensions and therefore became beneficiaries of the old-age grant. Therefore, the aim of the current government is to help reduce poverty amongst poor South Africans who meet the eligibility criteria. However, although the government's aim in equalising the old-age grant over the last two decades has been to mitigate poverty in old age, it has not been able to undo the previous disadvantage.

Worse still is the fact that the day on which old-age grant payment is made has become a monthly festivity, which illicitly benefits family members, vendors and local stores. Consequently, it has become a South African phenomenon that further abuses those who were abused and disadvantaged during the apartheid era. This is a crisis of epidemic proportions, which requires urgent government evaluation and intervention, as this situation is contrary to the government's objectives.

The number of the elderly who receive old-age grants in urban areas has also increased rapidly during the last few years. In terms of population analyses, the number of people aged sixty-five and over in South Africa doubled to one million from 1950 and 1980, which is indicative that they would depend on old-age grants (Marias 1988: 115). Since then, although there are seven other social grants, old-age grant recipients total three million as of 31 August 2014 (Ferreira 2015).

Old-Age Grant Days: Scenes of Festivity

Under closer observation, an intense beehive-like activity by vendors, small shops, large stores and taxi operators is detected on pay-out days. An atmosphere, reminiscent of the Christmas/holiday season, is created on this day each month. Senior citizens are dressed up and accompanied by some of their employed (but in the majority of cases unemployed) adult children, grandchildren or relatives who supposedly 'have their best interests at heart'. The visible intimacy observed is often a façade. Part of the reason for this (in some cases) may be, as with other forms of abuse, that victims hold the belief that it will stop (Duszak and Okulska 2011: 225). Either the family members' own vehicles are utilised, which results in some people staying out of work for the day, or family members hire vehicles that are paid for from the senior citizens' pensions. Minibus taxi drivers also make themselves available on the day to transport senior citizens, especially those who are unable to walk to their destinations, at raised rates.

The local halls where grants are paid are overcrowded with young and old individuals. Vendors also swarm into the areas. Multiple vehicles are parked nearby. Some vendors sell their produce from trucks. A festive 'braai' is held. A 'braai' is a cultural event that is arguably even more central to the South African identity than barbecues are to Australians (Pinchuck, McCrea and Reid 2002: 49). The braai is held at pay-out points each month, where some vendors sell ready-to-braai meat to senior citizens and their family members. Shops nearby display large signs detailing the goods they have for 'sale'. Pickpockets and robbers hang around to try their luck. In recent years, several instances have emerged and criminal cases were opened at local police stations in the West Rand, where senior citizens were smeared with 'black mixes' – an ointment or charm, became confused and were robbed of their cash at pay-out points or a few days afterwards. These crimes are primarily due to the lack of a police or security presence. Maria (interview, Dobsonville, South Africa 2015), a senior, remarks that 'on this day I feel special because I get much attention from my children and grandchildren and in the community, including vendors who sell diverse items'. Consequently, senior citizens are coerced into adopting irresponsible behaviour once they get their money. Some do not contribute to the welfare of their households, but indulge in alcohol abuse and other socially unacceptable activities. This study highlights experiences observed in a number of black townships or communities in Gauteng.

Vendors' Vibrant Market 'Sales'

At these vibrant markets, vendors sell diverse produce at what are termed 'cheap' prices. In most cases, vendors sell second hand goods and produce that is not fresh. Family members often coerce senior citizens into buying goods without ensuring that they are quality products. In some cases, the vendors indicate that their produce is fresh by displaying only a few at the top that are of good quality and fresh in order to lure senior citizens into buying, while the rest below are spoiled. Some senior citizens and family members remarked that 'the potatoes often look very good on top of the bag, but this is not the case beneath'. Alternatively, vendors have a sample bag, which is already open, and they throw all the potatoes out of the bag to show that the other bags are similar. Senior citizens remarked that 'they rob us and sell rotten or expired goods to us'. Some even lure the aged into purchasing items by lowering their 'cheap' prices further in order to ensure that the produce is purchased regardless of the fact that it is unhealthy and not suitable for human consumption.

Stores nearby also have a stake in the senior citizens' old-age grants. Stores 'reduce' prices dramatically to attract senior citizens. When the elderly enter a store to purchase maize-meal – a staple diet for the majority of South Africans – they may be unaware that the sell-by date is about to expire. This results in the aged and family members throwing away their money on old goods, manipulated by the buzzwords 'cheap days' (Edgeworth 2012: 119) or 'sales' as observed in South African societies. Many of the elderly do not look at the dates; I observed only a few who did. Family members, whose aim is to ensure that not too much of the grant is spent on food, often rush the elderly so that they do not have time to consider their purchases.

Local taxis also benefit. In their description of a typical grant day, Hebinck and Lent (2007: 329) quote Margaret, who lives in Guquka, describing the benefit grant days bring to taxi drivers 'who bring their taxis close to the pay point so that senior citizens do not have to walk to the taxi rank'. They confirm that the 'grant day is a good day for taxi men'. Taxi drivers also confirmed that grants days are good business days. Several taxi drivers remarked during an interview that: 'We are very busy on this day, it is not like other days during the month, we transport the elders wherever they want to go, we know they will pay and they do not complain about the amount we charge. We charge different prices; it only depends where they want to be dropped off' (Group interviews with taxi in Randfontein and Brandvlei, South Africa 2014–2015). Recently, some make use of the 'cheap-cheap *tuk-tuk* taxis that have taken over in Johannesburg' (Steyn 2013: 1).

The tuk-tuk taxi is a three-wheeler, commonly found in urban Asia. Some of the senior citizens remarked in interviews and others in surveys that: 'We pay the taxi or tuk-tuk drivers to take us wherever we need to go once we receive the grant. Many of us do not have family with vehicles, and we depend on the taxis to take us from one point to another, but they over-charge us, and they think that we are unaware' (Group interviews with Seniors in Randfontein and Dobsonville, South Africa 2016). Unfortunately, for the senior citizens, transportation is required if they have a few bags that they are unable to carry. They may pay as much as R60–80 for a single trip, while normal fares into town are R10 from Mohlakeng and R9 from Toekomsrus for a single trip.

The whole 'show' results in senior citizens spending much more than expected. Ironically, those who accompany them keep careful count of the amount being spent, since money lenders need to be paid and they themselves need to borrow some of the money. This entire 'festivity' places considerable pressure on senior citizens, some of whom are unable to count. Consequently, senior citizens benefit only marginally from their grant money. Two typically South African phenomena with regard to old-age grants in South Africa are as follows: first, as Clinton (1994: 616) observed, senior citizens who cannot afford to loan money are turned into money lenders by family members who 'borrow' and promise to return money; and, second, senior citizens fall victim or are lured into borrowing money from loan sharks.

Senior Citizens Forced to Become Money Lenders

Some senior citizens fall victim to adults in their own families who borrow from them and never pay the money back. Almost 76 per cent of senior citizens out of almost three hundred explored in five communities indicated that they were coerced into lending their grant money to family members. This occurs in the senior citizens' own households, regardless of their class status. Two groups of senior citizens are forced to become money lenders. The reason why I refer to the elderly who lend money to family members as 'money lenders' rather than loan sharks is because the elderly charge no interest on the money they lend to their relatives. The first group is senior citizens who are from marginally affluent families, while the second group includes senior citizens who are poor and are coerced – sometimes in abusive ways – to loan money to family members.

The first group often belong to money-sharing schemes referred to as 'societies' or *stokvels* in South Africa. It is estimated that *stokvels* in South Africa turn over R30 million a month (Mesthrie 2002: 413). Members pay a certain amount (R200–300) each. The amount they contribute each month is returned 10–12 times over, depending on the number of members of their society.

Some senior citizens fall under what Collins, Murdoch and Rutherford (2010: 51) refer to as 'obligatory lending'. The senior feels obliged to help out employed or unemployed family members who are in need. The senior may be in a position to help because they receive a small pension from their previous employers. While this is done willingly in the majority of cases, in some instances they are coerced into doing so, and while the money is repaid in some cases, it is not returned in others, even in affluent and supposedly 'caring' families.

The second group of senior citizens are worse off, are less privileged and cannot afford, as (Clinton 1994: 616) argues, to loan money to family members or any other individuals because their pensions can hardly sustain them throughout the month due to the number of family members who are dependent on them. Immediate and extended family members coerce and compel these senior citizens to lend money to them. This money is generally never repaid. In some communities, senior citizens who receive grants are bullied by younger members of their own households to support and sustain the youths' substance abuse habits. In the majority of the case studies conducted, it was established that the relatives of the elderly are the perpetrators of abuse and financial exploitation. Arditte (2014: 235) confirms this – culprits are usually very close family members.

This is a shameful situation, which requires prompt and urgent intervention on the part of state authorities, humanitarian organisations and society. It is a crisis, particularly when one takes into consideration the fact that the old-age grant is between a mere R1,400 and R1,470. These amounts are hardly sufficient to sustain one person on a monthly basis in the prevailing socio-economic circumstances. Instead of merely providing the grant to ensure the seniors' financial wellbeing, the government should ensure that their goals are adequately met and that the pensions are indeed benefiting the elderly, free from any abuse or exploitation.

Senior Citizens Fall Victim to Loan Sharks: The South African Situation

Senior citizens are lured into borrowing money to make ends meet and so fall victim to loan sharks. In this section, I distinguish between two phenomena in which senior citizens are directly targeted: first, the extent to which the senior citizens fall victim to loan sharks; and, second, how, as a result of family members, senior citizens are coerced into borrowing money from loan sharks. A striking observation in most South African neighbourhoods is the number of senior citizens present at loan sharks' homes on other days of the month. This happens just days after the old-age grant has been paid. Relatives of senior citizens in a specific loan shark's waiting room were loaning money on behalf of senior citizens when the following question was asked: 'Are you borrowing money for yourself or on behalf of someone else?'

Loan sharks, also known as *mashonisas*, as it will be applied in this chapter (the term can also be used as *omachonisas*) are individuals who loan money to individuals in African communities (Kelly-Louw 2009: 178). While quite a number of formal loan sharks or micro lenders have emerged in the country and are said to be benefit those who do not qualify for loans from banks, *mashonisas* are a law unto themselves. These local or informal loan sharks have ways of coercing individuals to pay back loans. They target low-income households, which are described by Mashigo (2012: 24) as those whose average monthly income is just below

R 1600. This is precisely the category into which the senior citizens fall. *The Economist* (2018: 29) asserts that 'if loans sharks are prosecuted it eliminates the victim's credit source'. Consequently, the extent to which the 'benefit' occurs has become a detriment to the aged.

Unlike Mashigo's (2012: 29–46) observation that '*mashonisas* own *spaza* shops', those observed in the communities researched do not own *spaza* or *tuck* shops; they are either employed or own other businesses, ranging from small to large, either in the public or private sectors. But, for some, money lending is their sole source of income. As a result, they charge exorbitant interest rates. This turns into a vicious cycle, from which the elderly are unable to escape, particularly when their grant is the only source of income for that family. In the communities observed, a number of senior citizens had fallen victim to these *mashonisas*. The resultant situation is not much different from the previous situation that existed during the colonial and apartheid eras.

The following question then arises: 'Are government officials and humanitarian organizations whose mandate it is to combat poverty and ensure the wellbeing of the aged not aware of this situation or are they just turning a blind eye?' This is an unjust situation – it cannot be condoned and should not be allowed to continue unabatedly. It is an indictment on civil society and our leaders in national government as long as this situation persists. It could be argued that stakeholders are not obliged to determine what should be done with the grants they provide. However, if these are not monitored in one way or another, it jeopardises the government's objectives. If no adequate steps are taken to protect senior citizens, the government's purposes are defeated and they are no better off than they were under the apartheid regime.

Conditions under Which Loan Sharks Lend

Loan sharks have several conditions under which they lend money to senior citizens and the unemployed. As Mashigo (2012: 40) noted, they 'do not require proof of employment. The modus operandi of *mashonisa's* or loan sharks is founded on the systemic retention of identity documents and grant cards, including SASSA cards. In the event of a client requiring their personal documents for any reason, certain preconditions must be adhered to'. Depending on the amount owed, personal, movable assets like televisions, DVD players, radio systems, microwaves and so on must be surrendered as security for the document while the money is being retrieved.

Two completely unethical situations occur: first, the amount paid to loan sharks is loaded with high interest, especially if the senior is unable to count; and, second, the full grant pay-out of the senior is handed over and the senior's identity document is returned to the loan shark. Squires (2004: 196) confirms this. This indicates that the elderly borrow more than the grant they receive and are then expected to loan more money. This is a vicious cycle, from which the senior cannot escape.

Old-Age Grants: Winners and Losers

While senior citizens are supposed to be the winners in terms of their grants and overall wellbeing, they tend to become losers. Exploitative practices show the moral decay prevalent in South African society. Unscrupulous 'criminal' elements become the 'winners' and senior citizens the victims, who are kept imprisoned in situations no different from those that existed in the colonial and apartheid eras they survived. Unscrupulous behaviour is driven solely by greed on the part of family members, vendors, loan sharks and others, as (Squires 2004: 27) indicates. In addition, local stores who sell goods at highly inflated 'sale' prices and taxi drivers who charge exorbitant amounts benefit. The abuse of the elderly was noted in the Debates on the National Council of Provinces in 1994 (Government Printer 2001: Issue 1–4). The fact that this issue remains a problem indicates the lack of regard for senior citizens.

Financial Abuse in Homes

Old-age grants put food on the tables of a significant number of South African households. With their state grants, the elderly feed and clothe either children who are young adults, or older children, as well as grandchildren whose parents have abandoned them. The grant is often the only income in such households. While many of the unemployed and, in some cases, children rely on old-age grants, the manner in which the aged are often coerced into providing money is seldom acknowledged. What is often absent in epistemologies is the conditions under which and the manner in which grants are eventually utilised in families. Seniors are often exploited to care for unemployed adults and children whose own parents should be responsible for their wellbeing, despite the fact that some parents 'collect' the child grant. Seniors are then coerced into providing for those who reside with them.

Abusive behaviour towards senior citizens commences immediately 'after the grant is used up'. One senior remarked that 'they do not really care about me. A few days before grant day they are really nice but after that, when my money is all spent, they are the same again – they do not care'. This behaviour change is indicative of the extent to which the grant goes beyond mere support for the elderly; sharing, particularly in African households, has been a norm for support in three-generation households (Cotter 2008: 115). It is 'a sign of strength of familial ties', as Kochendörfer-Lucius and Pleskovic (2007: 16) suggest. In interviews, senior citizens attested to the abuse and lack of care they receive on other days of the month. Supporting unemployed family members reduces the quality of life of the elderly themselves.

The World Bank (2013: 158–59) acknowledges that unemployment is high in South Africa and supporting unemployed family members drags many people into poverty, particularly families without any elderly members. When elderly people start receiving a grant, working-age family members also benefit from the grant. Vettori (2012: 196) equally highlights that 'the availability of the old-age grant seemingly has become more than a safety net; it is also a convenience for the unemployed who do not have an alternative income'. It is often a calamity when an elderly person, on whom individuals are dependent to sustain their livelihood, dies. The current high unemployment rates in South Africa enhance the challenges that senior citizens experience and place them at risk due to the grant they receive.

Supporting other unemployed people defeats the purpose and objective of the grants. The World Bank (2013) suggests that win-win investments should instead be favoured. Their view is that 'not only can public works offer employment to unemployed workers; which would in turn avert a crisis, but that it will positively enhance the livelihood of all affected parties'. South Africa has an Expanded Public Works Programme (EPWP 2013), which is a key government initiative. It originates from the Growth and Development Summit (GDS) of 2003. Key themes included are 'more jobs, better jobs, decent work for all'. The GDS came to a consensus that public works programmes 'can provide income relief through temporary work for the unemployed to carry out socially useful activities'.

The ANC (2002: 55) also revealed alarming levels of abuse and neglect by relatives, nursing homes, communities and government officials towards senior citizens. This is often hidden in the midst of façades observed for a few days around pay-out days. Social workers only intervene in cases of extreme emergency and only then become aware of the abuse not only of senior citizens but also of their grants. Only when crises occur are social workers made aware of the actual conditions under which senior citizens live. The Ministerial Committee on the Abuse, Neglect and Ill-Treatment of Older Persons presented its report in February 2001, reveal alarming levels of abuse and neglect by relatives, nursing homes, communities, government officials and service providers. The report indicates progress in the implementation of the Committee's recommendations, including problems faced by senior citizens. Almost fifteen years later, the abuse of older persons persists unabatedly.

What emerged in this study in five different communities in Gauteng was that almost 58 per cent of the elderly continue to experience abuse by those who are supposed to care for them. Some responses that stood out are quoted in the following paragraphs. Question 1 was: 'Have you witnessed any form of abuse of the elderly in your community, including abuse of their old-age grants during or after pay-out days?' The first is a response from Mpumi. Instead of simply marking 'strongly agree', the participant wrote at the bottom of the page: 'I have seen many forms of abuse, I cannot even count how many. Family members who are not in the least concerned about the senior citizens on other days of the month will demand part of the grants of their parents and grandparents.'

A number of people interviewed accused 'social workers and the police of being insensitive to the needs of senior citizens' (Maitse and Majake 2005: 36) and that, as a result, their wellbeing has been placed in jeopardy. Shara, a neighbour of a senior, indicated during interviews that 'my fellow neighbours and I have been aware of the abuse for a while now and we reported this to officials at pay points but they said they cannot do anything unless they see it happen. I have seen old people crying but it became clear that no one cares'. The officials' business is to pay out the grants on the day and they stated they cannot leave the elderly waiting to go outside in order to see the abuse. They remarked that 'we see these forms of abuse first hand and attempt to assist and report this, but there has been no response. Social workers and police only intervene when there is a severe crisis or near-death incident'. This response indicates frustration on the part of the participants of the continued abuse of the elderly. In February 2015, a neighbour remarked that:

> I have observed the abuse of the senior who lives next to me for a long time now, but I do not want to interfere, because here people gossip. A few of my friends are aware of the abuse. Just before grant day, the unemployed son, a middle-aged man, and a young adult woman, the granddaughter of the old women, accompany the old women to collect her grant but later during the day they are both intoxicated. The young lady's parents both died from HIV/AIDS because they failed to go for treatment at the local clinic and were addicted to alcohol. The young lady dropped out of school three years ago and is on drugs. These family members are both unemployed. Just a week

after grant day, there is little to eat and the old women has to ask from us, her neighbours. The unemployed son drinks alcohol and I am aware that he uses the money borrowed from us, to do so.

During the study, it became evident that many of the elderly found themselves in similar situations. I interviewed some of the elderly themselves. The responses received included that of Rachel, who appeared severely disturbed and said:

I cannot count and I am often surprised when I notice that after buying some food there is hardly any money left. I often complain that government does not really take care of us old people. How can they give us so little? My son said we only get R750. The money never goes up he says, but I heard on TV that it did go up, but he said I did not understand what was said … I buy food, pay rent and help my unemployed children with money to look for work, but they never seem to find work. Sometimes after my grant is paid they disappear for two days and return penniless. I have to feed and clothe them.

Another indicated that 'I owe money to the money lender, they have my ID book and I get it at the pay point. When he has been paid I have little left for food and my medicine, then I have to borrow again'. These are just some of the responses from participants that clearly indicate the extent of the abuse of the old-age grant.

Conclusion

Seniors are neglected when those who benefit from the state grant seem to have other interests. While 'familial is the route to go by' compared to public safety Kochendörfer-Lucius and Pleskovic (2007: 179) suggests, I suggest that we rethink this 'familial' phenomenon to benefit senior citizens. From a current African perspective and the case studies observed, based on the findings in this study, the situation which has developed around the old-age grant seems to be detrimental to the government's aim to assist. In relation to the elderly, South Africa requires stability and social justice that will protect senior citizens against the abuse of their grants. It is paramount to rethink the impact of the old-age grant and the manner in which the government goals are undermined by the current system. We have to make a decision to do what is right. Ralph Waldo Emerson (2010) asserts that 'once you make a decision, the universe conspires to make it happen'. We must show courage to be resilient and determined in our efforts to move away from economic deprivation and social marginalisation of the elderly. 'Defer no time, delays have dangerous ends' (Shakespeare 2004).

Humanitarians and politicians need to intervene by rectifying operations and inventing regulatory processes that would eradicate these social ills. Strict policies should be applied to restrict family members from abusing the elderly financially. Money lending to the elderly, particularly at the high rates charged by loan sharks, should be outlawed and perpetrators should be subjected to heavy fines. Urgent intervention is required at pay points and in the families where senior citizens are key financial contributors and support large and extended families (Dubow and Jeeves 2005: 49). Government intervention is urgently required. The task of visiting homes regularly and being present during pay-out days can be assigned to government officials. Undercover observers are urgently required at pay points. These moves could help curb the abuse of the elderly on pay-out days.

Gloria Sauti is an independent contractor in the department of Anthropology and Archeology at the University of South Africa (Unisa). She is an interdisciplinary scholar. Her research interests include social media, analysing social interactions, poverty among women, land, postcolonial racial identities and education. She holds a Ph.D. in social anthropology from the University of the Witwatersrand.

References

African National Congress (ANC). 2002. 'Umrabulo: Special 51st National Conference Edition', Issue 16, African National Congress, published by the African National Congress, University of Michigan.

Arditte, A.J. (ed.). 2014. *Family Problems: Stress, Risk, and Resilience*. Chichester: John Wiley & Sons.

Auer, P., and M. Fortuny. 2002. ILO Employment Paper, 'Ageing of the Labor Force in OECD Countries: Economic and Social Consequences. Employment Sector'. International Labour Office of Geneva. Retrieved 22 September 2018 from http://www.ilo.org/wcmsp5/groups/public/---ed_emp/documents/publication/wcms_142281.pdf.

Barrientos, A. 2003. 'What is the Impact of Non-contributory Pensions on Poverty? Estimates from Brazil and South Africa', *CPRC Working Paper* No. 33, Chronic Poverty Research Centre, Institute for Development Policy and Management. Manchester: University of Manchester.

Boyle, P., H. Keith and V. Robinson, et al. 2014. *Exploring Contemporary Migration*, 2nd ed. New York: Routledge.

Clinton, J.W. 1994. *Public Papers of the Presidents of the United States*, Government Printing Office, Washington. Retrieved 16 July 2014 from https://quod.lib.umich.edu/p/ppotpus/4733149.1994.001?view=toc.

Cohen, B., and J. Menken (eds). 2006. *Aging in Sub-Saharan Africa: Recommendations for Furthering Research*. National Research Council, South Africa. Retrieved 22 September 2018 from https://www.ncbi.nlm.nih.gov/books/NBK20306/pdf/Bookshelf_NBK20306.pdf.

Collins, D., J. Morduch and S. Rutherford. 2010. Portfolios of the Poor; How the Poor live on $2 Dollars a Day. Illustrated reprint. Princeton, NJ: Princeton University Press.

Cotter, A.-M. 2008. *Just a Number: An International Legal Analysis on Age Discrimination, Law and Discrimination*. London: Routledge.

Dubow, S., and A. Jeeves (eds). 2005. *South Africa's 1940's Worlds of Possibilities*. Cape Town: Double Storey Books, 49.

Duszak, A., and U. Okulska (eds). 2011. *Language, Culture and the Dynamics of Age*. Wiley and Sons, Oxford University Press. Retrieved 22 September 2018 from http://www.beckshop.de/fachbuch/inhaltsverzeichnis/9783110238105_TOC_001.pdf.

Edgeworth, M. 2012. *Tales and Novels Popular Tales, Containing Popular Tales, Vol. 1*. California: ULAN Press.

Emerson, R.W. 2010. 'Ralph Waldo Emerson Quotes', *Brainy Quote*. Retrieved 22 September 2018 from https://www.brainyquote.com/authors/ralph_waldo_emerson.

Expanded Public Works Programme (EPWP). 2013. *Integrated Grant Manual*, Department of Public Works, Pretoria Republic of South Africa. Retrieved 12 March 2015 from http://www.epwp.gov.za/documents.html.

Ferreira. L. 2015. 'Factsheets: Social Grants in South Africa – Separating Myth from Reality', *Africa Check*, 5 February. Retrieved 10 October 2015 fromhttps://africacheck.org/factsheets/separating-myth-from-reality-a-guide-to-social-grants-in-south-africa/.

Gillion C. 2000. 'The Development and Reform of Social Security Pensions: The Approach of the International Labor Office', *International Security Review* 53(1): 35–62.

Government Printer. 2001. *Debates of the National Council of Provinces (Hansard) Issue 1–4*. National Council of Provinces, Cape Town, South Africa.

Group Interviews with Senior citizens, 2014–2016, Randfontein and Dobsonville.

Group Interviews with Taxi Drivers 2014–2015, Randfontein and Brandvlei.

Hebinck, P.M., and P. C. Lent. (eds). 2007. *Livelihoods and Landscapes: The People of Guquka and their Resources*. Leiden: Brill.

Interview with Maria, 15 March 2015, Johannesburg, South Africa.

Interview with Mpumi, January 2015, Brandvlei, Gauteng, South Africa.

Interview with Rachel, February 2015, Snake Park – Soweto, Johannesburg, Gauteng, South Africa.

Interview with Shara, 25 April 2015 in Randfontein and Mohlakeng, South Africa.

Katzen, M. 1961. 'Industry in Greater Durban, Part 3'. Natal Town and Regional Planning Report, Vol. 3, Pietermaritzburg, South Africa.

Kelly-Louw, M. 2009. 'Prevention of Overindebtedness and Mechanisms for Resolving Overindebtedness of South African Consumers', in J. Niemi,

I. Ramsay and W.C. William (eds), *Consumer Credit, Debt and Bankruptcy*. Oxford: Hart Publishing, pp. 175–98.

Kochendörfer-Lucius, G., and B. Pleskovic. 2007. *Berlin Workshop Series 2007: Development and the Next Generation*. Washington DC: World Bank. Retrieved 22 September 2018 from https://openknowledge.worldbank.org/handle/10986/6808.

Lam, D., G. Leibbrandt and V. Ranchod. 2006. 'Labor Force Withdrawal of the Elderly in South Africa', in B. Cohen and J. Menken (eds), *Aging in Sub-Saharan Africa: Recommendations for Furthering Research*. Washington, DC: National Academies Press, pp. 214–249,

Lombard, A., and E. Kruger. 2009. 'Older Persons: The Case of South Africa', *Ageing International* 34(3): 119–35.

Maitse, T., and C. Majake. 2005. *Enquiry into the Gendered Lived Experience of Older Persons in Living Conditions of Poverty*. Braamfontein: Commission of Gender Equality.

Marias, H.C. 1988. ed., *South Africa: Perspectives on the Future*. Pine Town: Owen Burgess.

Marock, C., C. Harrison-Train, B. Soobrayan, and J. Gunthorpe. 2008. *SETA Review*. Cape Town: Development Policy Research Unit, University of Cape Town.

Mashigo, P. 2012. 'The Lending Practices of Township Micro-Lenders and Their Impact on the Low-Income Households in South Africa: A Case Study of Mamelodi Township', *New Contree* 65: 23–46.

May, T., and M. Williams. 2002. *Introduction to the Philosophy of Social Research*. New York: Routledge.

Mesthrie, R. (ed.). 2002. *Language in South Africa*. New York: Cambridge University Press.

Morduch, J., D. Collins, O. Ruthven and S. Rutherford. 2010. *Portfolios of the Poor: How the Poor Live on $2 a Day*. Princeton: Princeton University Press.

Ocampo, A.J. 2010. *Combatting, Poverty and Inequality: Structural Change, Social Policy and Politics*. Geneva: United Nations Research Institute for Social Development.

Pearson Education. 2011. *Sociology: Perspective, Theory, and Method, Social Science and its Methods*. University of Wisconsin, Whitewater.

Pelham, L. 2007. 'The Politics behind the Non-contributory Old Age Social Pension in Lesotho, Namibia and South Africa', *CPRC Working Paper* No. 83, Chronic Poverty Research Centre.

Pinchuck, T., B. McCrea, and D. Reid et al. 2002. *Rough Guides: The Routh Guide to South Africa*. Lesotho and Swaziland: APA Publications.

Seekings J., and N. Nattrass. 2015. *Policy, Politics and Poverty in South Africa*. Basingstoke: Palgrave Macmillan.

Shakespeare, W. 2004. 'William Shakespeare Quotes', Great - Quotes.com. Henry VI, Part 1. Retrieved from https://labs.jstor.org/shakespeare/henry_vi_part_1.

SASSA, South African Social Security Agency. 2015. 'You and Your Grants 2014/2015'. Retrieved July 2016 from https://africacheck.org/wp-content/uploads/2015/02/You-and-Your-Grants1.pdf.

Squires, D.G. (ed.). 2004. *Why the Poor Pay More: How to Stop Predatory Lending.* Westport, CT: Praeger.
Standing, G., and M. Samson. eds 2003. *A Basic Income Grant for South Africa.* Cape Town: University of Cape Town Press.
Steyn, L. 2013. 'Cheap-Cheap Tuk-Tuk Taxis Take over Jozi, Business', *Mail & Guardian*, 18 January.
Surrender, R. 2010. 'Social Assistance and Dependency in South Africa: An Analysis of Attitudes to Paid Work and Social Grants', *Journal of Social Policy* 39(2): 2013–21.
The Economist. 2018. 'In South Africa, More People have Loans than Jobs, Long Walk to Financial Ruin, Middle East and Africa', 18 January.
Vettori, S. (ed.). 2012. *Ageing Populations and Changing Labor Markets: Social and Economic Impacts of the Demographic Time Bomb.* Farnham: Gower.
World Bank. 2013. *World Development Report 2014, Risk and Opportunity: Managing Risk for Development.* Washington DC: World Bank.
Yeng, P. 2016. 'UK Welfare State "Mediocre" and in Need of Reform Think Tanks Find', *Independent,* 11 July, https://www.independent.co.uk/news/uk/home-news/welfare-state-uk-benefits-system-reform-international-longevity-centre-think-tank-a7130606.html.

Conclusion
The End of Development and the Rise of Decoloniality as the Future

Sabelo J. Ndlovu-Gatsheni and Busani Mpofu

Introduction

Rethinking development is fundamental to rethinking modernity. To rethink modernity entails provincialising and deprovincialising as decolonial processes. At the centre of both provincialising and deprovincialising is what has come to be termed 'de-Westernisation', that is, challenging and resisting the idea of Europe (real or imagined) as the origin of all positive human ideas, values and institutions as well as the centre of the world (Bhambra 2007; Waisbord and Mellado 2014). De-Westernisation is part of a broader project called decoloniality (Quijano 2000; Mignolo 2000). Decoloniality unmasks the very concept of modernity as it facilitates the end of privileging of Europe as the maker of universal history (Bhambra 2007; Grosfoguel 2007; Maldonado-Torres 2007). Development is one of those ideas and values that were claimed by Europe as endogenous and as absent in other parts of the world. Development has been portrayed as a normative European value ranking together with notions of modernity, social evolution, progress and emancipation. Here was born the linear idea and philosophy of human history, with Europe as the alpha and omega (Allen 2016). Thus, while development is a central part of Eurocentric, imperialist and colonial thought, decoloniality is a radical rejection of Eurocentrism and all those processes it enabled. The end of development as an imperial idea opens the way for the beginning of decoloniality as the future.

Scholars such as Amy Allen (2016) grappled with the idea of end of development in her book entitled *The End of Progress: Decolonizing the Normative Foundations of Critical Theory*. In this book, Allen mounted a systematic decolonial critique of the Frankfurt School and in particular its failure to take into account in its claimed critical theory such inimical processes as racism, enslavement, imperialism, colonialism and apartheid that were justified as part of the civilising mission and development. Allen (2016: 3) identifies prominent thinkers of the Frankfurt School such as Jurgen Habermas, Axel Honneth and Rainer Forst as examples of those theorists deeply wedded to the ideas of Eurocentrism and Enlightenment modernity – representing 'a developmental advance over premodern, nonmodern, or traditional forms of life, and, crucially, this idea plays an important role in grounding the normativity of critical theory for each thinker'.

On another level, Gurminder K. Bhambra (2007), building on the rich decolonial and postcolonial archive, directly confronted the very ideas of Europe with a view to demythologising 'the specialness of the West' in human history. She openly declared that: 'In contesting Eurocentrism, I contest the "fact" of the specialness of Europe – both in terms of its culture and its events; the "fact" of the autonomous development of events, concepts and paradigms; and ultimately, the "fact" of Europe itself as a coherent bounded entity giving form to the above' (Bhambra 2007: 5). Earlier on, Arturo Escobar (1995) had made the strongest argument about the need for the end of development and the beginning of post-development thought. Escobar interpreted development as a set of hegemonic discourses and practices cascading from the 'West' that profoundly enabled the making of what became known as the 'Third World' characterised by underdevelopment. He then posited three important arguments about development. The first was a call for decentring of development, that is, 'to displace it from its centrality in representations of and discussions about conditions in Asia, Africa and Latin America' (Escobar 1995: xii).

Based on this argument, Escobar called for an opening 'up of the discursive space to other ways of describing the conditions, less mediated by the premises and experiences of 'development' (1995: xii–xiii). The second intervention was a direct call for the end of development not so that there is a new search for 'development alternatives', but to enable 'alternatives to development' itself. The final intervention was to escalate the critique on development to the epistemological level (political economy of truth) and its imbrications with power. Even though the 'post-development' discourse was heavily criticised for overlooking poverty and capitalism as content of development, for being essentialist and for romanticising local traditions, the idea of development has continued to be the subject of further criticism, this time from a decolonial perspective.

Decolonial Confrontation with the Structure of Modern Powers

The Kenyan intellectual and novelist Ngugi wa Thiong'o (1986: 2) posited that African predicaments were 'often not a matter of personal choice', but were a product of a 'historical situation'. He identified imperialism and colonialism as well as neocolonialism not as mere slogans, but as 'real'. This meant that if the problems of development arose from a historical situation and were structural, then 'their solutions are not so much a matter of personal decision as that of fundamental social transformation of the structures of our societies starting with a real break with imperialism and its internal ruling allies. Imperialism and its comprador alliances in Africa can never develop the continent' (Ngugi wa Thiong'o 1986: xii). This structuralist decolonial argument raised the question of the possibilities and potentialities of African people being able to create African futures within a modern world system structured by global coloniality.

The decolonial perspective directly addresses the structural power problem known as global coloniality, that is, a modern global power structure that has been in place since the dawn of Euro-North Americancentric modernity. With the end of direct colonialism, global coloniality operated as an invisible power matrix that is shaping and sustaining asymmetrical power relations between the Global North and the Global South.

The decolonial perspective grapples with the interconnected and intertwined issues of coloniality of power, knowledge and being as constitutive elements of global coloniality as a power structure that makes it difficult for Africans to create their own futures. What Claude Ake (1979) described as knowledge for equilibrium continues to sustain the present status quo through colonisation of African imaginations of the future. This is why the concept of coloniality of knowledge is not only highlighted but also mobilised and utilised to systematically interrogate epistemicides that enabled the dominance of imperial/colonial reason, and explained how these processes culminated in the colonisation of African minds and the destabilisation of African imaginations of the future. Then there is the concept of coloniality of being, which is useful in revealing complex processes of subjection and subjectivity that play a role as Africans try to create African futures.

Gesturing into the Future

Being in control of the present and the future is part of taking charge of self-improvement. This is why the African Union's Agenda 2063 in its envisioning of an African future emphasises pan-African unity, integration, prosperity and peace. Africans have to drive the processes of self-improvement unencumbered by external forces of maintenance of the status quo. While global coloniality works through the division and atomisation of Africans, the African Union has identified pan-Africanism as the overarching ideological framework for unity, self-reliance, integration and solidarity (African Union 2013). Decoloniality emerges as the encapsulation of all those struggles ranged against coloniality of power, coloniality of knowledge and coloniality of being.

As Africans struggle to take charge of their future, they must be reminded of Karl Marx's arguments about people making history, but under circumstances they have not chosen. Global coloniality is the broader discursive terrain under which Africans have to make history. This entails struggling ceaselessly against global coloniality. When John Keegan (2002: 1) emphasised that we could write at least '[f]our times in the modern age men have sat down to reorder the world – at the Peace of Westphalia in 1648 after the Thirty Years War, at the Congress of Vienna in 1815 after the Napoleonic Wars, in Paris in 1919 after World War I, and in San Francisco in 1945 after World War II', he was explaining how global coloniality was invented together with its systems and orders. The invention of the modern global order is traceable to 1492, when Christopher Columbus claimed to have discovered a 'New World'. Europe became very active in formulating ways of managing and dominating the expanded modern world. For Africa, the Berlin Conference of 1884–85 at which leading European powers met to partition Africa among themselves is a major world ordering process. The Berlin Consensus, which Adekeye Adebajo correctly articulated as 'the Curse of Berlin', formed a major component of the invention of global coloniality as a modern power structure.

The laying down of systems and orders was always underpinned by what John M. Headley (2008) celebrated as 'the Europeanization of the world'. This Europeanisation of the world entailed reducing African people to the position of bystanders in the making of history. This was achieved through such processes as the racialisation of the human population, and the enslavement and colonisation of Africans. These processes practically colonised African imagination and disabled African agency. To take note of these processes is important because only a people who are free politically, socially, economically, ideologically and epistemologically are more able create their own futures and take charge of their destiny. While global coloniality intended to re-create Africans as permanent colonial subjects who would reproduce a colonial future that was inimical to their aspirations, African people consistently resisted the colonial framework and colonial library through launching antislavery revolts and anti-colonial nationalist-inspired decolonial struggles as part of their drive to create African futures. As noted by Kwame Nimako (2012), Africans tried to shape a world for themselves when they met at the First Pan-African Conference in London in 1900, at the Second Pan-African Conference in 1921 in London, Paris and Brussels, at the Third Pan-African Conference in 1923 in London and Lisbon, at the Fourth Pan-African Conference in 1927 in New York and at the Fifth Pan-African Conference in Manchester in 1945.

Continental African people worked together with those from the diaspora to try and create another future free from direct colonialism and indirect global coloniality. Pan-Africanism emerged within these struggles to imagine and create an African future (Ndlovu-Gatsheni 2013d, 2014c). The greatest challenge was that colonialism had already imposed colonial mindsets on the psyche of African people, which meant that they continued to reproduce coloniality as their future even after direct juridical colonialism has been dismantled (Ngugi wa Thiong'o 1986; Chinweizu 1987). What Frantz Fanon (1968) termed 'repetition without change' was a product of this pitfall of consciousness. Colonialism was not simply a process of conquest, annexation, occupation, settlement, domination and exploitation; it entailed emptying 'the native's brain of all form and content' on top of committing epistemicides such as distorting, disfiguring and eventually destroying the history of the colonised (Fanon 1968).

Outright capitulation to the dictates of global coloniality is always looming large over Africans. Globalisation and neoliberalism presents themselves as a reality to which Africans must adapt to rather than resist. Such defeatist discourse as 'There is No Alternative' (TINA) were meant to undercut resistance. Euro-North American-centric modernity also produces rhetoric of emancipation that hides its reality of coloniality as part of subverting decolonial resistance. Capitalism, globalisation, and neoliberalism are articulated from Europe and North America as natural processes that must not be contested. They are packaged as universal norms and values that every human being has to live by and practise.

Development exists as gift from Europe and North America. That gift is wrapped in capitalism, colonialism, neocolonialism and neoliberalism. Decolonial thinkers have identified racism, colonialism, neocolonialism and capitalism as major challenges preventing the emergence of a genuinely postcolonial world. Racism, the slave trade, imperialism, colonialism, apartheid and neocolonialism not only constitute global coloniality as a modern power structure but are also manifestations of the 'dark side/underside' of modernity (Mignolo 1995, 2000, 2011).

Thus, when decolonial thinkers, theorists and activists say that 'Another World is Possible', they are not talking about merely forecasting the supposedly 'mysterious' future; what they are talking about is that the present generation must mobilise itself and confront present structural and agential sources of social injustices, asymmetrical power structures, patriarchal ideologies, logics of capitalist exploitation, resilient imperial/colonial reason and racist articulations and practices (McNally 2005; de Santos 2008). What is underscored is that the African future will be a product of struggles for a decolonised new world system and a deimperialised global order. Clearly, such an envisaged new world system and its new global orders cannot be realised without decolonisation of power, knowledge and being. This is why it is pertinent for all those committed to fighting for better African futures have to understand fully the constitution of the present and at the same time comprehending how the modern world system works.

The Structural Cul-de-Sac

How the present 'global political' was constructed and constituted into the current asymmetrical modern power structure that is inherently Eurocentric constitute a structural straitjacket for African initiatives for self-improvement (Ndlovu-Gatsheni 2013a, 2013b). Michael Hardt and Antonio Negri (2000: 3) emphasised this point when they explained how Europe came to dominate and control the modern world by creating a global juridical formation consisting of what is known as the world order and world system. They have been defending these from the time they expanded out of Europe into other parts of the world and they have been imposing their systems and orders on other parts of the world.

While the modern world system is resistant to deimperialisation, its global order is equally resistant to decolonisation. Direct confrontation with the system and the order is depicted as terrorism. Antisystemic forces are constantly and systematically eliminated physically. Other moderate forces are disciplined and then accommodated into the very system and order they were resisting. Coloniality of power links the modern world system and its global orders. It is a structure of power that is defended by all means available including weapons of mass destruction (Quijano 2000, 2007; Ndlovu-Gatsheni 2013a, 2013b). Coloniality of power gave birth to a particular modern world system that Ramon Grosfoguel (2007, 2011) has characterised as racially hierarchised, patriarchal, sexist, heteronormative, Christian-centric, Euro-North American-centric, imperial, colonial and capitalist. Within this modern world system, coloniality of power exists as an entanglement of multiple and heterogeneous global hierarchies and hetararchies of sexual, political, epistemic, economic, spiritual, linguistic, aesthetic and racial forms of domination and exploitation (Grosfoguel 2007: 217).

In practice, the success of the coloniality of power depended on what Jack Goody (2006: 1) described as 'theft of history', that is, 'the take-over of history by the west' and the reconceptualisation and representation of human history 'according to what happened on the provincial scale of Europe' and 'then imposed upon the rest of the world'. This usurpation of human history by Europe and North America unfolded in terms of the colonisation of space (cartography, conquest and settlement), the colonisation of time (bifurcating it into ancient and modern epochs), the colonisation of being (classification and racial hierarchisation of human population according to race) and the colonisation of nature (subjecting it to the logic of capitalism and reducing it to a simple natural resource open for exploitation) (Ndlovu-Gatsheni 2013c).

Coloniality of power resulted not only in the 'theft of history' but also in the theft of the African future. African people became represented as bystanders in human history deserving to be civilised by Europeans and educated by Europeans within a world constructed and configured by Europeans. The present modern global power structure informed by coloniality has the United States and Europe at the apex. The emergence of new powers from the Global South such as China, Brazil and India has not yet deeply shaken the dominance of the United States and Europe. At the bottom is Africa and its people (Ndlovu-Gatsheni 2014a, 2014b). Decolonisation only led to the incorporation of African states at the lowest echelons of the asymmetrical modern global power structure without destroying global coloniality.

As a concept, coloniality of power enables us to understand deeply the structural cul-de-sac within which African leaders and their people try to create African futures. Ake (1981: 93) noted that 'the nationalist movement which arose from the contradictions of the colonial political economy achieved independence, not economic independence'. Both political and economic independence are essential prerequisites for launching genuine African futures. It is not clear whether African leaders and their people have managed to rise above the 'contradictions of the colonial political economy'. What is clear is that global coloniality produced a particular form of leadership in Africa – a petite bourgeoisie that could not invent or even transform political, economic and social institutions inherited from colonialism 'into its own image' so as to 'become socially hegemonic' (Nabudere 2011: 58; Taylor 2014: 5).

African leaders have only succeeded in staying in power through balancing internal and external forces, with the interests of external forces often outweighing those of internal constituencies in African leaders' political calculations. Thus, they preside over postcolonial states that are not entrenched in African society, but exist as 'a bureaucratic connivance' (Mafeje 1992: 31: Young 2012). Ralph Austen (1987: 271) clearly understood that the major economic problem facing African people is that of the asymmetrical relationship between the 'role of the continent in the world and the degree to which that world ... has penetrated Africa'. This perennial postcolonial problem compromises any initiatives aimed at creating African futures and, in particular, autonomous development.

African futures are entrapped within a system of structural dependence. African people and states in Africa lack autonomy, that is, 'a stable hegemonic project that binds different levels of society together' (Taylor 2014: 7). These realities, which are fundamentally informed and underpinned by global coloniality, need to be taken seriously as we grapple with the pertinent question of the possibilities of Africans creating their own futures. Today, this African possibility is posed in the context of the discourse of an Africa that is said to be rising economically.

What is clear in the discourse of Africa rising is the reality of diversifying dependency rather than a real leap into a better economic future (Taylor 2014). What is also clear is that whenever some African leaders attempted to articulate a vision of the future of their countries and the continent, either as individuals or as a collective, they have opted for 'Westernisation', that is, they push for 'economic growth within the context of the existing neocolonial economic structure' (Taylor 2014: 7). The current celebrated economic growth of Africa is not founded on any radical economic disobedience or questioning of the neoliberal market ideology; it is based on the increased sale of primary commodities and the importation and consumption of finished products from elsewhere.

The entry of Brazil, Russia, India and China (BRICS) into the African market has boosted this sale of primary commodities. There is no change in the forms of integration of Africa into the ever-evolving capitalist economy, making the notion of 'Africa Rising' to exist as only a slogan trumpeted by benefiting global corporations. Such blocs as BRICS are not about creating a radical change of the world system and its global orders; they are about making neoliberalism work more efficiently in accordance with the longstanding discourse of free trade (Taylor 2014: 156). Worse still, Africa is forced to celebrate an economic growth that is premised on a problematic 'intensification of resource extraction through diversification of partners, while inequality and unemployment increase and deindustrialization continues apace' (Taylor 2014: 160).

The narrative of 'Africa Rising' is blind to the problem of the new 'scramble' for African natural resources and the concomitant land grabbing that is articulated by advocates of neoliberalism as investment in land (Cotula 2013). Emerging powers from the Global South have joined the traditional Euro-North American powers and multinational corporations in this new scramble for African natural resources. Global coloniality deliberately creates celebrations of these false starts as it protects and diverts attention of antisystemic forces and formations from targeting the asymmetrical modern world system and its imperial global orders.

The Political Economy of Truth

Global coloniality is also sustained by a particular epistemology. African economic futures have remained trapped within the hegemonic Truman version of development, which is backed up by what Adebayo Adedeji termed the 'development merchant system' (DMS). The DMS is driven by the Breton Woods Institutions (BWI), which finance the implementation of exogenous development agenda (Adedeji 2002: 4). At the centre of the DMS is what David Slater termed 'imperiality of knowledge', which is constituted by 'interweaving of geopolitical power, knowledge and subordinating representation of the other' (Slater 2004: 223). The DMS maintains coloniality long after the dismantlement of administrative colonialism. It still approaches Africa as a space inhabited by a people 'shorn of the legitimate symbols of independent identity and authority' as well as a 'space ready to be penetrated, worked over, restructured and transformed' from outside (Slater 2004: 223). The DMS exists as a consortium of the International Monetary Fund (IMF), the World Bank, the World Trade Organization (WTO), international nongovernmental organisations (INGOs) and multinational corporations (MCs). They advance a 'Bretton Woods Paradigm' of the African future that is amenable to global coloniality (Therien 1999: 723–42).

What is worrying is that the African Union Agenda 2063 articulates the need for a paradigm shift in the economy and politics without necessarily elaborating upon a clear epistemological and ideological foundation for such a change. The question of epistemology is very important because from the start, the inscription of global coloniality commenced with 'a systematic repression, not only of the specific beliefs, ideas, images, symbols or knowledges that were not useful to global colonial domination, while at the same time colonizers were expropriating from the colonized their knowledge, especially in mining, agriculture, engineering as well as their products and work' (Quijano 2007: 169).

Epistemological colonisation that amounts to colonisation of the mind and imagination affected African 'modes of knowing, of producing knowledge, of producing perspectives, images and systems of images, symbols, modes of signification, over the resources, patterns, and instruments of formalized and objectivised expression', including intellectual and visual forms (Quijano 2007: 169). Having performed these epistemicides, the constructors and drivers of global coloniality proceeded to make their own patterns of producing knowledge and modes of knowing to be the only legitimate and scientific ways of understanding the world. They mystified their own patterns of knowing and knowledge production. However, they also tried to consistently place these Euro-North American-centric patterns 'far out of reach of the dominated' (Quijano 2007: 169).

When the Europeans decided to impart this knowledge on the colonised, they did so 'in a partial and selective way, in order to co-opt some of the dominated into their own power institutions' (Quijano 2007: 169). Consequently, they succeeded largely in transforming 'cultural Europeanisation' into 'an aspiration' of every African (Quijano 2007: 169). The long-term impact of this social engineering and epistemological process that was marked by epistemicides, displacements, expropriations and impositions invaded the core imaginary of the African psyche and culture to the extent that Africans today reproduce 'cultural Europeanisation' without the direct tutelage of Europeans.

The challenge facing Africans is how to undo this imperial/colonial epistemological damage as part of their drive to create decolonial futures. At the epistemological realm, Africans are still stuck in Euro-North American-centric thought. They somehow breathe it in on a daily basis because it is a major technology of domination. This is why the leading Egyptian economist and Marxist-decolonial thinker Samir Amin (1985) not only advocated for 'delinking' as part of enabling the Global South to escape from the constraints imposed by the world's economic system, but also highlighted the ubiquity and dominance of Euro-North Americancentric conventional classical economic thought in all the African attempts to chart an autonomous economic trajectory for the continent. Even the Lagos Plan of Action was informed by this thought (Amin 1990: 58).

The African epistemological predicament is further compounded by the fact that there is an increasing realisation that Euro-North Americancentric thought that has dominated the world for over five hundred years has now reached an epistemic crisis – a form of exhaustion and irrelevance.

Indeed, the promise of Euro-North American-centric epistemology to overcome all obstacles to human progress is today not taken seriously because it has mainly succeeded in creating modern problems such as pollution for which there are no modern solutions (Escobar 2004: 230).

This means that Africans can no longer rely solely on this epistemology in their endeavour to create African futures. Patrick Chabal made it clear that 'the social sciences we employ to explain what is happening domestically and overseas – are both historically and conceptually out of date' and he elaborated that the Euro-North American-centric 'theories are now obstacles to the understanding of what is going on in our societies and what we can do about it' (Chabal 2012: viii). His conclusion was that: 'The end of conceit is upon us. Western rationality must be rethought' (Chabal 2012: 335). The global financial crisis that hit Europe and North America in 2008 added to the questioning of the suitability of Euro-North American thought and epistemology in offering solutions to modern problems.

Releasing African Genius

The Eurocentric modernity inaugurated the colonisation of being through its social classification of human population according to race. While the processes of racialisation took different forms and assumed different terms across different colonial spaces, the logic and purpose remained the same. This was followed by racial hierarchisation of being according to race. White races claimed complete *being* for themselves and pushed African people into a perpetual state of *becoming* – a state of incompleteness (Ndlovu-Gatsheni 2013a, 2013b). This imperial reason was then used to consistently question the very humanity of African people in order to consign them to the status of inferiority. The overarching purpose of racial classification and racial hierarchisation was to construct a system of social differentiation between those who could own slaves and those who would be enslaved, and between those who could claim and own land and those who would be forced to work on it. It became a distinction in social category between those who could define others and those would always be the subjects and objects of definition (Martinot n.d.: 3).

The African subjectivity that emerged from these processes of racialisation and inferiorisation of blackness is one that has a diminished ontological density. It became a subjectivity that was said to be characterised by a catalogue of deficits and a series of lacks. Sabelo J. Ndlovu-Gatsheni (2013a) listed the deficits and lacks that were attributed to the African subject as ranging from lack of souls, writing, history, civilisation, development, democracy, human rights and ethics. This gave birth to the colonial idea of Africans as the condemned people of the earth, the anthropos of the planet, and the wretched of the earth that Frantz Fanon (1968) wrote about.

Race and colonial experience continue to define the interrelated conceptions of the African subject, its subjection and subjectivity (Ndlovu-Gatsheni 2013a, 2013b). The racist/imperial Manichean misanthropic scepticism was used to authorise such mistreatments of African people as enslavement, where black people were reduced to commodities that could be sold and bought and also reduced to the status of animals that could be forced to work for others. This is a central element of coloniality of being, which, according to Maldonado-Torres (2007: 255), 'refers to the normalization of extraordinary events that take place in war'. By this, he meant that African people whose very being was colonised became exposed to violence, murder, rape, exploitation, displacement, dispossession and other brutalities, including death. Concerning the treatment of African people, ethics were suspended.

What has compounded the phenomenon of coloniality of being is that the postcolonial state in Africa as an inherited institution continues to exert colonial-like brutalities on African people. The shooting of 34 black miners at Marikana by the South African police in 2012 confirmed Maldonado-Torres' (2007: 255) argument that black people endure 'hellish existence' in which 'killability' and 'rapeability' are normal states of life. Across the world, the life of a black person is the cheapest (most dispensable) (Magubane 2007). All this indicates that the problem of coloniality of being has a negative and disempowering bearing on the possibilities of African people creating their African futures. They cannot effectively create African futures if they have not regained their denied ontological density born out of an imposed inferiority complex.

Conclusion

The notion of development as a gift from Europe and North America has been discredited. The Truman version of development has long been countered by the Bandung decoloniality that targeted the world system and global orders of coloniality. It was clear that those who met at Bandung in 1955 realised that while coloniality of power was mainly about modern forms of domination, control and exploitation (power), coloniality of knowledge was about epistemological colonisation of the mind and imagination, and coloniality of being was about denial of the very humanity of African people through inferiorisation and dehumanisation. Decoloniality as the future confronts the structural cul-de-sac that is sustained by a combination of colonialities of power, being and knowledge. African genius remains entrapped within global coloniality. Thus, decoloniality has to be pursued as the future. The spirit and language of liberation informing socialisation of modern global power should be uncompromisingly anti-Eurocentrism, antisubject-object paradigm, anti-imperial, anti-colonial, anti-racist, anti-patriarchal, and anti-fundamentalist and anti-hegemonic.

Sabelo J. Ndlovu-Gatsheni is the Acting Executive Director of Change Management Unit (CMU), Vice Chancellor's Office at the University of South Africa (Unisa). He has published extensively on African history, African politics and development. His major publications include *The Ndebele Nation: Reflections on Hegemony, Memory and Historiography* (2009); *Do 'Zimbabweans' Exist? Trajectories of Nationalism, National Identity Formation and Crisis in a Postcolonial State* (2009); *Redemptive or Grotesque Nationalism? Rethinking Contemporary Politics in Zimbabwe* (2011); *Empire, Global Coloniality and African Subjectivity* (2013); *Coloniality of Power in Postcolonial Africa: Myths of Decolonization* (2013); *Nationalism and National Projects in Southern Africa: New Critical Reflections* (2013); and *Bondage of Boundaries and Identity Politics in Postcolonial Africa: The 'Northern Problem' and Ethno-futures* (2013).

Busani Mpofu is a senior researcher at AMRI, College of Graduate Studies, University of South Africa. His main research interests include Third World urbanisation and the history of African cities, urban poverty, inclusive development, development discourse and theory. His publications include 'The Urban Land Question, Land Reform and the Spectre of Extrajudicial Land Occupations in South Africa', *Africa Insight* (2017); and 'The Land Question, Agriculture, Industrialisation and the Economy in Zimbabwe: A Critical Reflection', in O. Akanle and J.O.T. Adesisa (eds), *Development of Africa: Issues, Diagnoses and Prognoses* (2018).

References

Adebajo, A. 2010. *The Curse of Berlin: Africa after the Cold War*. Scottsville: University of KwaZulu-Natal Press.

Adedeji, A. 2002. 'From the Lagos Plan of Action to the New Partnership for African Development and from the Final Act of Lagos to the Constitutive Act: Whither Africa?' Unpublished Keynote Address delivered at the African Forum for Envisioning Africa, Nairobi, Kenya, 26–29 April.

African Union. 2013. *Agenda 2063 Vision and Priorities: Unity, Prosperity and Peace.* Addis Ababa: African Union.
Ake, C. 1979. *Social Science as Imperialism: The Theory of Political Development.* Ibadan: University of Ibadan Press.
_____. 1981. *A Political Economy of Africa.* Lagos: Longman Nigeria.
Allen, A. 2016. *The End of Progress: Decolonizing the Normative Foundations of Critical Theory.* New York: Columbia University Press.
Amin, S. 1985. *Delinking: Towards a Polycentric World: Translated by Michael Wolfers.* London: Zed Books.
_____. 1990. *Maldevelopment: Anatomy of a Global Failure.* Tokyo/London: United Nations University Press/Zed Books.
_____. 2009. *Eurocentrism*, 2nd edn. New York: Monthly Review Press.
Austen, R.A. 1987. *African Economic History: Internal Development and External Dependency.* London: James Currey.
Bhambra, G.K. 2007. *Rethinking Modernity: Postcolonialism and the Sociological Imagination.* Basingstoke: Palgrave Macmillan.
Blaut, J.M. 1993. *The Colonizer's Model of the World: Geographical and Eurocentric History.* New York: Guilford Press.
Cesaire, A. 2000. *Discourse on Colonialism.* Trans. Joan Pinkham. New introduction by Robin D.G. Kelley. New York: Monthly Review Press.
Chabal. P. 2012. *The End of Conceit: Western Rationality after Postcolonialism.* London a: Zed Books.
Chinweizu, 1987. *Decolonizing the African Mind.* Lagos: Pero Press.
Chomsky, N. 2011. *How the World Works.* London: Hamish Hamilton.
Comaroff, J., and J.L. Comaroff. 2012. *Theory from the South: Or, How Euro-America is Evolving towards Africa.* Boulder: Paradigm Publishers.
Cotula, L. 2013. *The Great African Land Grab? Agricultural Investments and the Global Food System.* London: Zed Books.
De Santos, B.S. 2007. 'Beyond Abyssal Thinking: From Global Lines to Ecologies of Knowledge', *Review* XXX(1): 45–89.
_____. 2008. *Another Knowledge is Possible: Beyond Northern Epistemologies.* London: Verso.
_____. 2014. *Epistemologies of the South: Justice against Epistemicide.* Boulder: Paradigm Publishers.
Dussel, E. 2011. *Politics of Liberation: A Critical World History*, trans. Thia Cooper. London: SCM Press.
Escobar, A. 1995. *Encountering Development: The Making and Unmaking of the Third World.* Princeton: Princeton University Press.
_____. 2004. 'Beyond the Third World: Imperial Globality, Global Coloniality and Anti-globalization Social Movements', *Third World Quarterly* 25(1): 207–30.
Fanon, F. 1968. *The Wretched of the Earth.* New York: Grove Press.
Frank, A.N. 2008. *ReORIENT: Global Economy in the Asian Age.* Berkeley: University of California Press.
Fukuyama, F. 1992. *The End of History and the Last Man.* London: Penguin.
Goody, J. 2006. *The Theft of History.* Cambridge: Cambridge University Press.
Grosfoguel, R. 2007. 'The Epistemic Decolonial Turn: Beyond Political-Economy Paradigms', *Cultural Studies* 21(2–3): 211–23.

Hardt, M., and A. Negri. 2000. *Empire*. Cambridge, MA: Harvard University Press.
Headley, J.M. 2008. *The Europeanization of the World: On the Origins of Human Rights and Democracy*. Princeton: Princeton University Press.
Keegan, J. 2002. 'Book Review: Paris 1919 by Margaret McMillan', *Washington Post*, 15 December.
Mafeje, A. 1992. *In Search of an Alternative: A Collection of Essays on Revolutionary Theory and Politics*. Harare: SAPES Books.
Magubane, B.M. 2007. *Race and the Construction of Dispensable Other*. Pretoria: UNISA Press.
Maldonado-Torres, N. 2007. 'On Coloniality of Being: Contributions to the Development of a Concept', *Cultural Studies* 21(2): 240–70.
_____. 2011. 'Thinking through the Decolonial Turn: Post-continental Interventions in Theory, Philosophy, and Critique – An Introduction', *Transmodernity: Journal of Peripheral Cultural Production of Luso-Hispanic World* 1(2): 1–23.
Martinot, S. n.d. 'The Coloniality of Power: Notes towards De-colonization', unpublished paper. San Francisco: San Francisco State University.
McNally, D. 2005. *Another World is Possible: Globalization and Anti-capitalism*. Winnipeg: ArbeiterRing Publishing.
Mignolo, W.D. 1995. *The Dark Side of Renaissance: Literacy, Territory, and Colonization*. Ann Arbor: University of Michigan Press.
_____. 2000. *Local Histories/Global Designs; Coloniality, Subaltern Knowledges, and Border Thinking*. Princeton: Princeton University Press.
_____. 2011. *The Dark Side of Western Modernity: Global Futures, Decolonial Options*. Durham, NC: Duke University Press.
Nabudere, D.W. 2011. *Archie Mafeje: Scholar, Activist and Thinker*. Pretoria: Africa Institute of South Africa.
Ndlovu-Gatsheni, S.J. 2009. 'Making Sense of Mugabeism in Local and Global Politics: "So Blair, Keep Your England and Let Me Keep My Zimbabwe"', *Third World Quarterly* 30(6): 1139–58.
_____. 2013a. *Coloniality of Power in Postcolonial Africa: Myths of Decolonization*. Dakar: CODESRIA Book Series.
_____. 2013b. *Empire, Global Coloniality and African Subjectivity*. Oxford: Berghahn Books.
_____. 2013c. 'The Entrapment of Africa within Global Colonial Matrices of Power: Eurocentrism, Coloniality and Deimperialization in the Twenty-First Century', *Journal of Developing Societies* 29(4): 331–53.
_____. 2013d. 'Decolonial Epistemic Perspective and Pan African Unity in the 21st Century', in M. Muchie, P. Lukhele-Olorunju and O. Akpor (eds), *The African Union Ten Years after: Solving African Problems with Pan-Africanism and the African Renaissance*. Pretoria: Africa Institute of South Africa, pp. 385–409.
_____. 2014a. 'What is beyond Discourses of Alterity? Reflections on the Constitution of the Present and Construction of African Subjectivity', in S. Osha (ed.), *The Social Contract in Africa*. Pretoria: Africa Institute of South Africa, pp. 111–30.

———. 2014b. 'Global Technologies of Domination: From Colonial Encounters to the Arab Spring', in E. Obadare and W. Willems (eds), *Civic Agency in Africa: Arts of Resistance in the 21st Century*. Oxford: James Currey, pp. 27–48.

———. 2014c. 'Pan-Africanism and the International System', in T. Murithi (ed.), *Handbook of Africa's International Relations*. London: Routledge, pp. 21–29.

Ngugi wa Thiong'o. 1986. *Decolonizing the Mind: The Politics of Language in African Literature*. London: James Currey.

Nimako, K. 2011. 'Reorienting the World: With or without Africa?' *Working Paper*. International Centre for Muslim and Non-Muslim Understanding: University of South Australia.

———. 2012. Presentation at the International Summer School on Decolonizing Power, Knowledge and Being. Barcelona, Spain, July.

Quijano, A. 2000. 'The Coloniality of Power and Social Classification', *Journal of World Systems* 6(2): 342–86.

———. 2007. 'Coloniality and Modernity/Rationality', *Cultural Studies* 21(2–3): 168–78.

Slater, D. 2004. *Geopolitics and the Post-colonial: Rethinking North-South Relations*. Malden, MA: Blackwell Publishing.

Taylor, I. 2014. *Africa Rising: BRICS – Diversifying Dependency*. Oxford: James Currey.

Therien, J.P. 1999. 'Beyond the North-South Divide: Two Tales of World Poverty', *Third World Quarterly* 20(4): 723–42.

Tlostanova, M.V., and W.D. Mignolo. 2012. *Learning to Unlearn: Decolonial Reflections from Eurasia and the Americas*. Columbus: Ohio State University Press.

Waisbord, S. and C. Mellado. 2014. 'De-Westernizing Communication Studies: A Reassessment', *Communication Theory* 24(4): 361–72.

Wallerstein, I. 1999. 'Introduction: Why Unthink?', in I. Wallerstein (ed.), *Unthinking Social Science: The Limits of Nineteenth-Century Paradigms*. Cambridge: Polity Press, pp. 1–30.

Young, C. 2012. *The Postcolonial State in Africa: Fifty Years of Independence, 1960–2010*. Madison: University of Wisconsin Press.

Index

Accelerated and Shared Growth Initiative-South Africa (ASGISA), 139
AfCFTA (African Continental Free Trade Area), 1
Africa, 1-5, 9-13, 17, 21-2, 24-5, 29-31, 34-42, 45-57, 59-69, 131-2, 146-7, 149-50, 257-8, 262-3, 265-7
  context of, 54-5, 62
  early, 65, 67
  poor people inhabit, 4
Africa-centred knowledges, 4, 23
Africa Rising, 1, 25, 258-9, 267
African and coloured communities, 185
African Capitalism, 24, 149
African Charter on Human and Peoples, 56, 68-9
African cities, 22, 106, 207, 209, 263
African communities, 14, 201, 240
African conceptions of development, 37
African continent, 31, 123
African Continental Free Trade Area (AfCFTA), 1
African countries, 12-13, 41, 56, 59, 61-3
  most, 19, 206-7
African development, 36
African development challenges, 37

African development malaise, 36
African economies, 40, 57
African elites, 19, 38-9, 141
African families, 20, 194, 197-8, 200-8, 210, 212, 222, 235
  black, 20-1, 198-9, 201, 209
  compelled, 235
  disadvantaged, 201
  excluded black, 197
  urban, 115
African family in South Africa, 198, 201, 207
African family policy, 20, 199, 209
African futures, 11, 69, 253, 255-8, 261-2
African governments, 54, 68
African history, 22, 46, 123, 263
African household structure, 206
African households, 202-3, 205-6, 242
African imaginations, 253
African intellectuals, 12, 49
African languages, 52, 63, 67
African leaders, 3, 17, 38-40, 50, 257-8
African market, 11, 258
African marriage, 202, 205-6, 211, 219
African middle class, 61
African modernity, 12, 65
African nation, 63, 65, 67, 70

African National Congress. *See* ANC
African National Congress Youth
    League (ANCYL), 132
African national project, 17, 37-9
African nationalism, 63
African natural resources, 28, 41, 259
African people, 11, 16, 32, 40, 45, 60,
    139, 186–7, 255, 257–8, 262
  black, 188
  entailed reducing, 254
  ordinary, 42
  pushed, 261
  very humanity of, 261–2
African people being, 253
African perspective, 20, 197, 199, 205,
    209, 211, 245
African political economies, 17, 68
African political power, 38
African politics, 22, 46, 263
African population, black, 180
African postcolonial state, 38
African predicaments, 11, 253
African Renaissance, 63, 266
African societies, 32, 64, 202–5, 211, 258
African states, 4, 12, 38, 40, 233, 257
African Studies, 48, 169, 172, 191
African subject, 261–2
African subjectivity, 22, 28, 46, 49, 124,
    261, 263, 266
African Union (AU), 1, 13, 22, 25, 131,
    254, 265–6
African Unity, 48, 66–7
Africans, 5, 11, 13, 21, 24, 31–3, 35, 42,
    61, 63, 65–6, 216–20, 235–6, 253–5,
    260–2
  atomisation of, 13, 254
  black, 21, 175, 180, 190, 218–20
Africans in South Africa, 13
Africa's development, 24, 49, 67–9, 125
Africa's poverty, 18
Africa's underdevelopment, 3
Afrikaners in South Africa, 119
Afro-capitalism, 63–4
age of global coloniality, 16, 28, 30, 32,
    34, 38, 40, 42, 44, 46, 48, 50
AIDS, 118, 223, 226, 228–30
AIDS epidemic in South Africa, 223

AIDS pandemic in South Africa, 225
Alex Renewal Project (ARP), 118
Alexander, Jocelyn, 137, 147, 153, 155–
    9, 161–3, 166–9
Alexandra, 18, 107, 110, 114–19, 124,
    126
Alexandra Township, 18, 105–7, 114,
    122
Alkire, S., 71–2, 82
Allen, Amy, 251, 265
ANC (African National Congress), 2,
    13, 117, 133, 138–9, 141, 145–7, 149,
    173–4, 180–1, 235, 243, 245
ANCYL (African National Congress
    Youth League), 132
apartheid, 11, 13, 30, 42, 112, 115-16,
    118, 120, 124–5, 137–9, 175–6, 180–
    1, 219, 222, 235–6
apartheid South Africa, 109
Arab Spring, 42–3, 267
Arab States, 58–9
architects of poverty, 24, 48, 149
ARP (Alex Renewal Project), 118
ASGISA (Accelerated and Shared
    Growth Initiative-South Africa),
    139
assessment of South Africa, 148
AU. *See* African Union
Authoritarianism, 39, 145–6

basic needs (BN), 5, 17, 71, 73, 75–6,
    83–4
BBBEE (Broad-Based Black Economic
    Empowerment), 19, 129, 133–4,
    137–42
BEE. *See* Black Economic
    Empowerment
black economic empowerment, 2, 19,
    129, 133, 138, 146, 148
Black Economic Empowerment (BEE),
    2, 19, 129, 133, 138, 140, 142–3, 146,
    148, 150
Black Economic Empowerment in
    South Africa, 150
black-on-black violence, 116–17
black people, 4, 33, 117, 139, 144, 184,
    188, 214, 217, 219, 222, 226, 262

black South African families, 198, 211
black tax, 222
black workers, 89, 116, 221, 236
blacks, 89, 91, 105–9, 111–12, 114–18, 121, 123–4, 141, 191, 205, 208, 233–6
    impoverishment of, 108
BN. *See* basic needs
BN approach, 75–6
BN strategy, 75–6
BNG (Breaking New Ground), 173, 179, 191
Bonner, P. and N. Nieftagodien, 114–17
Brazil, Russia, India and China (BRICS), 25, 258, 267
Brazil and South Africa, 246
Breaking New Ground (BNG), 173, 179, 191
BRICS (Brazil, Russia, India and China), 25, 258, 267
brigade, 159–60, 167
British South African Company, 154
Broad-Based Black Economic Empowerment. *See* BBBEE

Cameron, 73, 76, 79, 82, 84
Cape Town, 70, 83–4, 125–6, 148–9, 151, 169–70, 175, 179, 181, 185, 187, 191–3, 210, 229–30, 246–8
capital, 39, 60, 62, 64, 74, 78, 83, 100, 136, 141, 165
Capitalism, 12, 14, 43–4, 60, 64–5, 68, 71, 80, 113, 131, 165, 255, 257
Catholic Commission for Justice and Peace. *See* CCJP
CCJP (Catholic Commission for Justice and Peace), 159, 169
Central Intelligence Organisation (CIO), 159
Chile, 80, 82, 84
China, 11–13, 24–5, 75, 100–1, 171, 257
Chronic Poverty Research Centre, 246–7
CIO (Central Intelligence Organisation), 159
civil marriages in South Africa, 217
cohabiting, 213, 218–20, 226
Cold War, 6–7, 263

Colonial Zimbabwe, 89
Colonialism, 2–3, 11, 15, 18, 24, 28–34, 37, 39, 42, 45–7, 111–12, 139, 222, 235, 255
coloniality, 10, 12, 15, 24, 28–31, 34, 39, 44–5, 48–9, 109, 111–13, 253–5, 257, 262–3, 266–7
coloniality of being, 111, 253–4, 262
coloniality of knowledge, 253–4, 262
coloniality of power, 10, 28, 30–1, 39, 256–7
colonisation, 34, 40, 89, 113, 253–4, 257, 260
colony, 89
coloured people, 186–8
coloured population, 175–7, 180–2, 185, 192
coloured population in South Africa, 175
coloured townships, 175–6, 189
coloureds, 4, 20, 114, 175, 178–84, 186, 189, 217, 235
conceptualisation, 20–1, 51–3, 129, 197–8, 200–2, 204, 206, 208–10, 212
conflicts, 98, 101, 109–11, 155, 157–8, 161, 185, 191, 226
confrontation, 183–4
Congress of South African Trade Unions (COSATU), 138, 146
conquest, 33, 41, 255, 257
contestations, 133, 142, 192
Continental African people, 255
Contractual fascism, 109
contradictions, 1, 9, 75, 80, 129, 144, 257
COSATU (Congress of South African Trade Unions), 138, 146
countries, 2–3, 10–11, 18, 51–2, 59, 61, 63, 105–6, 143–5, 162, 165–6, 197–201, 203–4, 207–9, 233–4
    developing, 9, 15, 51, 56, 219, 233
criminal activity, 178, 188
cultures, 4, 25, 33, 53, 57, 62–3, 66–7, 69, 72, 82, 108, 111, 124–5, 210, 219
customary marriages, 216
    registered, 216–17

de-Westernisation, 44, 251

deaths, 94, 112, 118, 160
decolonial epistemic perspectives, 9–10, 16, 28, 30–1, 35
decolonial turn, 43–5, 48, 112, 125, 266
decoloniality, 44, 107, 113, 126, 251–2, 254, 256, 258, 260, 262–4, 266
decolonisation, 2, 6, 16, 19, 28, 35–7, 39, 42, 44, 133, 139, 256–7
decolonisation of development studies, 28, 30
deficits, 28, 30, 261
democracy, 35, 39, 41, 117, 143, 146, 148–50, 169, 219, 262, 266
Department of Social Development, 20, 23, 198, 210, 223, 225, 228
deprivation, 17–18, 72–3, 75–7, 87, 101, 119, 207
develop developmental states, 146
development, 1–13, 15–17, 19, 22–3, 28–33, 35–57, 59–63, 65–70, 82–5, 102–4, 150, 161–5, 251–2, 253–6, 262–4
   autonomous, 258
   constrained, 57
   development characterise, 17, 50
   effective, 63–4, 67
   late, 7
   objects of, 30–1
   pursuit of, 59
   spatial, 173, 186
   true, 59–60, 65–7
   unthinking, 1
development approach, socioeconomic, 51, 57, 64
development discourses, 4–5, 10, 15, 22, 29–30, 44, 55, 59–60, 209, 263
development doctrine, 34, 49
development ideology, 4–5, 8–10
development impasse, 29, 43
   global, 17
development in Africa, 47–8, 53, 56, 60, 63, 68
development literature, 18, 37
Development Planning, 53, 69
Development Planning Committee (DPC), 179

development policies, national socioeconomic, 200
development projects, 19, 39, 46, 129, 161
development question, composite, 167
development revolution, 14, 23
Development Studies, 5–6, 16, 25, 28–30, 35, 37, 41, 46, 49, 69, 83, 123, 126, 167, 210
   decolonising, 29, 31, 34
development theory, twentieth-century, 55
development trajectory, 46, 65, 131
developmental, 134
developmental states, 51, 131, 134, 145–6
   democratic, 145–7
Developmentalism, 23, 28–9, 37, 47, 53, 59
   age of, 55
disabilities, 7, 9, 13, 18, 198, 200, 234
discipline, 79, 152–3, 171
discipline and punishment, 19, 152, 154, 156, 158, 160, 162, 164, 166, 168, 170, 172, 174
discrimination, 56, 161, 173, 246
disengaging, 64–5
disparities, 162, 234–5
divorces, 92, 207, 216–17
DMS, 259
doctrines of development, 5, 23
domestic violence, 213, 226
DoSD, 198, 200–2, 209–10
DPC (Development Planning Committee), 179
droughts, 94, 163–4, 166, 170
Durban, 148–9, 201, 228–9

early literature on African families, 203
Economia, 48, 84
economic development, 18, 37, 57, 66, 200
   sustainable African, 64
Economic Freedom Fighters. *See* EFF
economic growth, 3, 5, 11, 15, 38, 48, 53, 59, 61, 73–4, 76, 83–4, 91, 140, 258

Index   271

Economic Structural Adjustment Programme. *See* ESAP
economics, 8, 10, 25, 41, 68, 76, 82–3, 103, 186
economists, 5, 8, 16, 23, 240, 248
economy, 4–5, 8, 11, 13–14, 19, 22, 28, 61, 91, 95, 99, 120, 133–5, 140–1, 151
  solidarity, 71, 78–81, 83
EFF (Economic Freedom Fighters), 129, 132–3, 138, 146
EFF in South Africa, 143
elections, 33, 93, 95, 100–1, 133, 135, 146, 148–9, 156–7, 159, 162, 168–9
  national, 156, 158
emancipation, 35, 80, 109–11, 251, 255
Empire, 22, 30–1, 36, 41, 46–7, 49, 124, 263, 266
empowerment, 16, 18–19, 72, 80–2, 127, 136
end of development, 251, 254, 256, 258, 260, 262, 264, 266
enunciation, 31, 45
epistemology, 24, 29, 31, 45, 113, 259, 261
EPWP (Expanded Public Works Programme), 243, 246
equality, 8, 45, 72, 74, 78, 110, 117
ESAP (Economic Structural Adjustment Programme), 91–2, 103, 143, 165
ethics, 83, 108, 110, 262
ethnic groups, 154, 186
ethnicity, 7, 9, 18–19, 38, 78, 153–6, 171, 192
ethnopolitics and regionalism, 19, 152, 154, 156, 158, 160, 162, 164, 166, 168, 170, 172, 174
Euro-American hegemony, 44, 46
Euro-American powers, 42–3
Europe, 12, 32, 43–4, 51, 108, 251, 254, 256–7
Europe and Central Asia, 58–9
Europe and North America, 255, 257, 261–2
Europeans, 31, 257, 260
Evidence, 73, 99, 103, 144, 146, 149, 161, 167, 212–13, 218–20, 223, 225–6
excerpts, 159–60

exclusion, 2, 20, 33, 60, 95, 117, 178–80, 189
Expanded Public Works Programme (EPWP), 243, 246
experts, 8, 10, 23, 34–5, 120
exploitation, 4, 28, 33, 35, 51–2, 56, 60–1, 72, 148, 235, 240, 255, 257, 262
extent, 2, 4, 8, 34–5, 42, 73–7, 115, 133, 155, 213, 222, 225, 227, 240, 242

factories, 89–90, 176
failure, 13, 15, 37–8, 40, 42, 99, 112, 156, 159, 163, 165–6, 200
family life, 197–8, 200–2, 211, 213
  damaged South African, 199
family members, 21, 178, 200, 231–2, 235, 237–40, 242–5
family organisations, 204, 206
family policy, 20–1, 197, 199, 202, 209
  black South African, 201
family policy in South Africa, 199
Fanon, Frantz, 44–5, 47, 107–13, 116, 121, 124, 131, 134, 141, 148, 255, 265
Fast Track Land Reform Program, 132, 134–5
Ferguson, James, 14–15, 21, 23, 29, 47
fertility, 211, 219, 224–5, 229
freedom, 8–9, 18, 28, 41, 53, 56, 59, 70, 77, 82, 84, 117, 150, 219, 224
Freedom Charter, 4, 138–40
FROLIZI (Front for the Liberation of Zimbabwe), 155
Front for the Liberation of Zimbabwe (FROLIZI), 155

GDP (gross domestic product), 93, 165
GDS (Growth and Development Summit), 243
gender, 7, 9, 14, 28, 31, 49, 78–9, 81, 87, 102–3, 105, 110, 229
General Household Survey (GHS), 179, 191
GHS (General Household Survey), 179, 191
global coloniality, 3, 11, 16, 28, 30, 32, 34, 36, 38, 40, 42, 44, 46, 253–5, 257–60

global imperial designs, 16, 28–30, 45
global orders, 256, 258–9, 262
Global South, 6–7, 14–15, 23, 28–9, 44–6, 54, 59, 113, 253, 257, 259–60
government, 21, 66–7, 95, 100–1, 116–18, 158, 163–8, 180–1, 186–7, 189–90, 213–14, 223–5, 231–2, 234–6, 244–5
  central, 164
Government of South Africa, 228
government officials, 168, 241, 243, 245
government policies, 116, 161, 178, 180
grants, 199–200, 208, 227, 231–5, 237–8, 240–5, 248
  housing subsidy, 178, 184–6
gross domestic product (GDP), 93, 165
Growth and Development Summit (GDS), 243

HDI (Human Development Index), 57
HDI level for Sub-Saharan Africa, 59
history of African cities, 22, 209, 263
HIV, 16, 21, 97, 118, 212–16, 221–3, 225–6, 228
  risk of, 21, 213, 215, 217
HIV/AIDS pandemic, 198, 200
HIV and AIDS in South Africa, 226
HIV infection, 95, 202, 215, 220–1, 223, 225–6
HIV-positive people in South Africa, 221
HIV response in South Africa, 216
housing, 20, 75, 90, 95, 97, 114, 116, 173, 175, 177–8, 180–1, 184–6, 188, 191, 197
housing allocations, 180–1, 184
human development, 15, 57–8, 103–4, 204
Human Development Index (HDI), 57
Human Sciences Research Council. *See* HSRC
Hunter, M., 221–2

IAABD (International Academy of African Business and Development), 82

IBDC (Indigenous Business Development Committee), 133
IBWO (Indigenous Business Women's Organisation), 134
identities, 18–20, 47, 125, 127, 171, 173, 178, 180–1, 188, 190
  racial, 184–5, 188–91, 245
ILO (International Labour Organization), 17, 75, 83
IMF (International Monetary Fund), 5–6, 8, 40, 42, 73, 259
IMF/World Bank regulation of African macro-economic policy, 140
Imperialism, 2, 11, 25, 31, 37, 61, 113, 253, 256, 265
impoverished areas, 20
inclusive development, 9, 17, 22, 50, 56, 60–3, 67–9, 143, 263
income, 72, 74–8, 80, 87, 91, 93, 96, 99, 139, 222, 232, 242–3
  source of, 189–90, 241
independence, 19, 48–9, 91, 94–5, 97, 135, 152–6, 158, 162–3, 202, 267
  economic, 257
  political, 13, 38, 57, 63
Indian descent in South Africa, 203
Indigenisation, 2, 16, 19, 133–5, 144
Indigenous Business Development Committee (IBDC), 133
Indigenous Business Women's Organisation (IBWO), 134
industry, 121, 131, 138, 165–6, 169
inequality, 2–5, 8–9, 11, 15–19, 35, 60, 69, 71–6, 78–84, 86, 88, 105–6, 117–18, 132–3, 139–42
Inequality in South Africa, 126
informal settlements, 176, 179–80, 184, 187–8, 221, 226
Institute for African Development, 70
Institute of South Africa, 24
interaction, 44, 101, 161, 167–8
International Academy of African Business and Development (IAABD), 82
International Labour Organization. *See* ILO
International Monetary Fund. *See* IMF

Index

jobs, 5, 74, 77, 79, 90, 100–2, 116, 118, 120, 126, 140, 149, 171, 185, 243
   formal, 90, 226
Johannesburg, 24, 48, 114, 116, 119, 121, 124–6, 148–9, 191, 210, 229, 232, 238, 246

knowledge, 4, 9–10, 23, 28, 30–1, 34, 44–7, 49, 107–9, 113, 125–6, 253–4, 259–60, 262–3, 265
knowledge production, 107, 111, 113, 260

land, 16, 19–20, 31–2, 66, 90, 93, 95, 102, 114, 133, 135, 163, 168, 187–9, 235
Land Apportionment Act, 89
land invasions, 181, 184, 188–9
land ownership, 135, 173, 176, 178, 180, 182, 184, 186, 188, 190, 192, 194, 196
land reform, 22, 81, 133–6, 153, 163, 172, 209, 263
law, 32, 72–3, 98, 106, 116, 142, 176, 198–9, 210, 235–6, 240, 246
less developed countries (LDCs), 73, 76
liberation, 45, 69, 82, 91, 133, 135, 139, 152, 228, 263, 265
loan sharks, 21, 239–42, 245
loans, 11, 240–1, 248
lobola, 21, 218–20, 222–4
low-density areas, 96–7

Malema, Julius, 132–3
Mamdani, Mahmood, 32–3, 36, 48
manifesto, 132–3, 135, 151
marginalisation, 20, 92, 142, 173, 178, 180, 188–9
markets, 12, 50, 56, 59, 64, 66–7, 76, 80, 96, 117, 135
marriage, 21, 57, 203–5, 207, 213–29
   protective effect of, 214–15
marriage rates, 21, 214, 218–19, 226
   low, 21, 214, 219–20
married people, 21, 213, 215, 220, 223
Matabeleland development question, 152–53
Matabeleland North, 160, 162
Matabeleland problem, 167

Matabeleland regions, 152, 160, 163, 165
Matabeleland South, 156, 160, 162, 165
Matabeleland Zambezi Water Project (MZWP), 164
Matabeleland Zambezi Water Trust (MZWT), 164
MDC (Movement for Democratic Change), 93, 95, 100–1, 129, 138, 143, 149, 157
migrant labour system, 198–9, 221–2
migrants, 89, 103, 146, 171, 176–7, 189, 205–6
Millennium Development Goals, 72, 103, 230
modern power structure, 11, 253–4, 256
modernity, 1, 11, 25, 29–31, 34, 37, 39, 43–4, 46, 50–1, 57, 65, 69, 111, 251
Movement for Democratic Change. See MDC
MPI (Multidimensional Poverty Index), 72, 82
Mugabe, Robert, 131–4, 150, 156, 168
Multidimensional Poverty Index (MPI), 72, 82
municipalities, 94, 120, 181, 185, 188–90

National Development Commission in South Africa, 145
National Development Plan. See NDP
national projects, 37, 47–8, 69
National Union of Miners in South Africa (NUMSA), 138
Ndebele, 153–4, 157–8, 163, 167
Ndebele votes, 156–7
NDP (National Development Plan), 126, 133, 139, 144, 150
NDR (National Democratic Revolution), 137, 139–40, 143, 147
NDR in South Africa, 144
neighbourhoods, most South African, 240
neighbours, 122, 169, 243–4
neocolonialism, 11, 30, 37, 253, 255–6
neoliberalism, 2, 7, 15, 34, 37, 39, 41–2, 131, 137, 146, 148, 228, 255, 259
neopatrimonialism, 57, 69

nonbeing, 18, 107, 109–11, 114, 123
  zone of, 18, 107, 110, 123
nuclear families, 20–1, 198, 201, 203–6, 208–9
NUMSA (National Union of Miners in South Africa), 138

OAU (Organization of the African Unity), 56
ODI (Overseas Development Institute), 75–6, 84
old-age grant dynamics, 232
old-age grants, 231, 233–6, 238, 240–5
older persons, 198, 200, 243, 247
Operation Murambatsvina, 18, 94–7, 100, 102, 104, 145
operations, 94, 96, 100, 155, 159, 165
  government by, 145–6
opulence, 18, 106–7
Organization of the African Unity (OAU), 56
Overseas Development Institute (ODI), 75–6, 84
ownership in South Africa, 20

Padayachee, V. 24, 149, 210
Pan-Africanism, 13, 48, 63, 254–5, 266–7
parents, 123, 181, 202, 242–3
parties, 2, 101, 109, 139, 145–6, 153, 157–8, 243
  political, 91, 99, 102, 133–5, 145, 156
party-state, 133, 136, 143–4
pass, 115–16, 118
People's Manifesto, 135, 151
Peoples' Rights, 56, 68–9
peri-urban areas, 94, 116
PET (Programa de Economia del Trabajo), 84
policies, 12, 40, 48, 57, 76, 131, 134–6, 138, 176, 179–80, 187–8, 197, 199–200, 213–14, 235–6
  economic, 43, 57, 63, 66, 139, 141, 143, 146
  family-related, 197, 209
political economy, 68, 83, 106, 129, 131, 133–4, 143–4, 146–7, 149, 169, 200, 257
  distinctive, 134–5

population, 2, 14, 19, 32, 93, 98, 105, 109, 114–15, 173, 204, 214, 217–18, 231, 233–4
population groups, 217–18, 220
post-apartheid South Africa, 129, 131, 139
post-development, 17, 50, 54
post-independence Africa, 17, 50–1, 57, 67
postcolonial Africa, 19, 47, 146, 152
postcolonial state, 19, 22, 37–9, 42, 46, 124, 146, 152, 158, 163, 167, 262–3
postcolonial State in Africa, 267
postcolonialism, 22, 43, 47, 265
poverty, 2, 5, 7–9, 13–19, 71–4, 76–88, 104–8, 110, 118–20, 126, 140–2, 207–8, 232–3, 235–6, 245–7
  absolute, 75
  coexistence of, 18, 105
  combat, 22, 234, 241
  extreme, 5, 61
  genesis of, 18, 106
  global, 4, 9
  regarding, 17, 71
poverty alleviation, 18, 75, 81, 232
poverty levels, 93, 140
poverty of theory, 18, 84, 105–6, 108, 110, 112, 114, 116, 118, 120, 122, 124, 126, 128, 130
poverty reduction, 15, 84, 235
power, 9–10, 12, 18–19, 22–3, 28–31, 34–5, 39, 48–9, 54–5, 69–70, 124–6, 141–3, 256–9, 262–3, 266–7
  colonial matrices of, 28–9, 45
  coloniality of, 29, 34, 39, 109, 253–4, 257, 262
  foreign, 3
  political, 137–8, 142
power relations, 71, 73, 78, 81
Pretoria Republic of South Africa, 246
Programa de Economia del Trabajo (PET), 84

Quijano, 28, 31, 41, 49, 108, 251, 256, 260, 267

race, 25, 30, 32, 38, 66, 78–9, 87, 103–4, 107, 109, 126, 137, 186, 192, 261–2

racial identities in South Africa, 188
racism, 11, 108–9, 125, 178, 185, 187, 255–6
Ramaphosa, Cyril, (South African State Deputy President), 141
RDP (Reconstruction and Development Programme), 139, 143
Reconstruction and Development Programme (RDP), 139, 143
regional integration, 24, 65–6
regionalism, 7, 18–19, 127, 152, 154–6, 158, 160, 162, 164, 166, 168, 170, 172, 174
regions, 10–11, 19, 44, 51–2, 57–9, 65, 67, 137, 152–4, 156–7, 161, 163, 166–7
Republic of South Africa, 20, 23, 126, 150, 198, 210, 227
Reserve Bank of Zimbabwe (RBZ), 135–6, 150
resources, 1, 38–9, 59–60, 66, 74, 77–8, 91–2, 99, 114, 167, 173, 175–6, 181, 185–6, 188
rethinking development, 27, 251
right to development, 55–6, 61
rights, 56, 60, 74, 110–11, 115, 146, 158
rural areas, 18, 89, 91–2, 94–6, 101, 157, 175–6, 207, 209, 225, 232
rural people, 96, 225
rural poverty, 18, 114, 125–6

SADC (Southern African Development Community), 13, 93, 147
SANAC (South African National AIDS Council), 226
SAPA (South African Press Association), 186, 192
SAPs (structural adjustment programmes), 7, 30, 34, 39–40, 42, 51, 55, 91–2
SAR (Southern African Report), 172
SARS (South African Revenue Service), 133
SASSA (South African Social Security Agency), 233–4, 248
settlers, white, 31–2, 119, 154
sexual partners, multiple, 212–13, 215–16, 221

single people, 212–13
social development, 20, 23, 51, 56, 77, 84, 197–8, 210, 223, 225, 228, 247
social grants, 199, 234–6, 248
social policy, 16, 20, 63, 65–6, 102, 144, 197–8, 201, 209–10, 235, 248
socialism, 43, 64–5
societies, 4, 8–11, 14, 19, 32, 37, 54–5, 63–4, 74–6, 79, 81–2, 119, 140–1, 202–3, 239–40
  classless, 65
socioeconomic and cultural barriers, 15, 19–20, 212
South Africa, 12–14, 18–21, 32–3, 83–4, 105–6, 122–3, 131–4, 137–46, 197–204, 207–9, 211–14, 216–18, 222–3, 228–39, 245–8
  new, 118
  pre-1994, 208
  racialised, 188
  sets, 18
  temporary, 200
  urban, 121
South Africa and China, 12
South Africa and Namibia, 14
South Africa and Zimbabwe, 2, 15, 33
South Africa in Africa, 24
South Africa turn, 239
South African, 2–3, 11–12, 81, 103, 106, 137–8, 140–1, 145, 147, 175, 180, 231–2, 234–6, 238–9, 242
  black, 141–2, 175, 188, 233, 235
  elderly, 234
  ensured white, 122
  fortunate, 234
  married, 215
  older black, 207
  poor, 236
  poor black, 142
  senior, 234
  unmarried, 215
  white, 116
South African Association of Political Studies, 68
South African Broadcasting Corporation, 145
South African case, 208

South African destabilisation strategies, 161
South African family, 24, 198, 210
South African identity, 237
South African Institute of Race Relations, 24, 199, 210
South African National AIDS Council (SANAC), 226
South African population, 235
South African Revenue Service (SARS), 133
South African situation, 240
South African Social Security Agency. See SASSA
South African universities, 3
South African War, 119
South Africa's approach to social policy, 235
South Africa's decolonisation, 141
South Africa's Eastern Cape Province, 205
South Africa's senior citizens, 234
Southern Africa, 2, 11–12, 14, 19, 53, 66, 69, 81–2, 106, 129, 132–3, 146–8, 169, 233
Southern African, 13, 21, 80, 146
Southern African Development Community. See SADC
Southern African political economy, 131
Southern African Report (SAR), 172
Southern Africa's development, 146
Southern Rhodesia, 89, 154
Soweto in South Africa, 132
Spectre of Extrajudicial Land Occupations in South Africa, 22, 209, 263
SSA (State Security Agency), 145
State Building and Democracy in Southern Africa, 169
state grants, 235–6, 242, 244
state institutions, 145, 168
state ownership, 65–6
state power, 134, 136, 143
State Security Agency (SSA), 145
Statistics South Africa, 144, 150, 191, 214, 216–17, 222–23, 229

status, economic, 5, 223
strategies, 15, 19, 76, 160, 162, 200
structural adjustment programmes. See SAPs
structures, 11, 18, 30, 34, 37, 68, 87, 98, 108–9, 112, 177, 181, 189–90, 198–9, 204
  informal, 94, 178, 188–9
study, 20–1, 24, 28, 134, 165, 175, 182, 192, 198–9, 201, 212–16, 218–21, 231–2, 234–5, 243–5
Sub-Saharan Africa, 57–9
sustainable development, 1, 5, 70, 80, 83

tenants, 96, 176–8, 181, 185–6, 189–90
theory, 18, 26, 47, 70, 84, 104–6, 108, 110, 112, 114, 116, 118, 120, 124–6, 128–30
theory of poverty, 18, 105–6, 108, 110, 112, 114, 116, 118, 120, 122, 124, 126, 128, 130
thinking, 4, 15–17, 33, 36, 40–1, 45–6, 48, 61, 65–6, 107, 113, 125, 142, 167, 266
  post-development, 54
Third World, 4–5, 22–3, 30, 48, 51, 55, 59, 64, 68, 209, 265
thought
  strong, 34–5
  weak, 34–6
trade, 12, 60, 65, 82, 99, 138, 142
  cross-border, 92–3
transformation, 3, 25, 32, 59, 81, 83, 126, 147, 167, 211
transmodernity, 48, 125, 266
trickle down theory, 71, 73, 75, 81

UN (United Nations), 5, 56, 75, 83, 94, 103–4, 137
underdevelopment, 1–2, 18, 29, 37, 42, 51, 54, 83–4, 106, 143
understanding, 9–10, 16, 20, 88, 153, 197–8, 200, 202, 204–6, 208, 210, 212, 214–15, 229, 260–1
  historical, 21, 202, 209
Union of South Africa, 48
unions, 115, 162, 225–6
  formal, 215, 223, 225–6

ruling Zimbabwe African National, 129
United Nations. *See* UN
United Nations Research Institution for Social Development (UNRISD), 83–4
United States and Europe, 257
unity, pan-African, 13, 63, 66, 254
university, 3–4, 25, 48, 108, 147, 245
University of Zimbabwe, 102
unmarried people, 215–16, 220
UNRISD (United Nations Research Institution for Social Development), 83–4
urban poverty, 16, 18, 22, 92, 101, 105, 123, 209, 263
urban poverty in Zimbabwe, 17, 87
urbanisation, 75, 103–4, 119, 121, 207

vacant land, 187, 189
violence, 28, 33, 49, 87, 95, 110–11, 114, 123, 133–4, 143, 145, 147, 159, 167–70, 184
  structural, 112, 118
voting, 102, 156, 158

war, 91, 101, 108, 111, 119, 144, 154, 156, 159, 168, 262
water crisis, 164
wealth, 35, 74, 76, 78, 89, 108, 116, 139, 222
wedding ceremonies, 220, 222
wellbeing, 9, 22, 52, 61, 66, 76, 200, 207, 232, 235, 241–3
  socioeconomic, 222, 224
West, 7, 10, 41–2, 51, 54, 59, 107, 113, 154
Western, 13, 39–40, 205
Western Cape, 176, 184–5
Western societies, 46, 202
White Paper, 20, 198–9, 201–2, 209–10
White Paper on Families in South Africa, 23, 200, 210, 223, 225–6, 228
whites, 89–90, 107–9, 111, 116, 121–3, 134, 136, 138, 158, 175, 180, 191, 208, 233–5
wife, 100, 206, 216, 219, 221–2

women, 60, 69, 77, 80, 82, 89–93, 99, 102–3, 144–5, 160, 205, 207–8, 221, 229–30, 244–5
  never-married, 205–6
  young, 60, 92
workers, 4, 32, 74, 78–80, 89–91, 109, 141, 171, 207, 236
  black female, 89–90
  social, 243–4
  urban, 90, 93
  white, 89, 121–2, 235
world, 4, 9, 24, 32, 45–6, 59–61, 64–5, 67, 108–9, 111–13, 233, 251, 254–8, 260, 265–7
  developing, 30, 54, 56, 82, 229, 233
world capitalist system, 59–60
world systems, modern, 11, 253, 256–7
World Trade Organization (WTO), 8, 259
WTO (World Trade Organization), 8, 259

yards, 176–7, 179, 181, 185, 189–91

ZANLA (Zimbabwe African National Liberation Army), 155–6
ZANU (Zimbabwe African National Union), 91, 95, 99–102, 129, 131–3, 135–6, 138, 143, 145, 151–2, 154–8, 162–3, 166–8
ZAPU (Zimbabwe African People's Union), 91, 101, 154, 156–9, 162, 168–9, 171
ZIMASSET (Zimbabwe Agenda for Sustainable Social Economic Transformation), 145
Zimbabwe, 11–12, 18–19, 22, 32, 89–90, 92–6, 98–100, 102–4, 129, 131–8, 143–50, 153–4, 159–60, 164–5, 167–72
  post–independence, 136, 161
Zimbabwe African National Liberation Army. *See* ZANLA
Zimbabwe African National Union. *See* ZANU
Zimbabwe African National Union-Patriotic Front, 2

Zimbabwe African People's Union. *See* ZAPU
Zimbabwe Agenda for Sustainable Social Economic Transformation (ZIMASSET), 145
Zimbabwe and South Africa, 2, 18–19, 131, 143–4, 150, 170
Zimbabwe-People First (ZPF), 101
Zimbabwe People's Revolutionary Army (ZIPRA), 155–6
Zimbabwe Unity Movement (ZUM), 157

Zimbabwe's development challenges, 15
Zimbabwe's independence, 155, 166
ZIPRA (Zimbabwe People's Revolutionary Army), 155–6
zone of being, 18, 45, 107, 109–10, 119, 123
zone of nonbeing, 114
ZPF (Zimbabwe-People First), 101

www.ingramcontent.com/pod-product-compliance
Lightning Source LLC
Chambersburg PA
CBHW070913030426
42336CB00014BA/2398